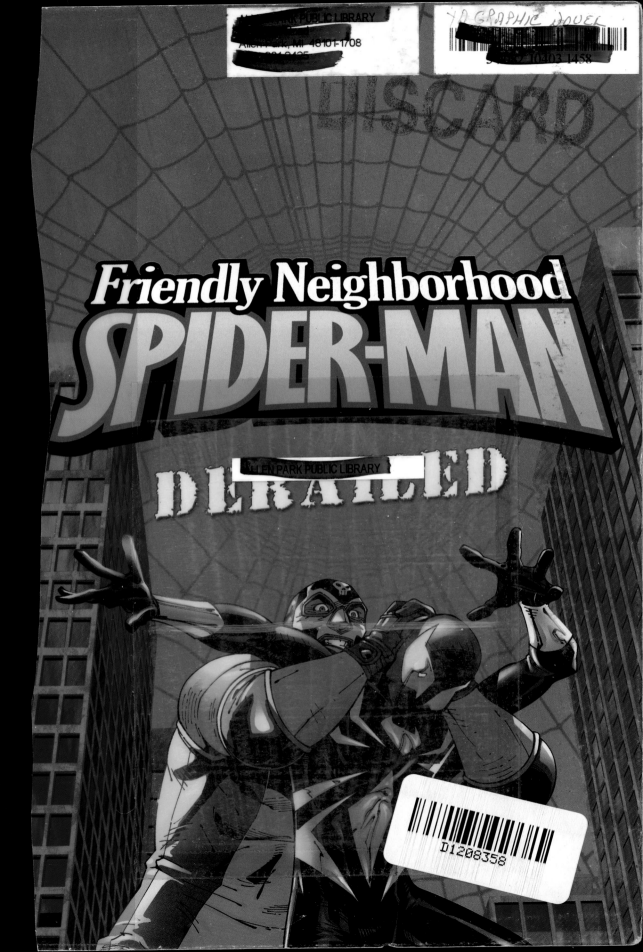

Friendly Neighborhood
SPIDER-MAN

DERAILED

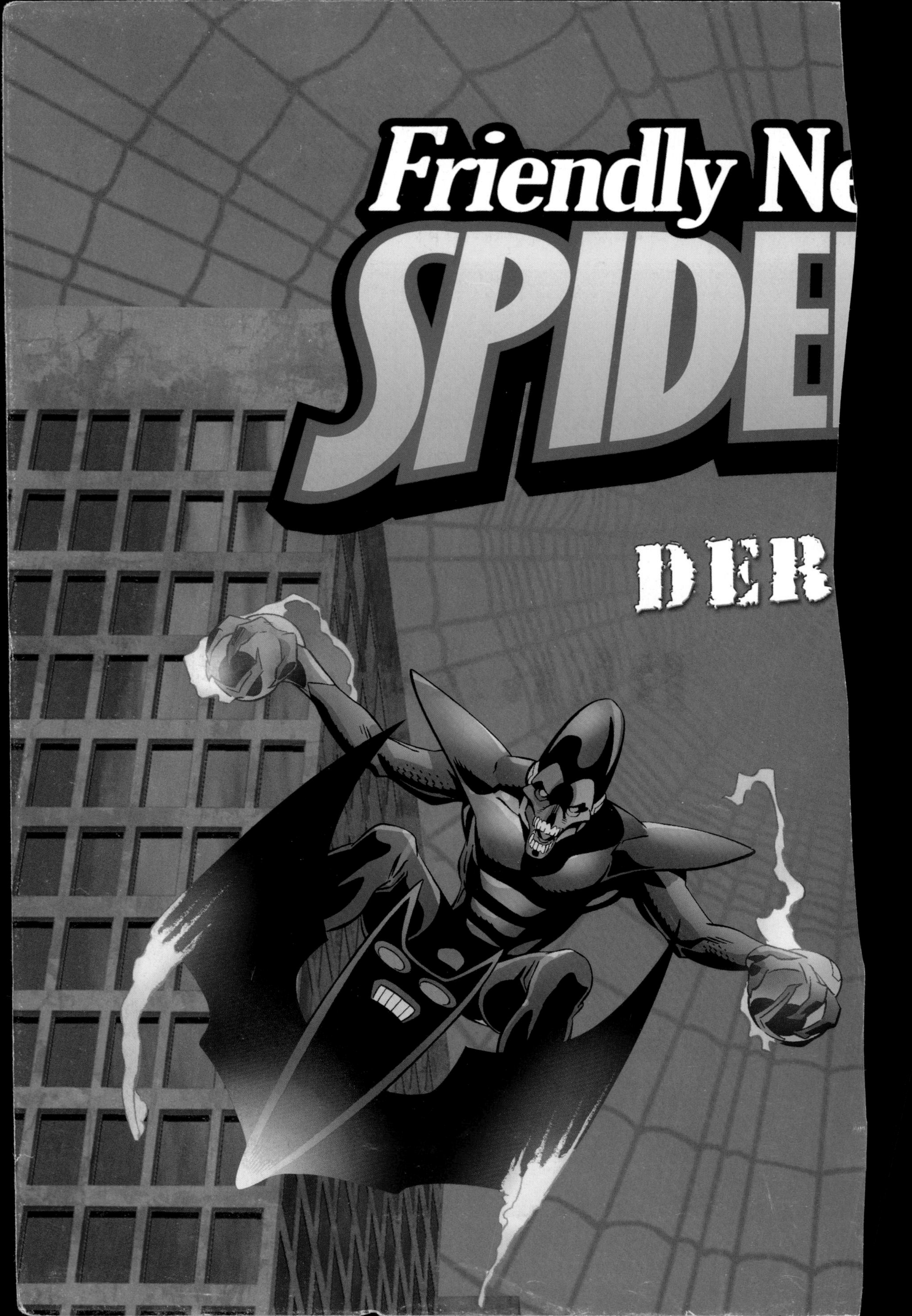
Friendly Ne
SPIDE
DER

ghborhood
R-MAN

ILED

Writer: Peter David
Pencils: Mike Wieringo & Roger Cruz
Inks: Karl Kesel, Oclair Albert,
Victor Olazaba & Mike Manley

Colors: Paul Mounts & Chris Sotomayor
Letters: Virtual Calligraphy's Cory Petit
Assistant Editors: Molly Lazer,
Aubrey Sitterson & Michael O'Connor
Associate Editor: Andy Schmidt
Editors: Tom Brevoort & Axel Alonso

Collection Editor: Jennifer Grünwald
Assistant Editor: Michael Short
Senior Editor, Special Projects: Jeff Youngquist
Vice President of Sales: David Gabriel
Production: Jerry Kalinowski
Book Designer: Dayle Chesler
Vice President of Creative: Tom Marvelli

Editor in Chief: Joe Quesada
Publisher: Dan Buckley

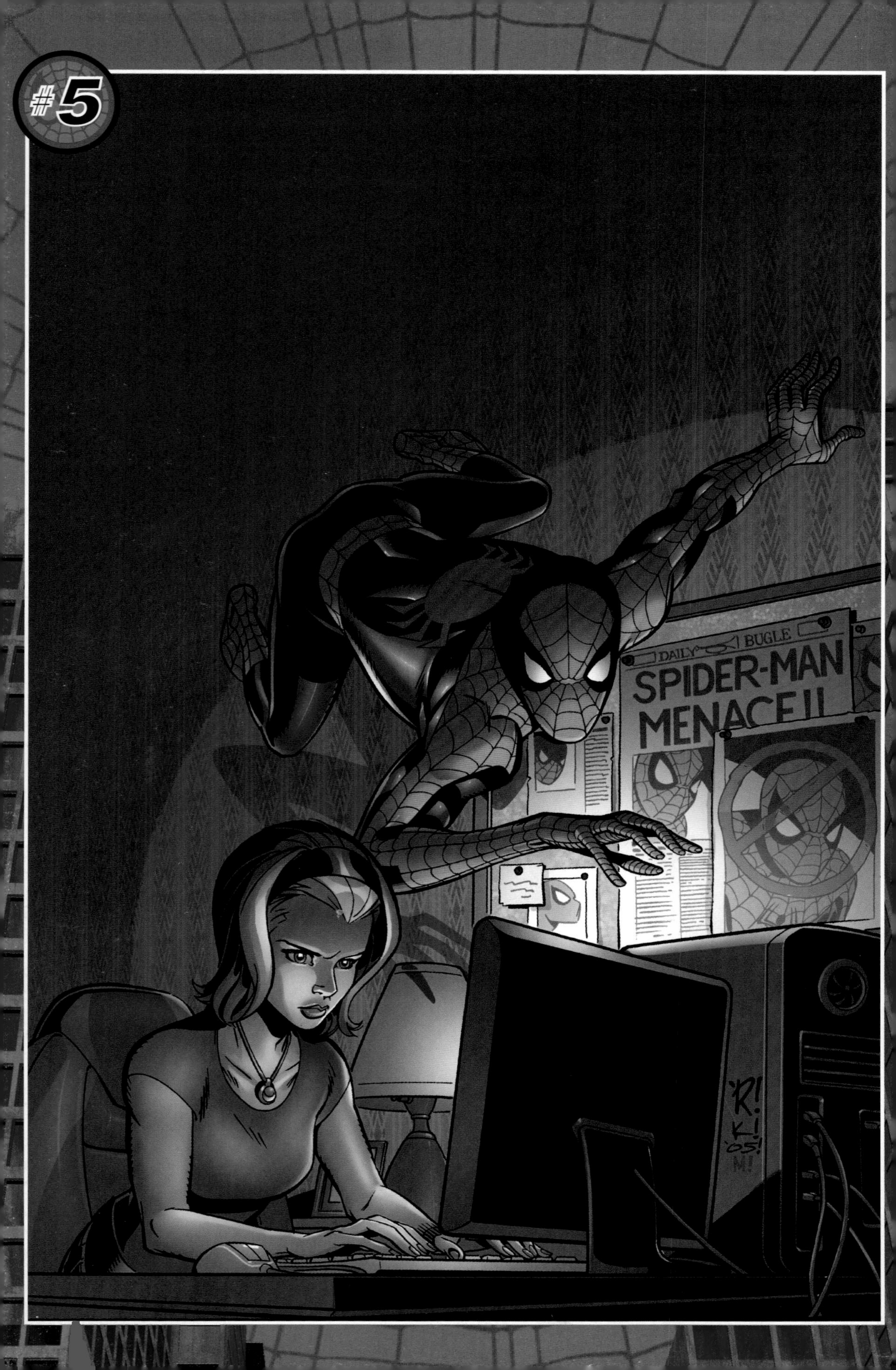
#5
DAILY BUGLE
SPIDER-MAN
MENACE!!

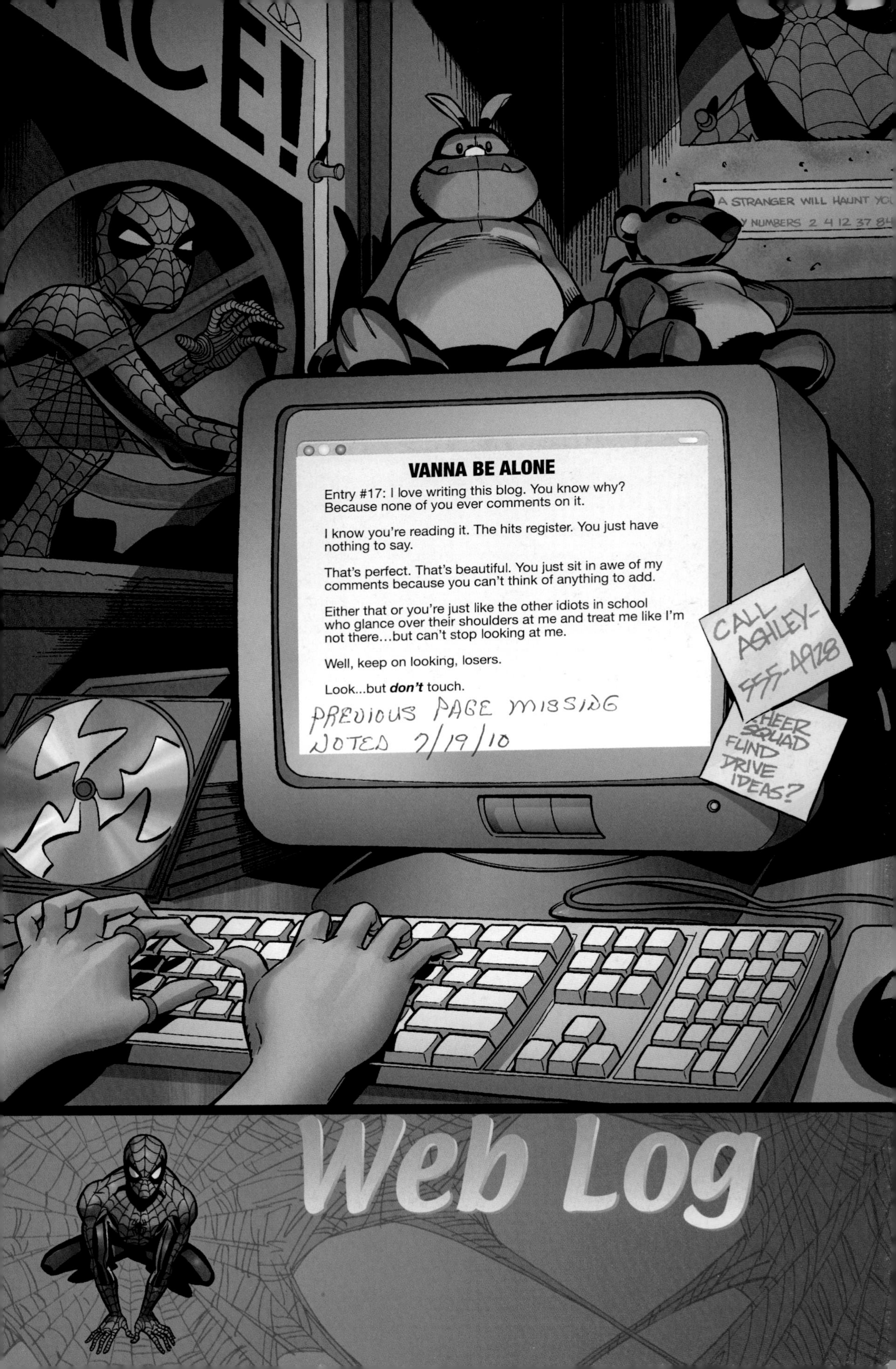
VANNA BE ALONE
Entry #17: I love writing this blog. You know why? Because none of you ever comments on it.
I know you're reading it. The hits register. You just have nothing to say.
That's perfect. That's beautiful. You just sit in awe of my comments because you can't think of anything to add.
Either that or you're just like the other idiots in school who glance over their shoulders at me and treat me like I'm not there...but can't stop looking at me.
Well, keep on looking, losers.
Look...but ***don't*** touch.
CALL ASHLEY-555-4928
CHEER SQUAD FUND DRIVE IDEAS?
Web Log

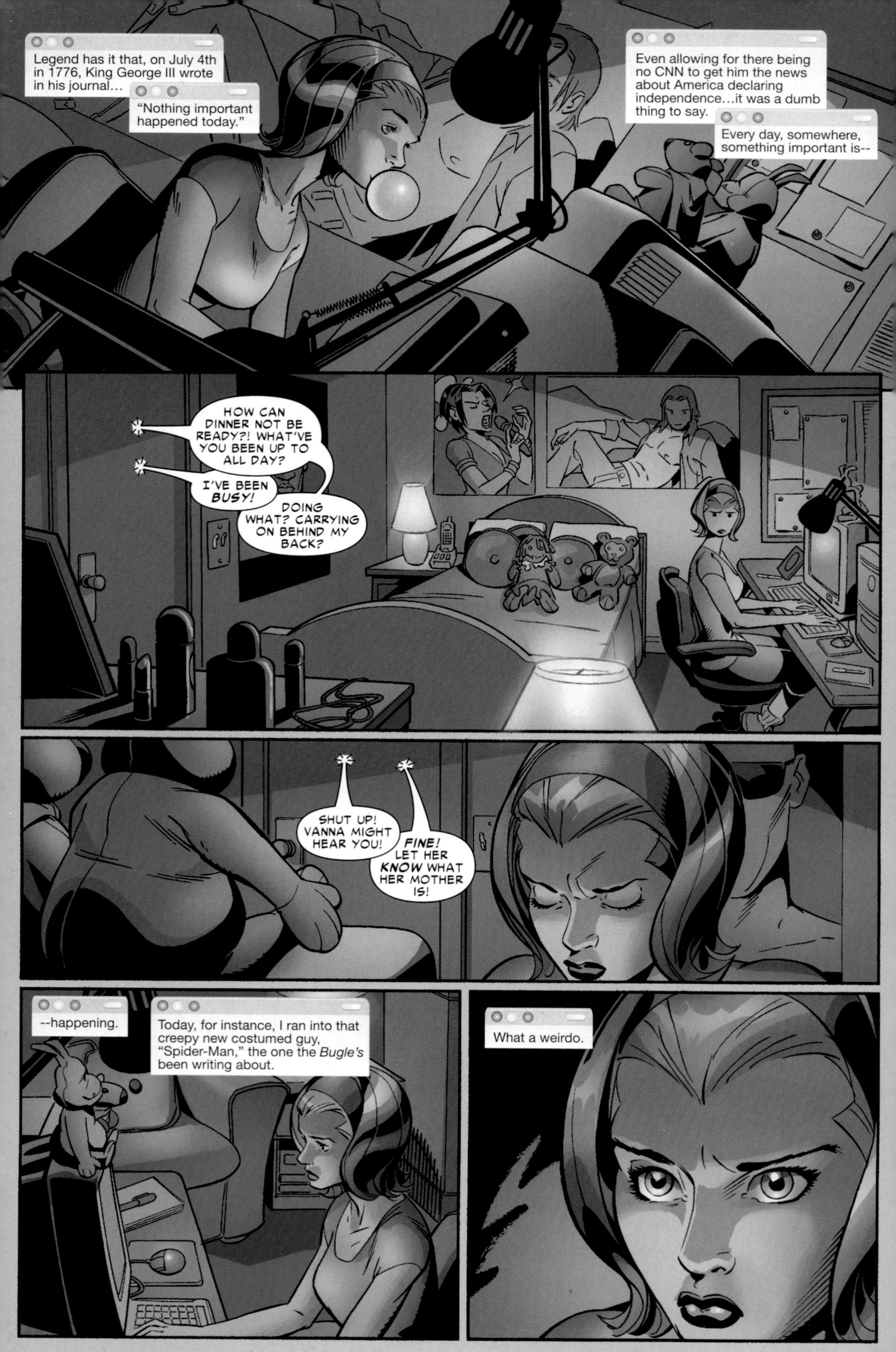
Legend has it that, on July 4th in 1776, King George III wrote in his journal…
"Nothing important happened today."
Even allowing for there being no CNN to get him the news about America declaring independence…it was a dumb thing to say.
Every day, somewhere, something important is--
HOW CAN DINNER NOT BE READY?! WHAT'VE YOU BEEN UP TO ALL DAY?
I'VE BEEN *BUSY!*
DOING WHAT? CARRYING ON BEHIND MY BACK?
SHUT UP! VANNA MIGHT HEAR YOU!
FINE! LET HER *KNOW* WHAT HER MOTHER IS!
--happening.
Today, for instance, I ran into that creepy new costumed guy, "Spider-Man," the one the *Bugle's* been writing about.
What a weirdo.

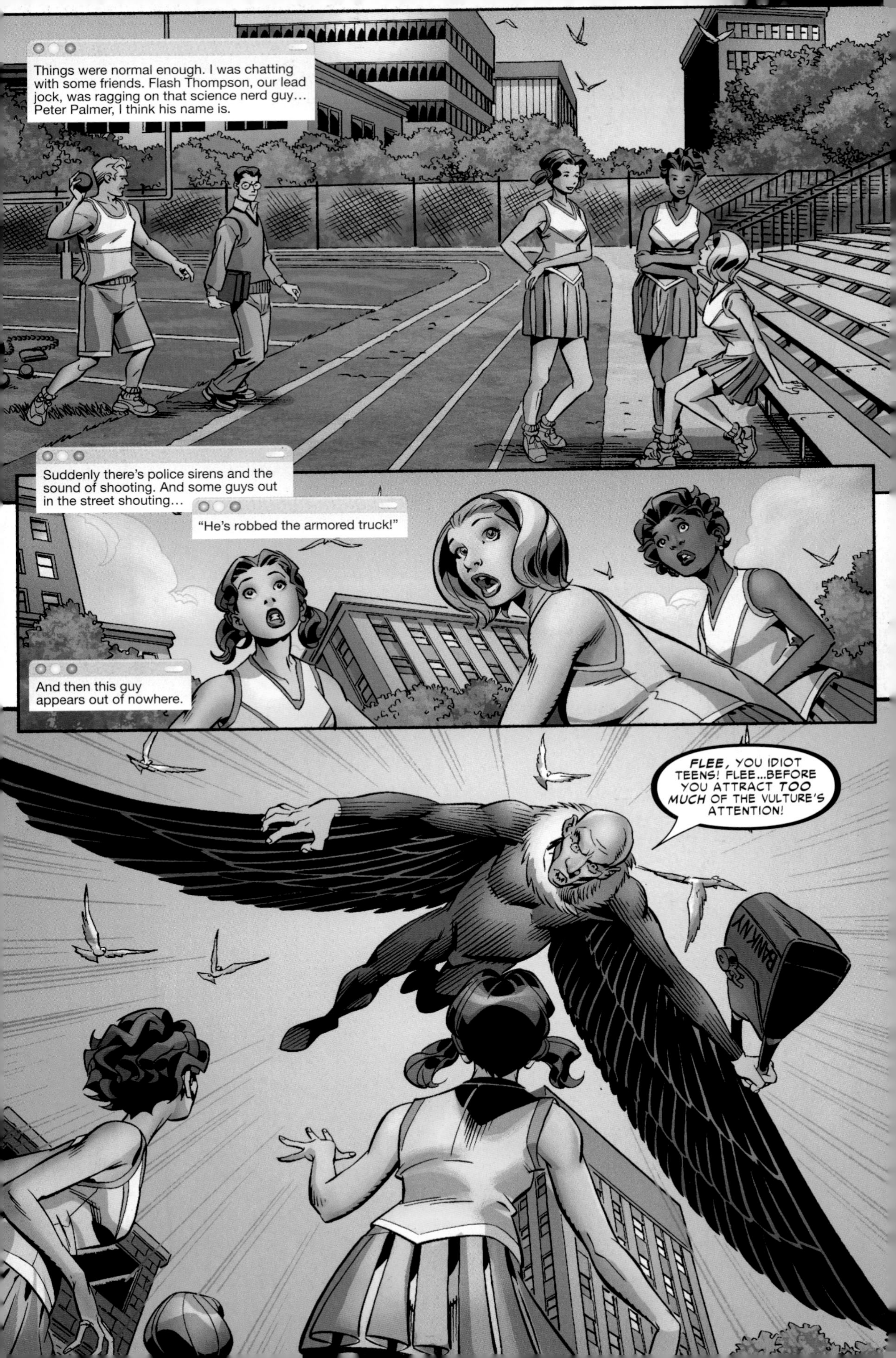

Things were normal enough. I was chatting with some friends. Flash Thompson, our lead jock, was ragging on that science nerd guy… Peter Palmer, I think his name is.
Suddenly there's police sirens and the sound of shooting. And some guys out in the street shouting…
"He's robbed the armored truck!"
And then this guy appears out of nowhere.
FLEE, YOU IDIOT TEENS! FLEE...BEFORE YOU ATTRACT TOO MUCH OF THE VULTURE'S ATTENTION!
BANK NY

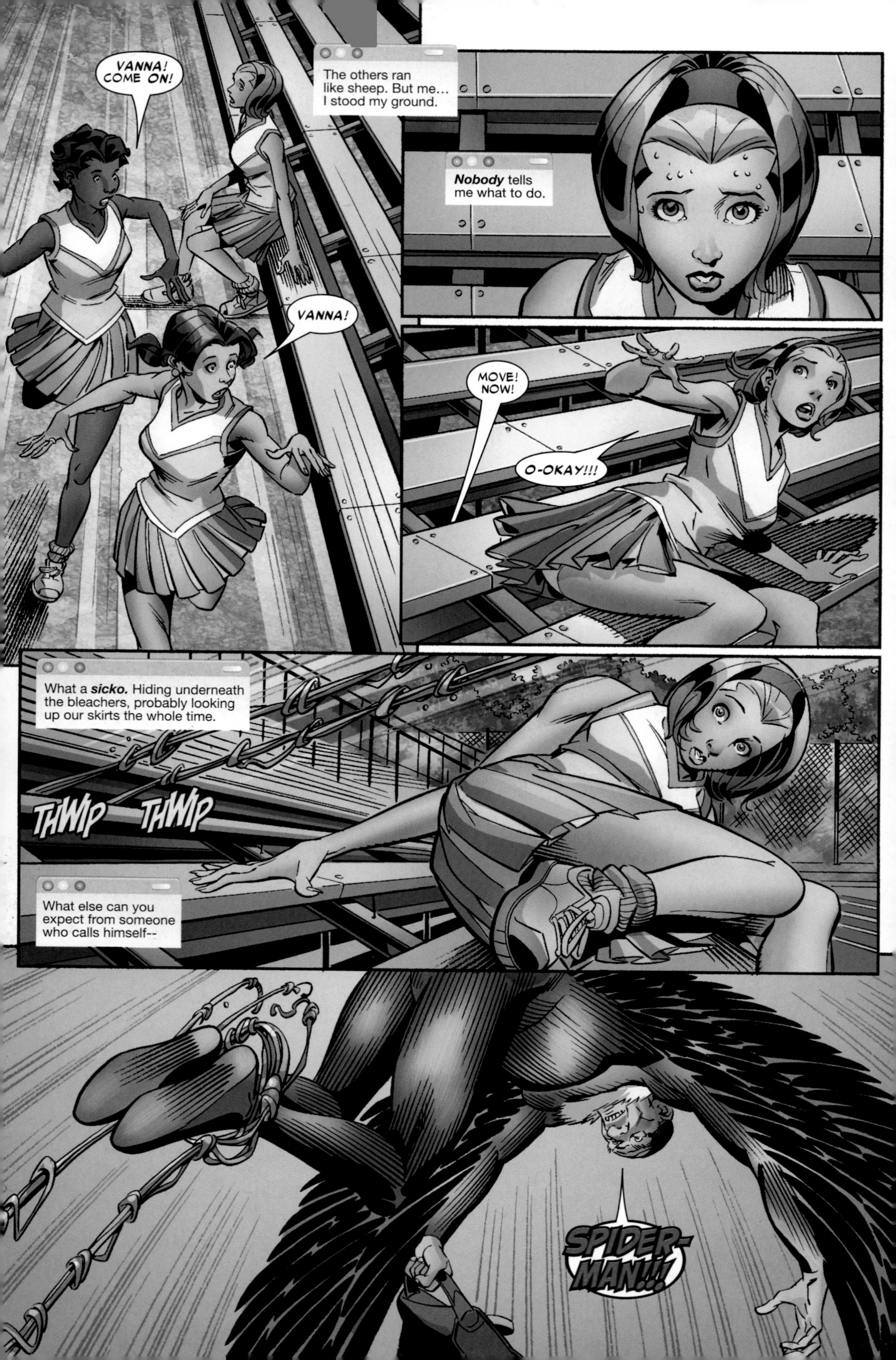
VANNA! COME ON!
The others ran like sheep. But me... I stood my ground.
VANNA!
Nobody tells me what to do.
MOVE! NOW!
O-OKAY!!!
What a sicko. Hiding underneath the bleachers, probably looking up our skirts the whole time.
THWIP THWIP
What else can you expect from someone who calls himself--
SPIDER-MAN!!!

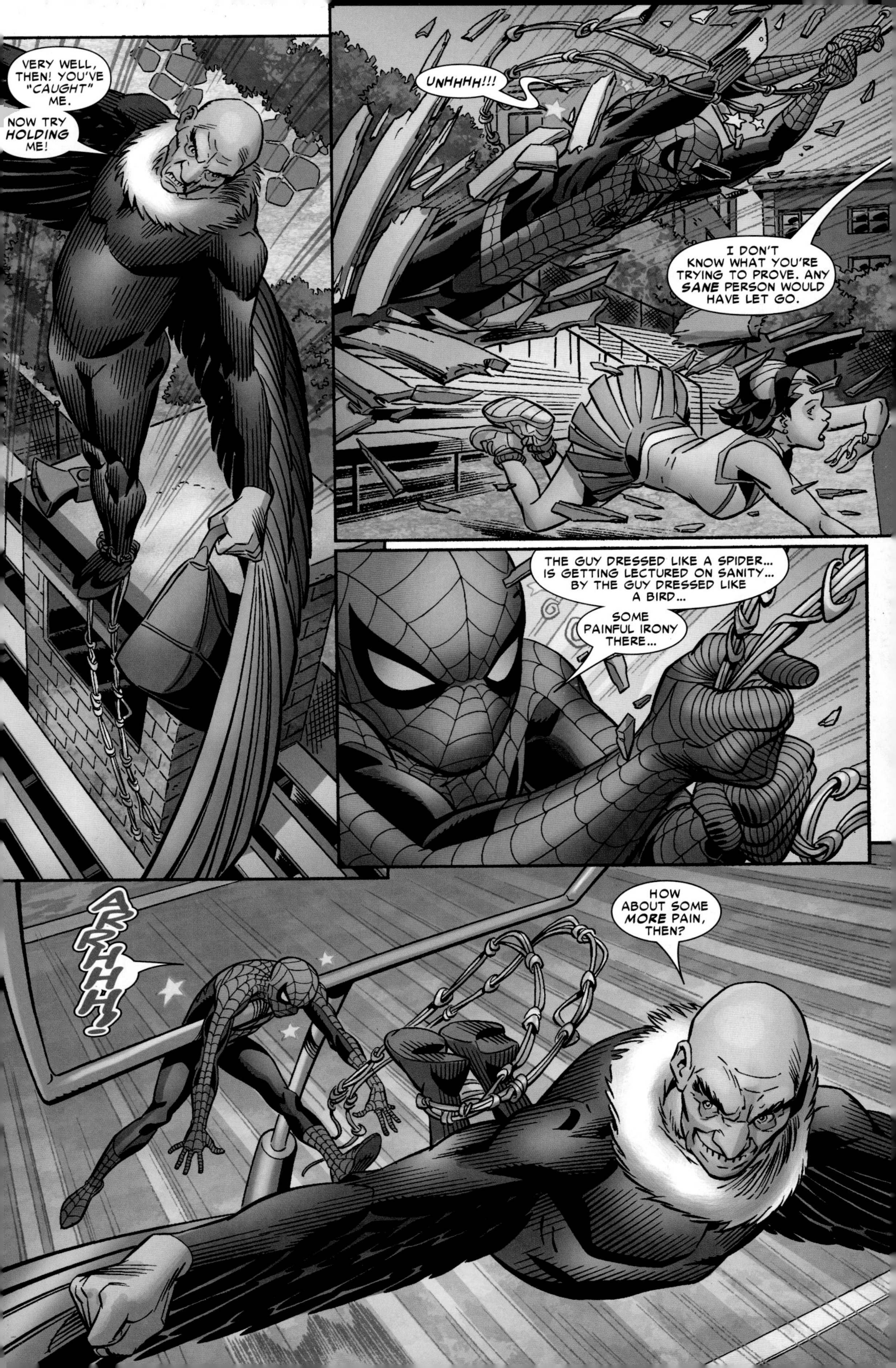
VERY WELL, THEN! YOU'VE "CAUGHT" ME.
NOW TRY HOLDING ME!
UNHHHH!!!
I DON'T KNOW WHAT YOU'RE TRYING TO PROVE. ANY SANE PERSON WOULD HAVE LET GO.
THE GUY DRESSED LIKE A SPIDER... IS GETTING LECTURED ON SANITY... BY THE GUY DRESSED LIKE A BIRD...
SOME PAINFUL IRONY THERE...
ARHHH!
HOW ABOUT SOME MORE PAIN, THEN?

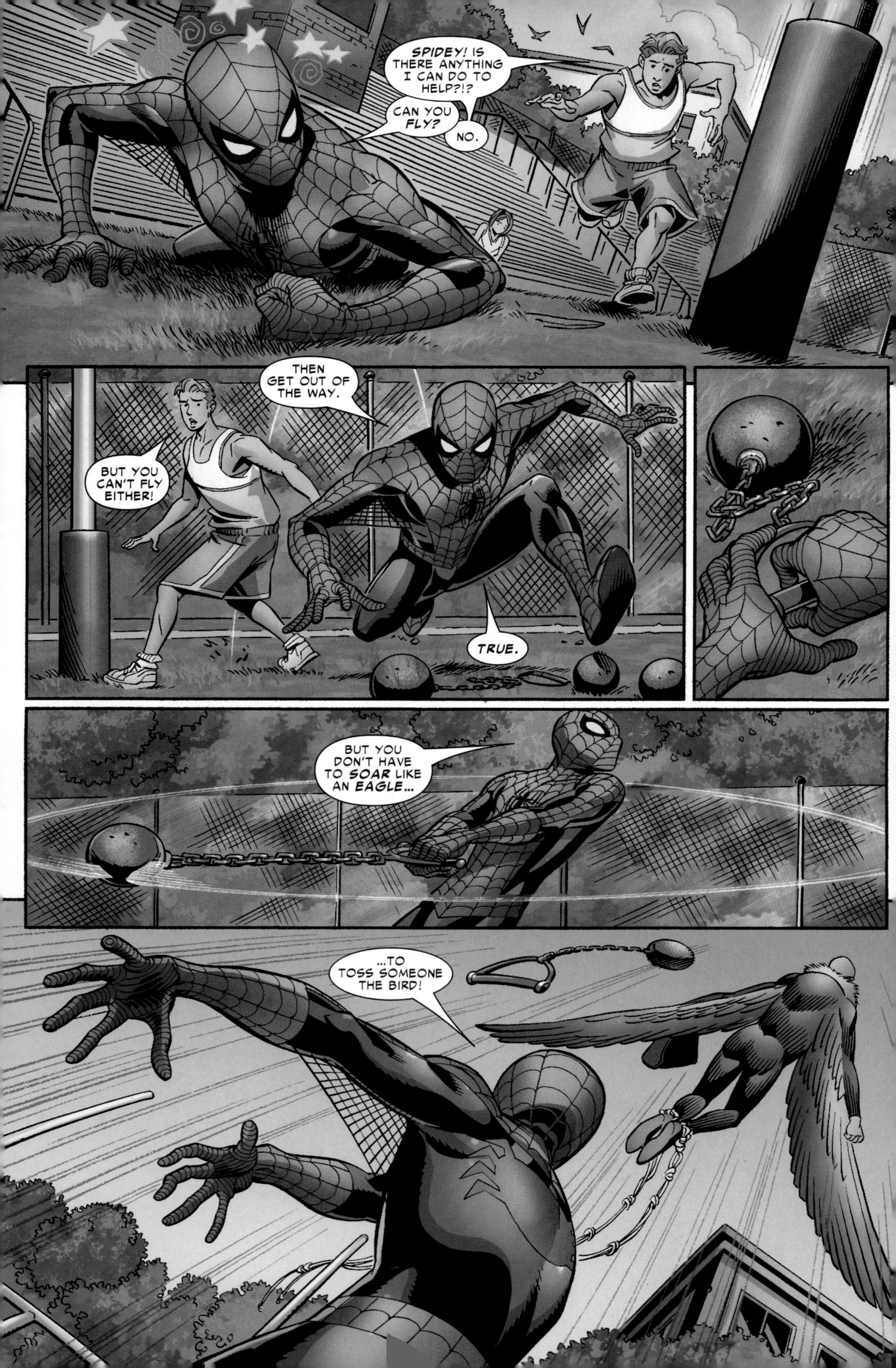
SPIDEY! IS THERE ANYTHING I CAN DO TO HELP?!?
CAN YOU FLY?
NO.
THEN GET OUT OF THE WAY.
BUT YOU CAN'T FLY EITHER!
TRUE.
BUT YOU DON'T HAVE TO SOAR LIKE AN EAGLE...
...TO TOSS SOMEONE THE BIRD!

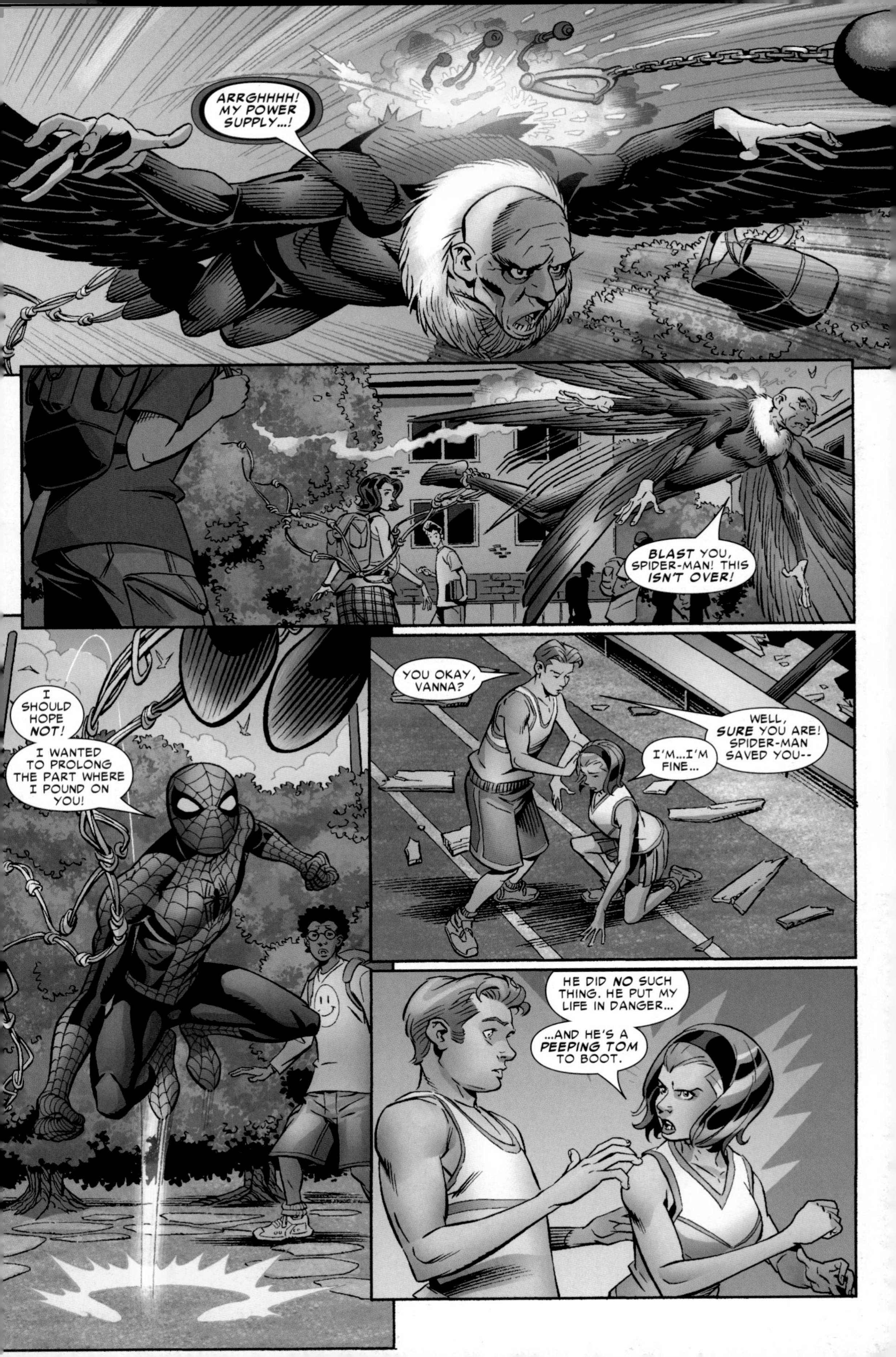
ARRGHHHH! MY POWER SUPPLY...!
BLAST YOU, SPIDER-MAN! THIS ISN'T OVER!
I SHOULD HOPE NOT!
I WANTED TO PROLONG THE PART WHERE I POUND ON YOU!
YOU OKAY, VANNA?
I'M...I'M FINE...
WELL, SURE YOU ARE! SPIDER-MAN SAVED YOU--
HE DID NO SUCH THING. HE PUT MY LIFE IN DANGER...
...AND HE'S A PEEPING TOM TO BOOT.

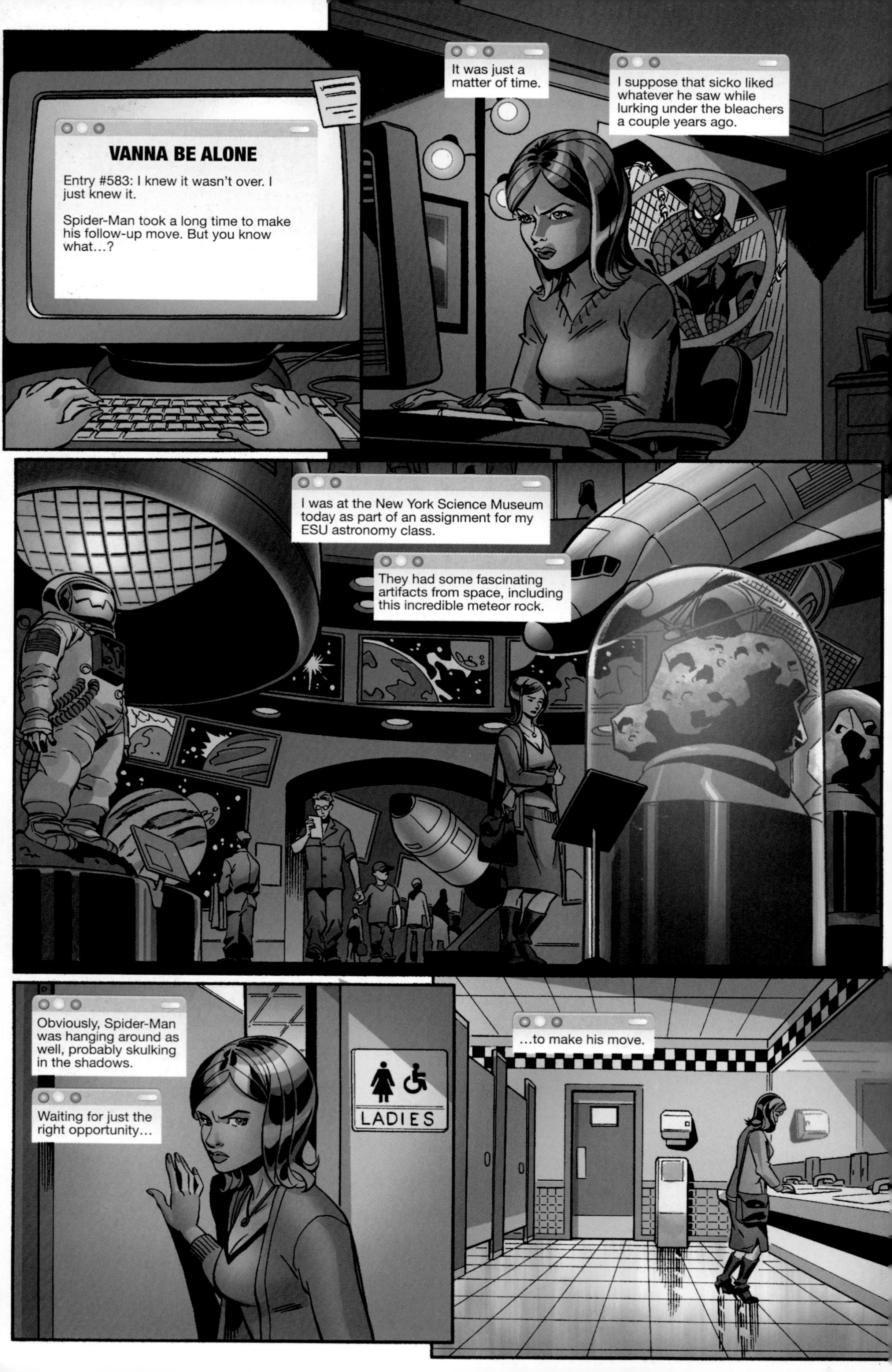
VANNA BE ALONE
Entry #583: I knew it wasn't over. I just knew it.
Spider-Man took a long time to make his follow-up move. But you know what…?
It was just a matter of time.
I suppose that sicko liked whatever he saw while lurking under the bleachers a couple years ago.
I was at the New York Science Museum today as part of an assignment for my ESU astronomy class.
They had some fascinating artifacts from space, including this incredible meteor rock.
Obviously, Spider-Man was hanging around as well, probably skulking in the shadows.
Waiting for just the right opportunity…
LADIES
…to make his move.

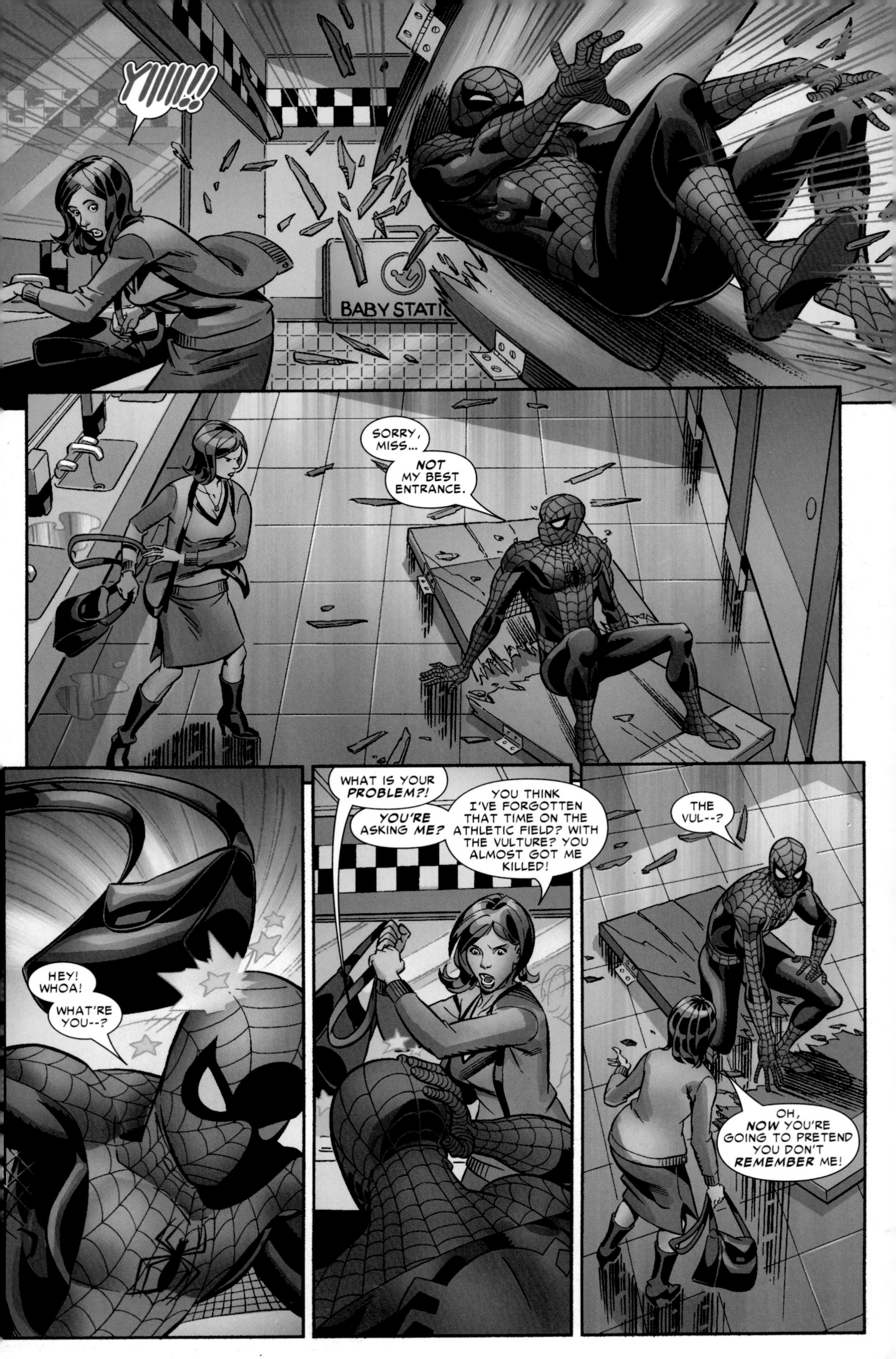
YIIIII!!
BABY STATIO
SORRY, MISS... NOT MY BEST ENTRANCE.
HEY! WHOA!
WHAT'RE YOU--?
WHAT IS YOUR PROBLEM?!
YOU'RE ASKING ME?
YOU THINK I'VE FORGOTTEN THAT TIME ON THE ATHLETIC FIELD? WITH THE VULTURE? YOU ALMOST GOT ME KILLED!
THE VUL--?
OH, NOW YOU'RE GOING TO PRETEND YOU DON'T REMEMBER ME!

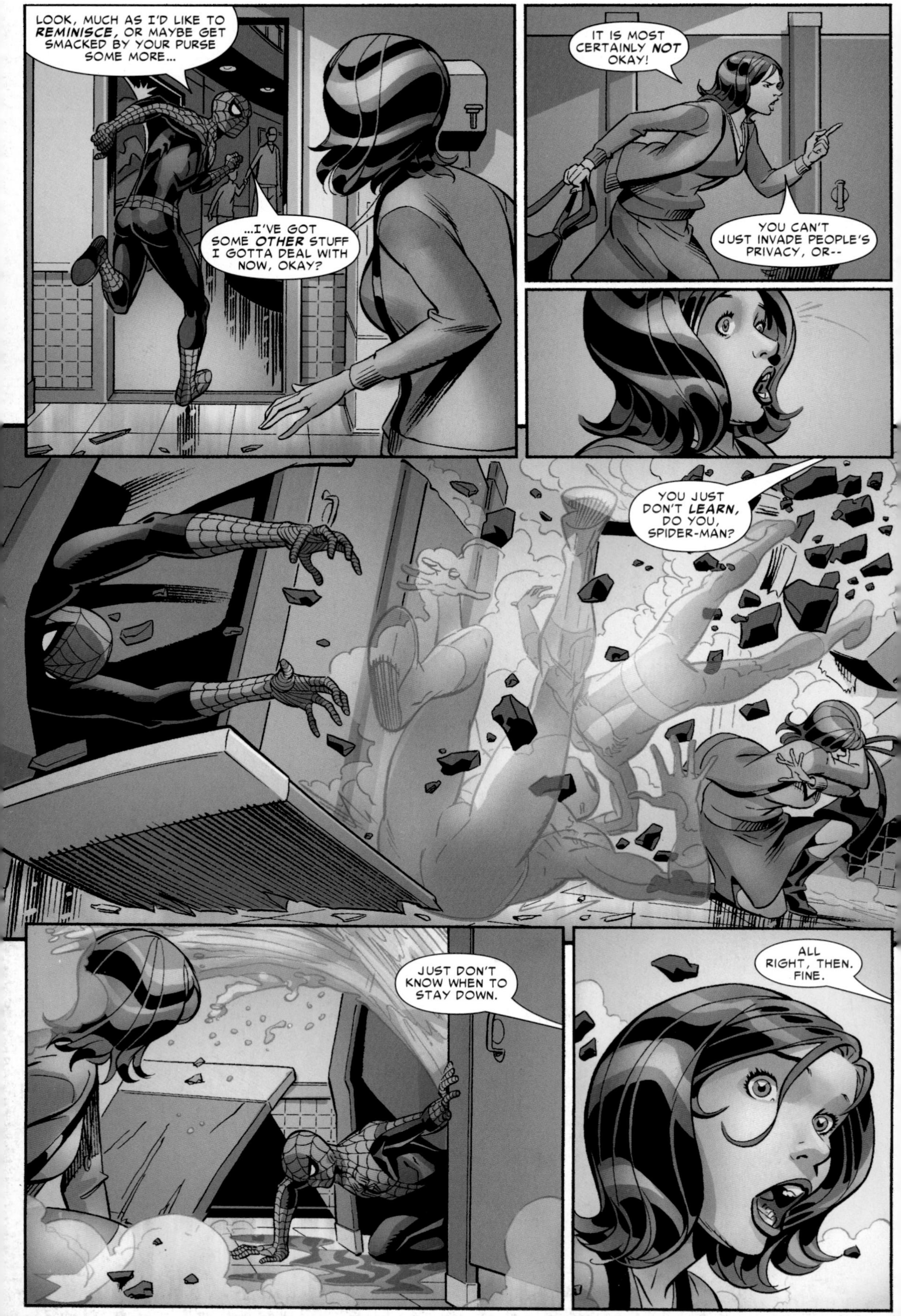
LOOK, MUCH AS I'D LIKE TO REMINISCE, OR MAYBE GET SMACKED BY YOUR PURSE SOME MORE...
...I'VE GOT SOME OTHER STUFF I GOTTA DEAL WITH NOW, OKAY?
IT IS MOST CERTAINLY NOT OKAY!
YOU CAN'T JUST INVADE PEOPLE'S PRIVACY, OR--
YOU JUST DON'T LEARN, DO YOU, SPIDER-MAN?
JUST DON'T KNOW WHEN TO STAY DOWN.
ALL RIGHT, THEN. FINE.

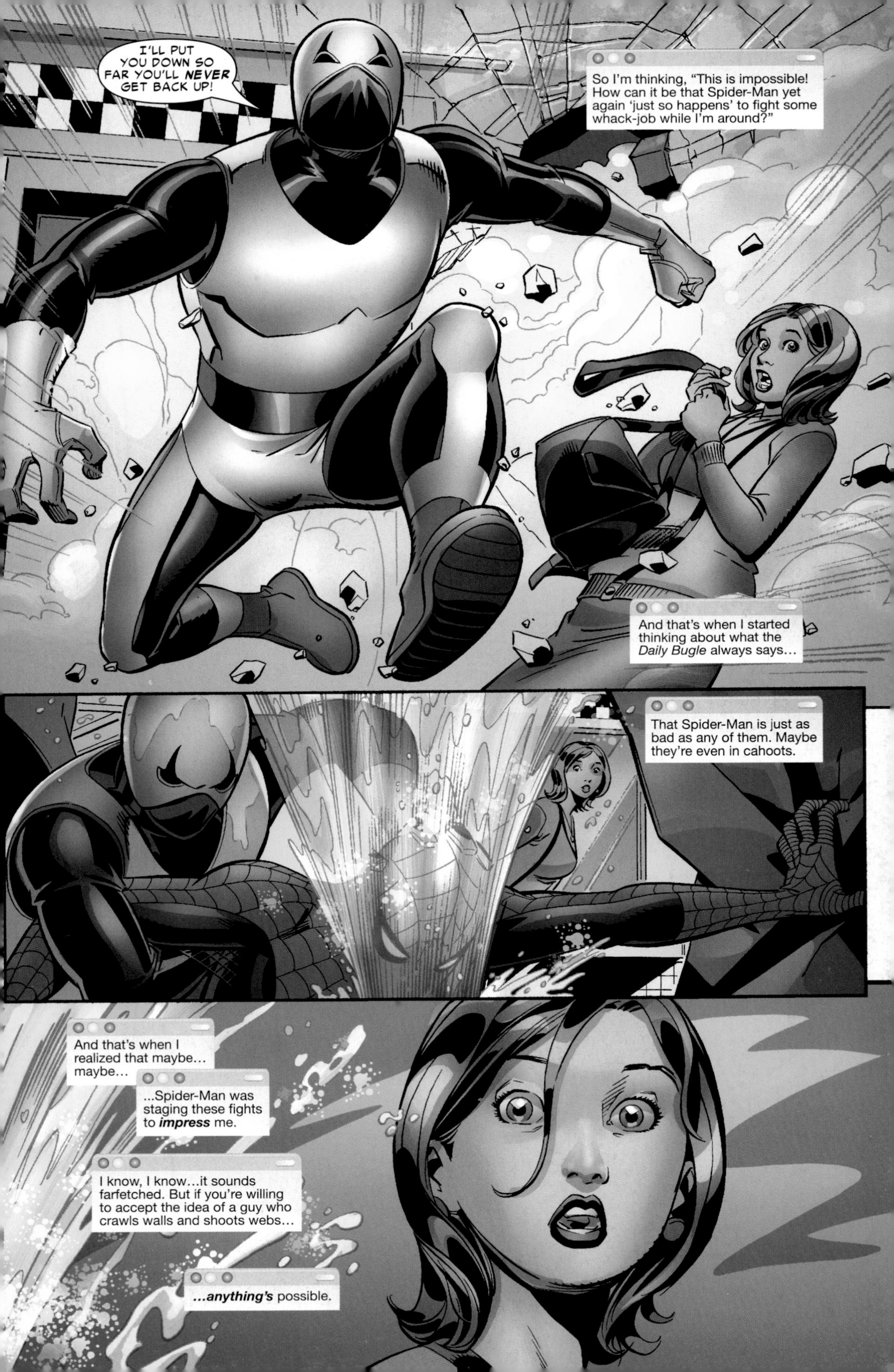
I'LL PUT YOU DOWN SO FAR YOU'LL NEVER GET BACK UP!
So I'm thinking, "This is impossible! How can it be that Spider-Man yet again 'just so happens' to fight some whack-job while I'm around?"
And that's when I started thinking about what the Daily Bugle always says…
That Spider-Man is just as bad as any of them. Maybe they're even in cahoots.
And that's when I realized that maybe… maybe…
...Spider-Man was staging these fights to impress me.
I know, I know…it sounds farfetched. But if you're willing to accept the idea of a guy who crawls walls and shoots webs…
…anything's possible.

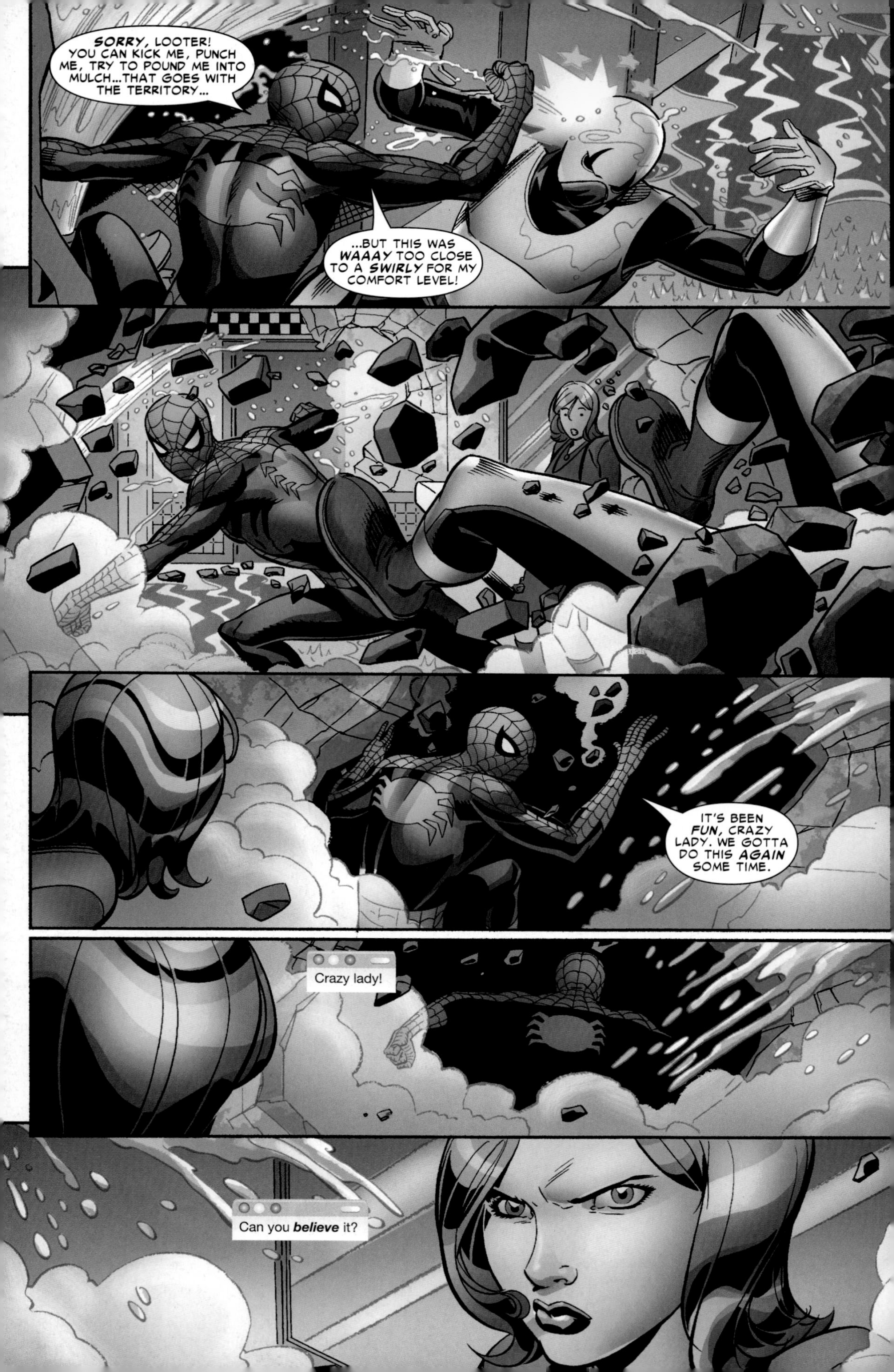
SORRY, LOOTER! YOU CAN KICK ME, PUNCH ME, TRY TO POUND ME INTO MULCH...THAT GOES WITH THE TERRITORY...
...BUT THIS WAS WAAAY TOO CLOSE TO A SWIRLY FOR MY COMFORT LEVEL!
IT'S BEEN FUN, CRAZY LADY. WE GOTTA DO THIS AGAIN SOME TIME.
Crazy lady!
Can you believe it?

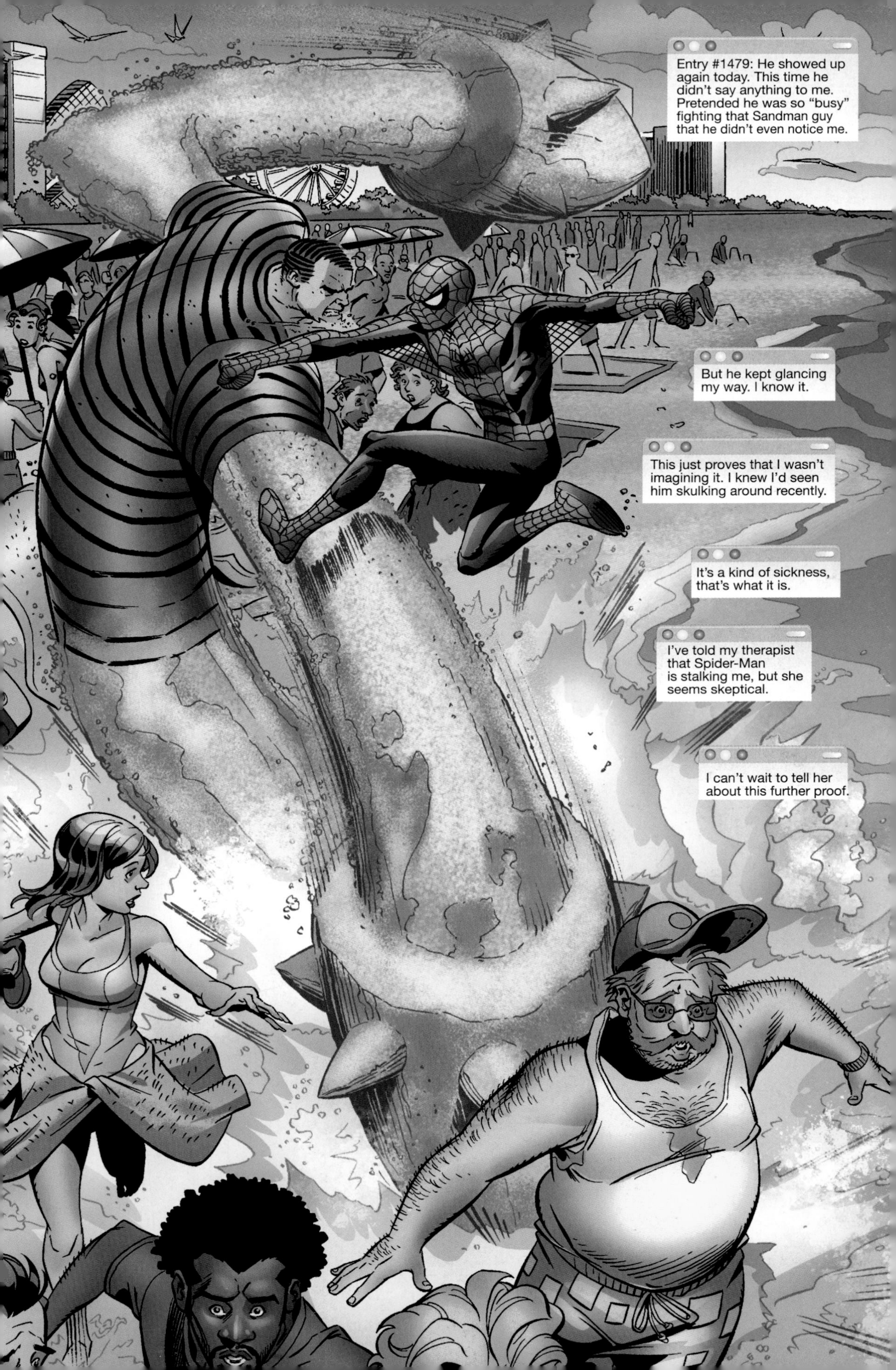
Entry #1479: He showed up again today. This time he didn't say anything to me. Pretended he was so "busy" fighting that Sandman guy that he didn't even notice me.
But he kept glancing my way. I know it.
This just proves that I wasn't imagining it. I knew I'd seen him skulking around recently.
It's a kind of sickness, that's what it is.
I've told my therapist that Spider-Man is stalking me, but she seems skeptical.
I can't wait to tell her about this further proof.

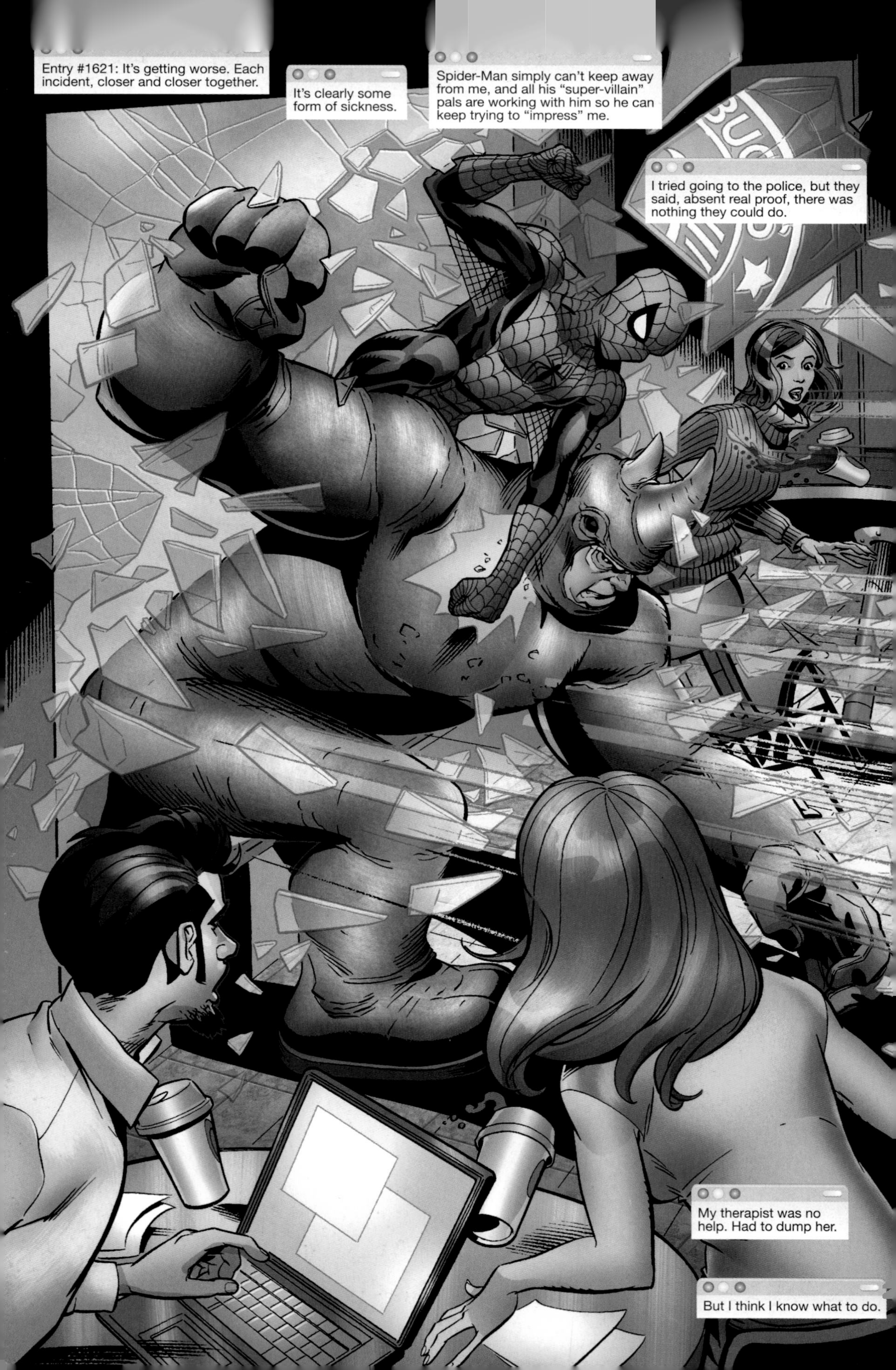
Entry #1621: It's getting worse. Each incident, closer and closer together.
It's clearly some form of sickness.
Spider-Man simply can't keep away from me, and all his "super-villain" pals are working with him so he can keep trying to "impress" me.
I tried going to the police, but they said, absent real proof, there was nothing they could do.
My therapist was no help. Had to dump her.
But I think I know what to do.

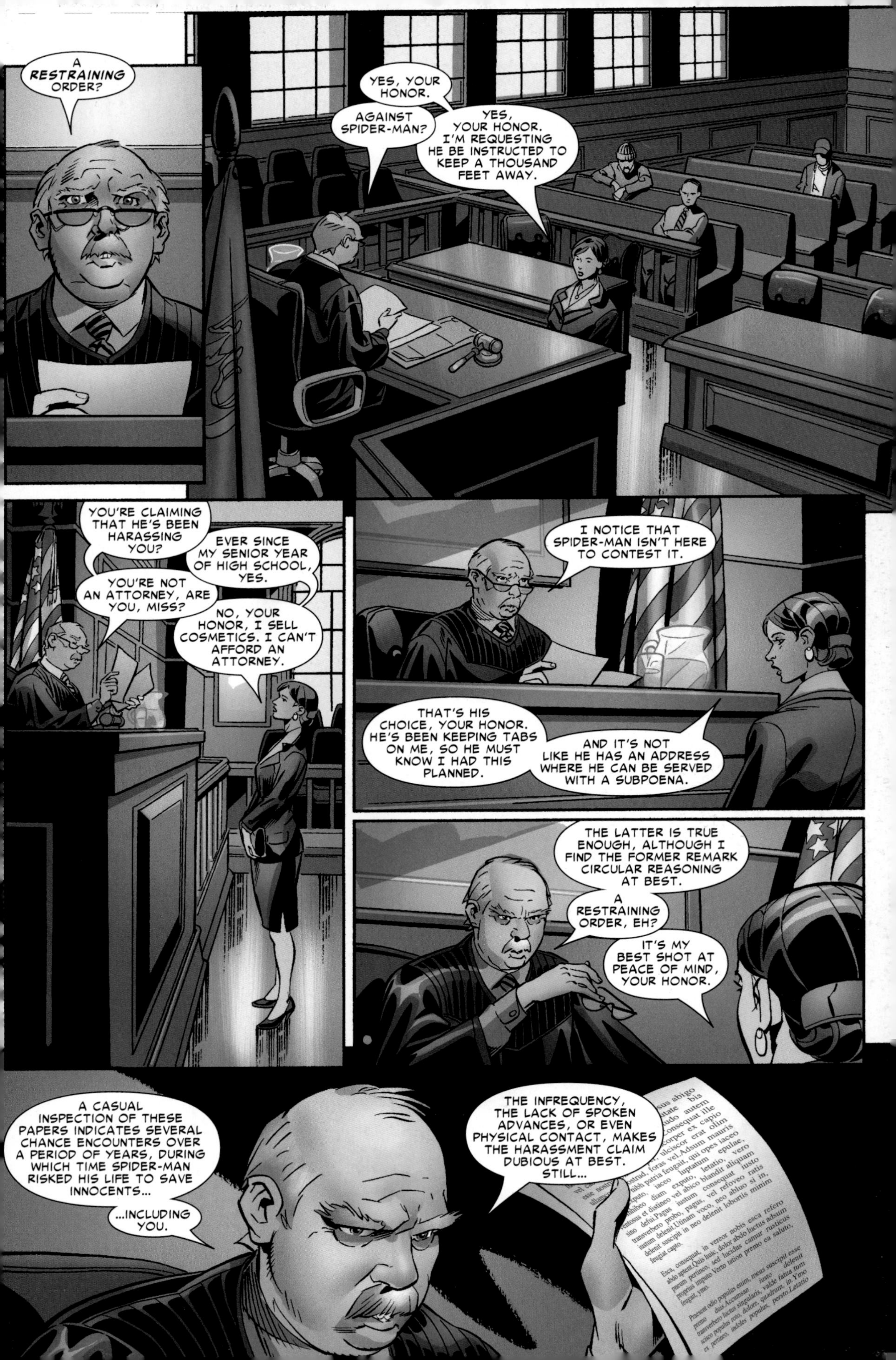

A RESTRAINING ORDER?
YES, YOUR HONOR.
AGAINST SPIDER-MAN?
YES, YOUR HONOR. I'M REQUESTING HE BE INSTRUCTED TO KEEP A THOUSAND FEET AWAY.
YOU'RE CLAIMING THAT HE'S BEEN HARASSING YOU?
EVER SINCE MY SENIOR YEAR OF HIGH SCHOOL, YES.
YOU'RE NOT AN ATTORNEY, ARE YOU, MISS?
NO, YOUR HONOR, I SELL COSMETICS. I CAN'T AFFORD AN ATTORNEY.
I NOTICE THAT SPIDER-MAN ISN'T HERE TO CONTEST IT.
THAT'S HIS CHOICE, YOUR HONOR. HE'S BEEN KEEPING TABS ON ME, SO HE MUST KNOW I HAD THIS PLANNED.
AND IT'S NOT LIKE HE HAS AN ADDRESS WHERE HE CAN BE SERVED WITH A SUBPOENA.
THE LATTER IS TRUE ENOUGH, ALTHOUGH I FIND THE FORMER REMARK CIRCULAR REASONING AT BEST.
A RESTRAINING ORDER, EH?
IT'S MY BEST SHOT AT PEACE OF MIND, YOUR HONOR.
A CASUAL INSPECTION OF THESE PAPERS INDICATES SEVERAL CHANCE ENCOUNTERS OVER A PERIOD OF YEARS, DURING WHICH TIME SPIDER-MAN RISKED HIS LIFE TO SAVE INNOCENTS...
...INCLUDING YOU.
THE INFREQUENCY, THE LACK OF SPOKEN ADVANCES, OR EVEN PHYSICAL CONTACT, MAKES THE HARASSMENT CLAIM DUBIOUS AT BEST. STILL...

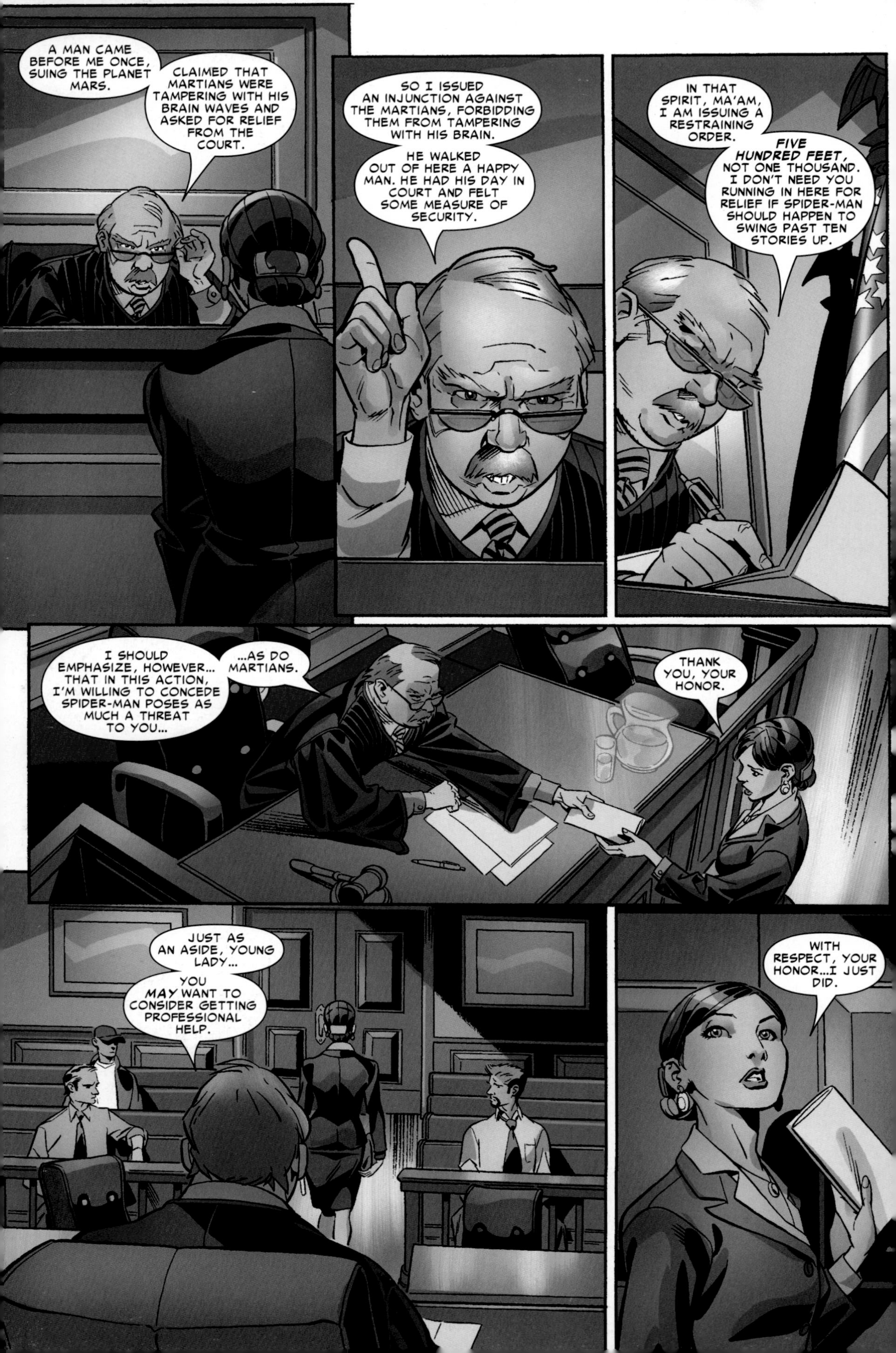
A MAN CAME BEFORE ME ONCE, SUING THE PLANET MARS.
CLAIMED THAT MARTIANS WERE TAMPERING WITH HIS BRAIN WAVES AND ASKED FOR RELIEF FROM THE COURT.
SO I ISSUED AN INJUNCTION AGAINST THE MARTIANS, FORBIDDING THEM FROM TAMPERING WITH HIS BRAIN.
HE WALKED OUT OF HERE A HAPPY MAN. HE HAD HIS DAY IN COURT AND FELT SOME MEASURE OF SECURITY.
IN THAT SPIRIT, MA'AM, I AM ISSUING A RESTRAINING ORDER.
FIVE HUNDRED FEET, NOT ONE THOUSAND. I DON'T NEED YOU RUNNING IN HERE FOR RELIEF IF SPIDER-MAN SHOULD HAPPEN TO SWING PAST TEN STORIES UP.
I SHOULD EMPHASIZE, HOWEVER... THAT IN THIS ACTION, I'M WILLING TO CONCEDE SPIDER-MAN POSES AS MUCH A THREAT TO YOU...
...AS DO MARTIANS.
THANK YOU, YOUR HONOR.
JUST AS AN ASIDE, YOUNG LADY...
YOU MAY WANT TO CONSIDER GETTING PROFESSIONAL HELP.
WITH RESPECT, YOUR HONOR...I JUST DID.

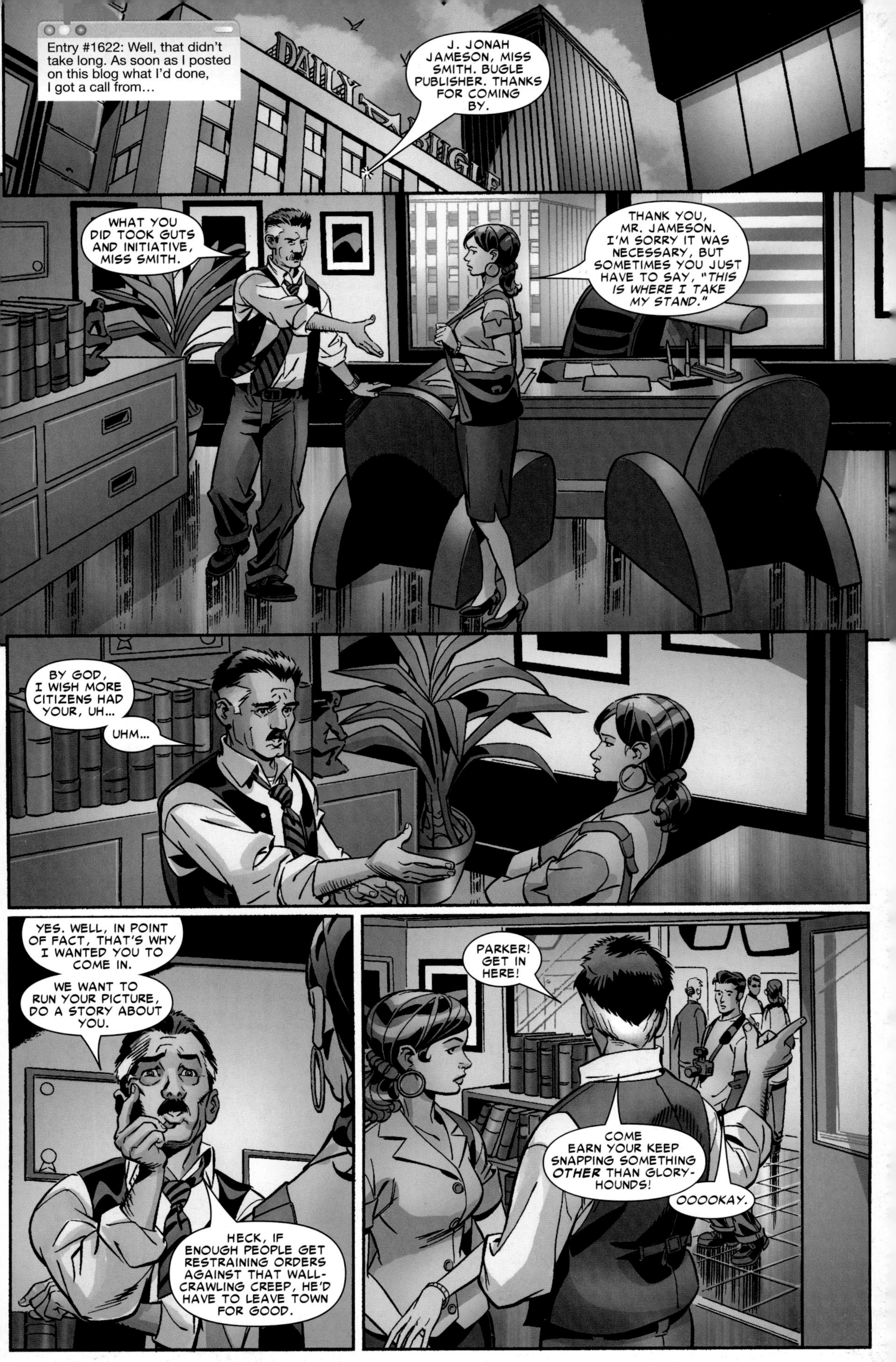
Entry #1622: Well, that didn't take long. As soon as I posted on this blog what I'd done, I got a call from…
DAILY BUGLE
J. JONAH JAMESON, MISS SMITH. BUGLE PUBLISHER. THANKS FOR COMING BY.
WHAT YOU DID TOOK GUTS AND INITIATIVE, MISS SMITH.
THANK YOU, MR. JAMESON. I'M SORRY IT WAS NECESSARY, BUT SOMETIMES YOU JUST HAVE TO SAY, "THIS IS WHERE I TAKE MY STAND."
BY GOD, I WISH MORE CITIZENS HAD YOUR, UH...
UHM...
YES. WELL, IN POINT OF FACT, THAT'S WHY I WANTED YOU TO COME IN.
WE WANT TO RUN YOUR PICTURE, DO A STORY ABOUT YOU.
HECK, IF ENOUGH PEOPLE GET RESTRAINING ORDERS AGAINST THAT WALL-CRAWLING CREEP, HE'D HAVE TO LEAVE TOWN FOR GOOD.
PARKER! GET IN HERE!
COME EARN YOUR KEEP SNAPPING SOMETHING OTHER THAN GLORY-HOUNDS!
OOOOKAY.

THIS WOMAN HAD THE *GUTS* TO CHALLENGE SPIDER-MAN IN COURT! HOLD UP THE RESTRAINING ORDER, VANNA.

YEAH? YOU *CHALLENGED* HIM? FACE TO... UH...MASK?

NO, BUT I WISH HE *HAD* SHOWN UP. I'D HAVE LOVED TO SETTLE THE SCORE WITH--

HAVE, UH...WE MET?

NOPE. YOU DON'T KNOW ME AT ALL.

FWASH

DAILY BUGLE

JUDGE TO WALL-CRAWLER "BUG OFF"

orem ipsum dolor sit amet, consectetuer adipiscing elit. Duis vel eros. Nunc nibh ante, fermentum a, tricies et, congue ac, quam. Maecenas in elit. Praesent ut augue ut nonummy lobortis, risus turpis iaculis nibh, sagittis euismod felis ullentesque vel diam. Ut porta, velit on nonummy lobortis, risus turpis culis nibh, sagittis euismod felis ulm eget pede. Sed lacus ligula. terdum vel, condimentum cursus, onsec vel, justo. Donec ondimentum. Pellentesque tellus agna, faucibus in, porttitor in, olestie egestas, nunc. Fusce viverra.

auris sit amet orci sed justo ndrerit molestie. Vestibulum luctus sum eget nunc. Sed vehicula ingilla orci. Donec eu mauris et nisl gnissim aliquet. Sed egestas lacus eros. Suspendisse potenti. In etium dolor malesuada nunc. uspendisse vitae tellus eget neque napat faucibus. Sed accumsan sum sed diam luctus consequat. ellentesque commodo. Ut et quam as nisl hendrerit hendrerit. Cras venenatis risus non erat. Aliquam erat alupat. Suspendisse ut leo. Quisque ipsen. Pellentesque non neque.

estibulum ante ipsum primis in acibus orci luctus et ultrices posuere abilia Curae; Donec rhoncus. Morbi risus. Nulla dolor eros, pulvinar dipitate, dapibus ut, rhoncus vitae, nus. Ut volutpat. Ut laoreet. ivamus id arcu. Nullam orci. Nulla ellisi. Cras turpis. Sed blandit. urabitur rutrum. Vestibulum ante nodio molestie imperdiet. Etiam bh eros, dictum at, molestie id, actor et, felis. Suspendisse risus eus, dictum vitae, imperdiet quis, trices et, lorem. Duis pellentesque cus vel risus.

tiam mollis nunc sodales nisl. hasellus eget tellus. Class aptent citi sociosqu ad litora torquent per mubia nostra, per inceptos ymenaeos. Etiam vestibulum. Sed enenatis lacus suscipit leo. Aenean id ante ac dui laoreet it risus. aliquam a ligula. In risus. uspendisse urna. Pellentesque idimentum mollis neque. Aenean wallis suscipit leo. Vivamus sed bus at nibh aliquet interdum. Cras actor, massa et ultrices pharetra, ibero velit pellentesque elit, vitae. Aenean vel arcu non nisl hendrerit vestibulum. Donec dignissim

Lorem ipsum dolor sit amet, consectetuer adipiscing elit. Duis vel eros. Nunc nibh ante, fermentum a, ultricies et, congue ac, quam. Maecenas in elit. Praesent ut augue quis urna convallis venenatis. Praesent hendrerit tincidunt felis. Pellentesque vel diam. Ut porta, velit non nonummy lobortis, risus turpis iaculis nibh, sagittis euismod felis ullem eget pede. Sed lacus ligula, interdum vel, condimentum cursus, laoreet vel, justo. Donec condimentum. Pellentesque tellus magna, faucibus in, porttitor in, molestie egestas, nunc. Fusce viverra.

Vestibulum ante ipsum primis in faucibus orci luctus et ultrices posuere cubilia Curae; Donec rhoncus. Morbi eu risus. Nulla dolor eros, pulvinar vulputate, dapibus ut, rhoncus vitae, purus. Ut volutpat. Ut laoreet. Vivamus id arcu. Nullam orci. Nulla facilisi. Cras turpis. Sed blandit. Curabitur rutrum. Vestibulum ut quam non odio molestie imperdiet. Etiam nibh eros, dictum at, molestie id, auctor et, felis. Suspendisse risus eros, dictum vitae, imperdiet quis, ultrices et, lorem. Duis pellentesque lacus vel risus.

Etiam mollis nunc sodales nisl. Phasellus eget tellus. Class aptent taciti sociosqu ad litora torquent per conubia nostra, per inceptos hymenaeos. Etiam vestibulum. Sed

Mauris sit amet orci a hendrerit molestie. Vestibul ipsum eget nunc. Sed fringilla orci. Donec eu maur dignissim aliquet. Sed eger eu eros. Suspendisse pu pretium dolor malesuad Suspendisse vitae tellus eg temp or faucibus. Sed ipsum sed diam luctus c Pellentesque commodo. Ut quis nisl hendrerit hendr accumsan risus non erat. Ali volutpat. Suspendisse ut leo sapien. Pellentesque non nea

Vestibulum ante ipsum p faucibus orci luctus et ultrice cubilia Curae; Donec rhonc eu risus. Nulla dolor eros vulputate, dapibus ut, rhone purus. Ut volutpat. Ut lao Vivamus id arcu. Nullam o facilisi. Cras turpis. Sed Curabitur rutrum. Vestibul non odio molestie imperdie nibh eros, dictum at, mo auctor et, felis. Suspendiss lacus, dictum vitae, imperd ultrices et, lorem. Duis pel lacus vel risus.

Maecenas nisi vel sapie accumsan. Aenean ut velit auctor fermentum. Maecen Quisque consequat, odio a la vulputate, dolor tortor ull tortor, tempus ullamcorper sit amet nibh. Sed augu consectetuer ac, lobortis a a, dolor. Mauris et velit sodales blandit. Quisque lig lobortis libero sed enim pede enim, eleifend eu, pla egestas sed, neque. Curabiti vel elit, pulvinar , Mauris et velit sed sapien. Mauris vestibulum faucib

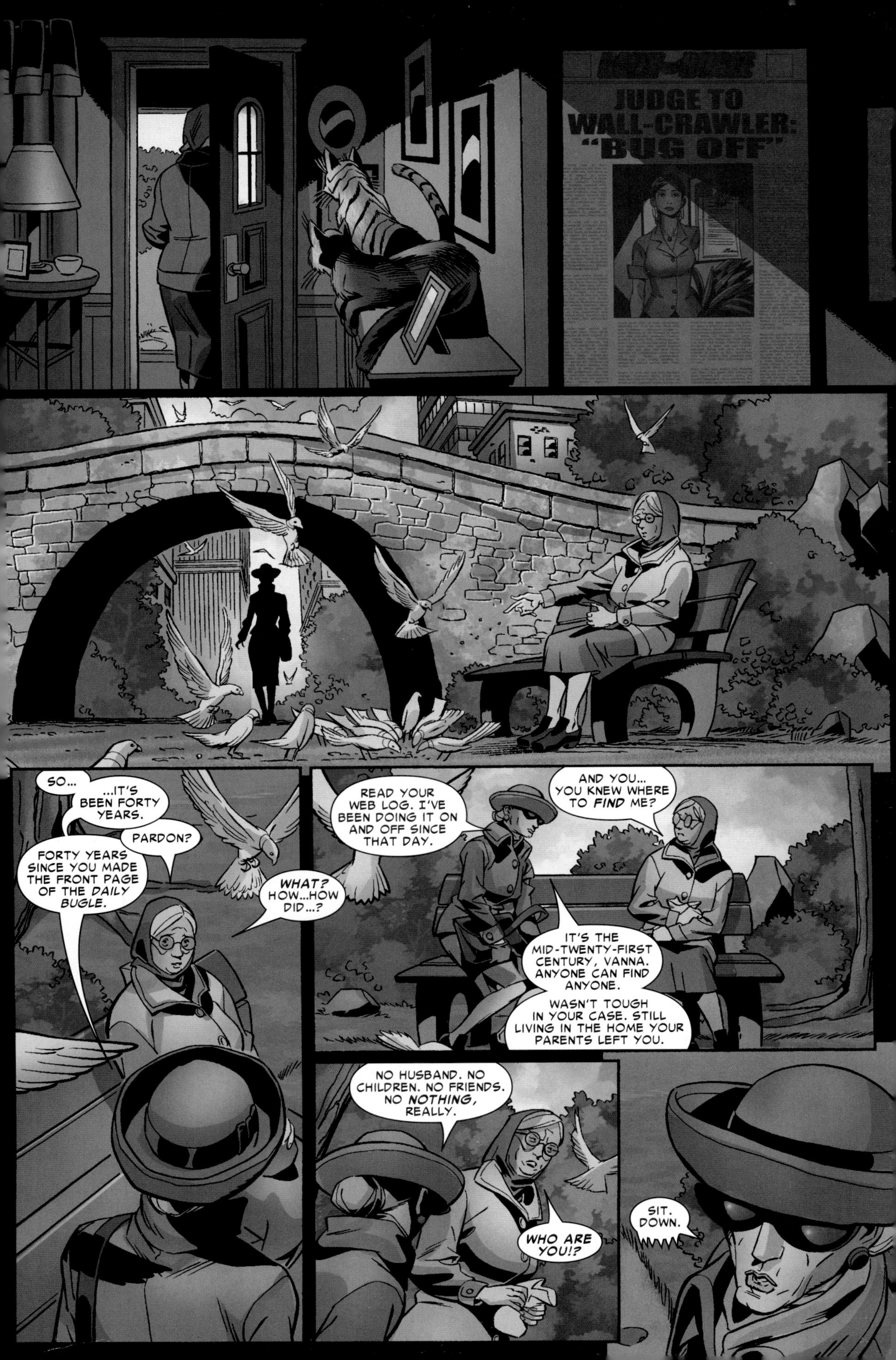
JUDGE TO WALL-CRAWLER: "BUG OFF"
SO...
...IT'S BEEN FORTY YEARS.
PARDON?
FORTY YEARS SINCE YOU MADE THE FRONT PAGE OF THE *DAILY BUGLE*.
WHAT? HOW...HOW DID...?
READ YOUR WEB LOG. I'VE BEEN DOING IT ON AND OFF SINCE THAT DAY.
AND YOU... YOU KNEW WHERE TO *FIND* ME?
IT'S THE MID-TWENTY-FIRST CENTURY, VANNA. ANYONE CAN FIND ANYONE.
WASN'T TOUGH IN YOUR CASE. STILL LIVING IN THE HOME YOUR PARENTS LEFT YOU.
NO HUSBAND. NO CHILDREN. NO FRIENDS. NO *NOTHING*, REALLY.
WHO ARE YOU!?
SIT. DOWN.

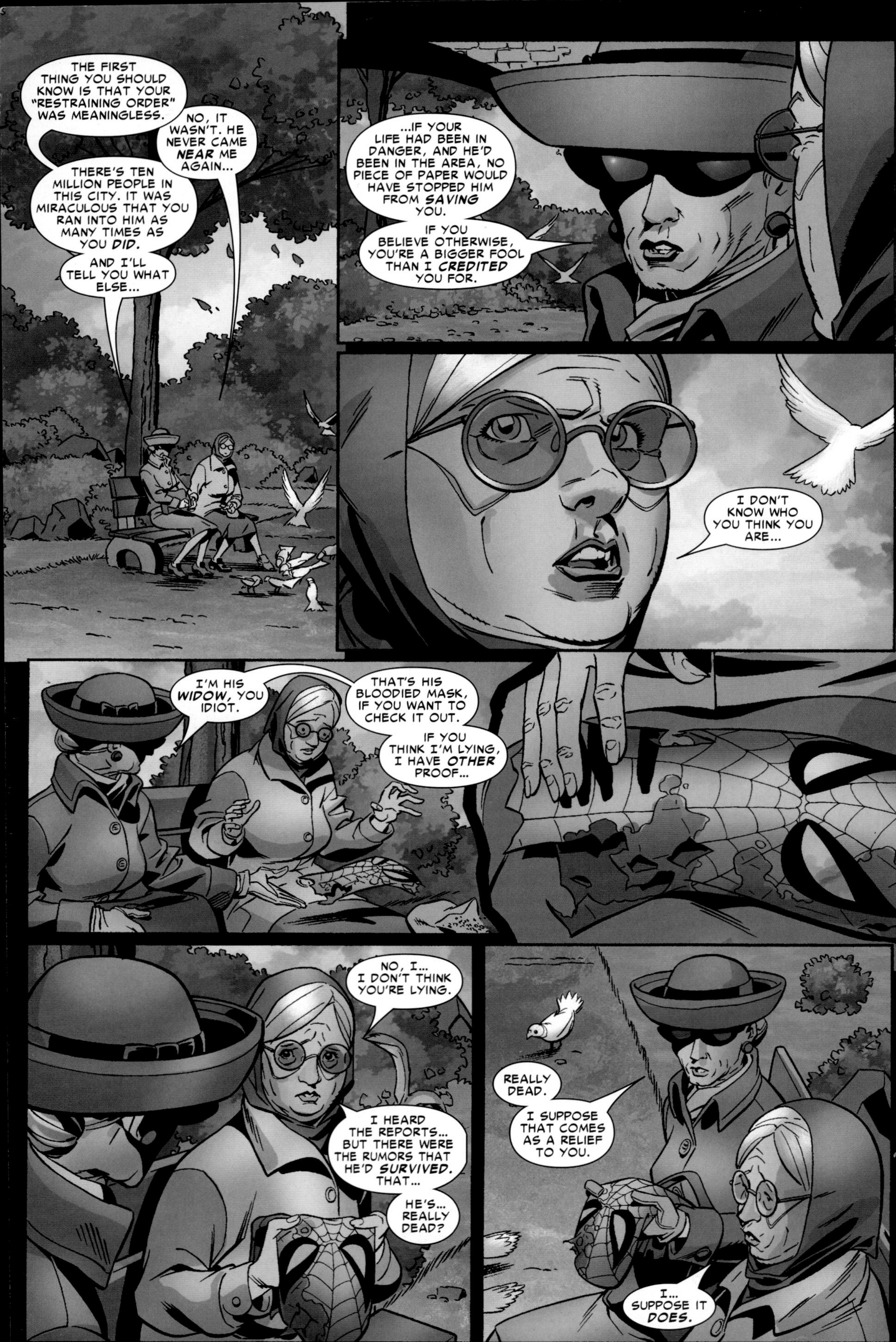
THE FIRST THING YOU SHOULD KNOW IS THAT YOUR "RESTRAINING ORDER" WAS MEANINGLESS.
NO, IT WASN'T. HE NEVER CAME NEAR ME AGAIN...
THERE'S TEN MILLION PEOPLE IN THIS CITY. IT WAS MIRACULOUS THAT YOU RAN INTO HIM AS MANY TIMES AS YOU DID.
AND I'LL TELL YOU WHAT ELSE...
...IF YOUR LIFE HAD BEEN IN DANGER, AND HE'D BEEN IN THE AREA, NO PIECE OF PAPER WOULD HAVE STOPPED HIM FROM SAVING YOU.
IF YOU BELIEVE OTHERWISE, YOU'RE A BIGGER FOOL THAN I CREDITED YOU FOR.
I DON'T KNOW WHO YOU THINK YOU ARE...
I'M HIS WIDOW, YOU IDIOT.
THAT'S HIS BLOODIED MASK, IF YOU WANT TO CHECK IT OUT.
IF YOU THINK I'M LYING, I HAVE OTHER PROOF...
NO, I... I DON'T THINK YOU'RE LYING.
I HEARD THE REPORTS... BUT THERE WERE THE RUMORS THAT HE'D SURVIVED. THAT...
HE'S... REALLY DEAD?
REALLY DEAD.
I SUPPOSE THAT COMES AS A RELIEF TO YOU.
I... SUPPOSE IT DOES.

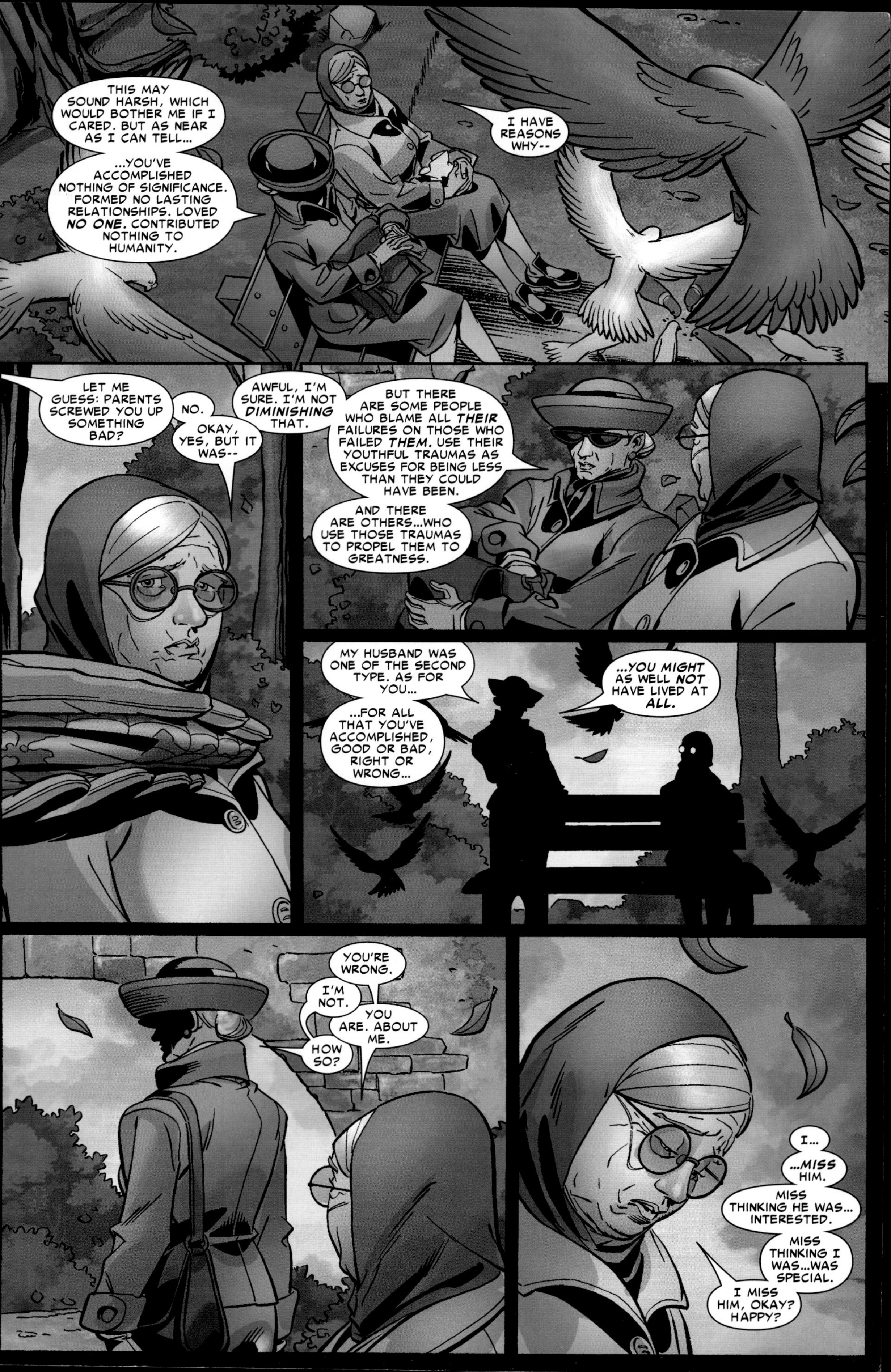
THIS MAY SOUND HARSH, WHICH WOULD BOTHER ME IF I CARED. BUT AS NEAR AS I CAN TELL...
...YOU'VE ACCOMPLISHED NOTHING OF SIGNIFICANCE. FORMED NO LASTING RELATIONSHIPS. LOVED NO ONE. CONTRIBUTED NOTHING TO HUMANITY.
I HAVE REASONS WHY--
LET ME GUESS: PARENTS SCREWED YOU UP SOMETHING BAD?
NO.
OKAY, YES, BUT IT WAS--
AWFUL, I'M SURE. I'M NOT DIMINISHING THAT.
BUT THERE ARE SOME PEOPLE WHO BLAME ALL THEIR FAILURES ON THOSE WHO FAILED THEM. USE THEIR YOUTHFUL TRAUMAS AS EXCUSES FOR BEING LESS THAN THEY COULD HAVE BEEN.
AND THERE ARE OTHERS...WHO USE THOSE TRAUMAS TO PROPEL THEM TO GREATNESS.
MY HUSBAND WAS ONE OF THE SECOND TYPE. AS FOR YOU...
...FOR ALL THAT YOU'VE ACCOMPLISHED, GOOD OR BAD, RIGHT OR WRONG...
...YOU MIGHT AS WELL NOT HAVE LIVED AT ALL.
YOU'RE WRONG.
I'M NOT.
YOU ARE. ABOUT ME.
HOW SO?
I...
...MISS HIM.
MISS THINKING HE WAS... INTERESTED.
MISS THINKING I WAS...WAS SPECIAL.
I MISS HIM, OKAY? HAPPY?

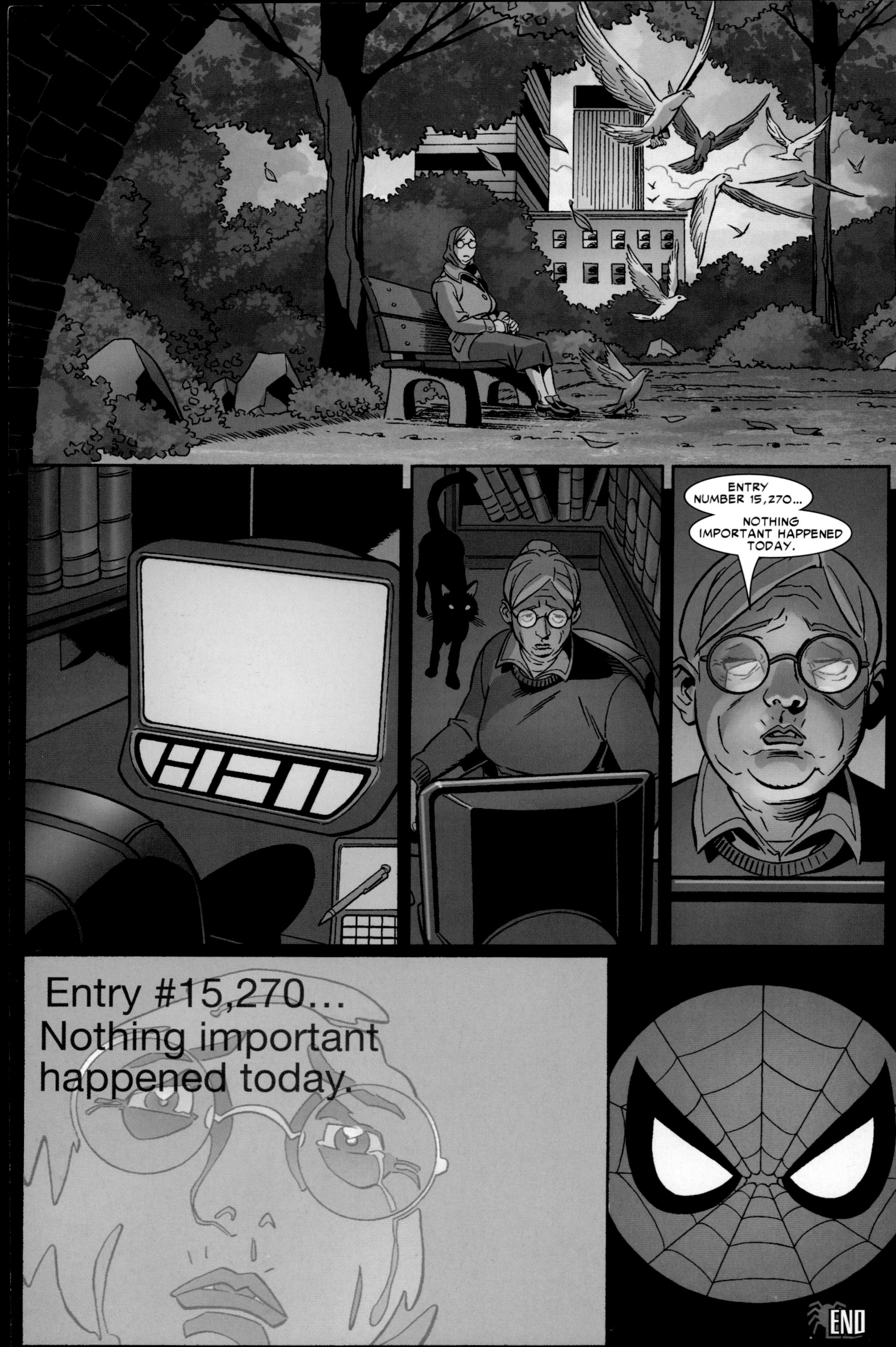
ENTRY NUMBER 15,270...
NOTHING IMPORTANT HAPPENED TODAY.
Entry #15,270…
Nothing important happened today.
END

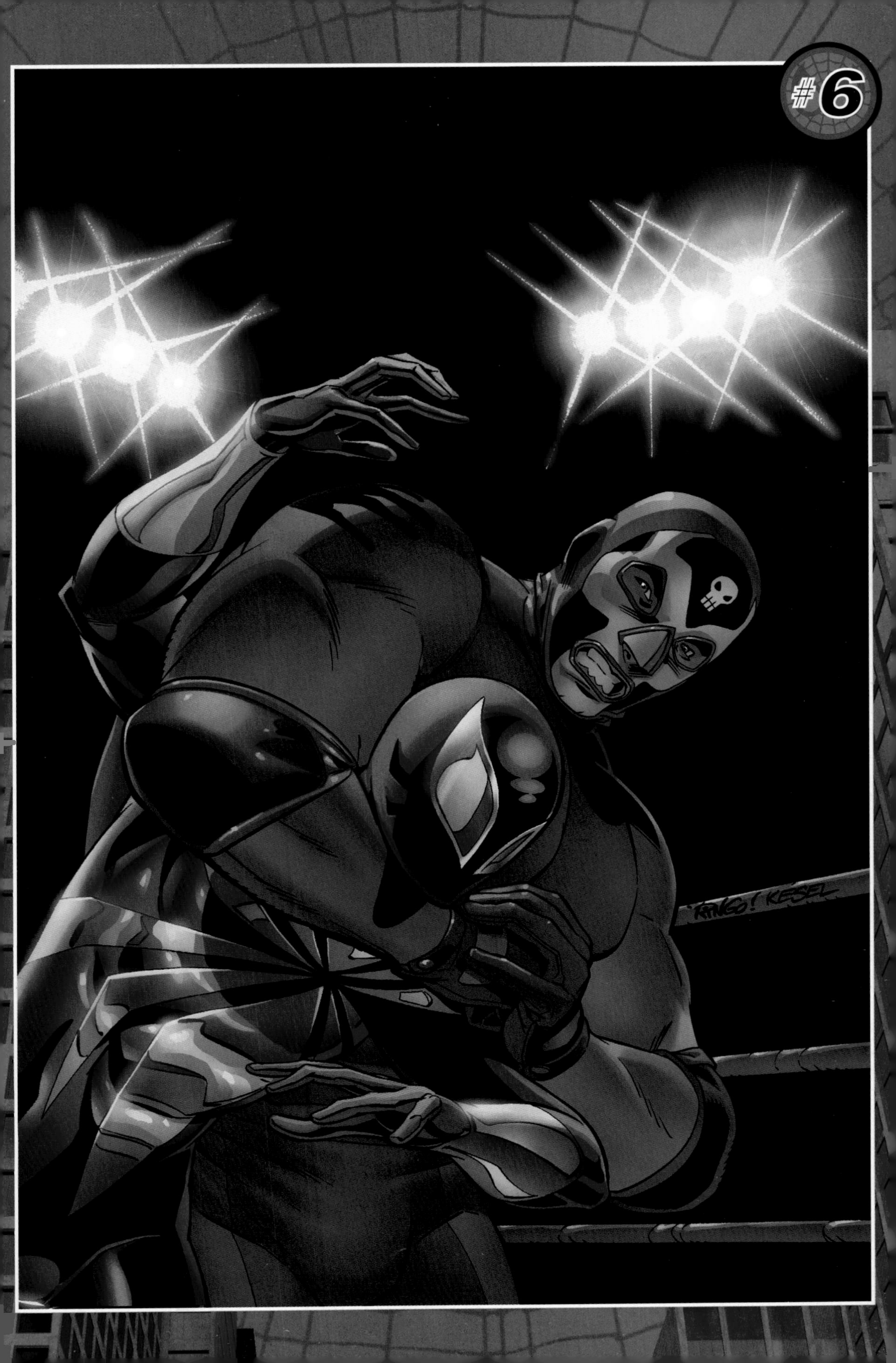

#6
RINGO! KESEL

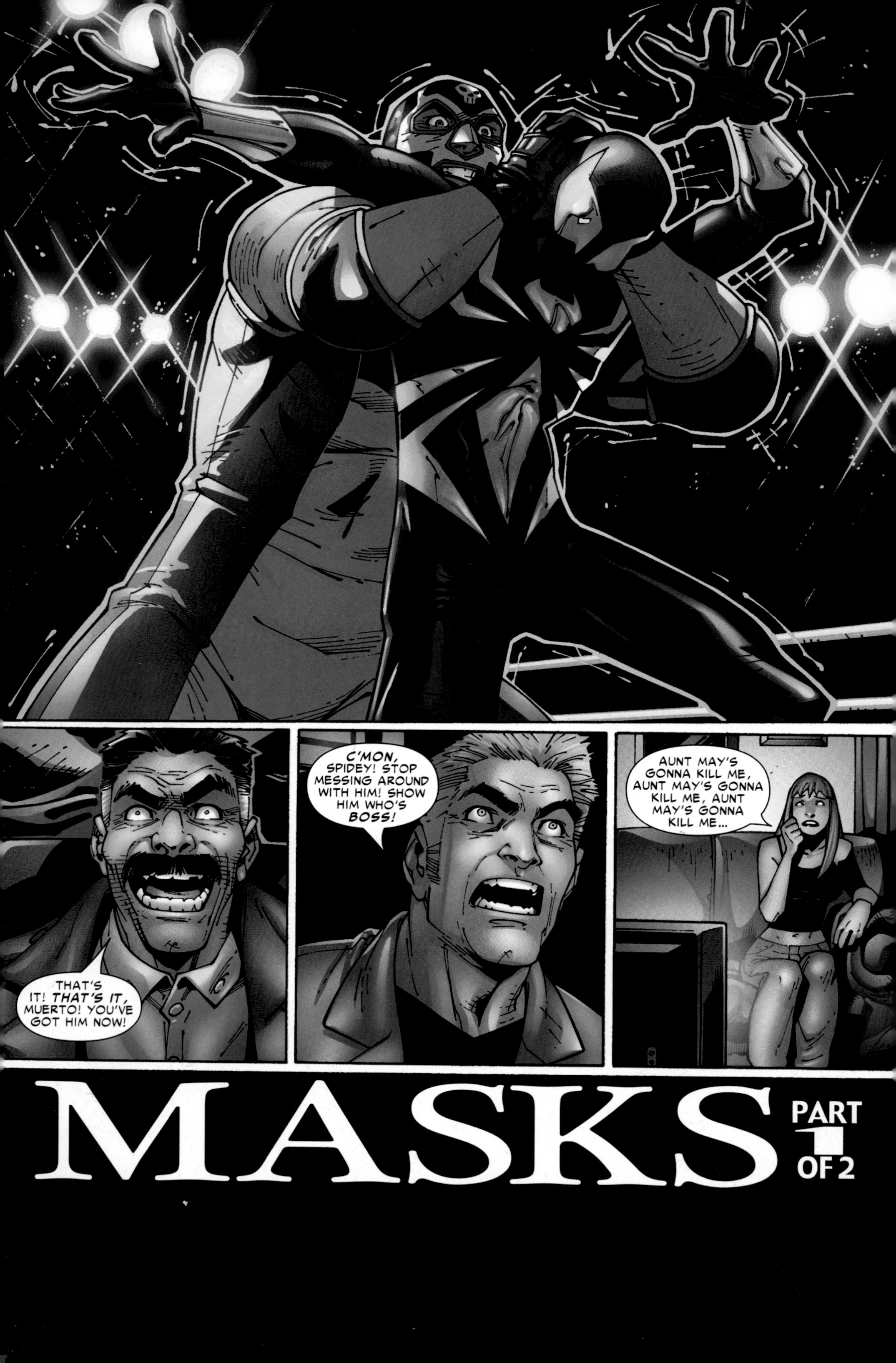
THAT'S IT! THAT'S IT, MUERTO! YOU'VE GOT HIM NOW!
C'MON, SPIDEY! STOP MESSING AROUND WITH HIM! SHOW HIM WHO'S BOSS!
AUNT MAY'S GONNA KILL ME, AUNT MAY'S GONNA KILL ME, AUNT MAY'S GONNA KILL ME...

MASKS PART 1 OF 2

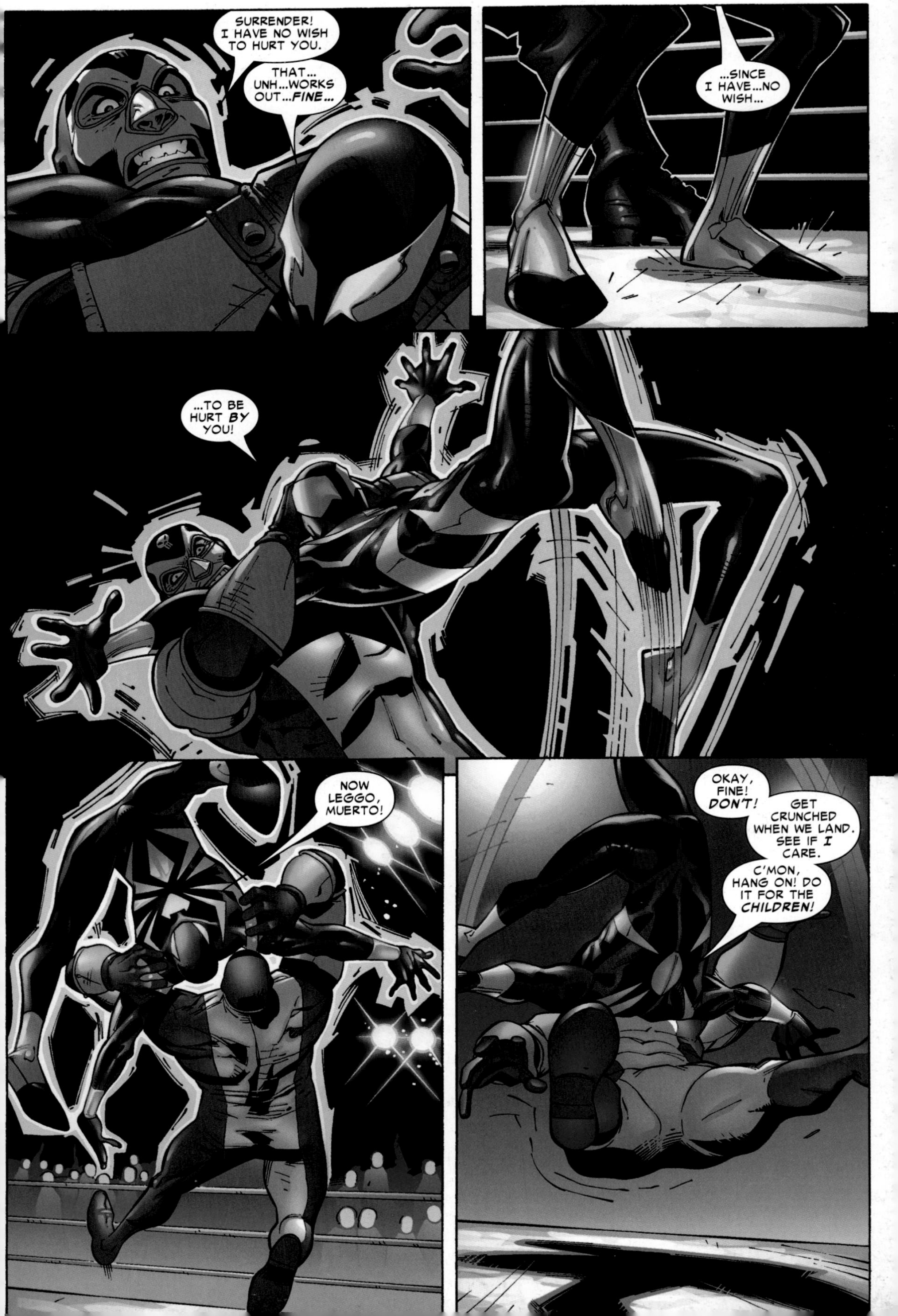
SURRENDER! I HAVE NO WISH TO HURT YOU.
THAT... UNH...WORKS OUT...FINE...
...SINCE I HAVE...NO WISH...
...TO BE HURT BY YOU!
NOW LEGGO, MUERTO!
OKAY, FINE! DON'T!
GET CRUNCHED WHEN WE LAND. SEE IF I CARE.
C'MON, HANG ON! DO IT FOR THE CHILDREN!

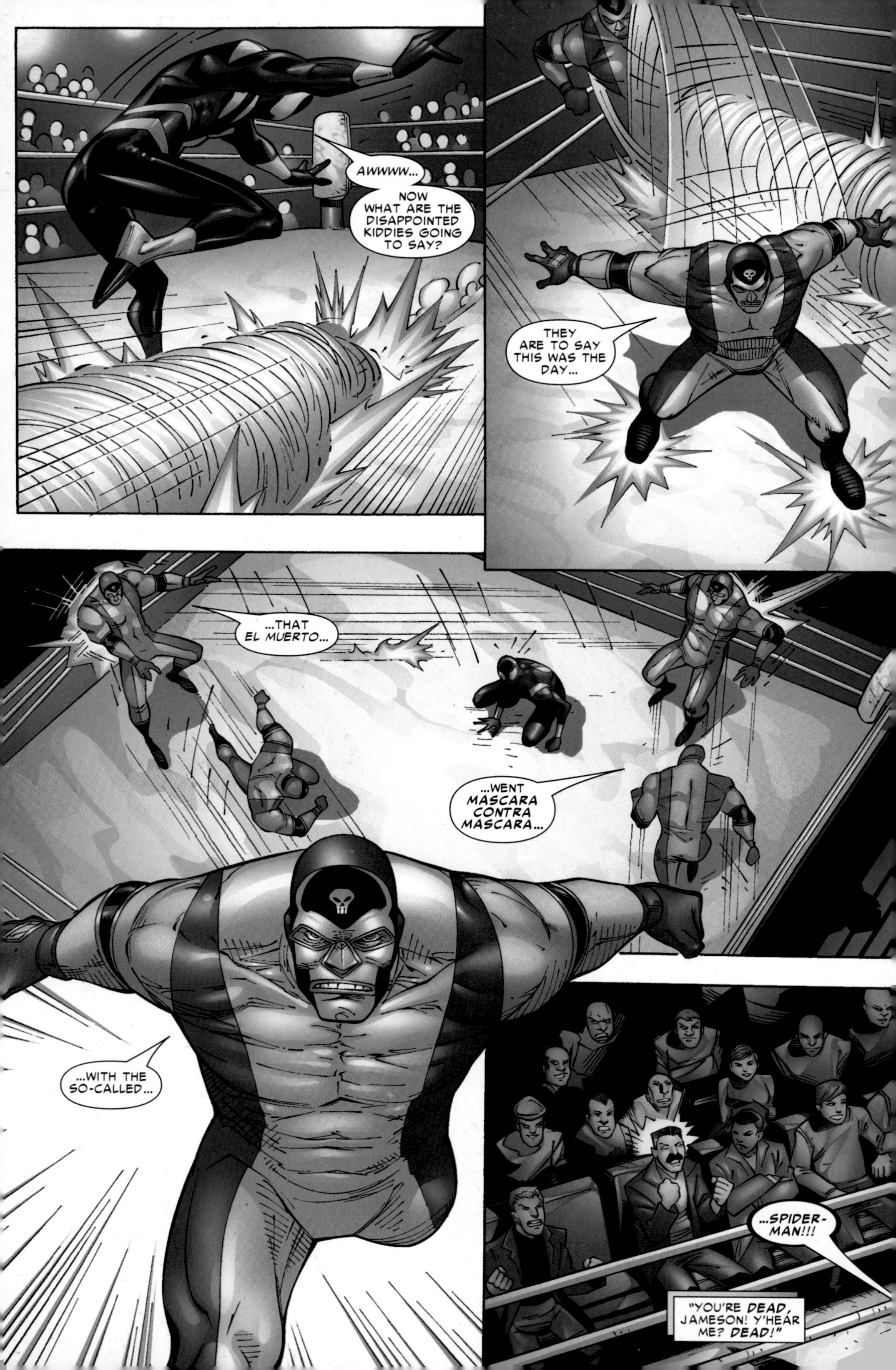
AWWWW...
NOW WHAT ARE THE DISAPPOINTED KIDDIES GOING TO SAY?
THEY ARE TO SAY THIS WAS THE DAY...
...THAT EL MUERTO...
...WENT MASCARA CONTRA MASCARA...
...WITH THE SO-CALLED...
...SPIDER-MAN!!!
"YOU'RE DEAD, JAMESON! Y'HEAR ME? DEAD!"

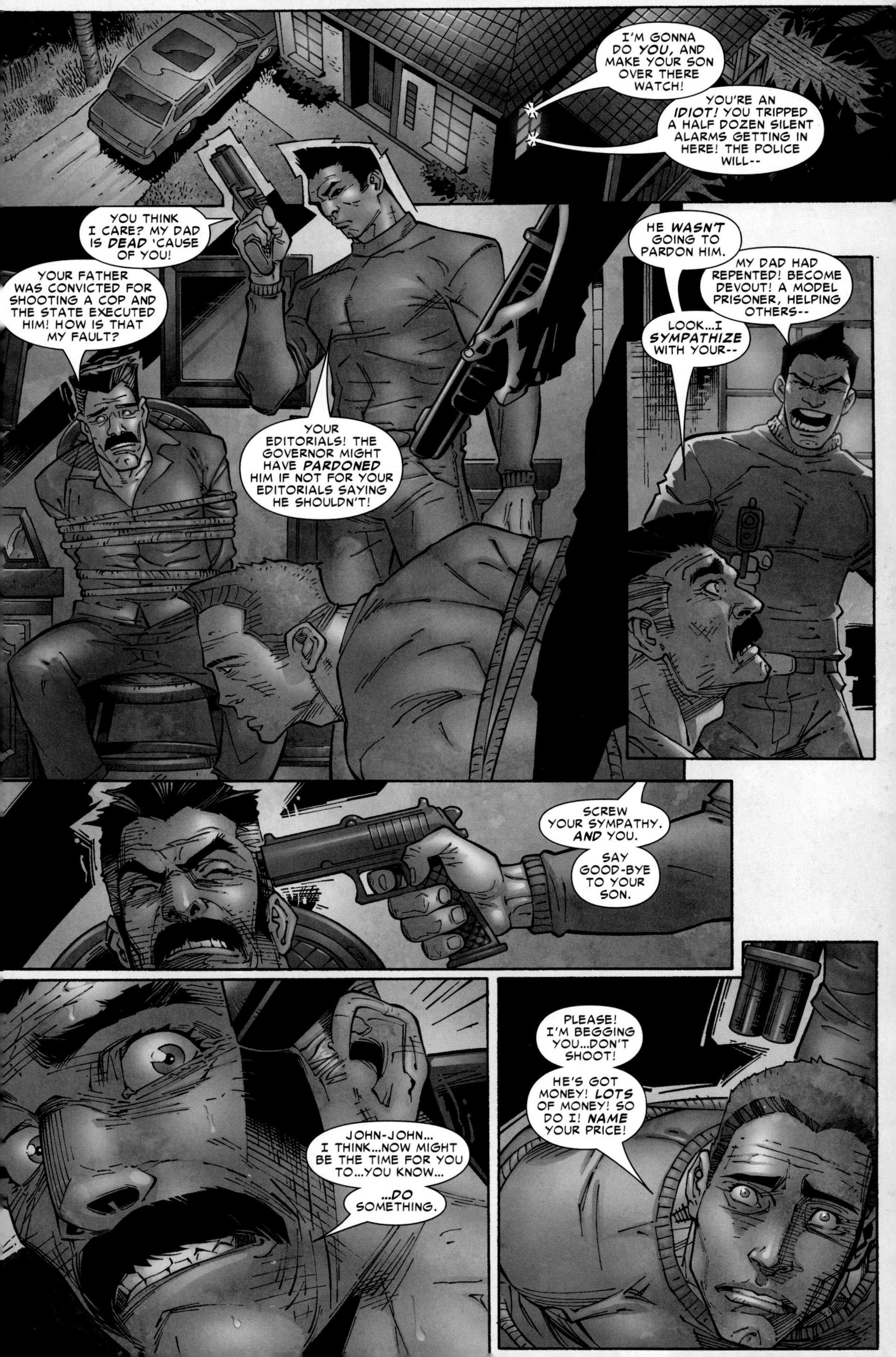
I'M GONNA DO *YOU*, AND MAKE YOUR SON OVER THERE WATCH!
YOU'RE AN ***IDIOT!*** YOU TRIPPED A HALF DOZEN SILENT ALARMS GETTING IN HERE! THE POLICE WILL--
YOU THINK I CARE? MY DAD IS ***DEAD*** 'CAUSE OF YOU!
YOUR FATHER WAS CONVICTED FOR SHOOTING A COP AND THE STATE EXECUTED HIM! HOW IS THAT MY FAULT?
YOUR EDITORIALS! THE GOVERNOR MIGHT HAVE ***PARDONED*** HIM IF NOT FOR YOUR EDITORIALS SAYING HE SHOULDN'T!
HE ***WASN'T*** GOING TO PARDON HIM.
MY DAD HAD REPENTED! BECOME DEVOUT! A MODEL PRISONER, HELPING OTHERS--
LOOK...I ***SYMPATHIZE*** WITH YOUR--
SCREW YOUR SYMPATHY. ***AND*** YOU.
SAY GOOD-BYE TO YOUR SON.
JOHN-JOHN... I THINK...NOW MIGHT BE THE TIME FOR YOU TO...YOU KNOW...
...DO SOMETHING.
PLEASE! I'M BEGGING YOU...DON'T SHOOT!
HE'S GOT MONEY! ***LOTS*** OF MONEY! SO DO I! ***NAME*** YOUR PRICE!

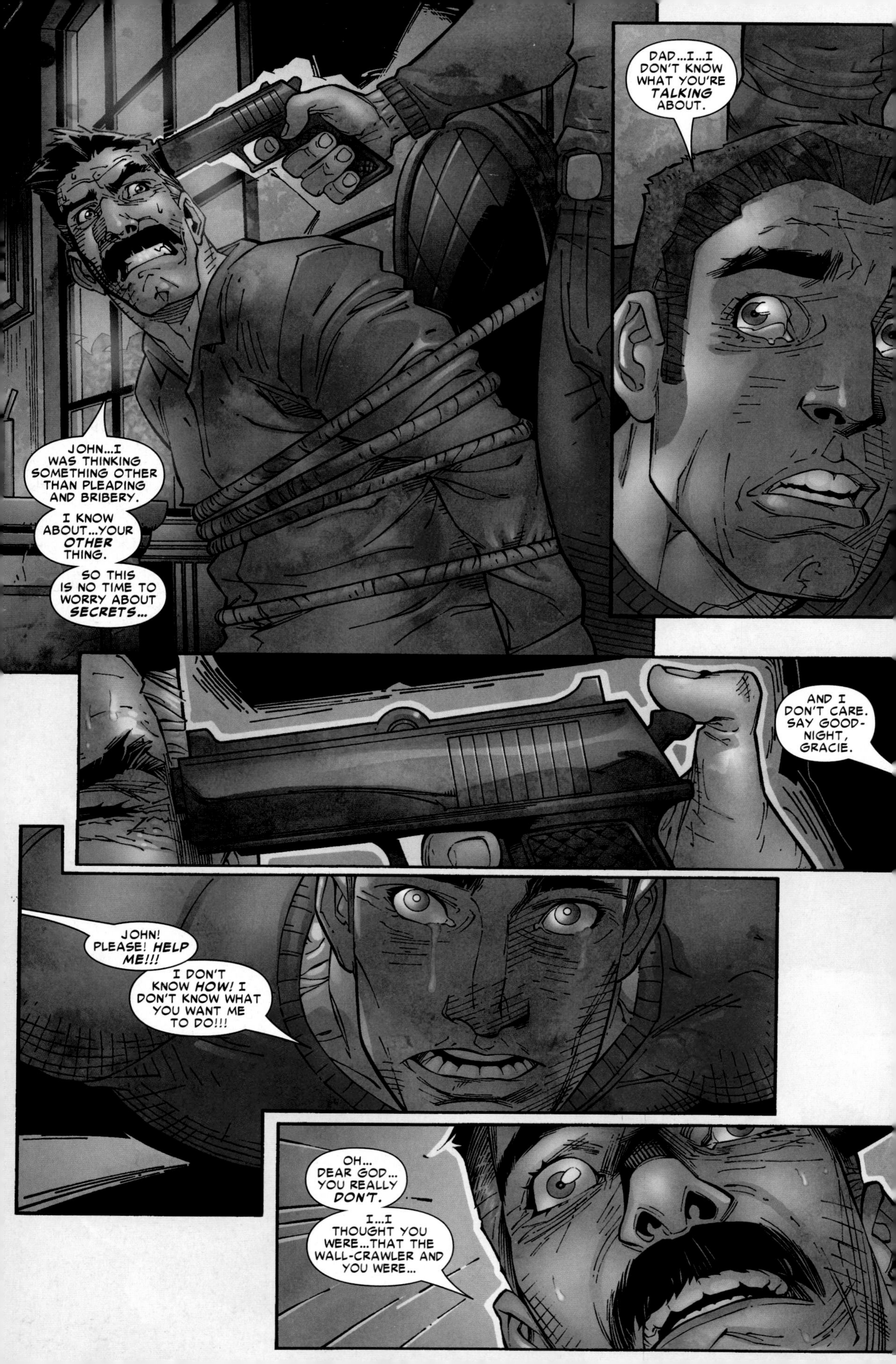
JOHN...I WAS THINKING SOMETHING OTHER THAN PLEADING AND BRIBERY.
I KNOW ABOUT...YOUR OTHER THING.
SO THIS IS NO TIME TO WORRY ABOUT SECRETS...
DAD...I...I DON'T KNOW WHAT YOU'RE TALKING ABOUT.
AND I DON'T CARE. SAY GOOD-NIGHT, GRACIE.
JOHN! PLEASE! HELP ME!!!
I DON'T KNOW HOW! I DON'T KNOW WHAT YOU WANT ME TO DO!!!
OH... DEAR GOD... YOU REALLY DON'T.
I...I THOUGHT YOU WERE...THAT THE WALL-CRAWLER AND YOU WERE...

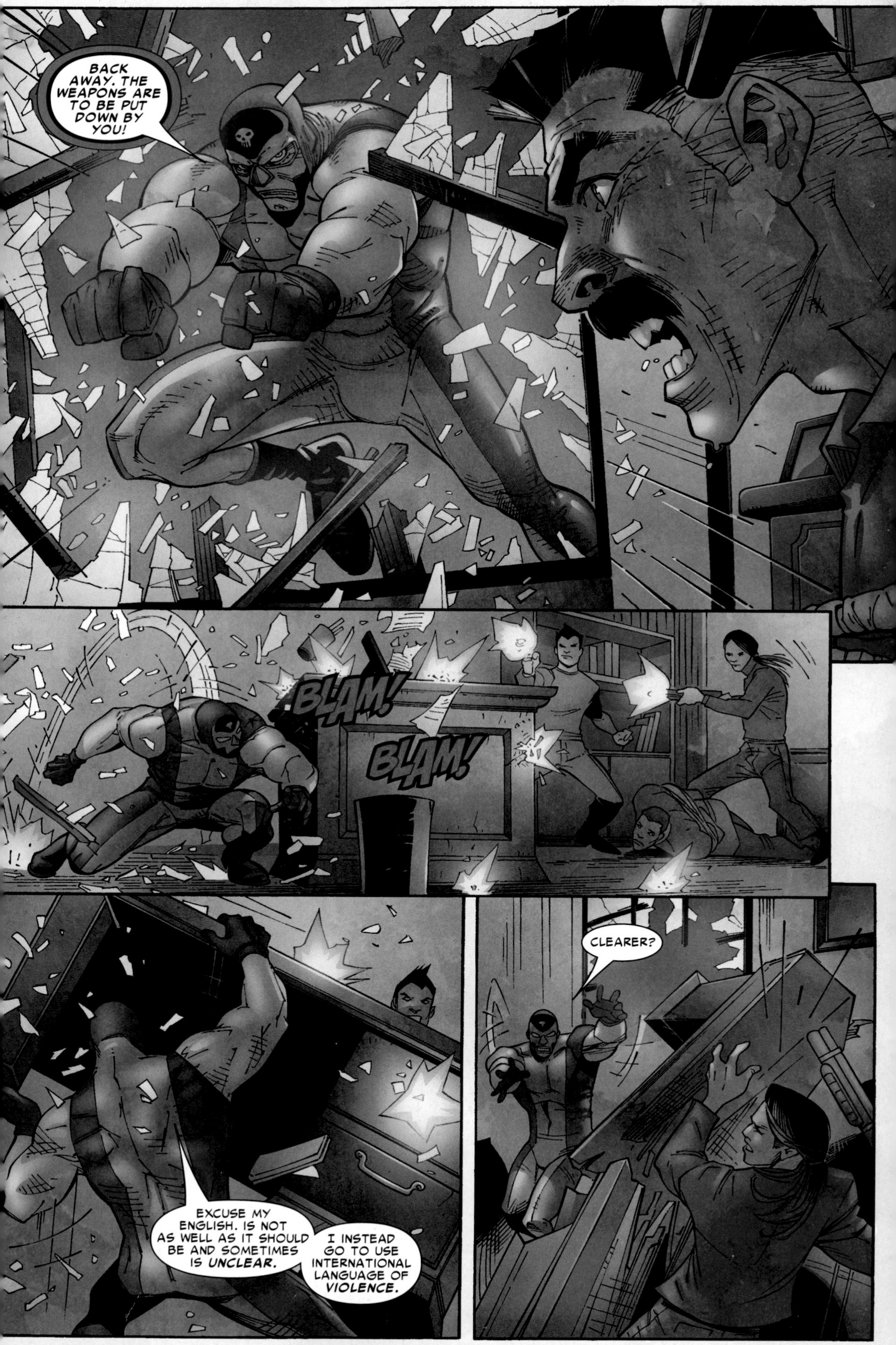
BACK AWAY. THE WEAPONS ARE TO BE PUT DOWN BY YOU!
BLAM!
BLAM!
EXCUSE MY ENGLISH. IS NOT AS WELL AS IT SHOULD BE AND SOMETIMES IS UNCLEAR.
I INSTEAD GO TO USE INTERNATIONAL LANGUAGE OF VIOLENCE.
CLEARER?

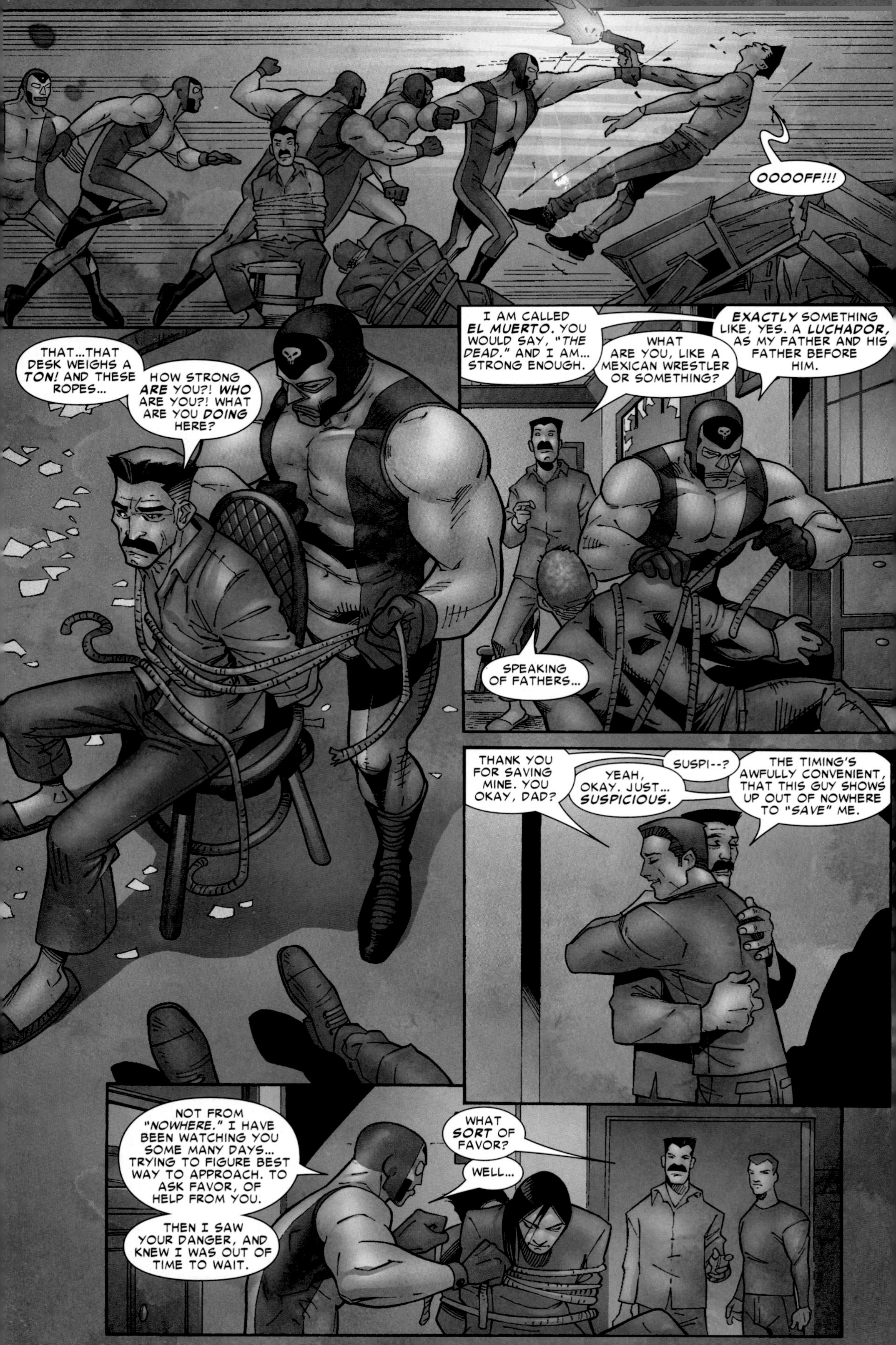
OOOOFF!!!
THAT...THAT DESK WEIGHS A TON! AND THESE ROPES...
HOW STRONG ARE YOU?! WHO ARE YOU?! WHAT ARE YOU DOING HERE?
I AM CALLED EL MUERTO. YOU WOULD SAY, "THE DEAD." AND I AM... STRONG ENOUGH.
WHAT ARE YOU, LIKE A MEXICAN WRESTLER OR SOMETHING?
EXACTLY SOMETHING LIKE, YES. A LUCHADOR, AS MY FATHER AND HIS FATHER BEFORE HIM.
SPEAKING OF FATHERS...
THANK YOU FOR SAVING MINE. YOU OKAY, DAD?
SUSPI--?
YEAH, OKAY. JUST... SUSPICIOUS.
THE TIMING'S AWFULLY CONVENIENT, THAT THIS GUY SHOWS UP OUT OF NOWHERE TO "SAVE" ME.
NOT FROM "NOWHERE." I HAVE BEEN WATCHING YOU SOME MANY DAYS... TRYING TO FIGURE BEST WAY TO APPROACH. TO ASK FAVOR, OF HELP FROM YOU.
THEN I SAW YOUR DANGER, AND KNEW I WAS OUT OF TIME TO WAIT.
WHAT SORT OF FAVOR?
WELL...

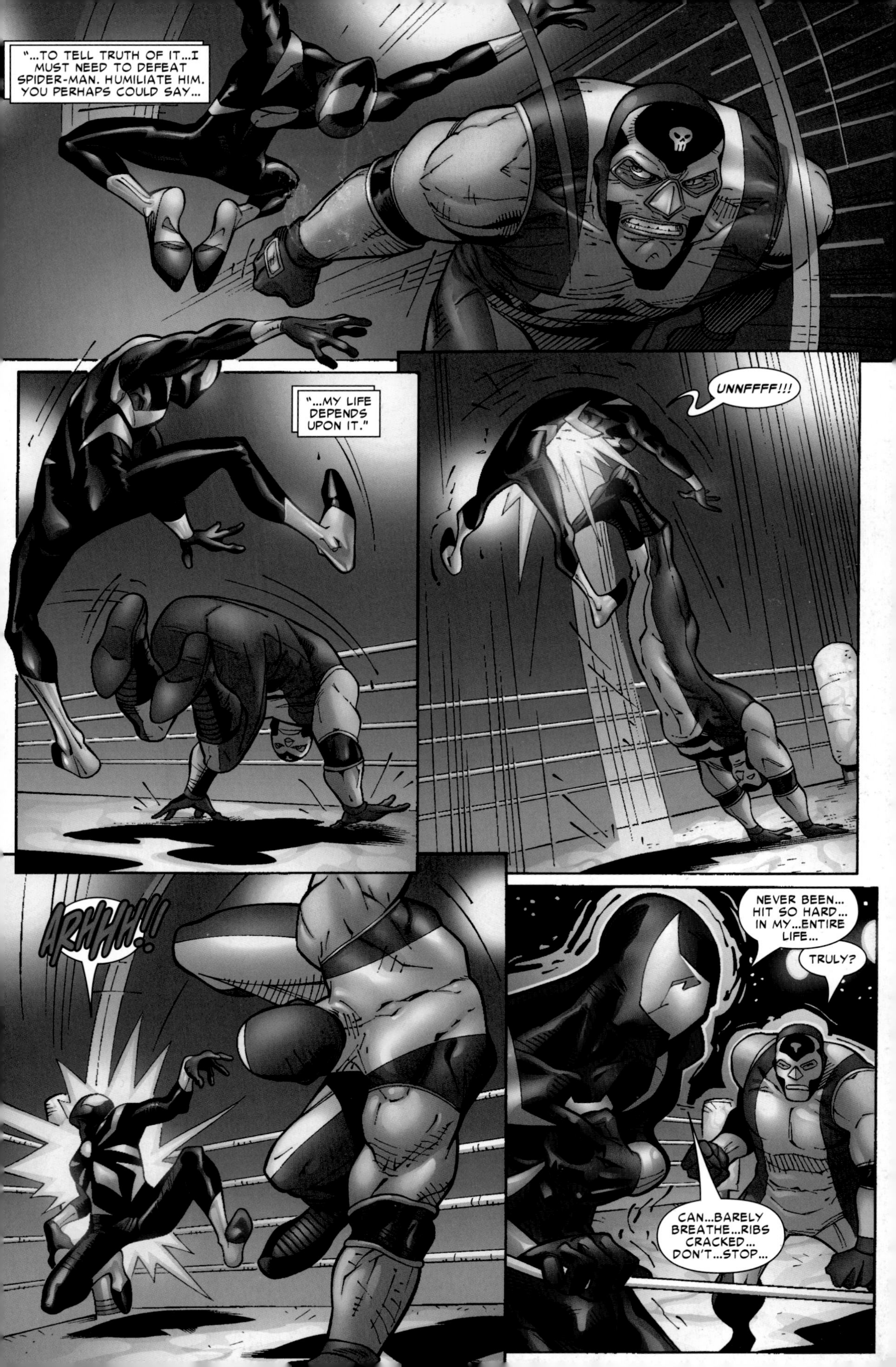
"...TO TELL TRUTH OF IT...I MUST NEED TO DEFEAT SPIDER-MAN. HUMILIATE HIM. YOU PERHAPS COULD SAY...
"...MY LIFE DEPENDS UPON IT."
UNNFFFF!!!
ARHHH!!!
NEVER BEEN... HIT SO HARD... IN MY...ENTIRE LIFE...
TRULY?
CAN...BARELY BREATHE...RIBS CRACKED... DON'T...STOP...

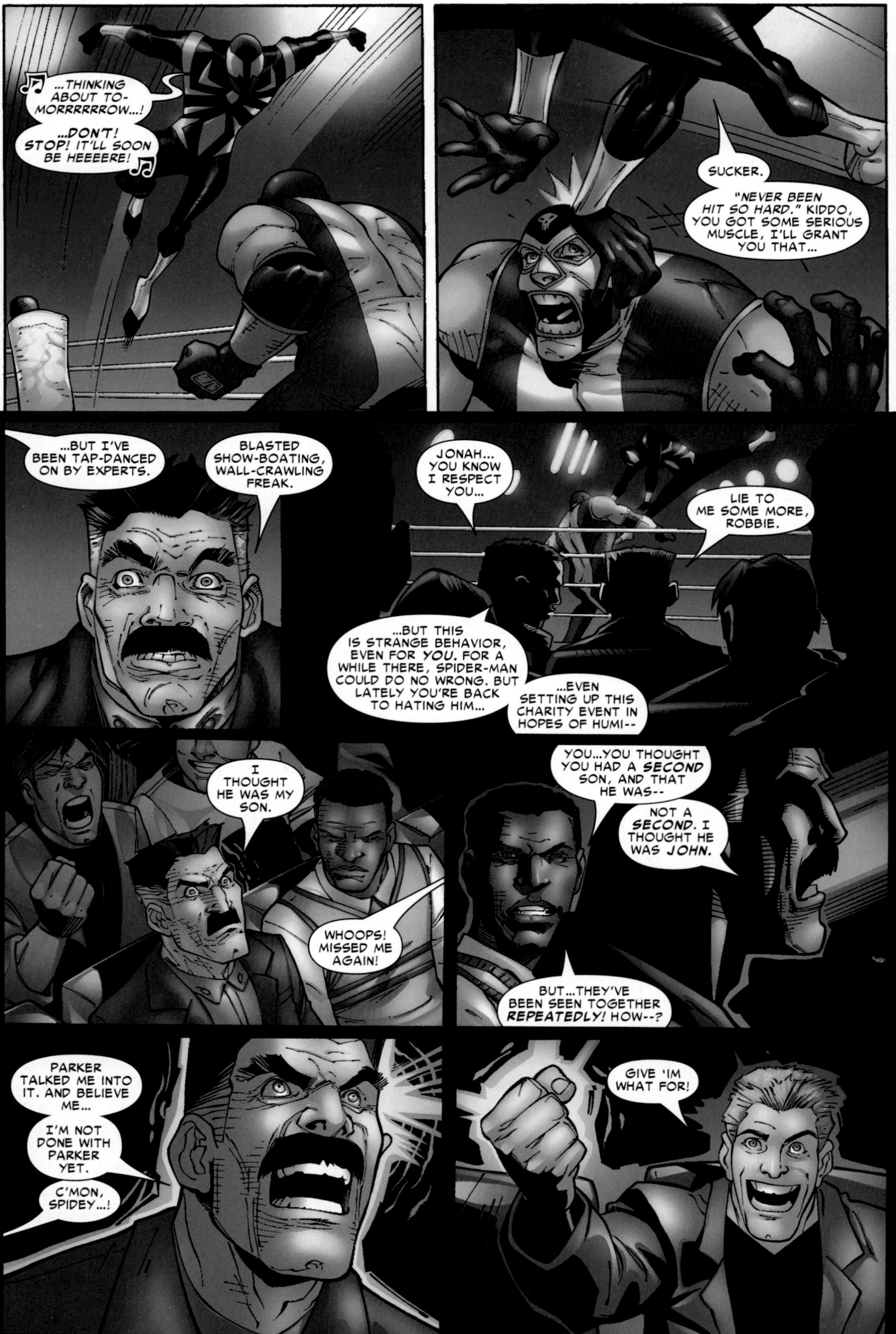
...THINKING ABOUT TO-MORRRRRROW...!
...DON'T! STOP! IT'LL SOON BE HEEEERE!
SUCKER.
"NEVER BEEN HIT SO HARD." KIDDO, YOU GOT SOME SERIOUS MUSCLE, I'LL GRANT YOU THAT...
...BUT I'VE BEEN TAP-DANCED ON BY EXPERTS.
BLASTED SHOW-BOATING, WALL-CRAWLING FREAK.
JONAH... YOU KNOW I RESPECT YOU...
LIE TO ME SOME MORE, ROBBIE.
...BUT THIS IS STRANGE BEHAVIOR, EVEN FOR YOU. FOR A WHILE THERE, SPIDER-MAN COULD DO NO WRONG. BUT LATELY YOU'RE BACK TO HATING HIM...
...EVEN SETTING UP THIS CHARITY EVENT IN HOPES OF HUMI--
I THOUGHT HE WAS MY SON.
WHOOPS! MISSED ME AGAIN!
YOU...YOU THOUGHT YOU HAD A SECOND SON, AND THAT HE WAS--
NOT A SECOND. I THOUGHT HE WAS JOHN.
BUT...THEY'VE BEEN SEEN TOGETHER REPEATEDLY! HOW--?
PARKER TALKED ME INTO IT. AND BELIEVE ME...
I'M NOT DONE WITH PARKER YET.
C'MON, SPIDEY...!
GIVE 'IM WHAT FOR!

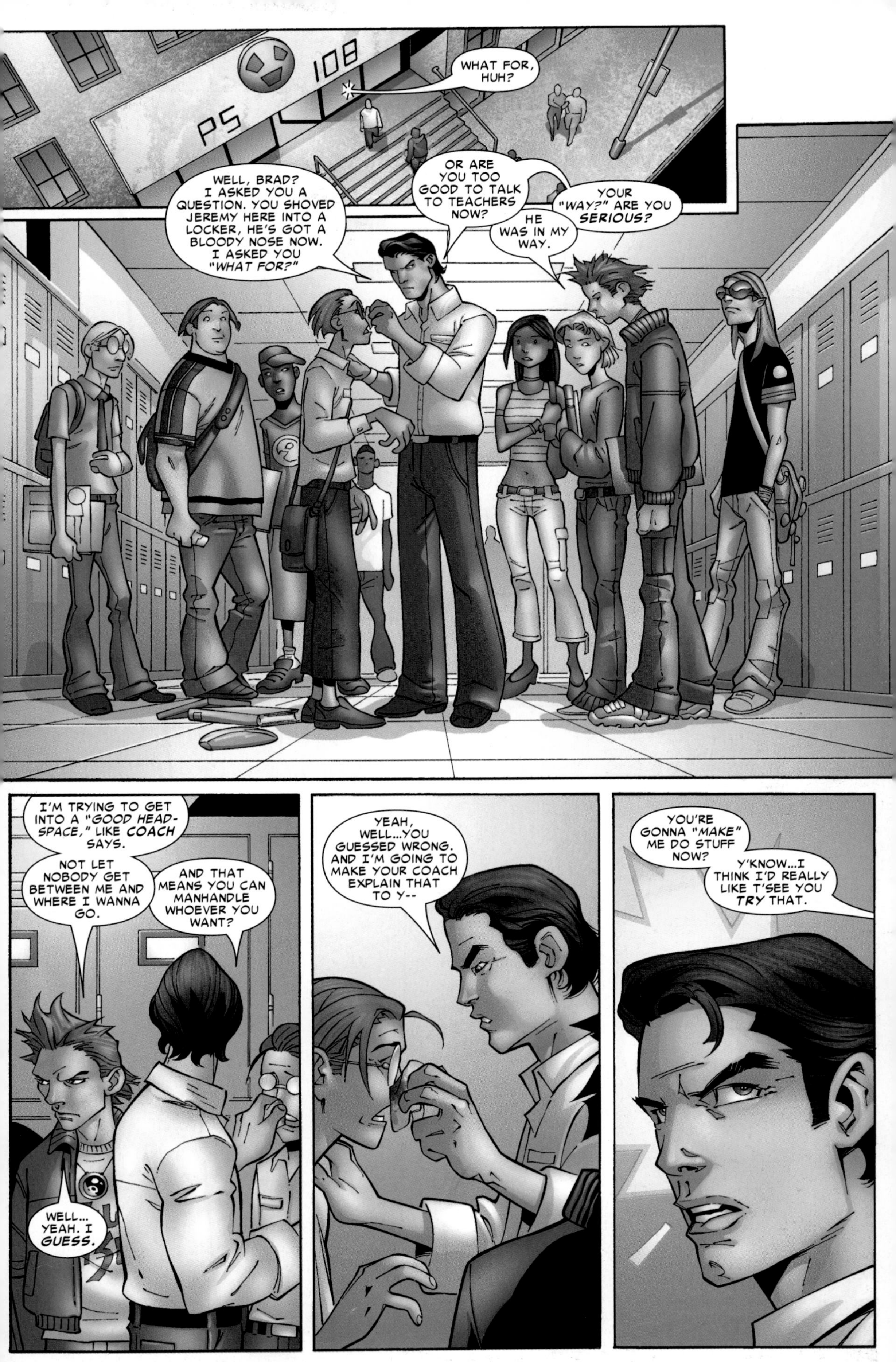
PS 108
WHAT FOR, HUH?
WELL, BRAD? I ASKED YOU A QUESTION. YOU SHOVED JEREMY HERE INTO A LOCKER, HE'S GOT A BLOODY NOSE NOW. I ASKED YOU "WHAT FOR?"
OR ARE YOU TOO GOOD TO TALK TO TEACHERS NOW?
HE WAS IN MY WAY.
YOUR "WAY?" ARE YOU SERIOUS?
I'M TRYING TO GET INTO A "GOOD HEAD-SPACE," LIKE COACH SAYS.
NOT LET NOBODY GET BETWEEN ME AND WHERE I WANNA GO.
AND THAT MEANS YOU CAN MANHANDLE WHOEVER YOU WANT?
WELL... YEAH. I GUESS.
YEAH, WELL...YOU GUESSED WRONG. AND I'M GOING TO MAKE YOUR COACH EXPLAIN THAT TO Y--
YOU'RE GONNA "MAKE" ME DO STUFF NOW?
Y'KNOW...I THINK I'D REALLY LIKE T'SEE YOU TRY THAT.

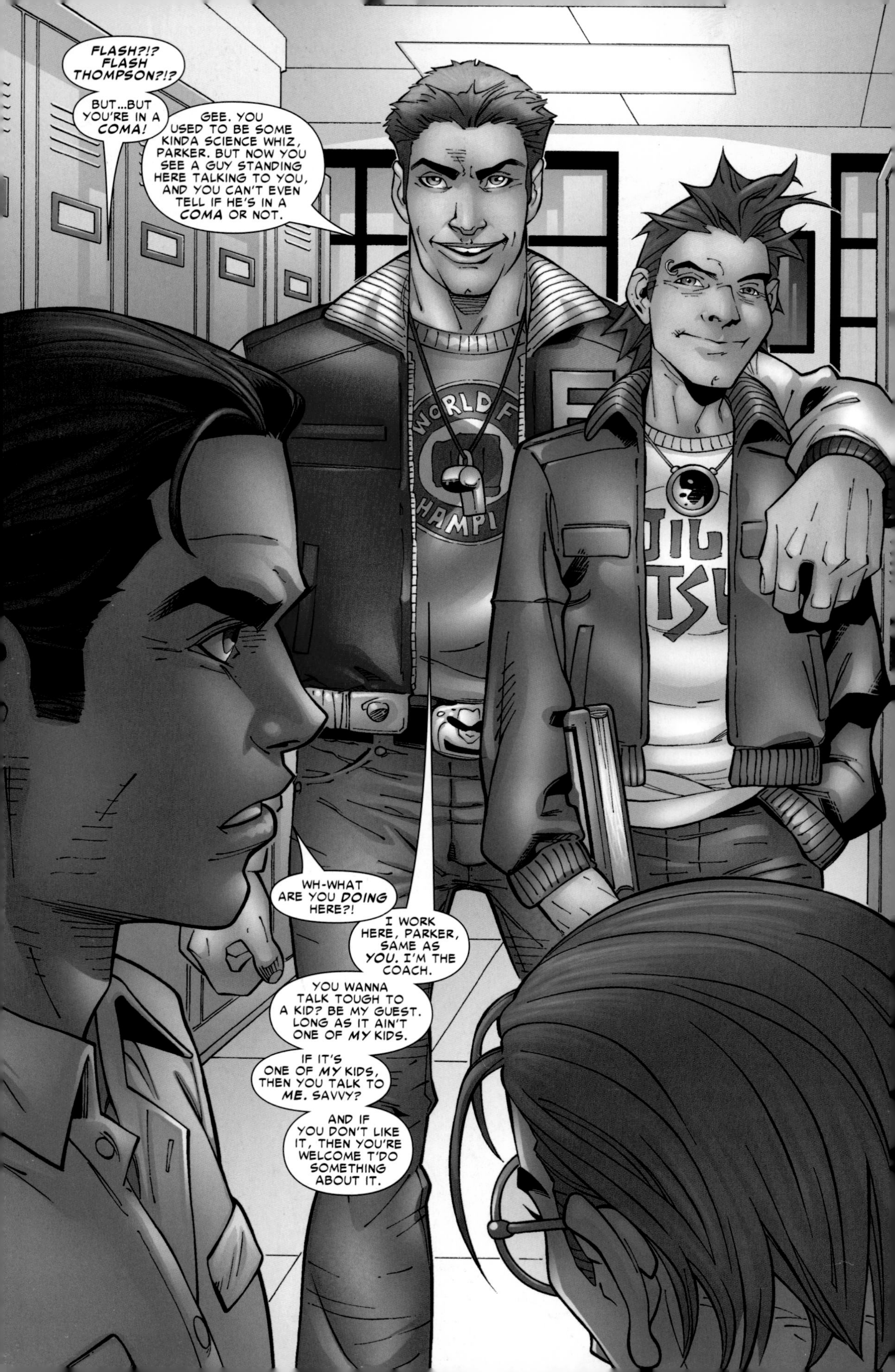
FLASH?!? FLASH THOMPSON?!?
BUT...BUT YOU'RE IN A COMA!
GEE. YOU USED TO BE SOME KINDA SCIENCE WHIZ, PARKER. BUT NOW YOU SEE A GUY STANDING HERE TALKING TO YOU, AND YOU CAN'T EVEN TELL IF HE'S IN A COMA OR NOT.
WH-WHAT ARE YOU DOING HERE?!
I WORK HERE, PARKER, SAME AS YOU. I'M THE COACH.
YOU WANNA TALK TOUGH TO A KID? BE MY GUEST. LONG AS IT AIN'T ONE OF MY KIDS.
IF IT'S ONE OF MY KIDS, THEN YOU TALK TO ME. SAVVY?
AND IF YOU DON'T LIKE IT, THEN YOU'RE WELCOME T'DO SOMETHING ABOUT IT.

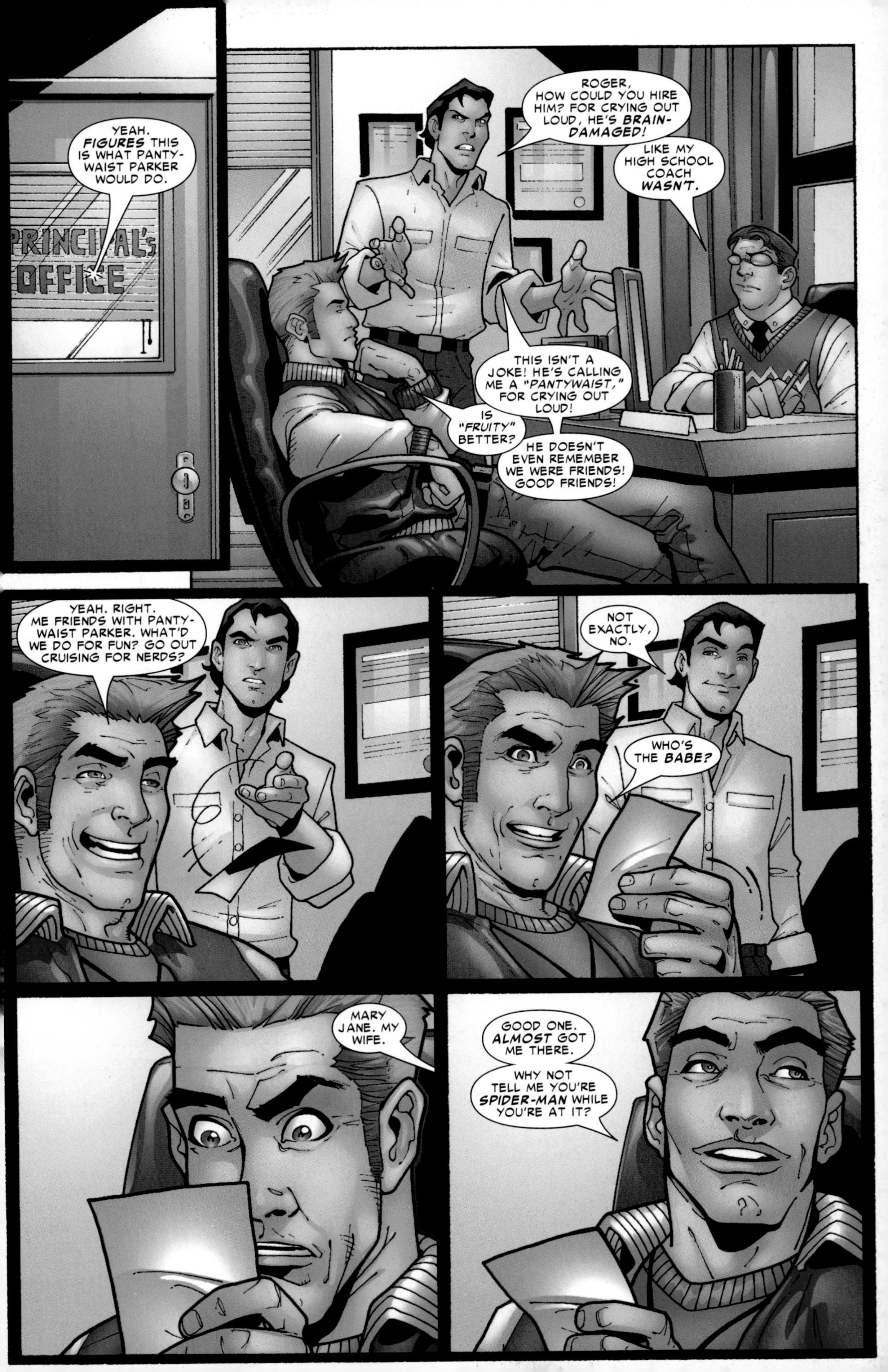
YEAH. FIGURES THIS IS WHAT PANTY-WAIST PARKER WOULD DO.
PRINCIPAL'S OFFICE
ROGER, HOW COULD YOU HIRE HIM? FOR CRYING OUT LOUD, HE'S BRAIN-DAMAGED!
LIKE MY HIGH SCHOOL COACH WASN'T.
THIS ISN'T A JOKE! HE'S CALLING ME A "PANTYWAIST," FOR CRYING OUT LOUD!
IS "FRUITY" BETTER?
HE DOESN'T EVEN REMEMBER WE WERE FRIENDS! GOOD FRIENDS!
YEAH. RIGHT. ME FRIENDS WITH PANTY-WAIST PARKER. WHAT'D WE DO FOR FUN? GO OUT CRUISING FOR NERDS?
NOT EXACTLY, NO.
WHO'S THE BABE?
MARY JANE. MY WIFE.
GOOD ONE. ALMOST GOT ME THERE.
WHY NOT TELL ME YOU'RE SPIDER-MAN WHILE YOU'RE AT IT?

FLASH. WAIT UP.

AW, GEEZ. LOOK, PARKER, I *TOLD* THE PRINCIPAL I'D TALK TO MY KID, SET 'IM STRAIGHT. WHAT *MORE* DO YOU WANT?

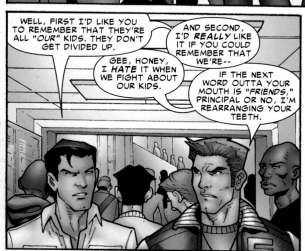

WELL, FIRST I'D LIKE YOU TO REMEMBER THAT THEY'RE ALL *"OUR"* KIDS. THEY DON'T GET DIVIDED UP.

AND SECOND, I'D *REALLY* LIKE IT IF YOU COULD REMEMBER THAT WE'RE--

GEE, HONEY, I *HATE* IT WHEN WE FIGHT ABOUT OUR KIDS.

IF THE NEXT WORD OUTTA YOUR MOUTH IS *"FRIENDS,"* PRINCIPAL OR NO, I'M REARRANGING YOUR TEETH.

YOU KNOW WHAT? IT FIGURES THAT YEARS WORTH OF YOUR MEMORIES COULD BE WIPED OUT... BUT YOUR SPIDER-MAN HERO WORSHIP IS INTACT.

IT'S NOT *"WORSHIP."* HE'S THE MAN, THAT'S ALL.

THAT'S HOW I KNOW HE'S GONNA DO THE WRESTLING THING.

OH, YOU HEARD ABOUT THAT?

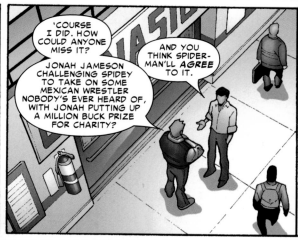

'COURSE I DID. HOW COULD ANYONE MISS IT?

JONAH JAMESON CHALLENGING SPIDEY TO TAKE ON SOME MEXICAN WRESTLER NOBODY'S EVER HEARD OF, WITH JONAH PUTTING UP A MILLION BUCK PRIZE FOR CHARITY?

AND YOU THINK SPIDER-MAN'LL *AGREE* TO IT.

A MILLION BUCKS FOR CHARITY AND A CHANCE TO MAKE OL' HITLER MUSTACHE-FACE LOOK LIKE A CHUMP?

WHAT'S NOT TO LIKE?

NOT THAT YOU'D UNDERSTAND THAT. LATER, *"PETEY."*

HUNH.

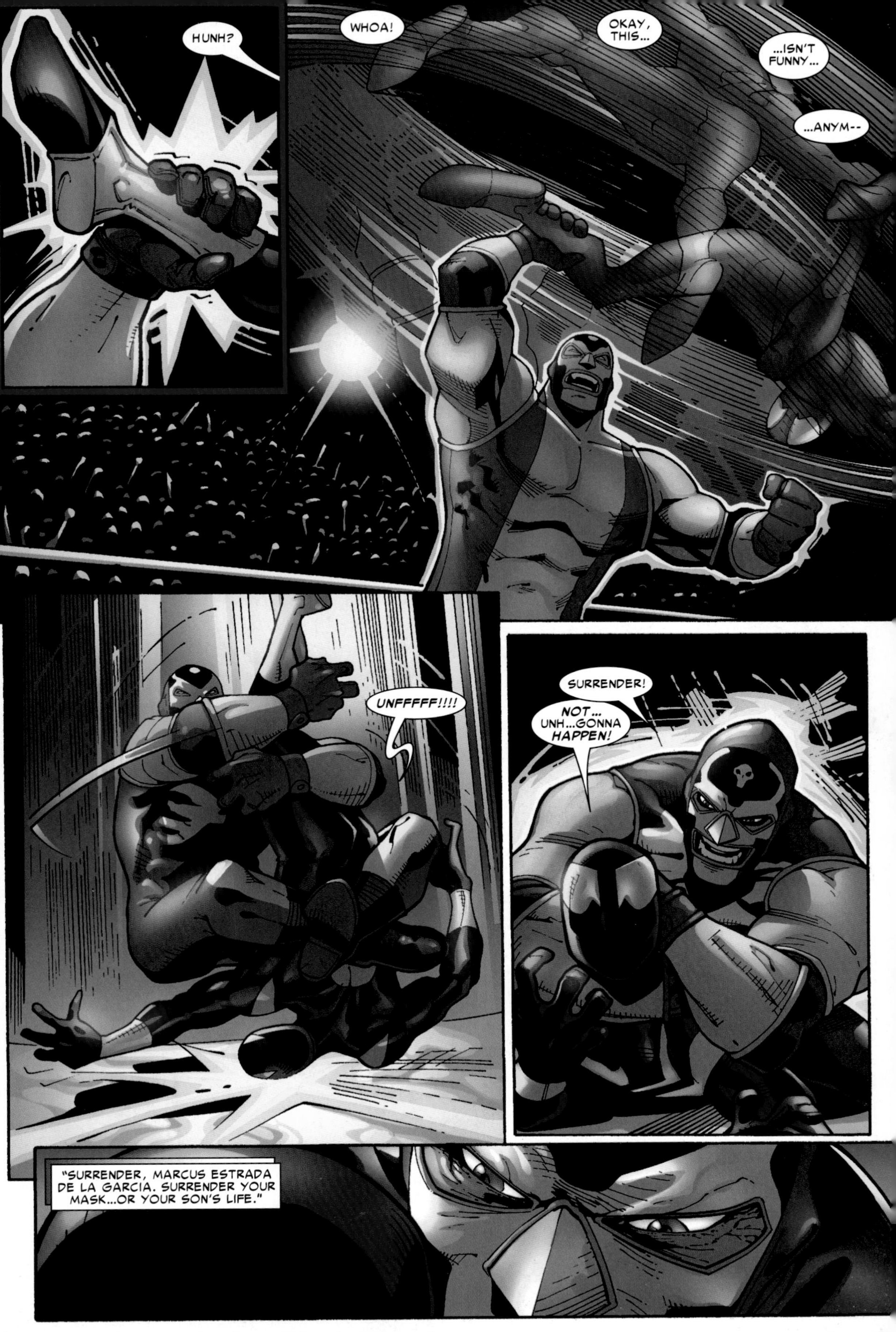
HUNH?
WHOA!
OKAY, THIS...
...ISN'T FUNNY...
...ANYM--
UNFFFFF!!!!
SURRENDER!
NOT... UNH...GONNA HAPPEN!
"SURRENDER, MARCUS ESTRADA DE LA GARCIA. SURRENDER YOUR MASK...OR YOUR SON'S LIFE."

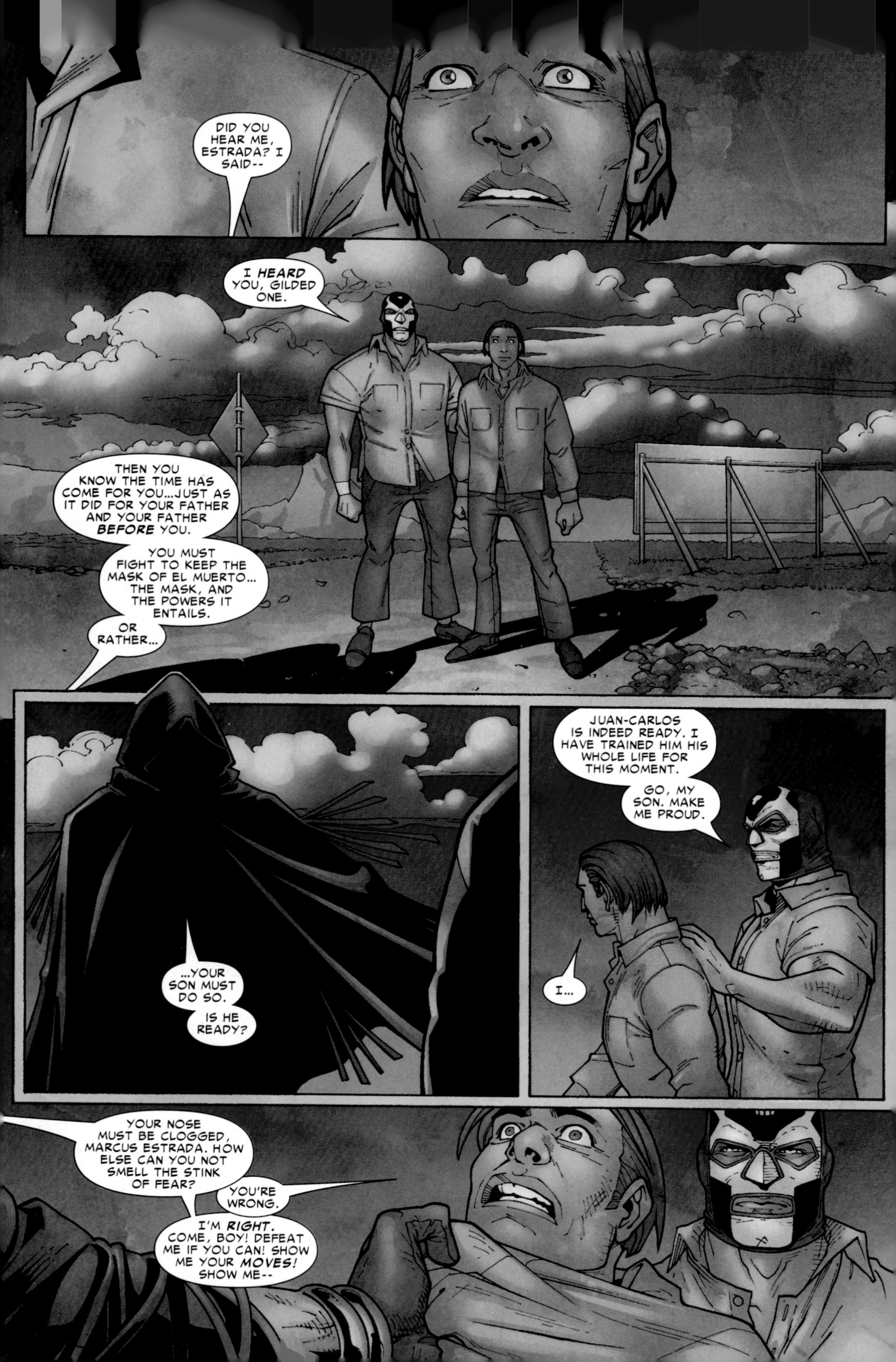
DID YOU HEAR ME, ESTRADA? I SAID--
I HEARD YOU, GILDED ONE.
THEN YOU KNOW THE TIME HAS COME FOR YOU...JUST AS IT DID FOR YOUR FATHER AND YOUR FATHER BEFORE YOU.
YOU MUST FIGHT TO KEEP THE MASK OF EL MUERTO... THE MASK, AND THE POWERS IT ENTAILS.
OR RATHER...
...YOUR SON MUST DO SO.
IS HE READY?
JUAN-CARLOS IS INDEED READY. I HAVE TRAINED HIM HIS WHOLE LIFE FOR THIS MOMENT.
GO, MY SON. MAKE ME PROUD.
I...
YOUR NOSE MUST BE CLOGGED, MARCUS ESTRADA. HOW ELSE CAN YOU NOT SMELL THE STINK OF FEAR?
YOU'RE WRONG.
I'M RIGHT. COME, BOY! DEFEAT ME IF YOU CAN! SHOW ME YOUR MOVES! SHOW ME--

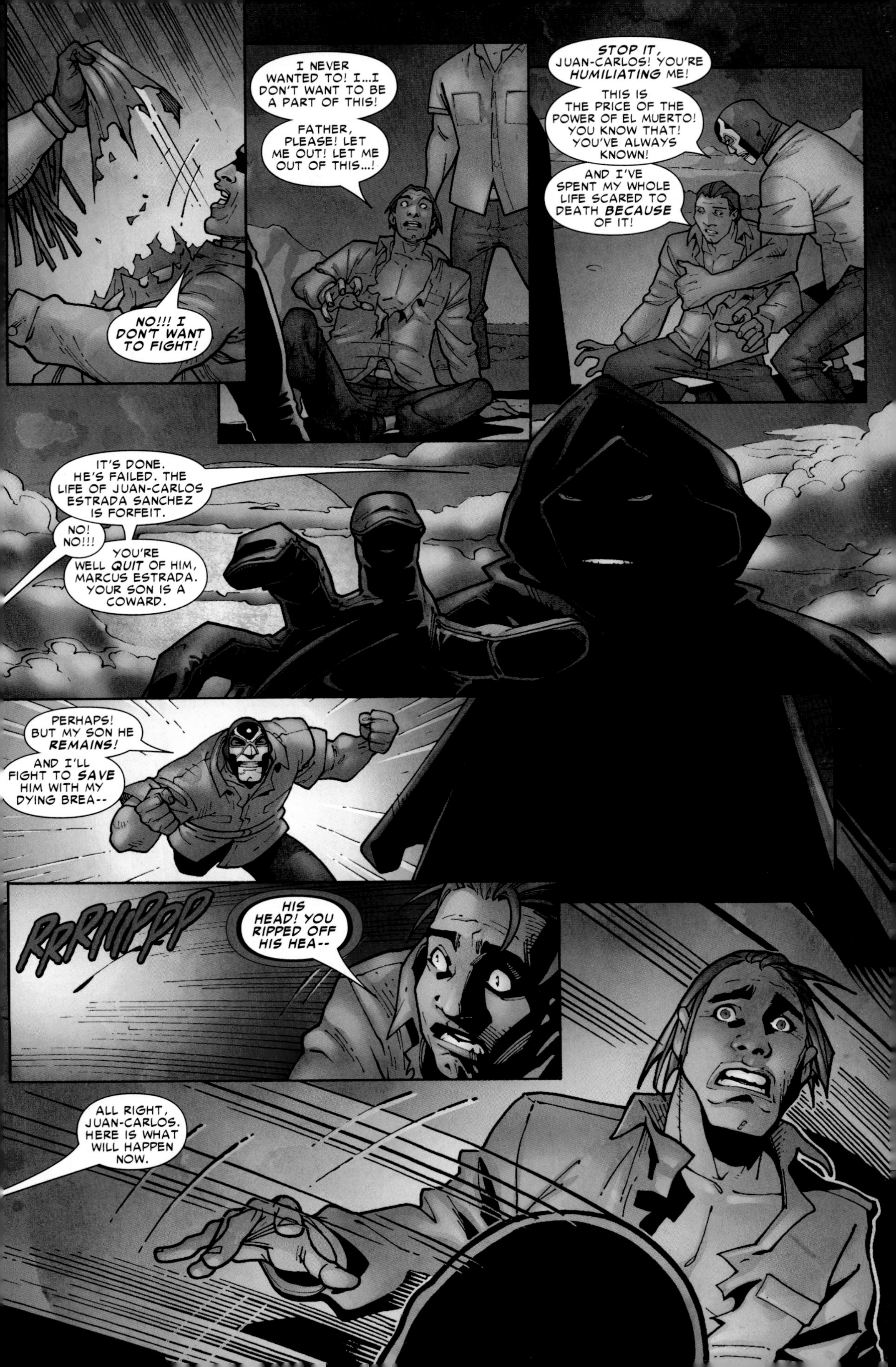
NO!!! I DON'T WANT TO FIGHT!
I NEVER WANTED TO! I...I DON'T WANT TO BE A PART OF THIS!
FATHER, PLEASE! LET ME OUT! LET ME OUT OF THIS...!
STOP IT, JUAN-CARLOS! YOU'RE HUMILIATING ME!
THIS IS THE PRICE OF THE POWER OF EL MUERTO! YOU KNOW THAT! YOU'VE ALWAYS KNOWN!
AND I'VE SPENT MY WHOLE LIFE SCARED TO DEATH BECAUSE OF IT!
IT'S DONE. HE'S FAILED. THE LIFE OF JUAN-CARLOS ESTRADA SANCHEZ IS FORFEIT.
NO! NO!!!
YOU'RE WELL QUIT OF HIM, MARCUS ESTRADA. YOUR SON IS A COWARD.
PERHAPS! BUT MY SON HE REMAINS!
AND I'LL FIGHT TO SAVE HIM WITH MY DYING BREA--
RRRIIIPPP
HIS HEAD! YOU RIPPED OFF HIS HEA--
ALL RIGHT, JUAN-CARLOS. HERE IS WHAT WILL HAPPEN NOW.

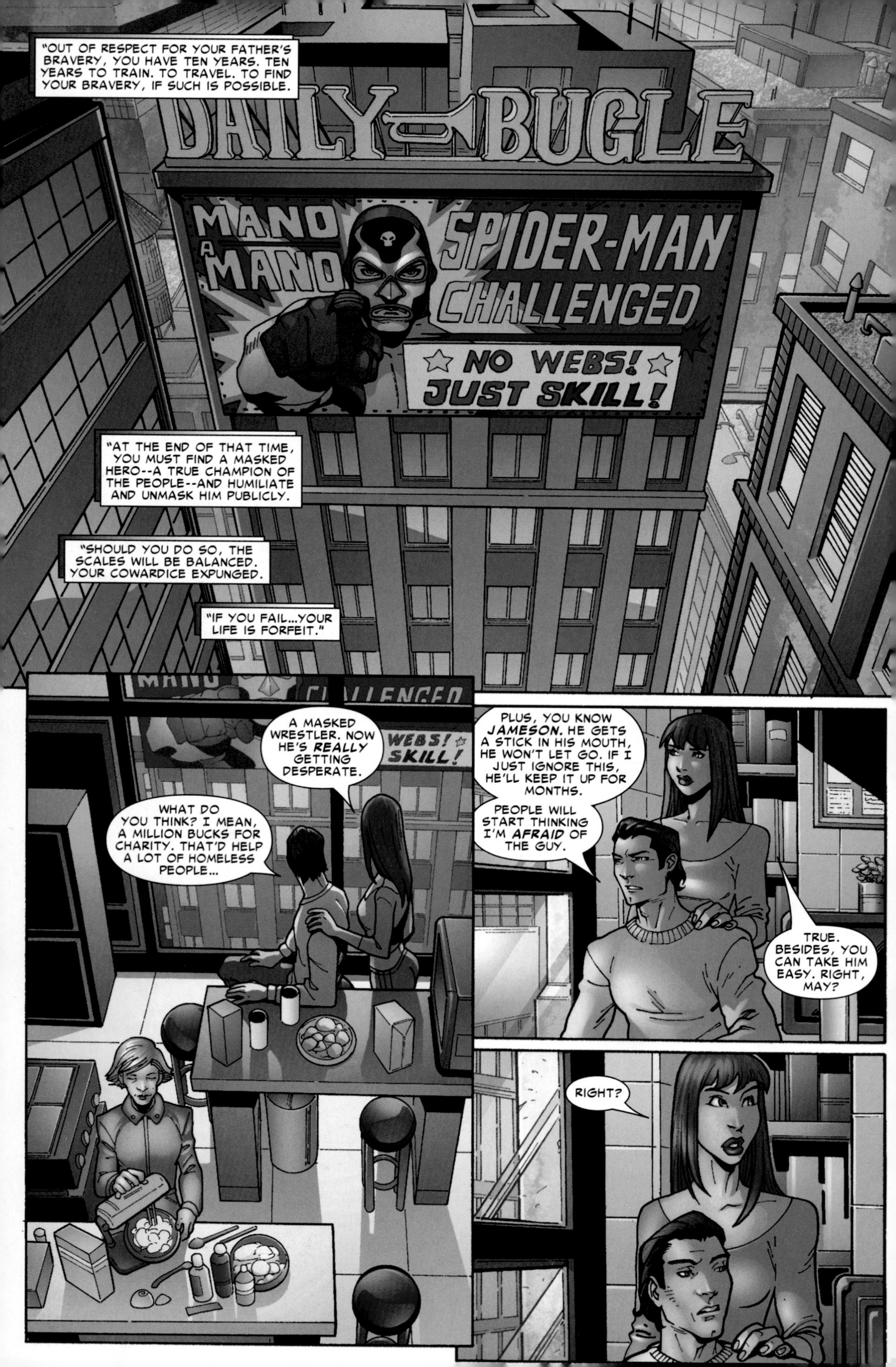
"OUT OF RESPECT FOR YOUR FATHER'S BRAVERY, YOU HAVE TEN YEARS. TEN YEARS TO TRAIN. TO TRAVEL. TO FIND YOUR BRAVERY, IF SUCH IS POSSIBLE.
DAILY BUGLE
MANO A MANO
SPIDER-MAN CHALLENGED
NO WEBS! JUST SKILL!
"AT THE END OF THAT TIME, YOU MUST FIND A MASKED HERO--A TRUE CHAMPION OF THE PEOPLE--AND HUMILIATE AND UNMASK HIM PUBLICLY.
"SHOULD YOU DO SO, THE SCALES WILL BE BALANCED. YOUR COWARDICE EXPUNGED.
"IF YOU FAIL...YOUR LIFE IS FORFEIT."
A MASKED WRESTLER. NOW HE'S *REALLY* GETTING DESPERATE.
WHAT DO YOU THINK? I MEAN, A MILLION BUCKS FOR CHARITY. THAT'D HELP A LOT OF HOMELESS PEOPLE...
PLUS, YOU KNOW *JAMESON*. HE GETS A STICK IN HIS MOUTH, HE WON'T LET GO. IF I JUST IGNORE THIS, HE'LL KEEP IT UP FOR MONTHS.
PEOPLE WILL START THINKING I'M *AFRAID* OF THE GUY.
TRUE. BESIDES, YOU CAN TAKE HIM EASY. RIGHT, MAY?
RIGHT?

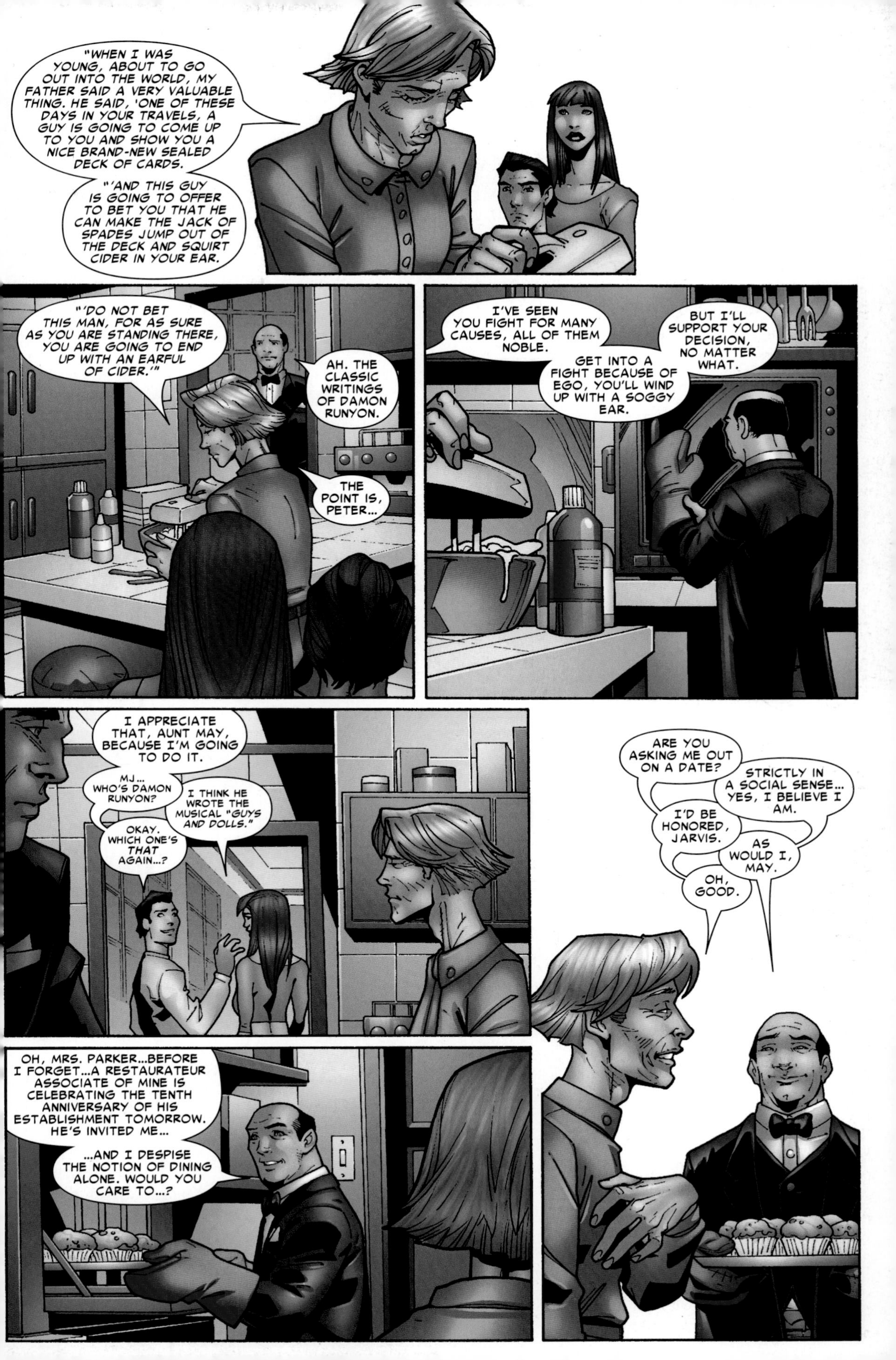
"WHEN I WAS YOUNG, ABOUT TO GO OUT INTO THE WORLD, MY FATHER SAID A VERY VALUABLE THING. HE SAID, 'ONE OF THESE DAYS IN YOUR TRAVELS, A GUY IS GOING TO COME UP TO YOU AND SHOW YOU A NICE BRAND-NEW SEALED DECK OF CARDS.
"'AND THIS GUY IS GOING TO OFFER TO BET YOU THAT HE CAN MAKE THE JACK OF SPADES JUMP OUT OF THE DECK AND SQUIRT CIDER IN YOUR EAR.
"'DO NOT BET THIS MAN, FOR AS SURE AS YOU ARE STANDING THERE, YOU ARE GOING TO END UP WITH AN EARFUL OF CIDER.'"
AH. THE CLASSIC WRITINGS OF DAMON RUNYON.
THE POINT IS, PETER...
I'VE SEEN YOU FIGHT FOR MANY CAUSES, ALL OF THEM NOBLE.
GET INTO A FIGHT BECAUSE OF EGO, YOU'LL WIND UP WITH A SOGGY EAR.
BUT I'LL SUPPORT YOUR DECISION, NO MATTER WHAT.
I APPRECIATE THAT, AUNT MAY, BECAUSE I'M GOING TO DO IT.
MJ... WHO'S DAMON RUNYON?
I THINK HE WROTE THE MUSICAL "GUYS AND DOLLS."
OKAY. WHICH ONE'S *THAT* AGAIN...?
OH, MRS. PARKER...BEFORE I FORGET...A RESTAURATEUR ASSOCIATE OF MINE IS CELEBRATING THE TENTH ANNIVERSARY OF HIS ESTABLISHMENT TOMORROW. HE'S INVITED ME...
...AND I DESPISE THE NOTION OF DINING ALONE. WOULD YOU CARE TO...?
ARE YOU ASKING ME OUT ON A DATE?
STRICTLY IN A SOCIAL SENSE... YES, I BELIEVE I AM.
I'D BE HONORED, JARVIS.
AS WOULD I, MAY.
OH, GOOD.

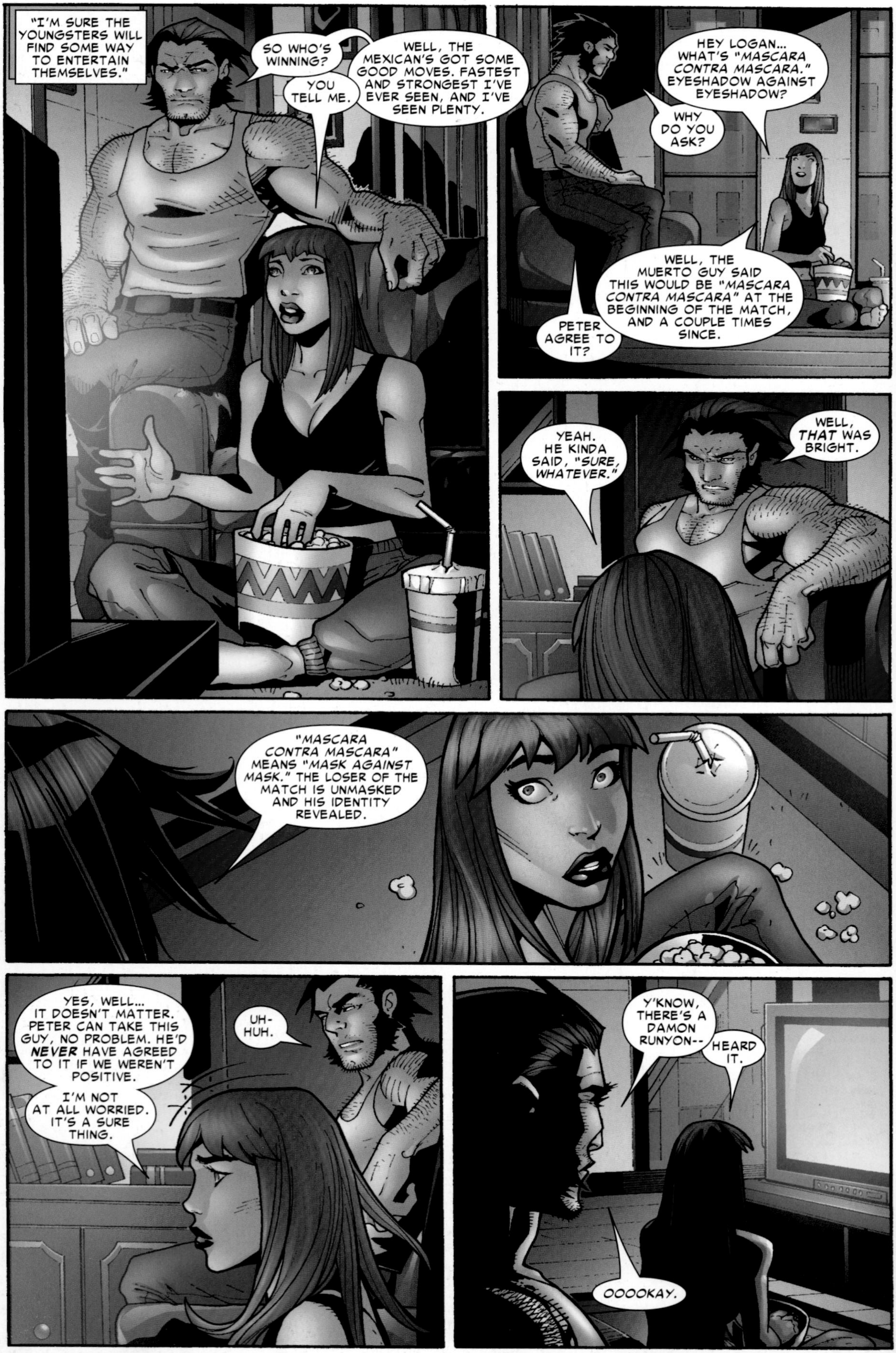
"I'M SURE THE YOUNGSTERS WILL FIND SOME WAY TO ENTERTAIN THEMSELVES."
SO WHO'S WINNING?
YOU TELL ME.
WELL, THE MEXICAN'S GOT SOME GOOD MOVES. FASTEST AND STRONGEST I'VE EVER SEEN, AND I'VE SEEN PLENTY.
HEY LOGAN... WHAT'S "MASCARA CONTRA MASCARA." EYESHADOW AGAINST EYESHADOW?
WHY DO YOU ASK?
WELL, THE MUERTO GUY SAID THIS WOULD BE "MASCARA CONTRA MASCARA" AT THE BEGINNING OF THE MATCH, AND A COUPLE TIMES SINCE.
PETER AGREE TO IT?
YEAH. HE KINDA SAID, "SURE, WHATEVER."
WELL, THAT WAS BRIGHT.
"MASCARA CONTRA MASCARA" MEANS "MASK AGAINST MASK." THE LOSER OF THE MATCH IS UNMASKED AND HIS IDENTITY REVEALED.
YES, WELL... IT DOESN'T MATTER. PETER CAN TAKE THIS GUY, NO PROBLEM. HE'D NEVER HAVE AGREED TO IT IF WE WEREN'T POSITIVE.
I'M NOT AT ALL WORRIED. IT'S A SURE THING.
UH-HUH.
Y'KNOW, THERE'S A DAMON RUNYON--
HEARD IT.
OOOOKAY.

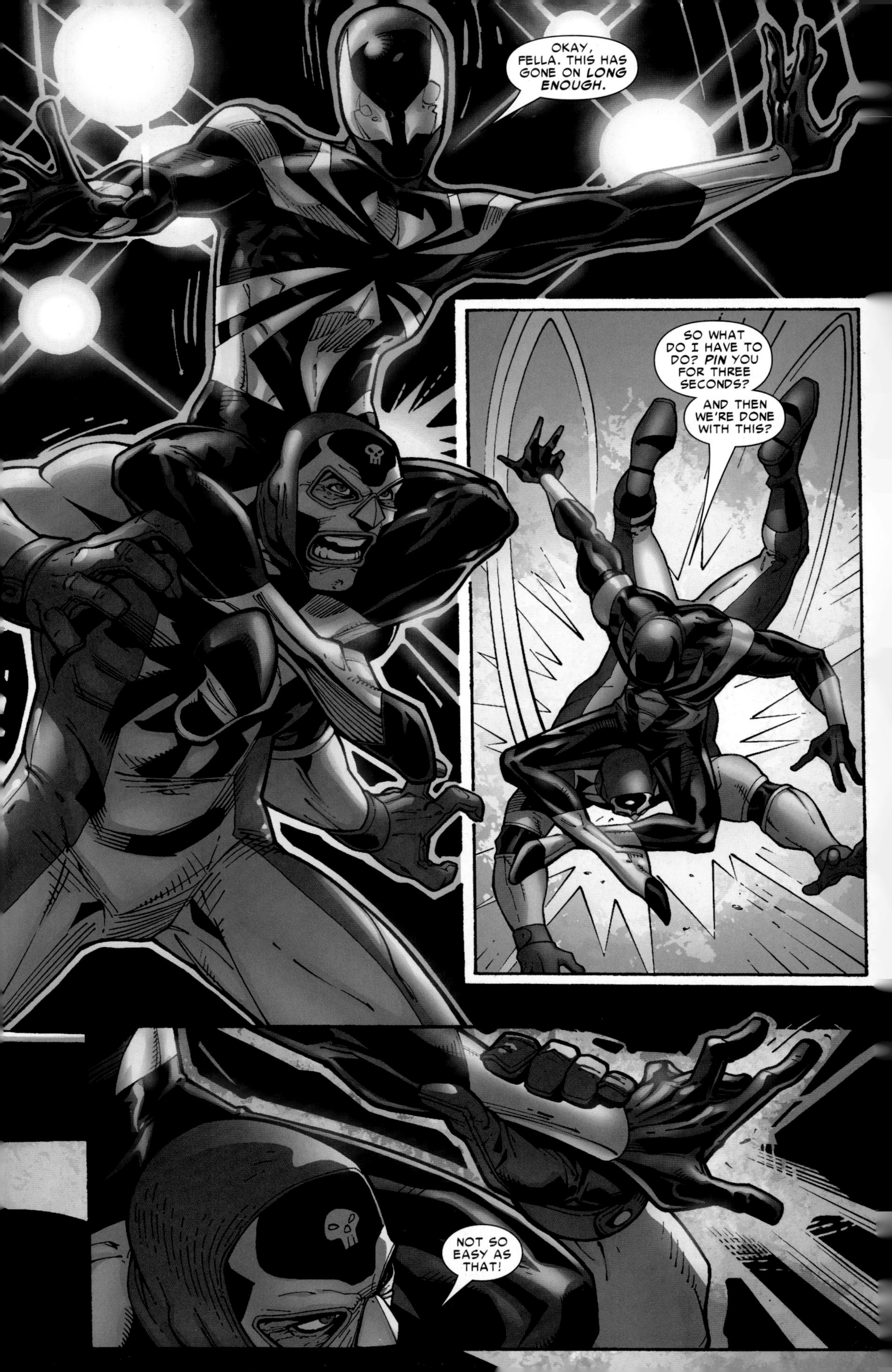
OKAY, FELLA. THIS HAS GONE ON LONG ENOUGH.
SO WHAT DO I HAVE TO DO? PIN YOU FOR THREE SECONDS?
AND THEN WE'RE DONE WITH THIS?
NOT SO EASY AS THAT!

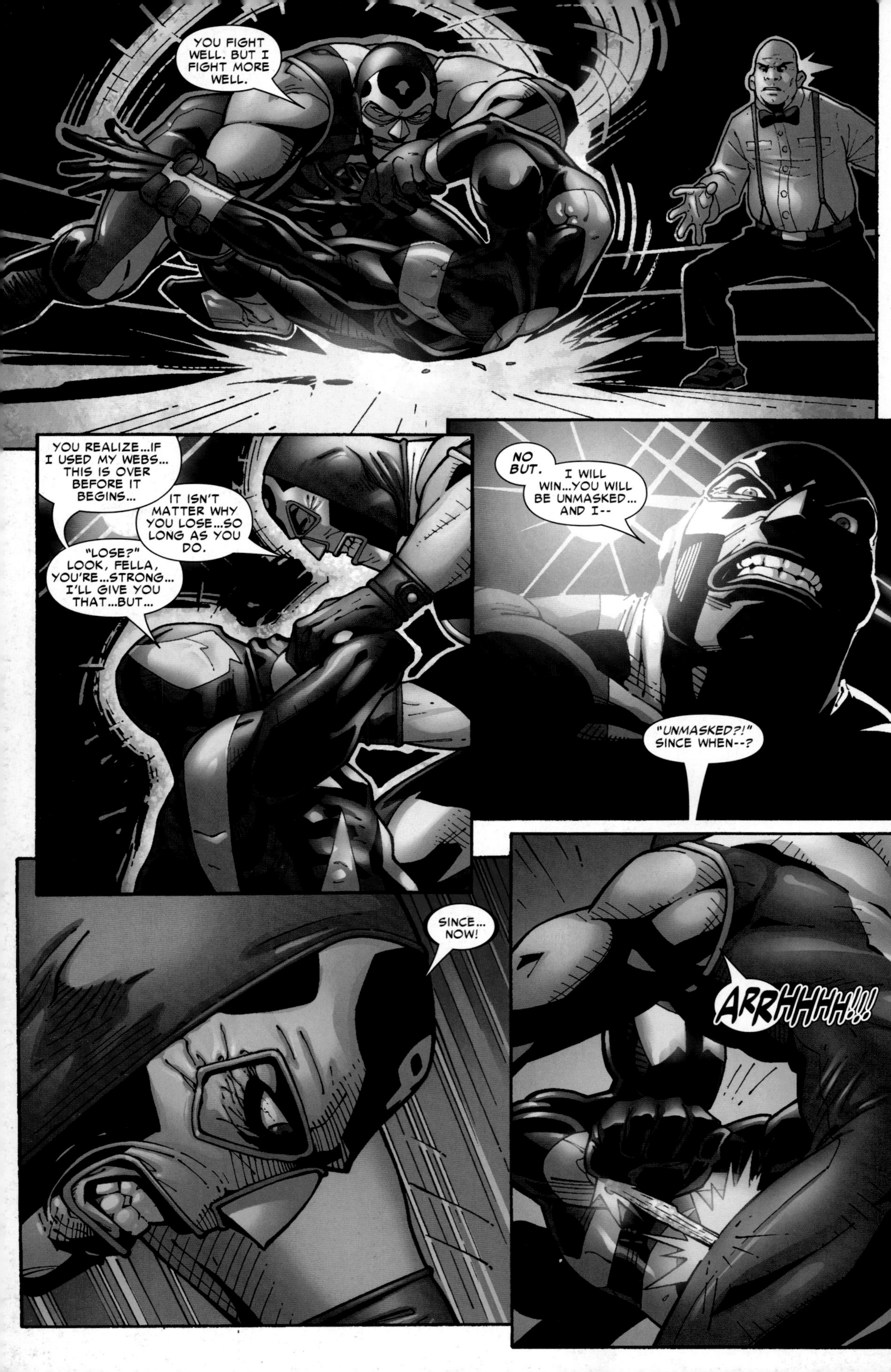
YOU FIGHT WELL. BUT I FIGHT MORE WELL.
YOU REALIZE...IF I USED MY WEBS... THIS IS OVER BEFORE IT BEGINS...
IT ISN'T MATTER WHY YOU LOSE...SO LONG AS YOU DO.
"LOSE?" LOOK, FELLA, YOU'RE...STRONG... I'LL GIVE YOU THAT...BUT...
NO BUT.
I WILL WIN...YOU WILL BE UNMASKED... AND I--
"UNMASKED?!" SINCE WHEN--?
SINCE... NOW!
ARRHHHH!!!

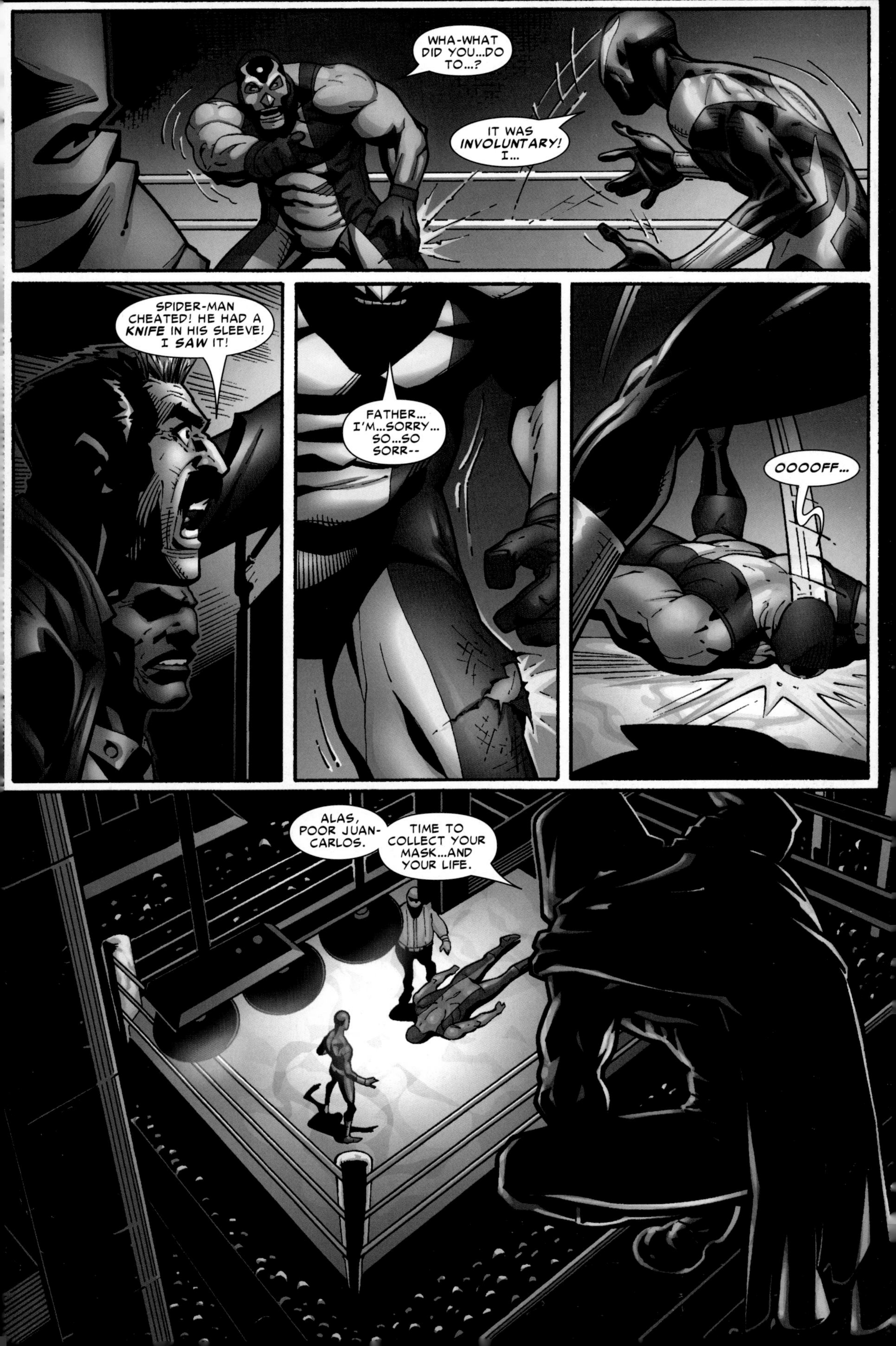
WHA-WHAT DID YOU...DO TO...?
IT WAS INVOLUNTARY! I...
SPIDER-MAN CHEATED! HE HAD A KNIFE IN HIS SLEEVE! I SAW IT!
FATHER... I'M...SORRY... SO...SO SORR--
OOOOFF...
ALAS, POOR JUAN-CARLOS.
TIME TO COLLECT YOUR MASK...AND YOUR LIFE.

#7

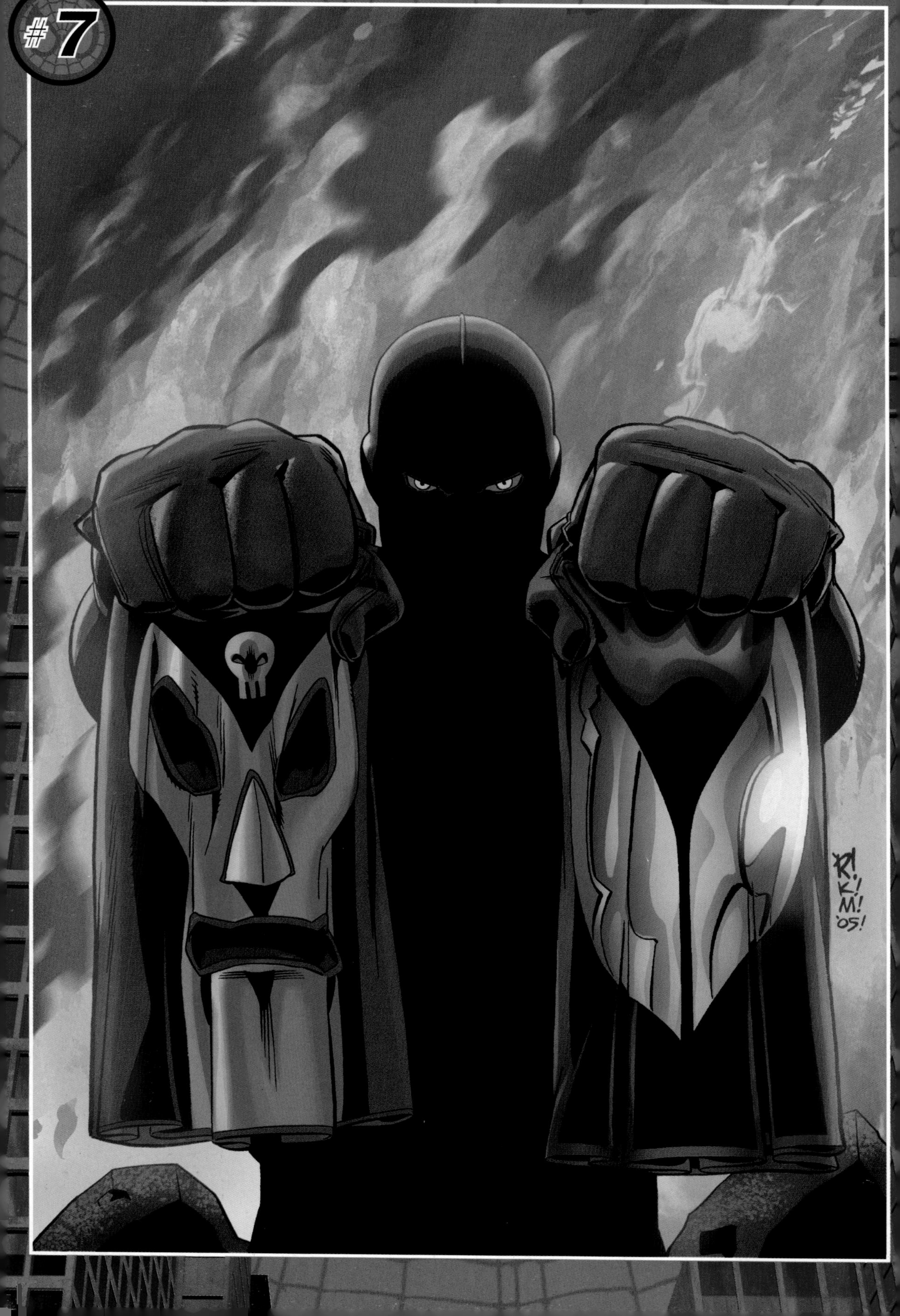
R!
K!
M!
'05!

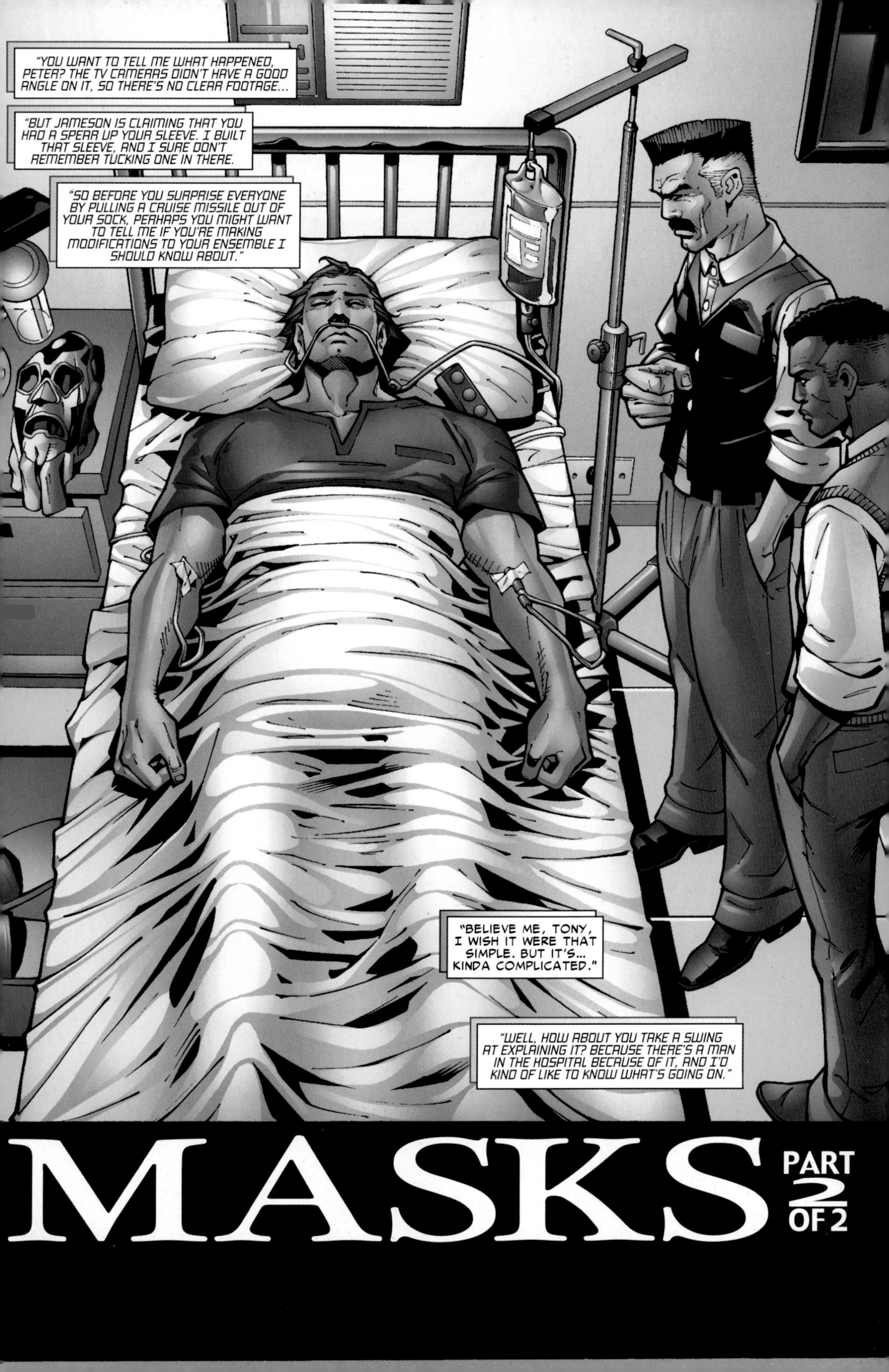
"YOU WANT TO TELL ME WHAT HAPPENED, PETER? THE TV CAMERAS DIDN'T HAVE A GOOD ANGLE ON IT, SO THERE'S NO CLEAR FOOTAGE...
"BUT JAMESON IS CLAIMING THAT YOU HAD A SPEAR UP YOUR SLEEVE. I BUILT THAT SLEEVE, AND I SURE DON'T REMEMBER TUCKING ONE IN THERE.
"SO BEFORE YOU SURPRISE EVERYONE BY PULLING A CRUISE MISSILE OUT OF YOUR SOCK, PERHAPS YOU MIGHT WANT TO TELL ME IF YOU'RE MAKING MODIFICATIONS TO YOUR ENSEMBLE I SHOULD KNOW ABOUT."
"BELIEVE ME, TONY, I WISH IT WERE THAT SIMPLE. BUT IT'S... KINDA COMPLICATED."
"WELL, HOW ABOUT YOU TAKE A SWING AT EXPLAINING IT? BECAUSE THERE'S A MAN IN THE HOSPITAL BECAUSE OF IT, AND I'D KIND OF LIKE TO KNOW WHAT'S GOING ON."
MASKS
PART 2 OF 2

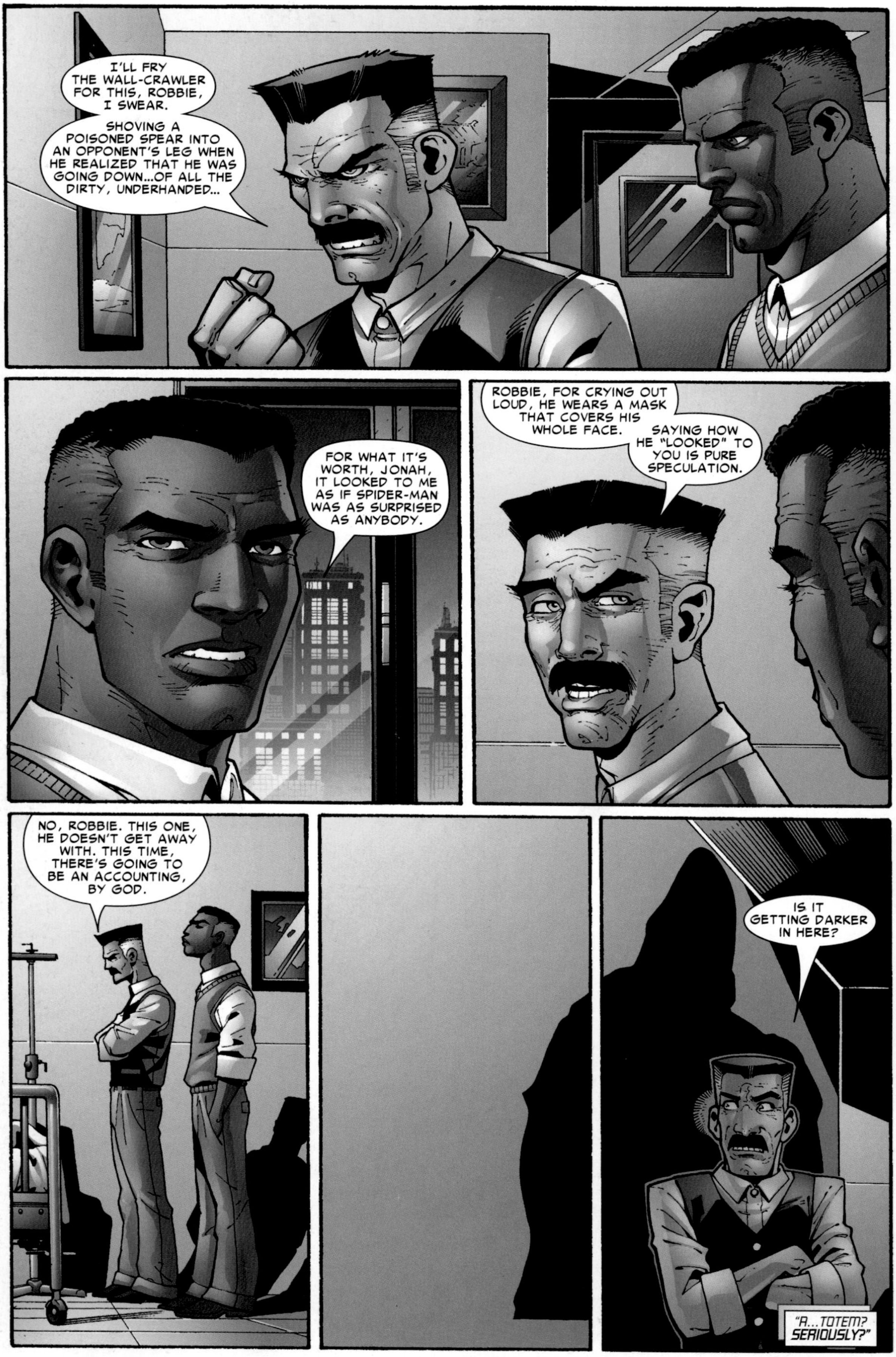
I'LL FRY THE WALL-CRAWLER FOR THIS, ROBBIE, I SWEAR.
SHOVING A POISONED SPEAR INTO AN OPPONENT'S LEG WHEN HE REALIZED THAT HE WAS GOING DOWN...OF ALL THE DIRTY, UNDERHANDED...
FOR WHAT IT'S WORTH, JONAH, IT LOOKED TO ME AS IF SPIDER-MAN WAS AS SURPRISED AS ANYBODY.
ROBBIE, FOR CRYING OUT LOUD, HE WEARS A MASK THAT COVERS HIS WHOLE FACE.
SAYING HOW HE "LOOKED" TO YOU IS PURE SPECULATION.
NO, ROBBIE. THIS ONE, HE DOESN'T GET AWAY WITH. THIS TIME, THERE'S GOING TO BE AN ACCOUNTING, BY GOD.
IS IT GETTING DARKER IN HERE?
"A...TOTEM? SERIOUSLY?"

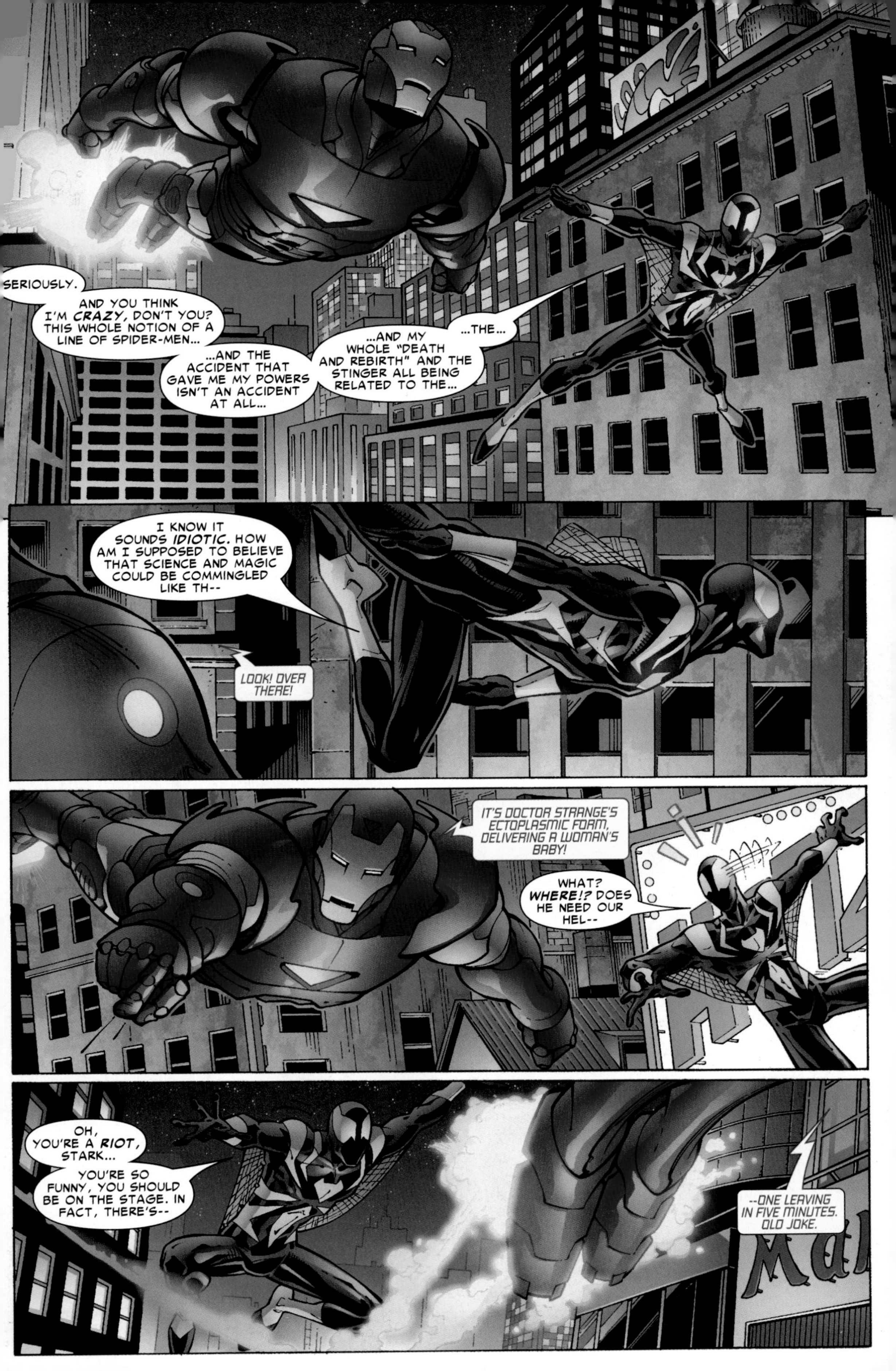
SERIOUSLY.
AND YOU THINK I'M CRAZY, DON'T YOU? THIS WHOLE NOTION OF A LINE OF SPIDER-MEN...
...AND THE ACCIDENT THAT GAVE ME MY POWERS ISN'T AN ACCIDENT AT ALL...
...AND MY WHOLE "DEATH AND REBIRTH" AND THE STINGER ALL BEING RELATED TO THE...
...THE...
I KNOW IT SOUNDS IDIOTIC. HOW AM I SUPPOSED TO BELIEVE THAT SCIENCE AND MAGIC COULD BE COMMINGLED LIKE TH--
LOOK! OVER THERE!
IT'S DOCTOR STRANGE'S ECTOPLASMIC FORM, DELIVERING A WOMAN'S BABY!
WHAT? WHERE!? DOES HE NEED OUR HEL--
OH, YOU'RE A RIOT, STARK...
YOU'RE SO FUNNY, YOU SHOULD BE ON THE STAGE. IN FACT, THERE'S--
--ONE LEAVING IN FIVE MINUTES. OLD JOKE.

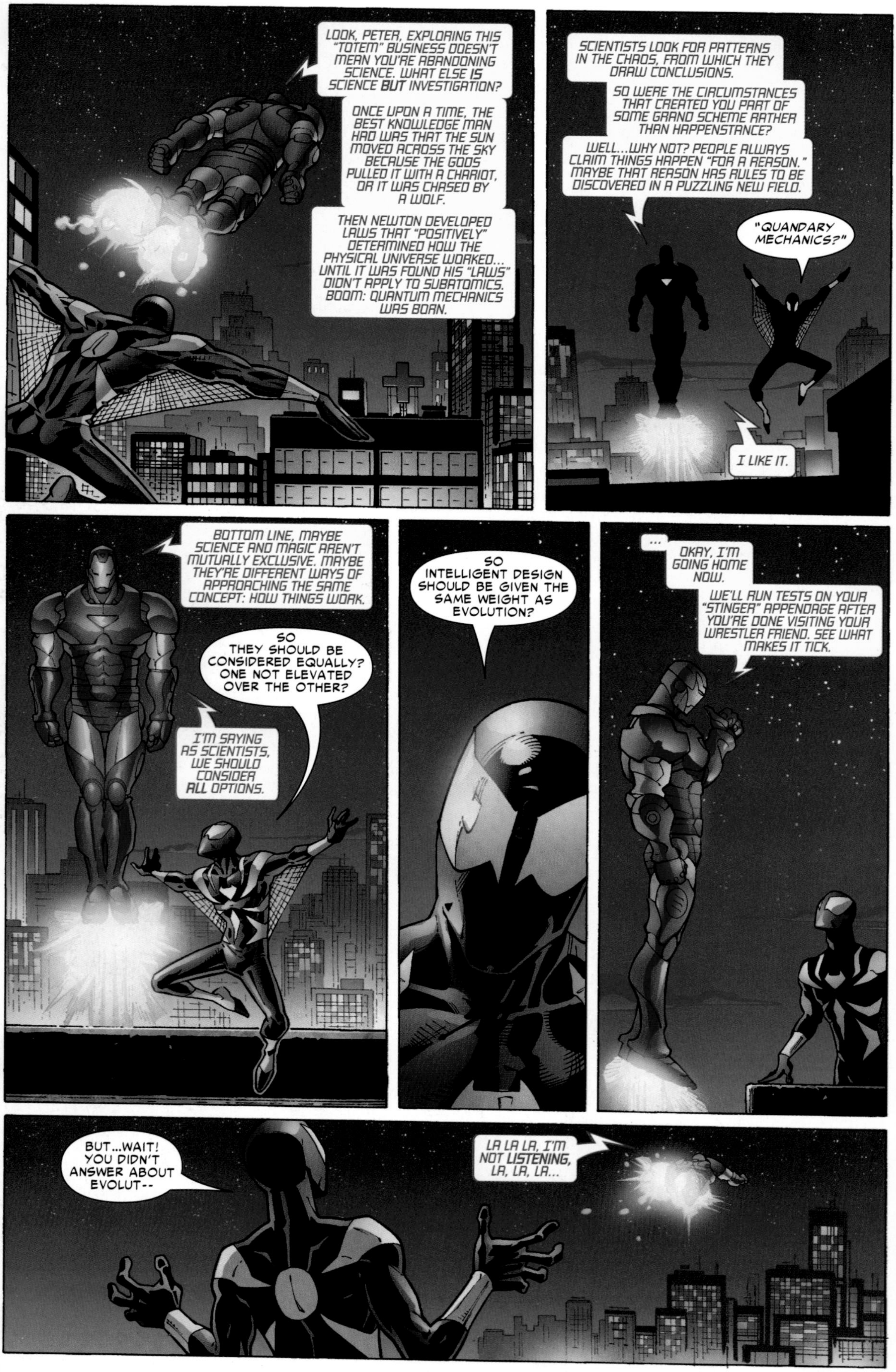
LOOK, PETER, EXPLORING THIS "TOTEM" BUSINESS DOESN'T MEAN YOU'RE ABANDONING SCIENCE. WHAT ELSE **IS** SCIENCE **BUT** INVESTIGATION?
ONCE UPON A TIME, THE BEST KNOWLEDGE MAN HAD WAS THAT THE SUN MOVED ACROSS THE SKY BECAUSE THE GODS PULLED IT WITH A CHARIOT, OR IT WAS CHASED BY A WOLF.
THEN NEWTON DEVELOPED LAWS THAT "POSITIVELY" DETERMINED HOW THE PHYSICAL UNIVERSE WORKED... UNTIL IT WAS FOUND HIS "LAWS" DIDN'T APPLY TO SUBATOMICS. BOOM: QUANTUM MECHANICS WAS BORN.
SCIENTISTS LOOK FOR PATTERNS IN THE CHAOS, FROM WHICH THEY DRAW CONCLUSIONS.
SO WERE THE CIRCUMSTANCES THAT CREATED YOU PART OF SOME GRAND SCHEME RATHER THAN HAPPENSTANCE?
WELL...WHY NOT? PEOPLE ALWAYS CLAIM THINGS HAPPEN "FOR A REASON." MAYBE THAT REASON HAS RULES TO BE DISCOVERED IN A PUZZLING NEW FIELD.
"QUANDARY MECHANICS?"
I LIKE IT.
BOTTOM LINE, MAYBE SCIENCE AND MAGIC AREN'T MUTUALLY EXCLUSIVE. MAYBE THEY'RE DIFFERENT WAYS OF APPROACHING THE SAME CONCEPT: HOW THINGS WORK.
SO THEY SHOULD BE CONSIDERED EQUALLY? ONE NOT ELEVATED OVER THE OTHER?
I'M SAYING AS SCIENTISTS, WE SHOULD CONSIDER **ALL** OPTIONS.
SO INTELLIGENT DESIGN SHOULD BE GIVEN THE SAME WEIGHT AS EVOLUTION?
...
OKAY, I'M GOING HOME NOW.
WE'LL RUN TESTS ON YOUR "STINGER" APPENDAGE AFTER YOU'RE DONE VISITING YOUR WRESTLER FRIEND. SEE WHAT MAKES IT TICK.
BUT...WAIT! YOU DIDN'T ANSWER ABOUT EVOLUT--
LA LA LA, I'M NOT **LISTENING**, LA, LA, LA...

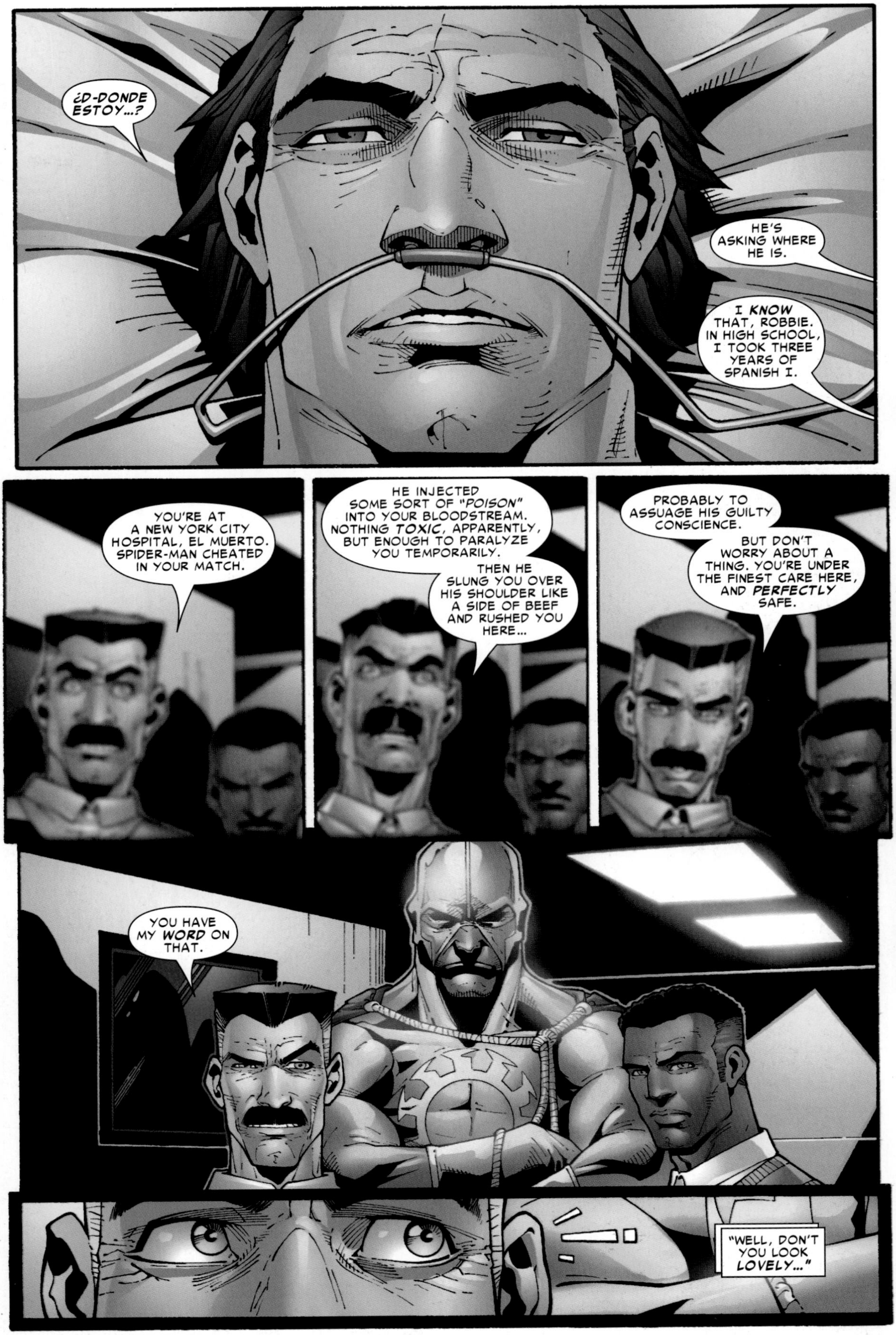
¿D-DONDE ESTOY...?
HE'S ASKING WHERE HE IS.
I KNOW THAT, ROBBIE. IN HIGH SCHOOL, I TOOK THREE YEARS OF SPANISH I.
YOU'RE AT A NEW YORK CITY HOSPITAL, EL MUERTO. SPIDER-MAN CHEATED IN YOUR MATCH.
HE INJECTED SOME SORT OF "POISON" INTO YOUR BLOODSTREAM. NOTHING TOXIC, APPARENTLY, BUT ENOUGH TO PARALYZE YOU TEMPORARILY.
THEN HE SLUNG YOU OVER HIS SHOULDER LIKE A SIDE OF BEEF AND RUSHED YOU HERE...
PROBABLY TO ASSUAGE HIS GUILTY CONSCIENCE.
BUT DON'T WORRY ABOUT A THING. YOU'RE UNDER THE FINEST CARE HERE, AND PERFECTLY SAFE.
YOU HAVE MY WORD ON THAT.
"WELL, DON'T YOU LOOK LOVELY..."

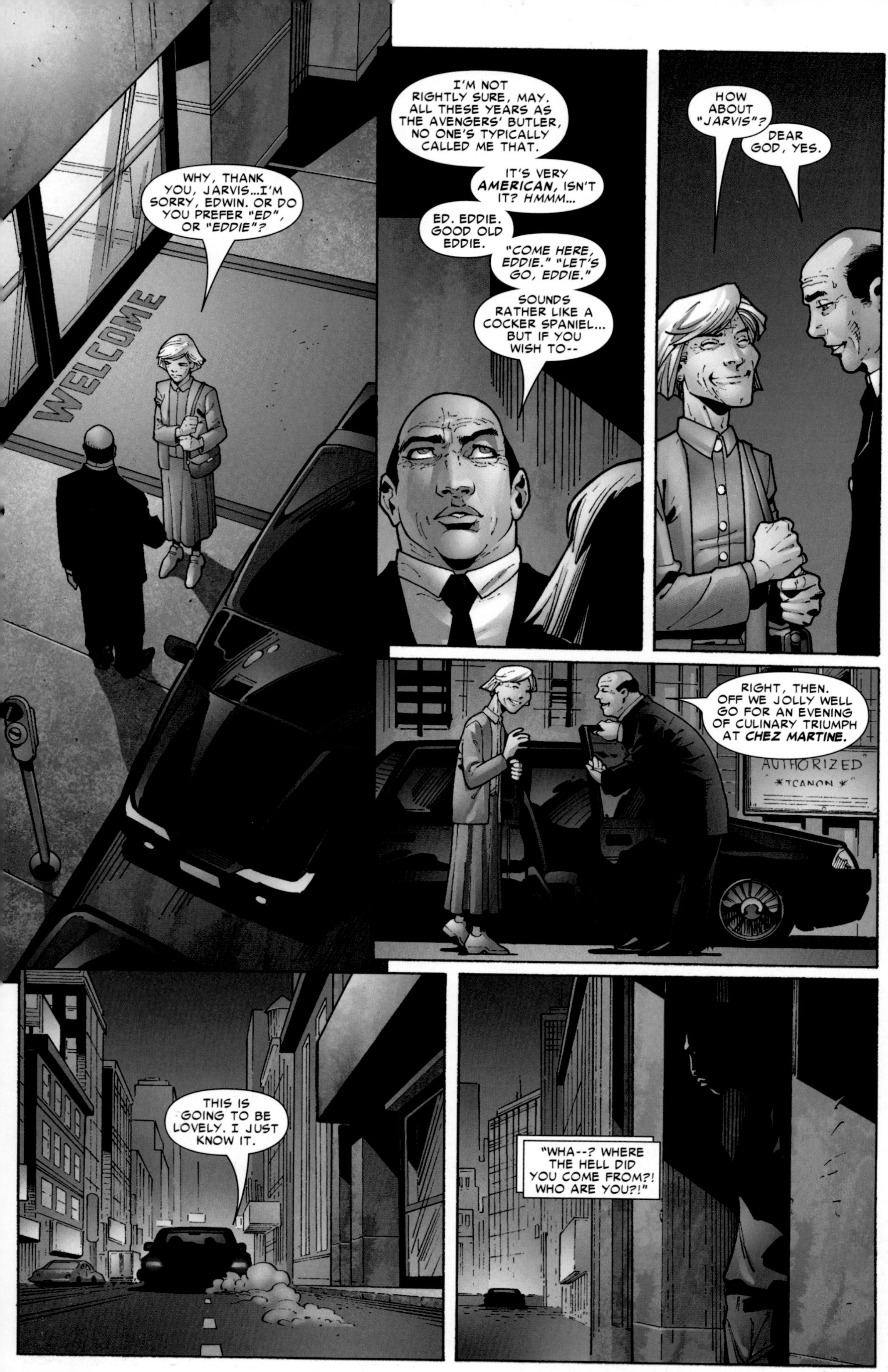

WHY, THANK YOU, JARVIS...I'M SORRY, EDWIN. OR DO YOU PREFER "ED", OR "EDDIE"?
WELCOME
I'M NOT RIGHTLY SURE, MAY. ALL THESE YEARS AS THE AVENGERS' BUTLER, NO ONE'S TYPICALLY CALLED ME THAT.
IT'S VERY AMERICAN, ISN'T IT? HMMM...
ED. EDDIE. GOOD OLD EDDIE.
"COME HERE, EDDIE." "LET'S GO, EDDIE."
SOUNDS RATHER LIKE A COCKER SPANIEL... BUT IF YOU WISH TO--
HOW ABOUT "JARVIS"?
DEAR GOD, YES.
RIGHT, THEN. OFF WE JOLLY WELL GO FOR AN EVENING OF CULINARY TRIUMPH AT CHEZ MARTINE.
AUTHORIZED
TCANON
THIS IS GOING TO BE LOVELY. I JUST KNOW IT.
"WHA--? WHERE THE HELL DID YOU COME FROM?! WHO ARE YOU?!"

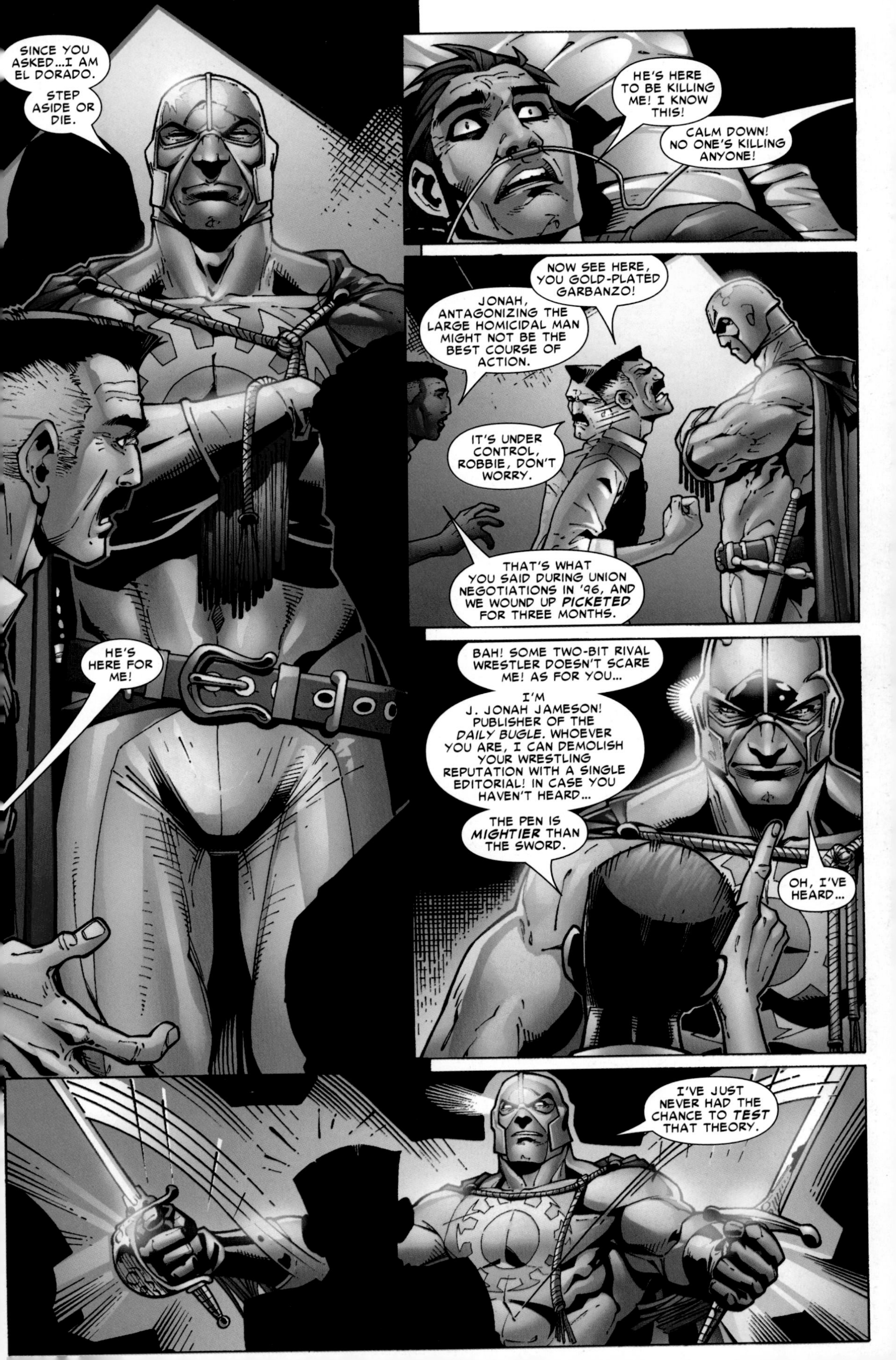
SINCE YOU ASKED...I AM EL DORADO.
STEP ASIDE OR DIE.
HE'S HERE FOR ME!
HE'S HERE TO BE KILLING ME! I KNOW THIS!
CALM DOWN! NO ONE'S KILLING ANYONE!
NOW SEE HERE, YOU GOLD-PLATED GARBANZO!
JONAH, ANTAGONIZING THE LARGE HOMICIDAL MAN MIGHT NOT BE THE BEST COURSE OF ACTION.
IT'S UNDER CONTROL, ROBBIE, DON'T WORRY.
THAT'S WHAT YOU SAID DURING UNION NEGOTIATIONS IN '96, AND WE WOUND UP PICKETED FOR THREE MONTHS.
BAH! SOME TWO-BIT RIVAL WRESTLER DOESN'T SCARE ME! AS FOR YOU...
I'M J. JONAH JAMESON! PUBLISHER OF THE DAILY BUGLE. WHOEVER YOU ARE, I CAN DEMOLISH YOUR WRESTLING REPUTATION WITH A SINGLE EDITORIAL! IN CASE YOU HAVEN'T HEARD...
THE PEN IS MIGHTIER THAN THE SWORD.
OH, I'VE HEARD...
I'VE JUST NEVER HAD THE CHANCE TO TEST THAT THEORY.

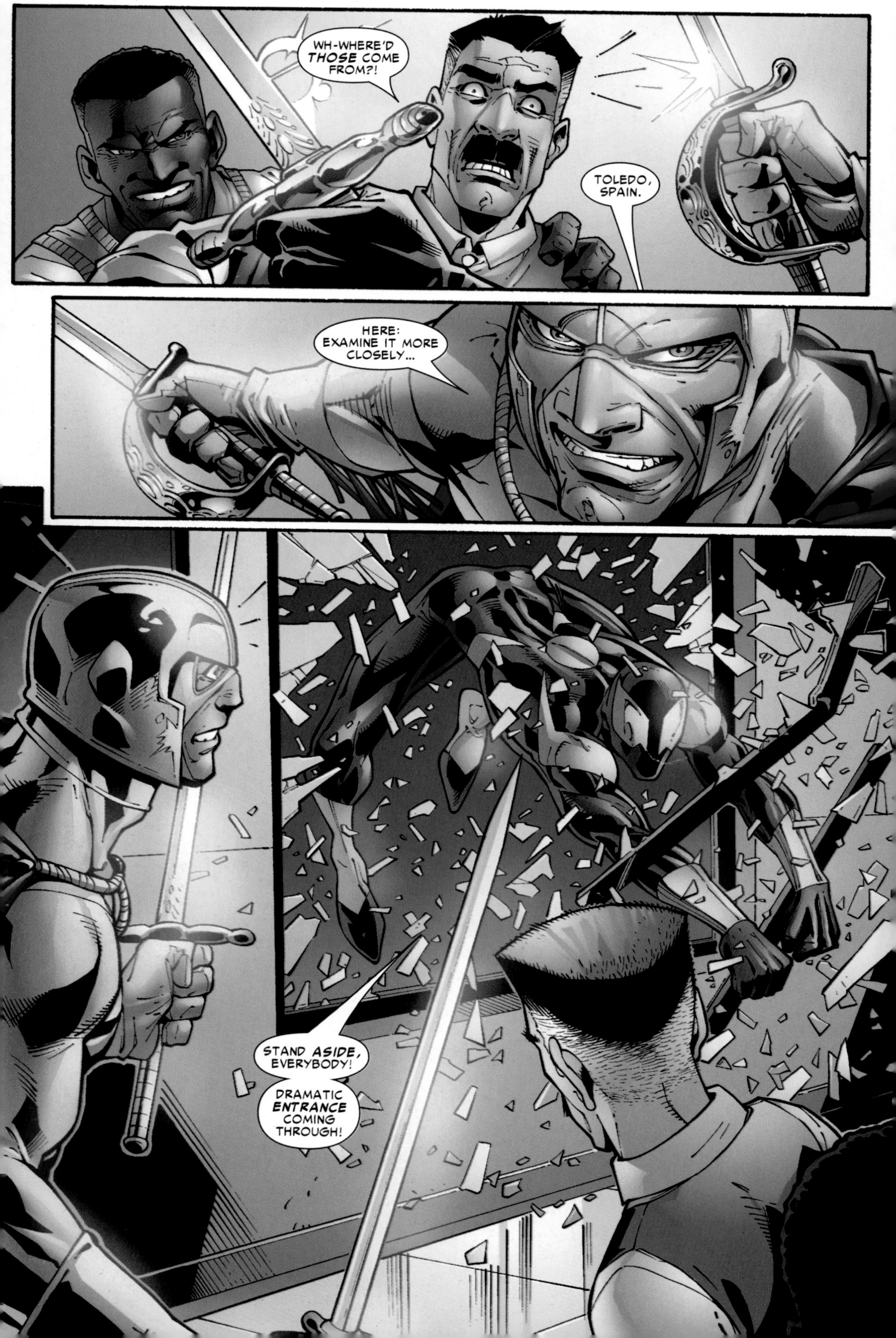
WH-WHERE'D THOSE COME FROM?!
TOLEDO, SPAIN.
HERE: EXAMINE IT MORE CLOSELY...
STAND ASIDE, EVERYBODY!
DRAMATIC ENTRANCE COMING THROUGH!

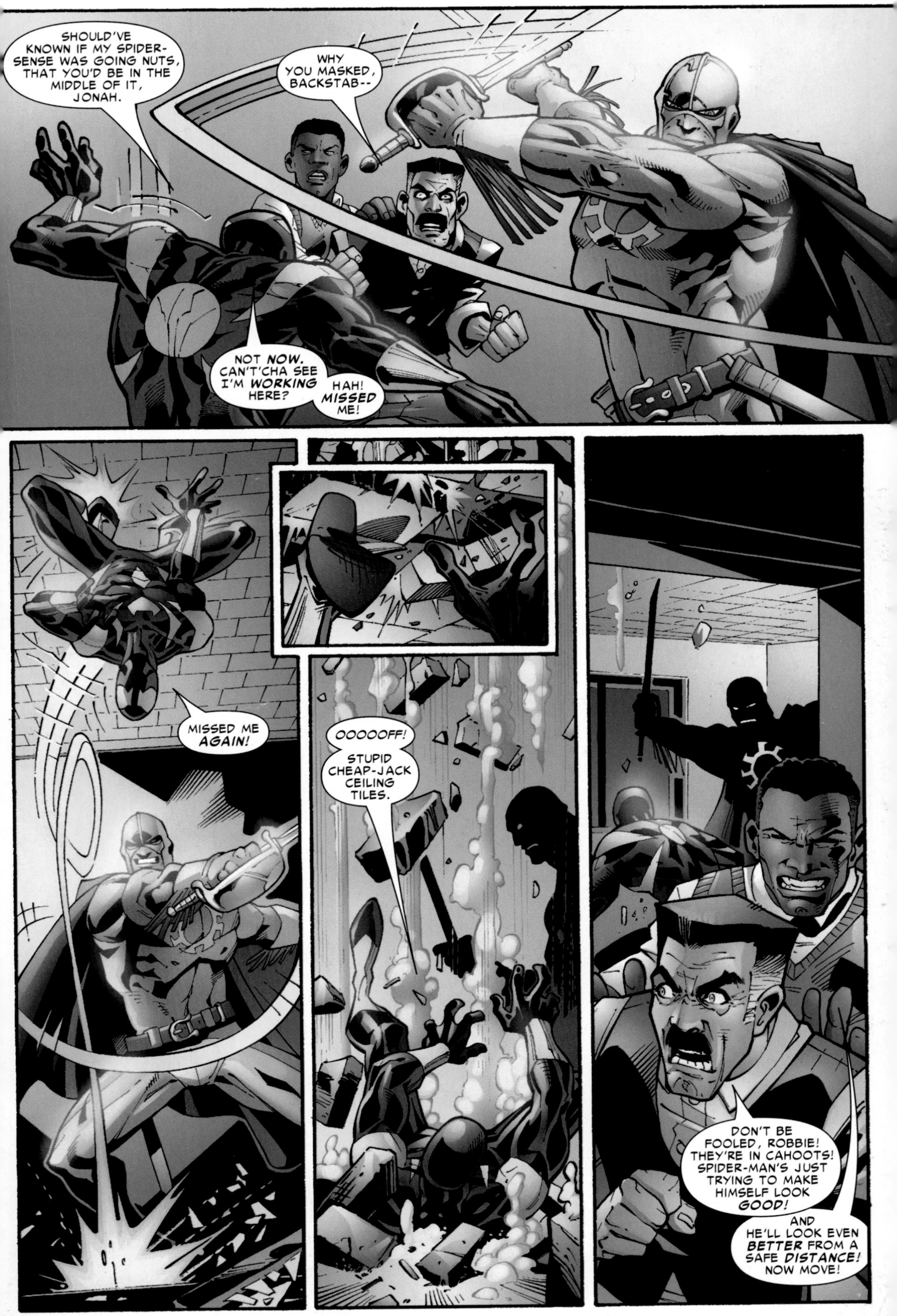
SHOULD'VE KNOWN IF MY SPIDER-SENSE WAS GOING NUTS, THAT YOU'D BE IN THE MIDDLE OF IT, JONAH.
WHY YOU MASKED, BACKSTAB--
NOT NOW. CAN'T'CHA SEE I'M WORKING HERE?
HAH! MISSED ME!
MISSED ME AGAIN!
OOOOOFF!
STUPID CHEAP-JACK CEILING TILES.
DON'T BE FOOLED, ROBBIE! THEY'RE IN CAHOOTS! SPIDER-MAN'S JUST TRYING TO MAKE HIMSELF LOOK GOOD!
AND HE'LL LOOK EVEN BETTER FROM A SAFE DISTANCE! NOW MOVE!

I *UNDERESTIMATED* YOU, JUAN-CARLOS! HERE I THOUGHT YOU HAD MERELY BEEN DEFEATED BY A MASKED OPPONENT, AND THUS FORFEITED YOUR LIFE...

BUT INSTEAD YOU SOMEHOW LURED HIM HERE AS AN OFFERING TO ME! I'M *HONORED.*

YOU MAY KEEP THE INHERITANCE OF YOUR FAMILY'S MASK. YOU WILL NOT BE AN ESPECIALLY ADMIRABLE EL MUERTO...BUT AT LEAST THE TRADITION WILL LIVE.

WHICH IS *MORE* THAN I CAN SAY FOR EL SPIDER-MAN--!

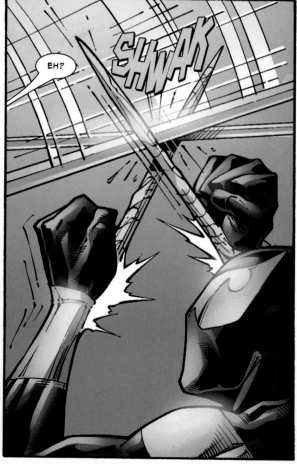

EH?

SHWAK

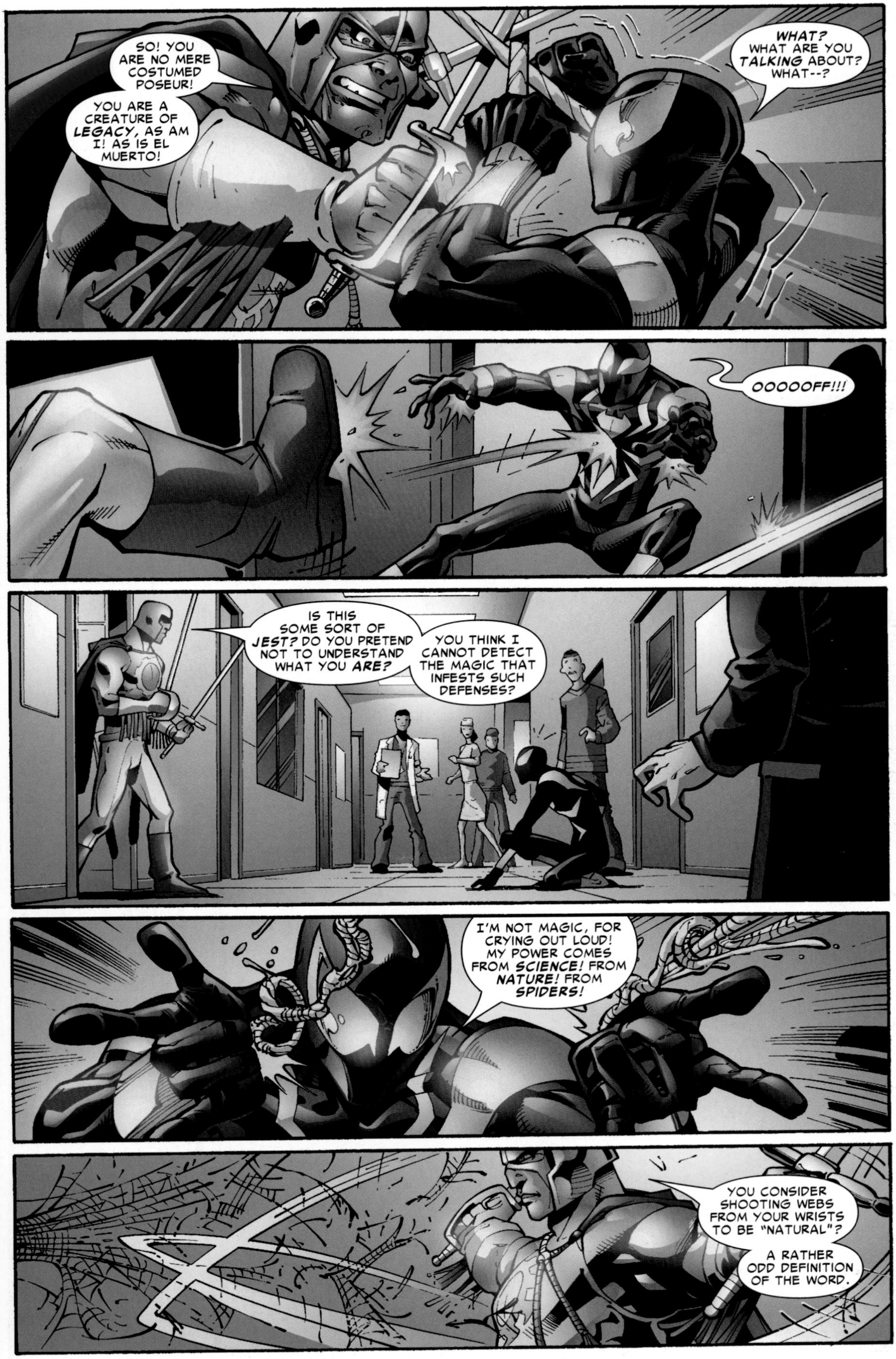
SO! YOU ARE NO MERE COSTUMED POSEUR!
YOU ARE A CREATURE OF LEGACY, AS AM I! AS IS EL MUERTO!
WHAT? WHAT ARE YOU TALKING ABOUT? WHAT--?
OOOOOFF!!!
IS THIS SOME SORT OF JEST? DO YOU PRETEND NOT TO UNDERSTAND WHAT YOU ARE?
YOU THINK I CANNOT DETECT THE MAGIC THAT INFESTS SUCH DEFENSES?
I'M NOT MAGIC, FOR CRYING OUT LOUD! MY POWER COMES FROM SCIENCE! FROM NATURE! FROM SPIDERS!
YOU CONSIDER SHOOTING WEBS FROM YOUR WRISTS TO BE "NATURAL"?
A RATHER ODD DEFINITION OF THE WORD.

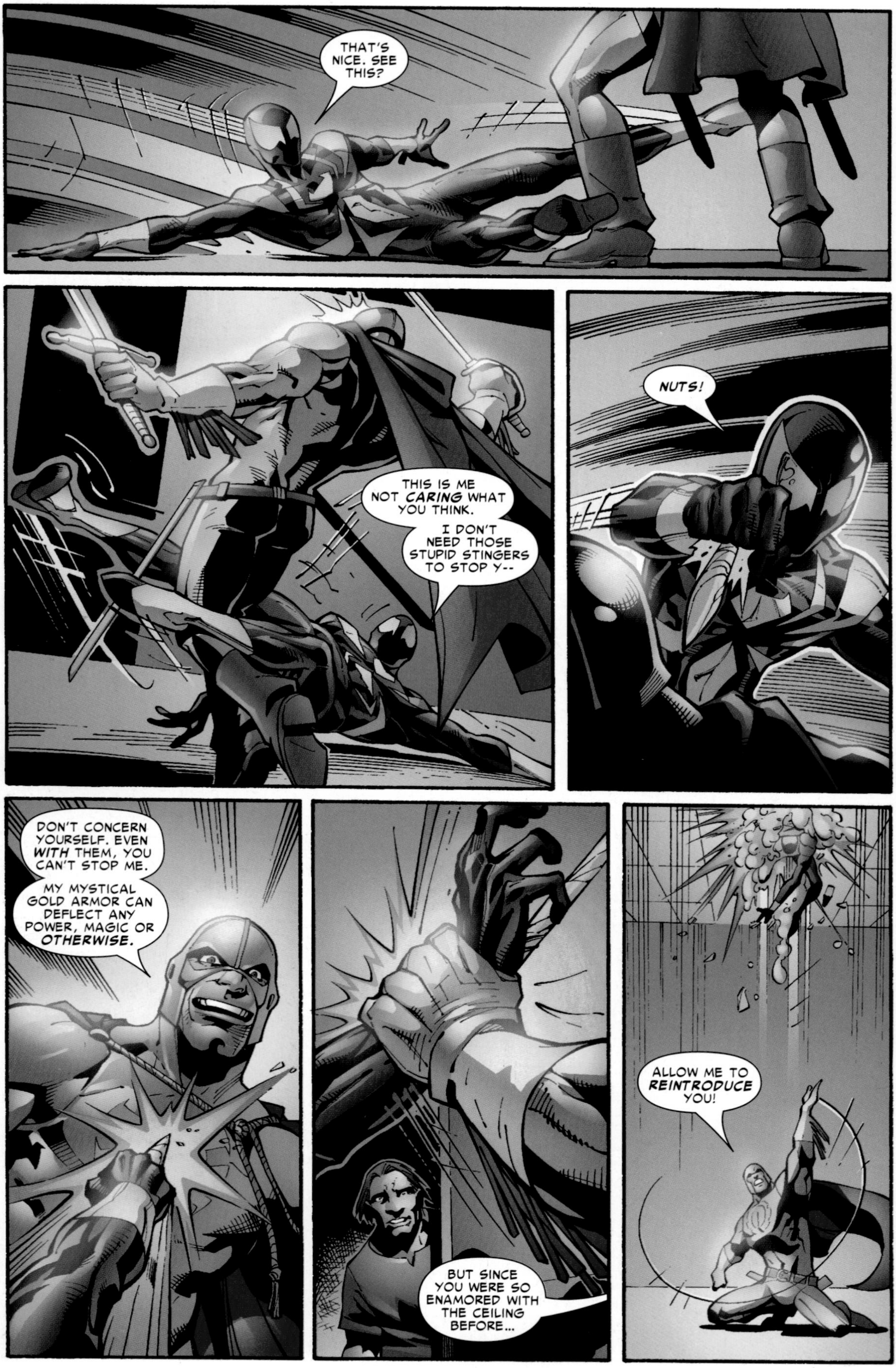
THAT'S NICE. SEE THIS?
THIS IS ME NOT CARING WHAT YOU THINK.
I DON'T NEED THOSE STUPID STINGERS TO STOP Y--
NUTS!
DON'T CONCERN YOURSELF. EVEN WITH THEM, YOU CAN'T STOP ME.
MY MYSTICAL GOLD ARMOR CAN DEFLECT ANY POWER, MAGIC OR OTHERWISE.
BUT SINCE YOU WERE SO ENAMORED WITH THE CEILING BEFORE...
ALLOW ME TO REINTRODUCE YOU!

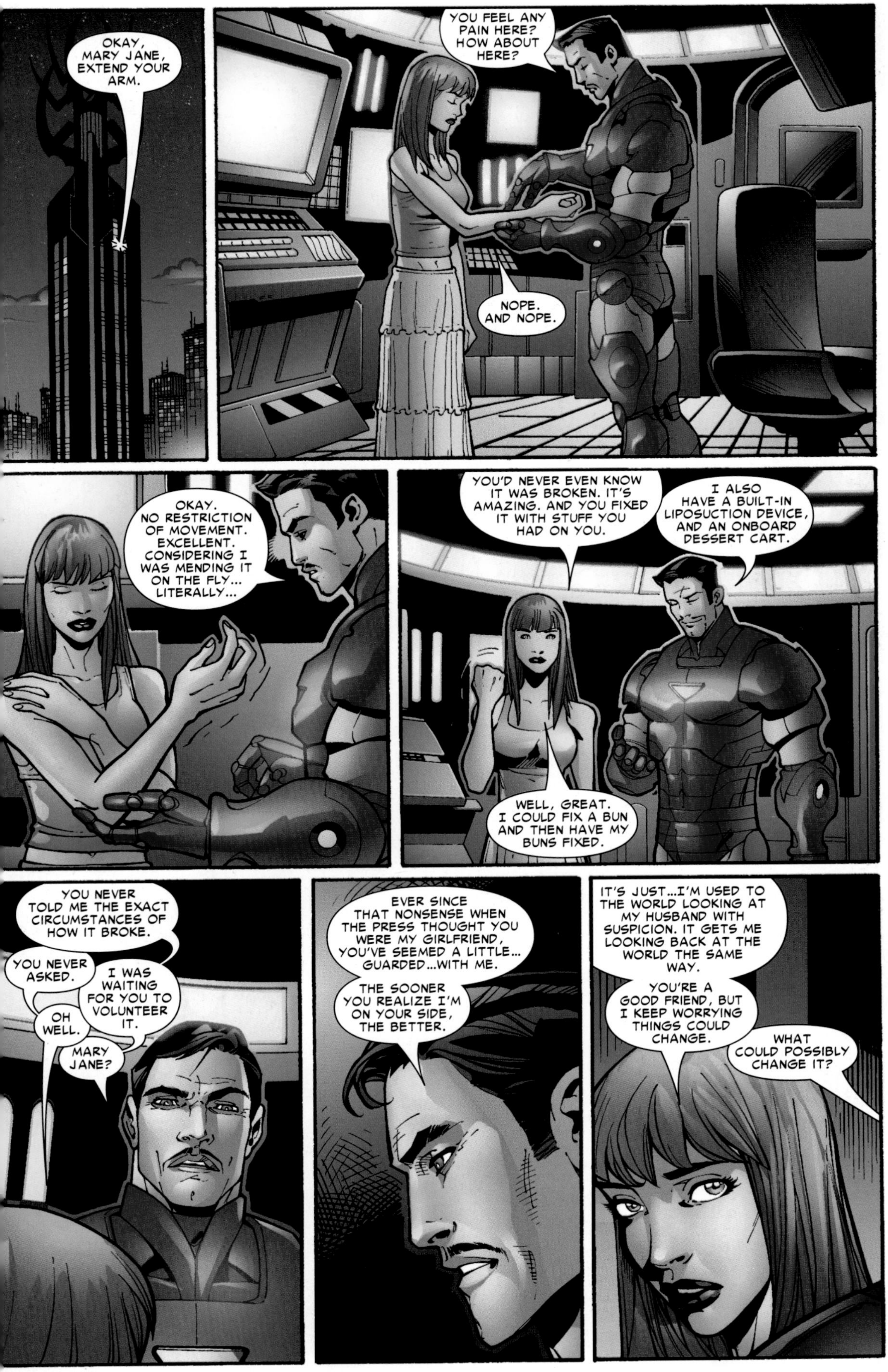

OKAY, MARY JANE, EXTEND YOUR ARM.
YOU FEEL ANY PAIN HERE? HOW ABOUT HERE?
NOPE. AND NOPE.
OKAY. NO RESTRICTION OF MOVEMENT. EXCELLENT. CONSIDERING I WAS MENDING IT ON THE FLY... LITERALLY...
YOU'D NEVER EVEN KNOW IT WAS BROKEN. IT'S AMAZING. AND YOU FIXED IT WITH STUFF YOU HAD ON YOU.
I ALSO HAVE A BUILT-IN LIPOSUCTION DEVICE, AND AN ONBOARD DESSERT CART.
WELL, GREAT. I COULD FIX A BUN AND THEN HAVE MY BUNS FIXED.
YOU NEVER TOLD ME THE EXACT CIRCUMSTANCES OF HOW IT BROKE.
YOU NEVER ASKED.
I WAS WAITING FOR YOU TO VOLUNTEER IT.
OH WELL.
MARY JANE?
EVER SINCE THAT NONSENSE WHEN THE PRESS THOUGHT YOU WERE MY GIRLFRIEND, YOU'VE SEEMED A LITTLE... GUARDED...WITH ME.
THE SOONER YOU REALIZE I'M ON YOUR SIDE, THE BETTER.
IT'S JUST...I'M USED TO THE WORLD LOOKING AT MY HUSBAND WITH SUSPICION. IT GETS ME LOOKING BACK AT THE WORLD THE SAME WAY.
YOU'RE A GOOD FRIEND, BUT I KEEP WORRYING THINGS COULD CHANGE.
WHAT COULD POSSIBLY CHANGE IT?

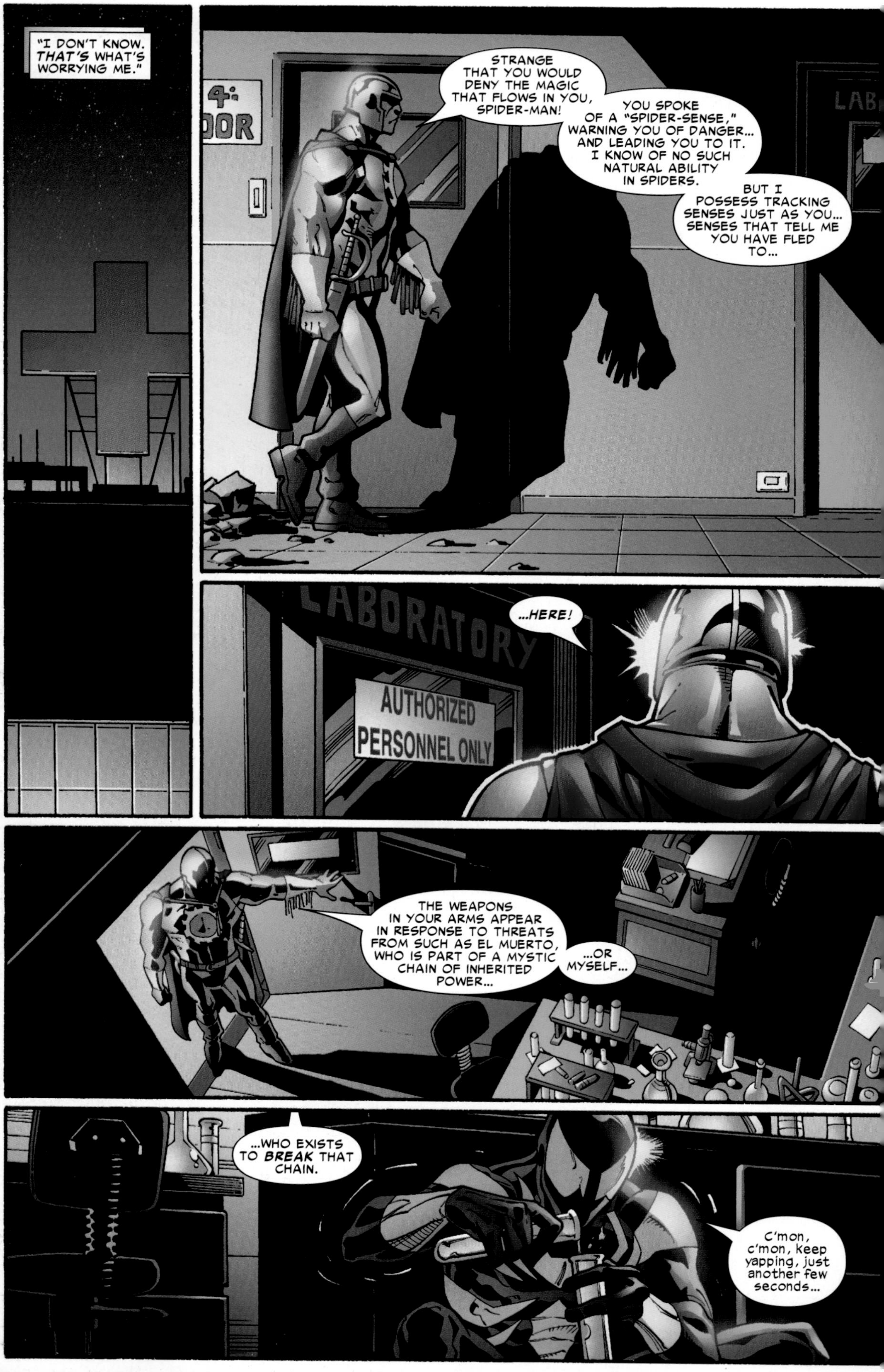
"I DON'T KNOW. THAT'S WHAT'S WORRYING ME."
STRANGE THAT YOU WOULD DENY THE MAGIC THAT FLOWS IN YOU, SPIDER-MAN!
YOU SPOKE OF A "SPIDER-SENSE," WARNING YOU OF DANGER... AND LEADING YOU TO IT. I KNOW OF NO SUCH NATURAL ABILITY IN SPIDERS.
BUT I POSSESS TRACKING SENSES JUST AS YOU... SENSES THAT TELL ME YOU HAVE FLED TO...
LABORATORY
AUTHORIZED PERSONNEL ONLY
...HERE!
THE WEAPONS IN YOUR ARMS APPEAR IN RESPONSE TO THREATS FROM SUCH AS EL MUERTO, WHO IS PART OF A MYSTIC CHAIN OF INHERITED POWER...
...OR MYSELF...
...WHO EXISTS TO BREAK THAT CHAIN.
C'mon, c'mon, keep yapping, just another few seconds...

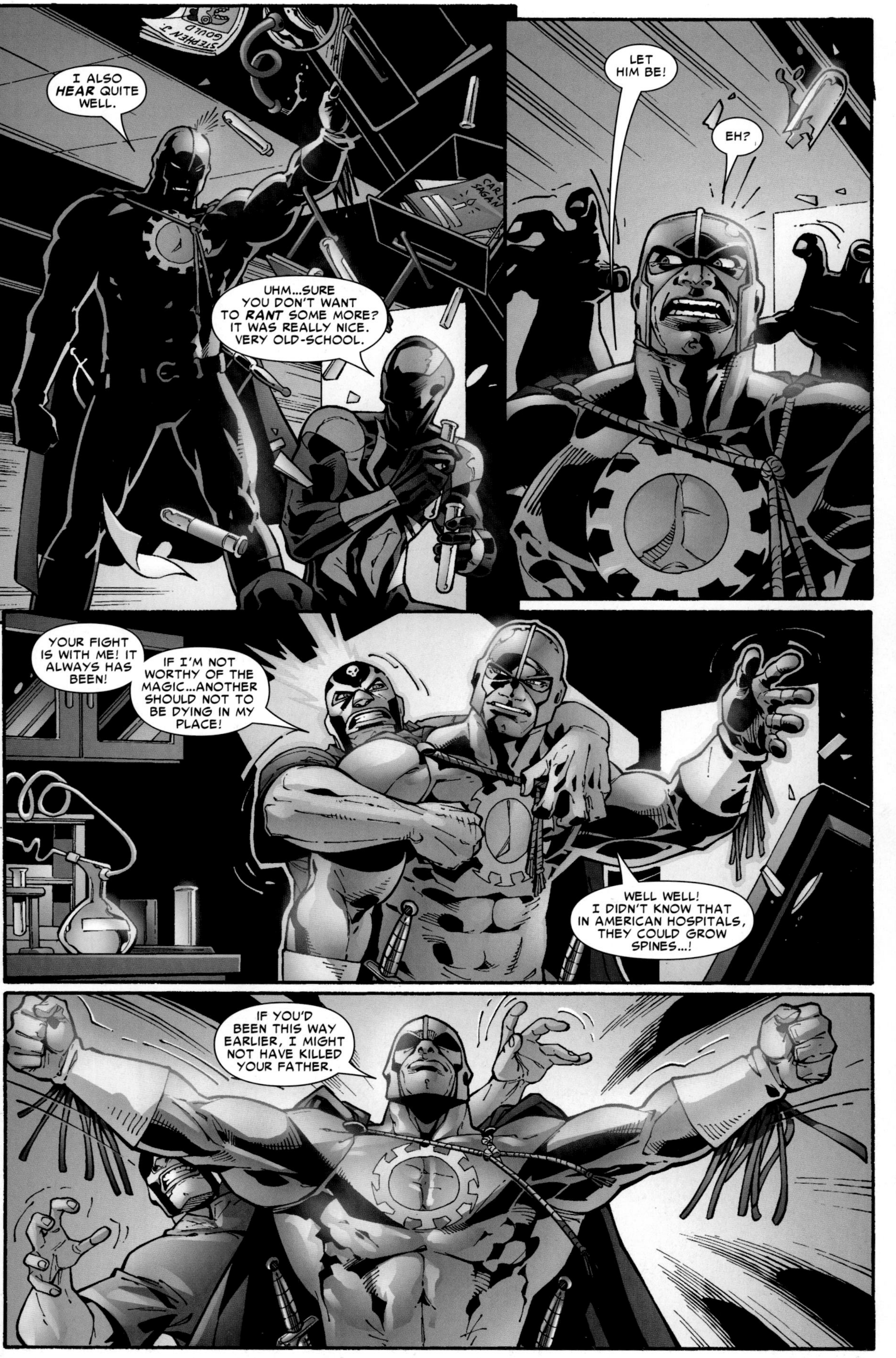

STEPHEN J. GOULD
I ALSO *HEAR* QUITE WELL.
CARL SAGAN
UHM...SURE YOU DON'T WANT TO *RANT* SOME MORE? IT WAS REALLY NICE. VERY OLD-SCHOOL.
LET HIM BE!
EH?
YOUR FIGHT IS WITH ME! IT ALWAYS HAS BEEN!
IF I'M NOT WORTHY OF THE MAGIC...ANOTHER SHOULD NOT TO BE DYING IN MY PLACE!
WELL WELL! I DIDN'T KNOW THAT IN AMERICAN HOSPITALS, THEY COULD GROW SPINES...!
IF YOU'D BEEN THIS WAY EARLIER, I MIGHT NOT HAVE KILLED YOUR FATHER.

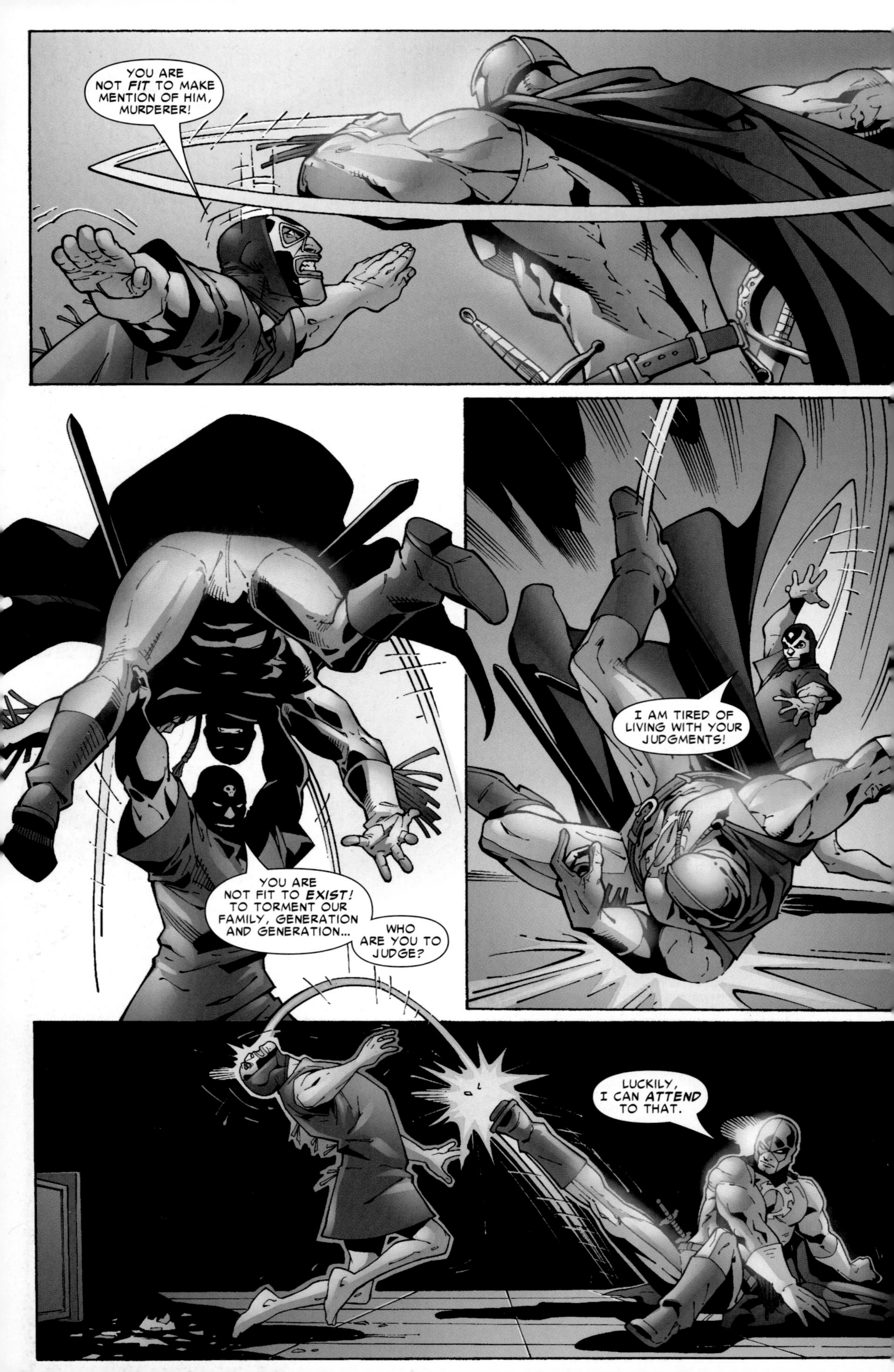
YOU ARE NOT FIT TO MAKE MENTION OF HIM, MURDERER!
YOU ARE NOT FIT TO EXIST! TO TORMENT OUR FAMILY, GENERATION AND GENERATION...
WHO ARE YOU TO JUDGE?
I AM TIRED OF LIVING WITH YOUR JUDGMENTS!
LUCKILY, I CAN ATTEND TO THAT.

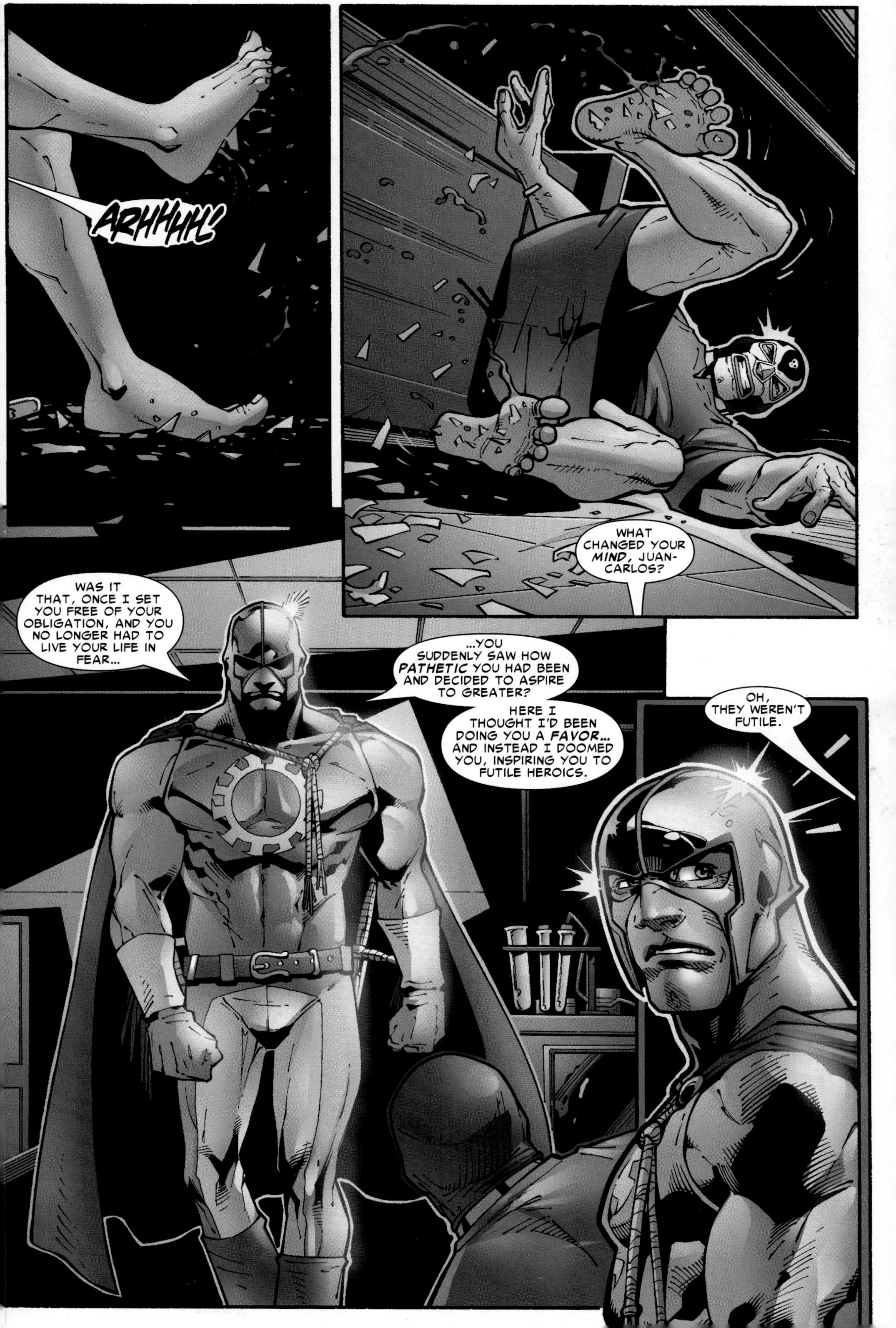
ARHHHH!
WHAT CHANGED YOUR MIND, JUAN-CARLOS?
WAS IT THAT, ONCE I SET YOU FREE OF YOUR OBLIGATION, AND YOU NO LONGER HAD TO LIVE YOUR LIFE IN FEAR...
...YOU SUDDENLY SAW HOW PATHETIC YOU HAD BEEN AND DECIDED TO ASPIRE TO GREATER?
HERE I THOUGHT I'D BEEN DOING YOU A FAVOR... AND INSTEAD I DOOMED YOU, INSPIRING YOU TO FUTILE HEROICS.
OH, THEY WEREN'T FUTILE.

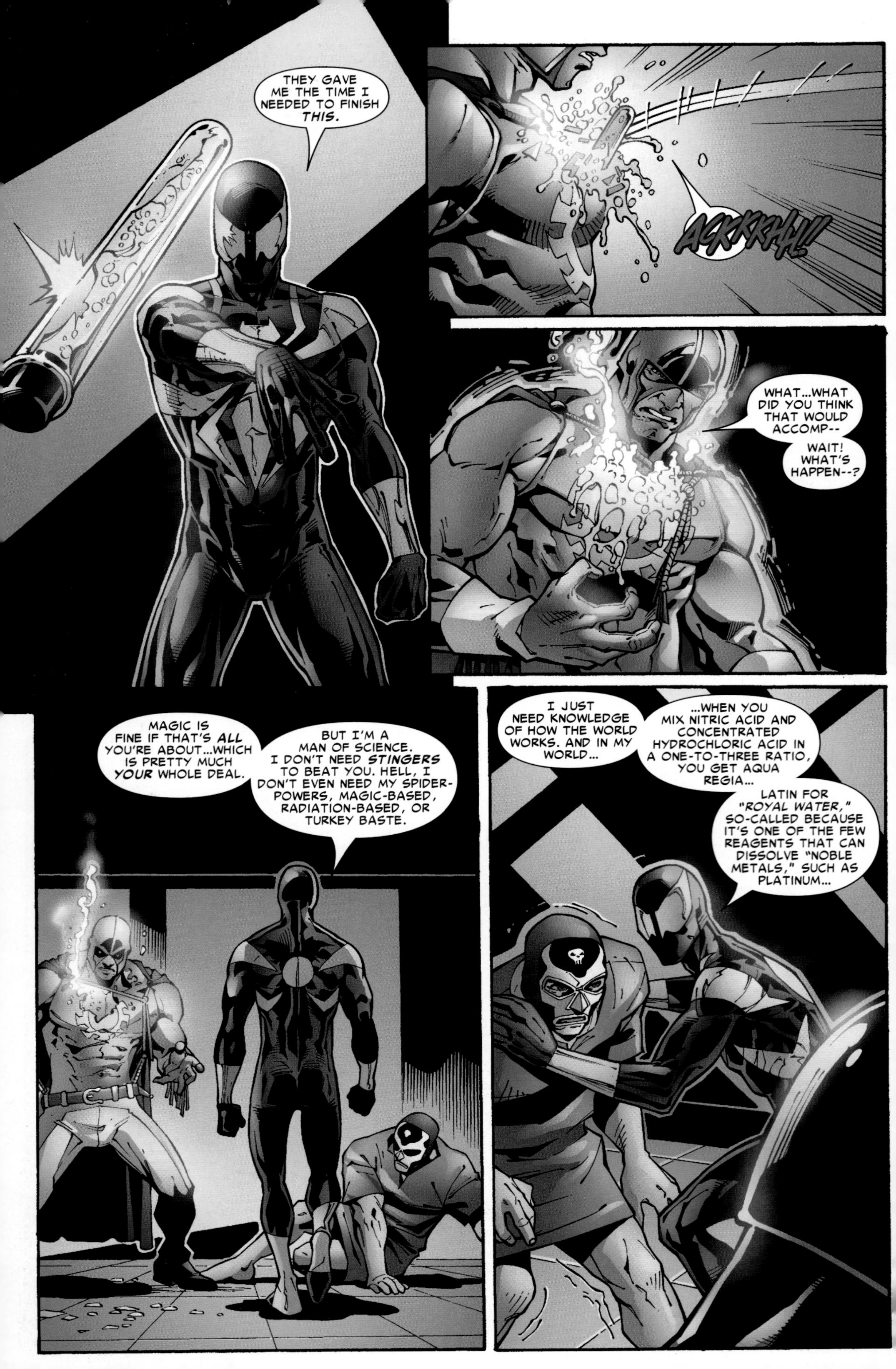
THEY GAVE ME THE TIME I NEEDED TO FINISH *THIS.*
ACKKKHH!
WHAT...WHAT DID YOU THINK THAT WOULD ACCOMP--
WAIT! WHAT'S HAPPEN--?
MAGIC IS FINE IF THAT'S *ALL* YOU'RE ABOUT...WHICH IS PRETTY MUCH *YOUR* WHOLE DEAL.
BUT I'M A MAN OF SCIENCE. I DON'T NEED *STINGERS* TO BEAT YOU. HELL, I DON'T EVEN NEED MY SPIDER-POWERS, MAGIC-BASED, RADIATION-BASED, OR TURKEY BASTE.
I JUST NEED KNOWLEDGE OF HOW THE WORLD WORKS. AND IN MY WORLD...
...WHEN YOU MIX NITRIC ACID AND CONCENTRATED HYDROCHLORIC ACID IN A ONE-TO-THREE RATIO, YOU GET AQUA REGIA...
LATIN FOR *"ROYAL WATER,"* SO-CALLED BECAUSE IT'S ONE OF THE FEW REAGENTS THAT CAN DISSOLVE "NOBLE METALS," SUCH AS PLATINUM...

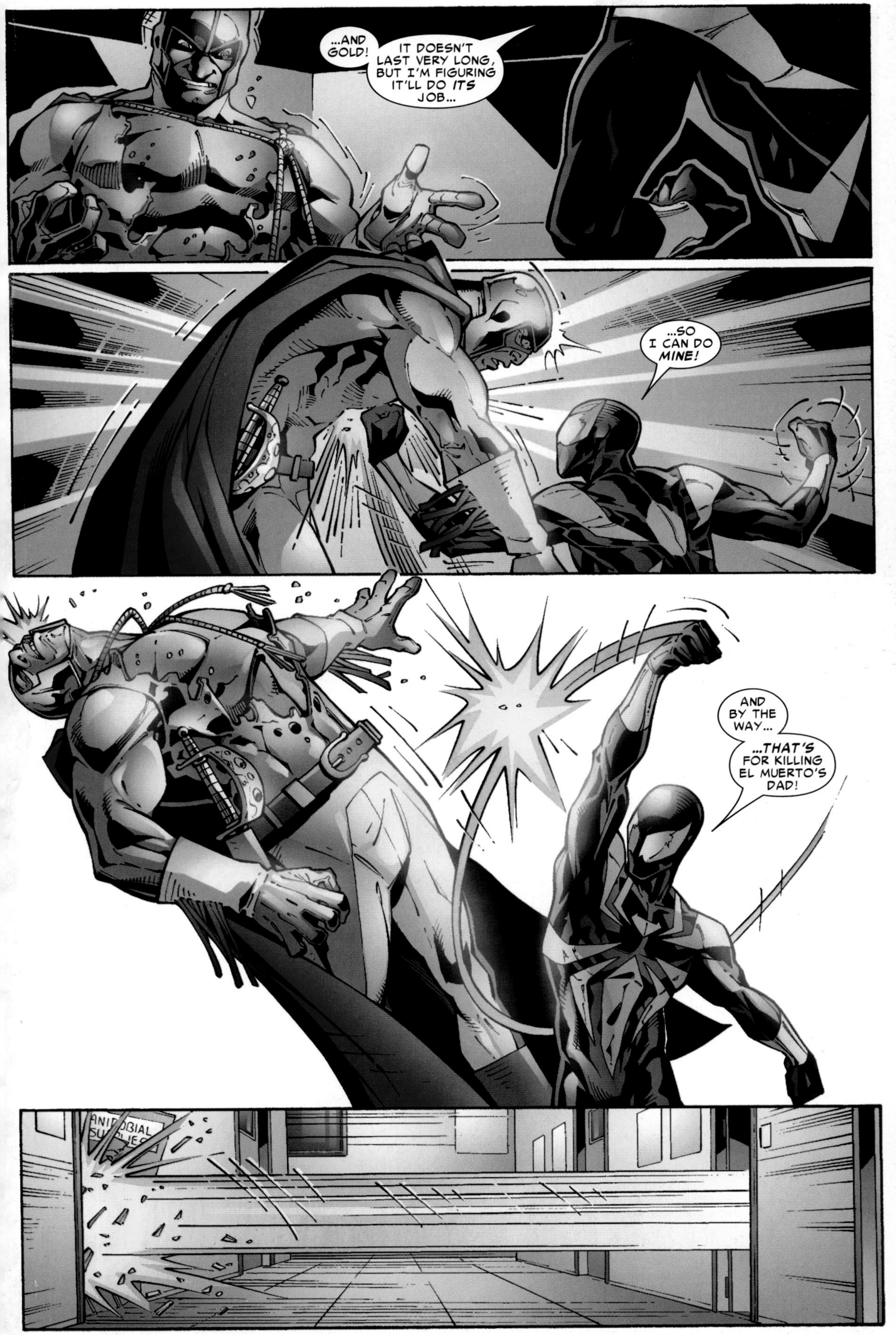
...AND GOLD!
IT DOESN'T LAST VERY LONG, BUT I'M FIGURING IT'LL DO *ITS* JOB...
...SO I CAN DO *MINE!*
AND BY THE WAY...
...*THAT'S* FOR KILLING EL MUERTO'S DAD!

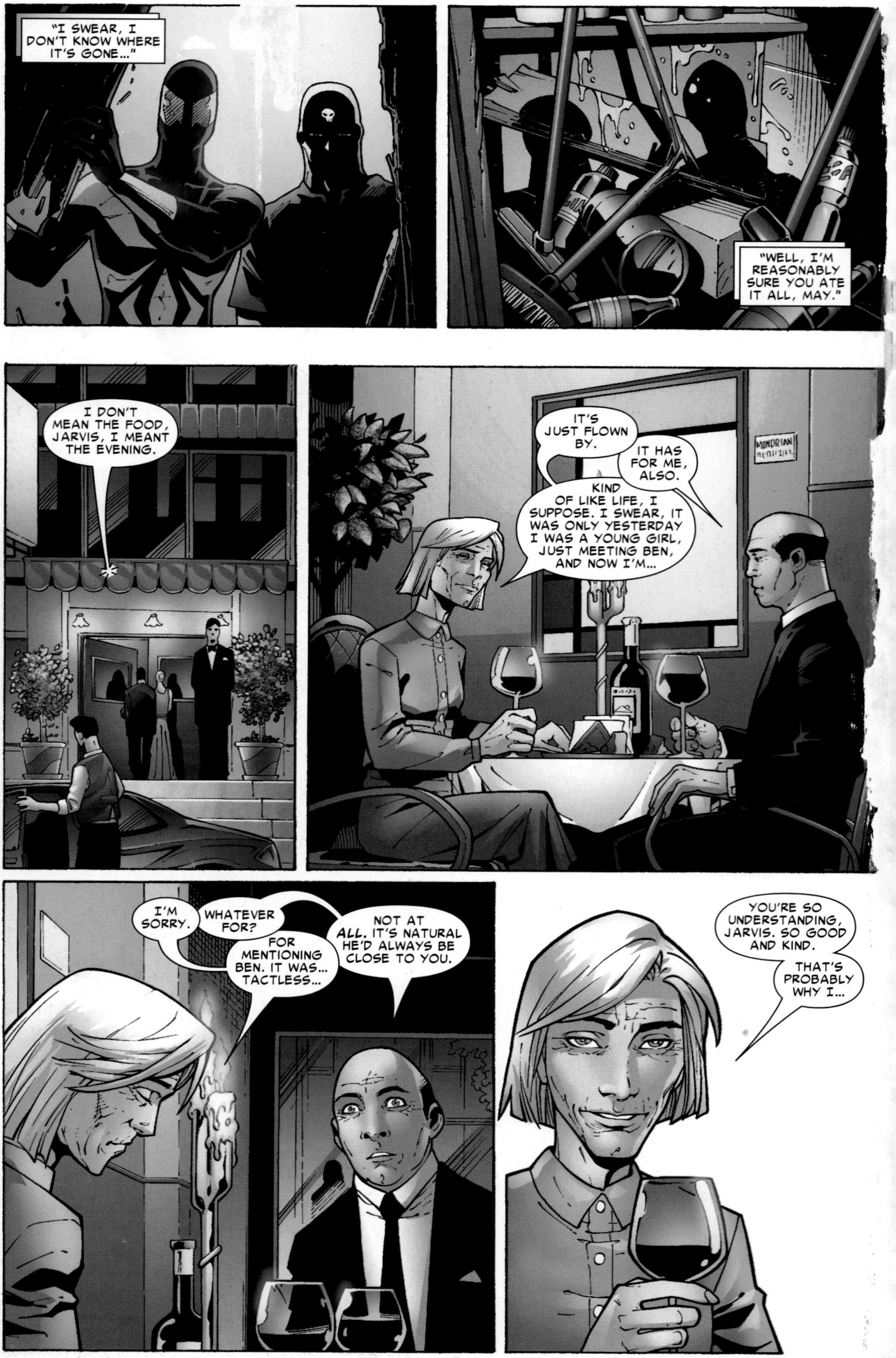
"I SWEAR, I DON'T KNOW WHERE IT'S GONE..."
"WELL, I'M REASONABLY SURE YOU ATE IT ALL, MAY."
I DON'T MEAN THE FOOD, JARVIS, I MEANT THE EVENING.
IT'S JUST FLOWN BY.
IT HAS FOR ME, ALSO.
KIND OF LIKE LIFE, I SUPPOSE. I SWEAR, IT WAS ONLY YESTERDAY I WAS A YOUNG GIRL, JUST MEETING BEN, AND NOW I'M...
MONDRIAN
I'M SORRY.
WHATEVER FOR?
FOR MENTIONING BEN. IT WAS... TACTLESS...
NOT AT ALL. IT'S NATURAL HE'D ALWAYS BE CLOSE TO YOU.
YOU'RE SO UNDERSTANDING, JARVIS. SO GOOD AND KIND.
THAT'S PROBABLY WHY I...

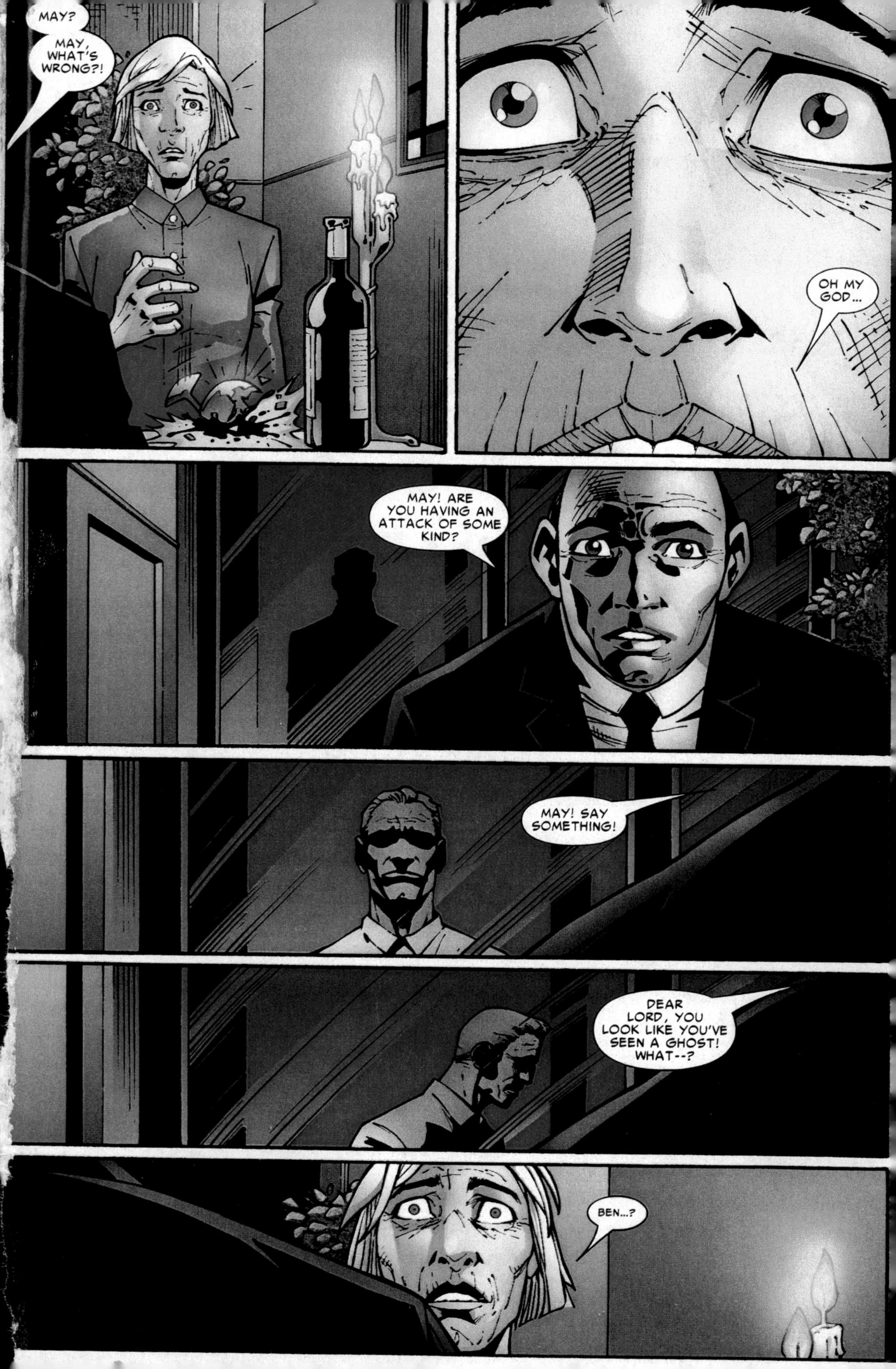
MAY?
MAY, WHAT'S WRONG?!
OH MY GOD...
MAY! ARE YOU HAVING AN ATTACK OF SOME KIND?
MAY! SAY SOMETHING!
DEAR LORD, YOU LOOK LIKE YOU'VE SEEN A GHOST! WHAT--?
BEN...?

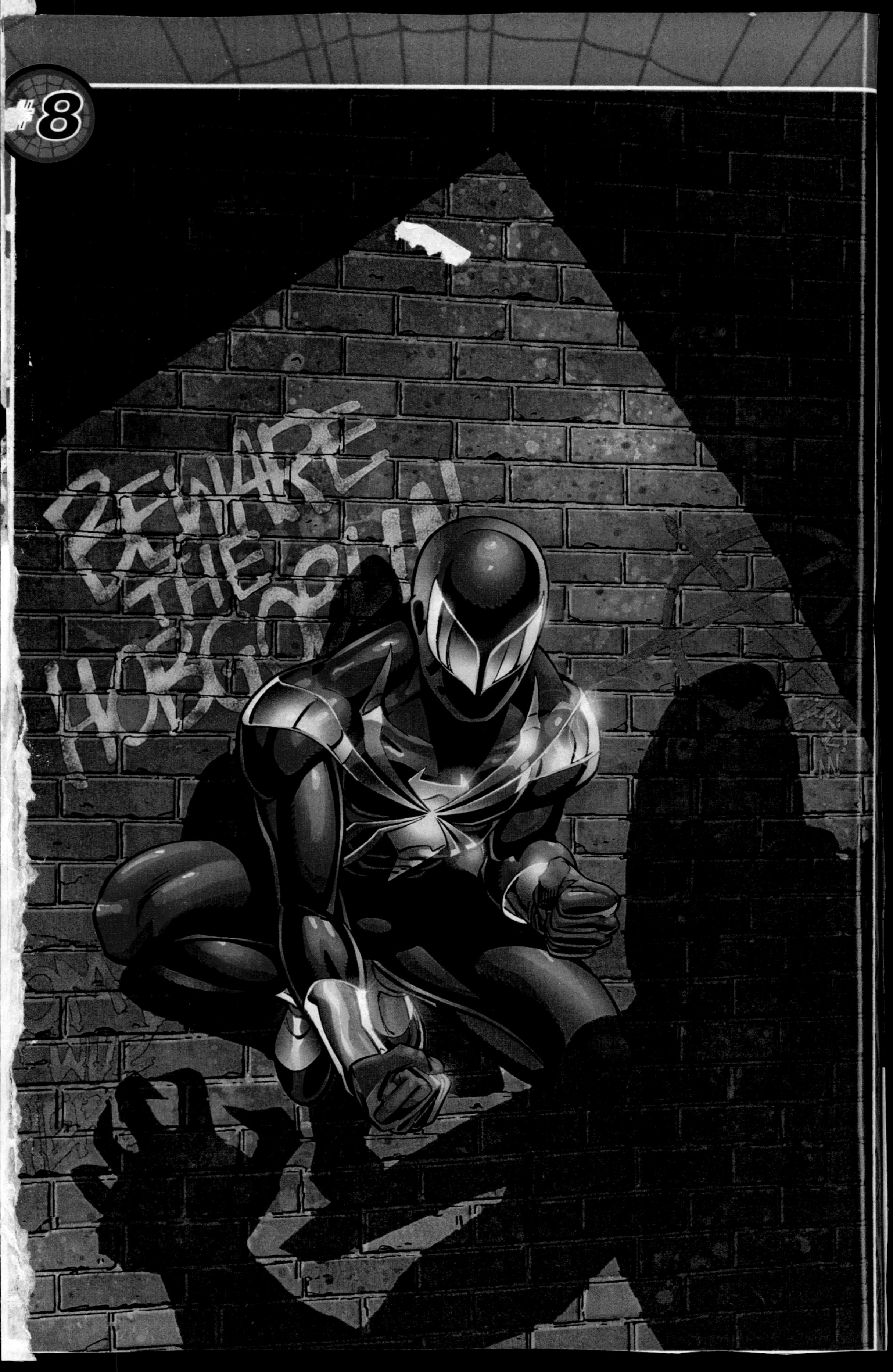
#8
BEWARE
THE

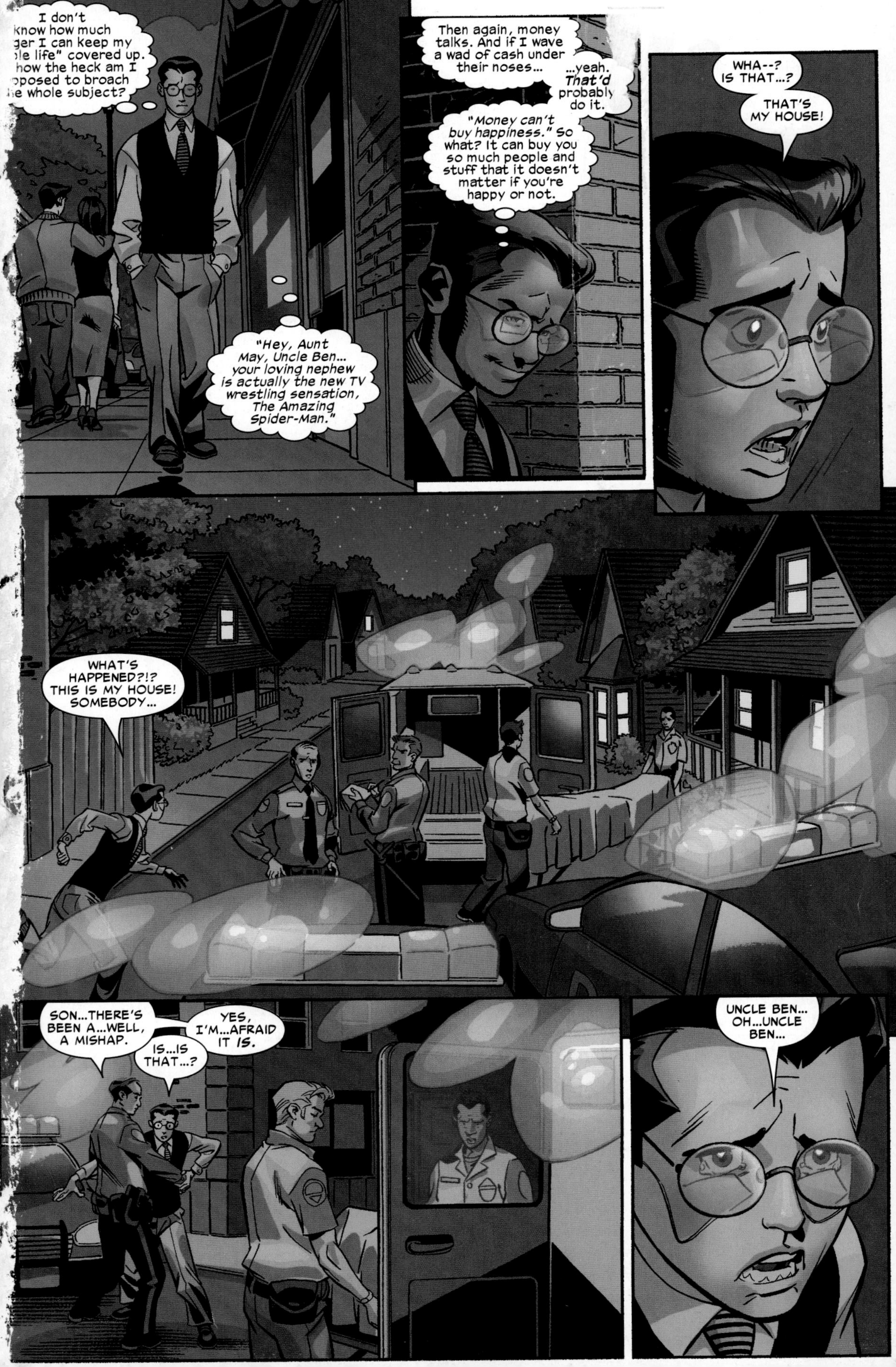

I don't know how much ger I can keep my ole life" covered up. how the heck am I pposed to broach e whole subject?
"Hey, Aunt May, Uncle Ben... your loving nephew is actually the new TV wrestling sensation, The Amazing Spider-Man."
Then again, money talks. And if I wave a wad of cash under their noses...
...yeah. That'd probably do it.
"Money can't buy happiness." So what? It can buy you so much people and stuff that it doesn't matter if you're happy or not.
WHA--? IS THAT...?
THAT'S MY HOUSE!
WHAT'S HAPPENED?!? THIS IS MY HOUSE! SOMEBODY...
SON...THERE'S BEEN A...WELL, A MISHAP.
IS...IS THAT...?
YES, I'M...AFRAID IT IS.
UNCLE BEN... OH...UNCLE BEN...

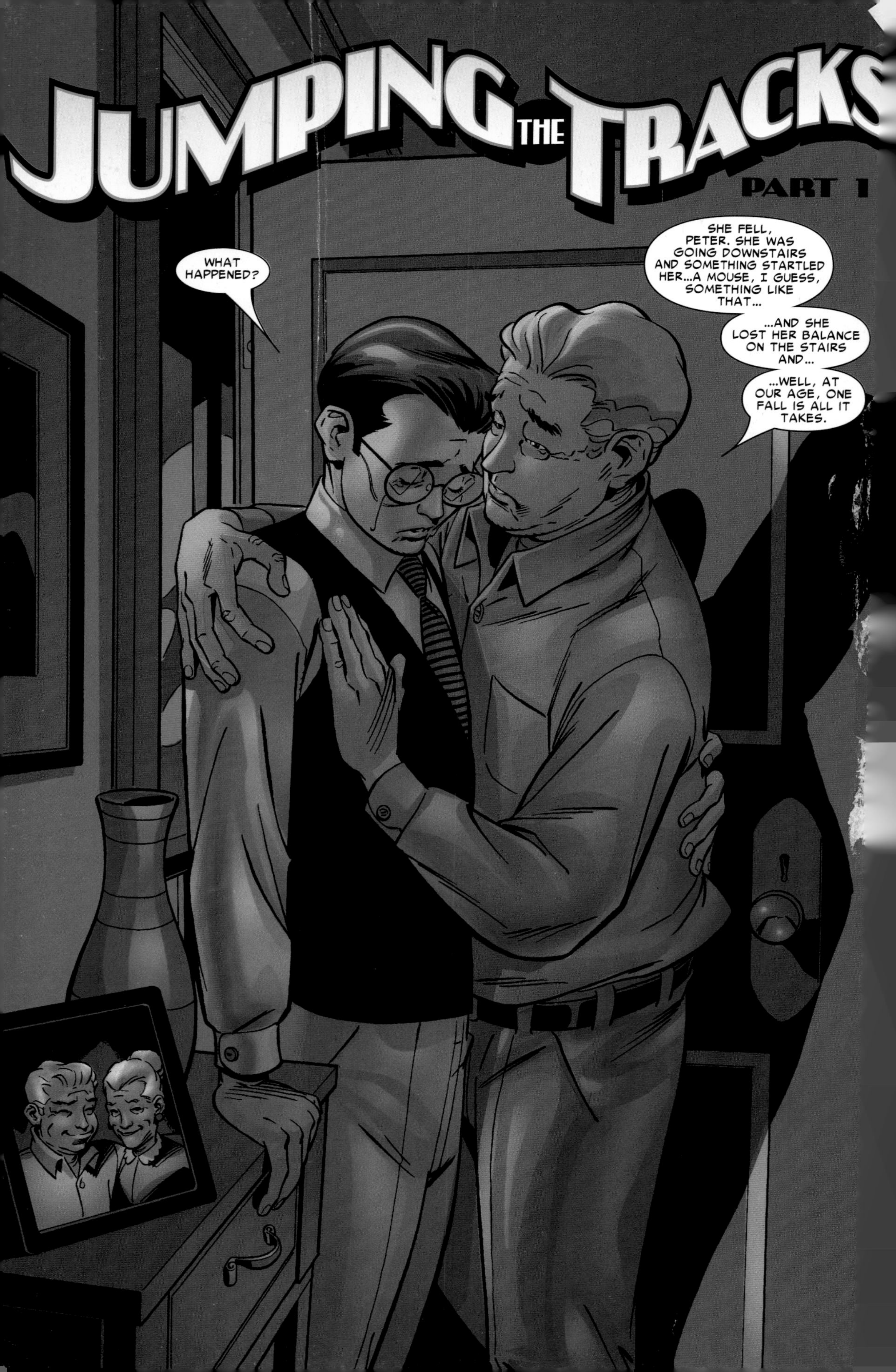
JUMPING THE TRACKS
PART 1
WHAT HAPPENED?
SHE FELL, PETER. SHE WAS GOING DOWNSTAIRS AND SOMETHING STARTLED HER...A MOUSE, I GUESS, SOMETHING LIKE THAT...
...AND SHE LOST HER BALANCE ON THE STAIRS AND...
...WELL, AT OUR AGE, ONE FALL IS ALL IT TAKES.

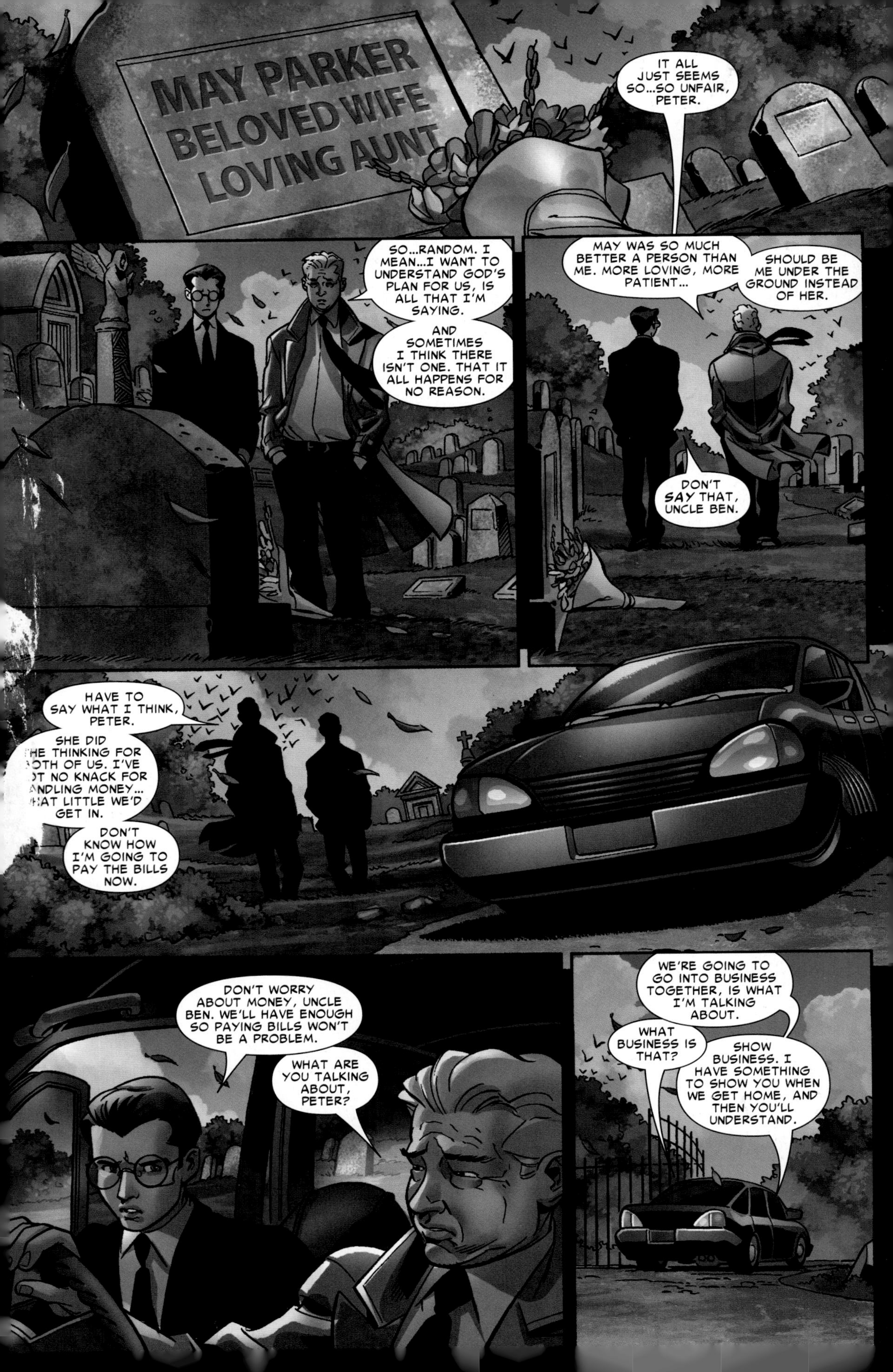
MAY PARKER
BELOVED WIFE
LOVING AUNT
IT ALL JUST SEEMS SO...SO UNFAIR, PETER.
SO...RANDOM. I MEAN...I WANT TO UNDERSTAND GOD'S PLAN FOR US, IS ALL THAT I'M SAYING.
AND SOMETIMES I THINK THERE ISN'T ONE. THAT IT ALL HAPPENS FOR NO REASON.
MAY WAS SO MUCH BETTER A PERSON THAN ME. MORE LOVING, MORE PATIENT...
SHOULD BE ME UNDER THE GROUND INSTEAD OF HER.
DON'T SAY THAT, UNCLE BEN.
HAVE TO SAY WHAT I THINK, PETER.
SHE DID HE THINKING FOR OTH OF US. I'VE OT NO KNACK FOR ANDLING MONEY... HAT LITTLE WE'D GET IN.
DON'T KNOW HOW I'M GOING TO PAY THE BILLS NOW.
DON'T WORRY ABOUT MONEY, UNCLE BEN. WE'LL HAVE ENOUGH SO PAYING BILLS WON'T BE A PROBLEM.
WHAT ARE YOU TALKING ABOUT, PETER?
WE'RE GOING TO GO INTO BUSINESS TOGETHER, IS WHAT I'M TALKING ABOUT.
WHAT BUSINESS IS THAT?
SHOW BUSINESS. I HAVE SOMETHING TO SHOW YOU WHEN WE GET HOME, AND THEN YOU'LL UNDERSTAND.

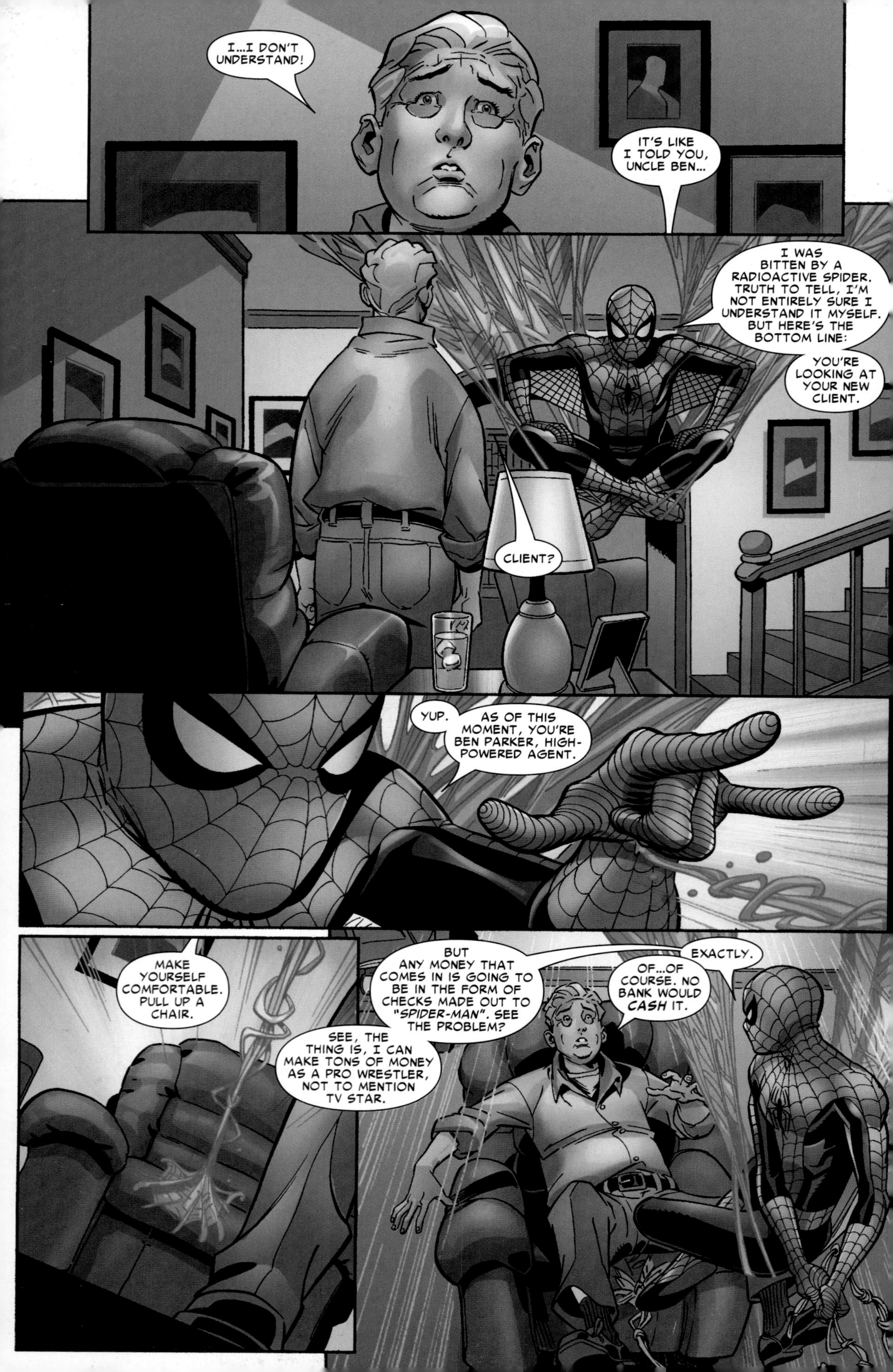
I...I DON'T UNDERSTAND!
IT'S LIKE I TOLD YOU, UNCLE BEN...
I WAS BITTEN BY A RADIOACTIVE SPIDER. TRUTH TO TELL, I'M NOT ENTIRELY SURE I UNDERSTAND IT MYSELF. BUT HERE'S THE BOTTOM LINE:
YOU'RE LOOKING AT YOUR NEW CLIENT.
CLIENT?
YUP.
AS OF THIS MOMENT, YOU'RE BEN PARKER, HIGH-POWERED AGENT.
MAKE YOURSELF COMFORTABLE. PULL UP A CHAIR.
SEE, THE THING IS, I CAN MAKE TONS OF MONEY AS A PRO WRESTLER, NOT TO MENTION TV STAR.
BUT ANY MONEY THAT COMES IN IS GOING TO BE IN THE FORM OF CHECKS MADE OUT TO "*SPIDER-MAN*". SEE THE PROBLEM?
OF...OF COURSE. NO BANK WOULD *CASH* IT.
EXACTLY.

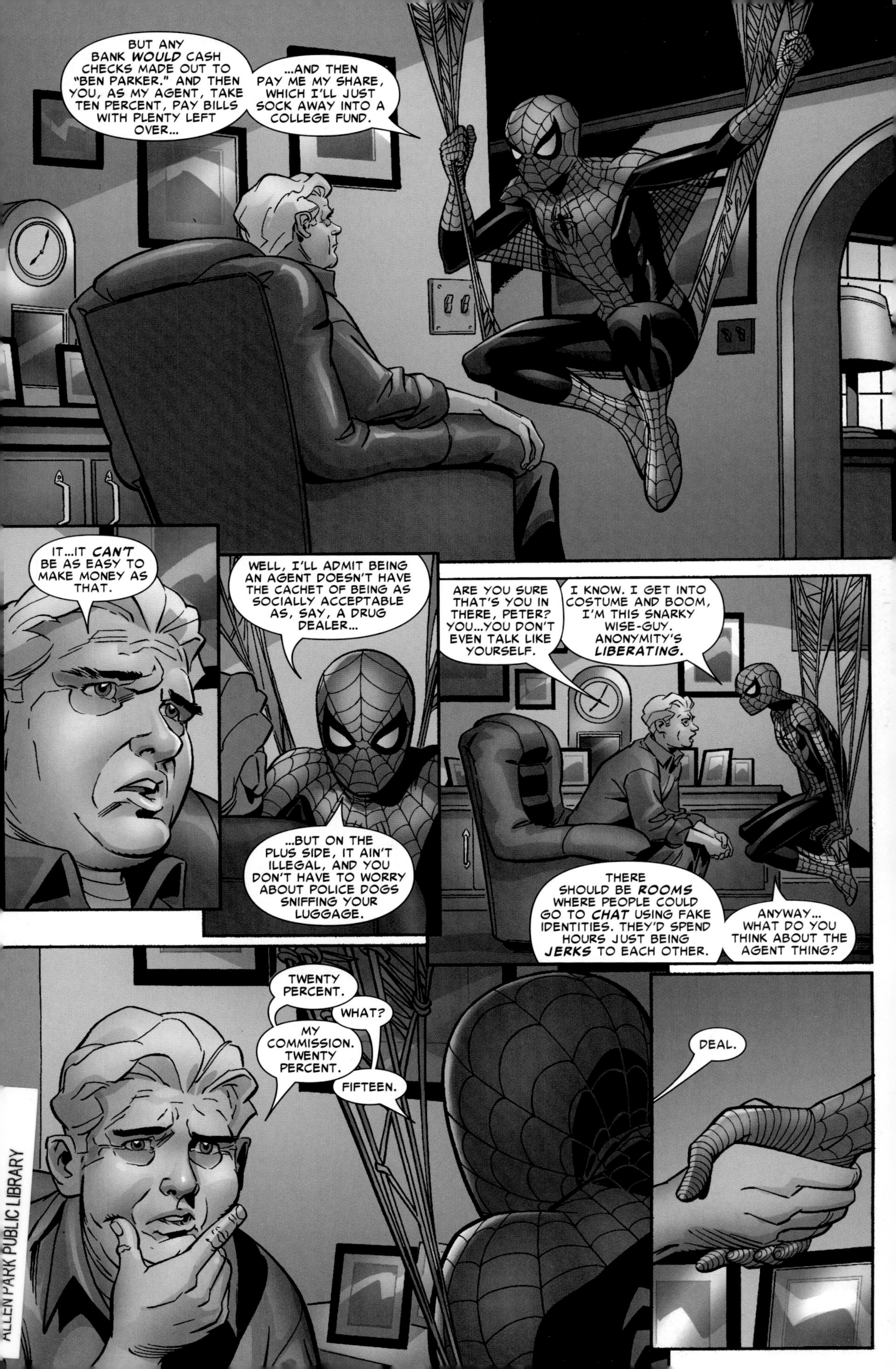

BUT ANY BANK WOULD CASH CHECKS MADE OUT TO "BEN PARKER." AND THEN YOU, AS MY AGENT, TAKE TEN PERCENT, PAY BILLS WITH PLENTY LEFT OVER...
...AND THEN PAY ME MY SHARE, WHICH I'LL JUST SOCK AWAY INTO A COLLEGE FUND.
IT...IT CAN'T BE AS EASY TO MAKE MONEY AS THAT.
WELL, I'LL ADMIT BEING AN AGENT DOESN'T HAVE THE CACHET OF BEING AS SOCIALLY ACCEPTABLE AS, SAY, A DRUG DEALER...
...BUT ON THE PLUS SIDE, IT AIN'T ILLEGAL, AND YOU DON'T HAVE TO WORRY ABOUT POLICE DOGS SNIFFING YOUR LUGGAGE.
ARE YOU SURE THAT'S YOU IN THERE, PETER? YOU...YOU DON'T EVEN TALK LIKE YOURSELF.
I KNOW. I GET INTO COSTUME AND BOOM, I'M THIS SNARKY WISE-GUY. ANONYMITY'S LIBERATING.
THERE SHOULD BE ROOMS WHERE PEOPLE COULD GO TO CHAT USING FAKE IDENTITIES. THEY'D SPEND HOURS JUST BEING JERKS TO EACH OTHER.
ANYWAY... WHAT DO YOU THINK ABOUT THE AGENT THING?
TWENTY PERCENT.
WHAT?
MY COMMISSION. TWENTY PERCENT.
FIFTEEN.
DEAL.

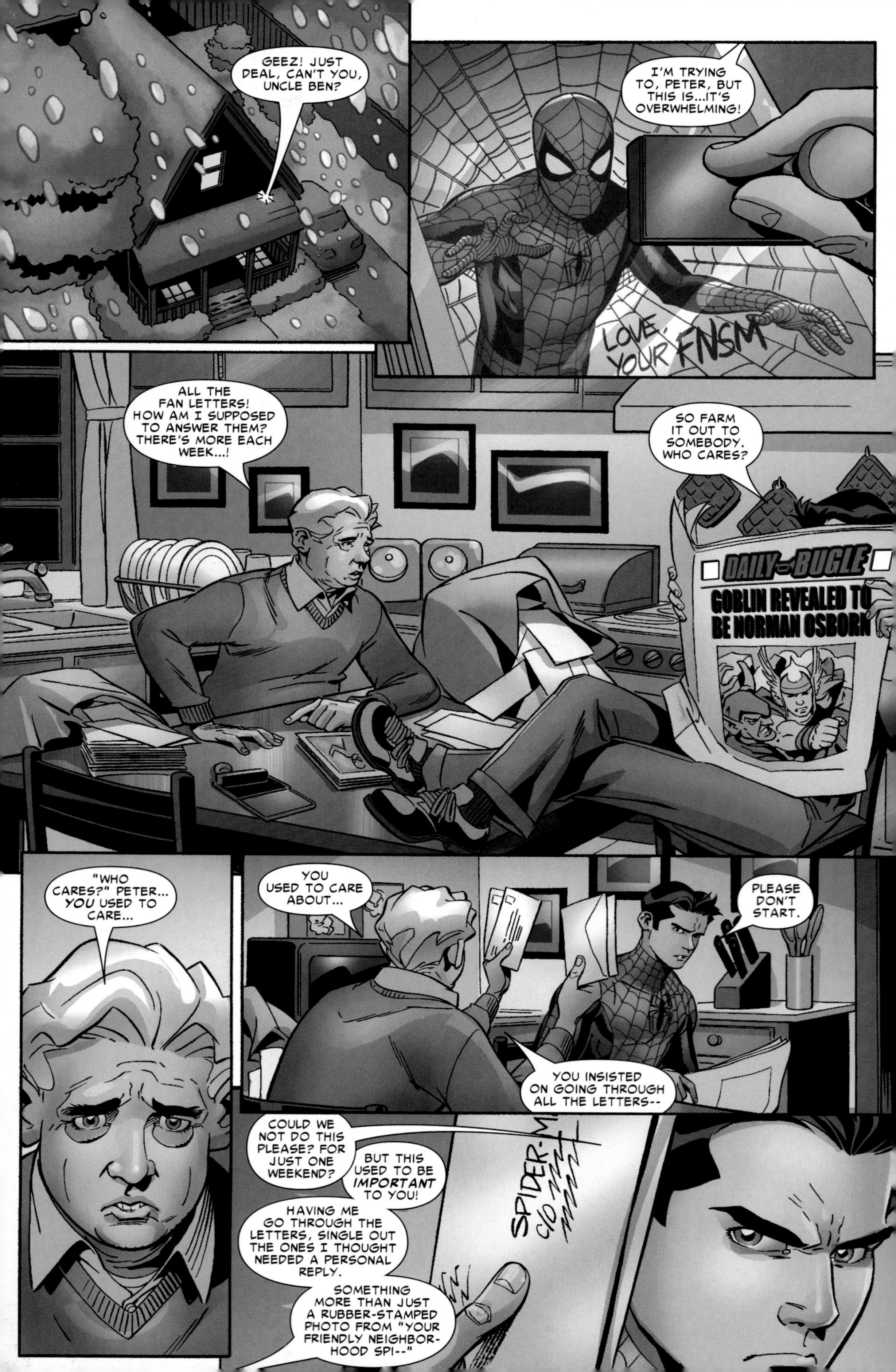
GEEZ! JUST DEAL, CAN'T YOU, UNCLE BEN?
I'M TRYING TO, PETER, BUT THIS IS...IT'S OVERWHELMING!
LOVE, YOUR FNSM
ALL THE FAN LETTERS! HOW AM I SUPPOSED TO ANSWER THEM? THERE'S MORE EACH WEEK...!
SO FARM IT OUT TO SOMEBODY. WHO CARES?
DAILY BUGLE
GOBLIN REVEALED TO BE NORMAN OSBORN
"WHO CARES?" PETER... *YOU* USED TO CARE...
YOU USED TO CARE ABOUT...
PLEASE DON'T START.
YOU INSISTED ON GOING THROUGH ALL THE LETTERS--
COULD WE NOT DO THIS PLEASE? FOR JUST ONE WEEKEND?
BUT THIS USED TO BE *IMPORTANT* TO YOU!
HAVING ME GO THROUGH THE LETTERS, SINGLE OUT THE ONES I THOUGHT NEEDED A PERSONAL REPLY.
SOMETHING MORE THAN JUST A RUBBER-STAMPED PHOTO FROM "YOUR FRIENDLY NEIGHBOR-HOOD SPI--"
SPIDER-M C/O

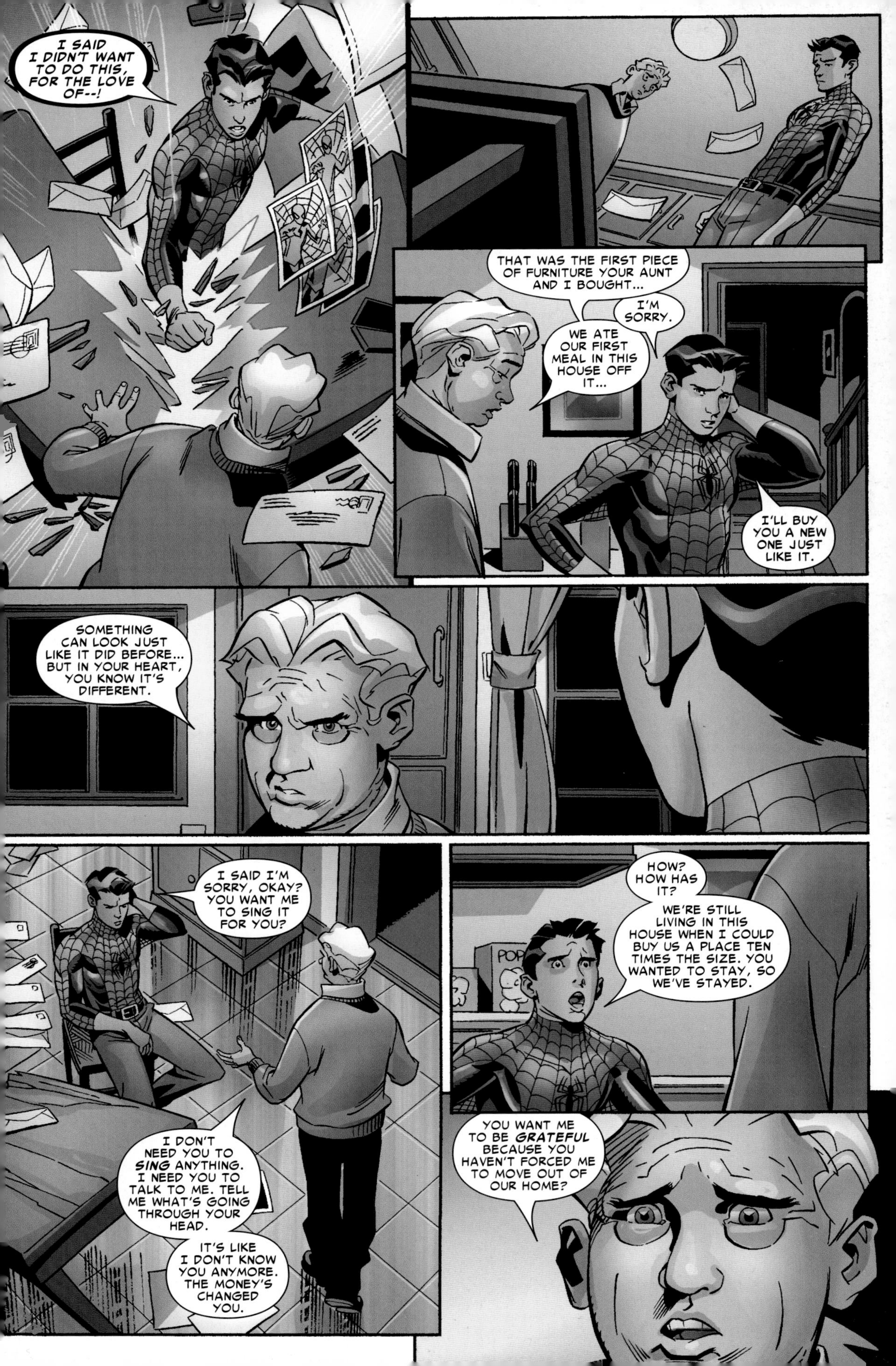
I SAID I DIDN'T WANT TO DO THIS, FOR THE LOVE OF--!
THAT WAS THE FIRST PIECE OF FURNITURE YOUR AUNT AND I BOUGHT...
I'M SORRY.
WE ATE OUR FIRST MEAL IN THIS HOUSE OFF IT...
I'LL BUY YOU A NEW ONE JUST LIKE IT.
SOMETHING CAN LOOK JUST LIKE IT DID BEFORE... BUT IN YOUR HEART, YOU KNOW IT'S DIFFERENT.
I SAID I'M SORRY, OKAY? YOU WANT ME TO SING IT FOR YOU?
I DON'T NEED YOU TO SING ANYTHING. I NEED YOU TO TALK TO ME. TELL ME WHAT'S GOING THROUGH YOUR HEAD.
IT'S LIKE I DON'T KNOW YOU ANYMORE. THE MONEY'S CHANGED YOU.
HOW? HOW HAS IT?
WE'RE STILL LIVING IN THIS HOUSE WHEN I COULD BUY US A PLACE TEN TIMES THE SIZE. YOU WANTED TO STAY, SO WE'VE STAYED.
YOU WANT ME TO BE GRATEFUL BECAUSE YOU HAVEN'T FORCED ME TO MOVE OUT OF OUR HOME?

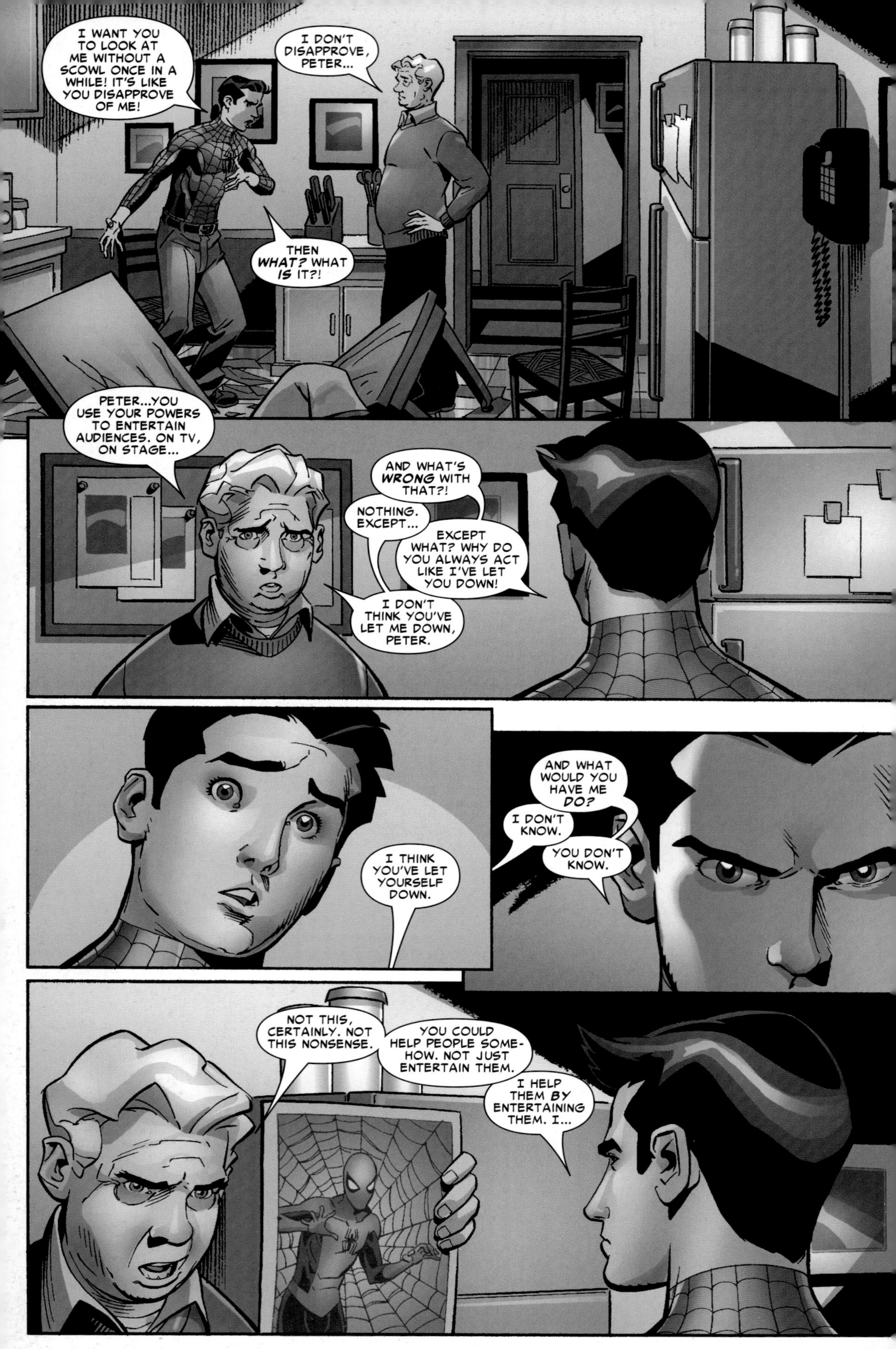
I WANT YOU TO LOOK AT ME WITHOUT A SCOWL ONCE IN A WHILE! IT'S LIKE YOU DISAPPROVE OF ME!
I DON'T DISAPPROVE, PETER...
THEN *WHAT?* WHAT *IS* IT?!
PETER...YOU USE YOUR POWERS TO ENTERTAIN AUDIENCES. ON TV, ON STAGE...
AND WHAT'S *WRONG* WITH THAT?!
NOTHING. EXCEPT...
EXCEPT WHAT? WHY DO YOU ALWAYS ACT LIKE I'VE LET YOU DOWN!
I DON'T THINK YOU'VE LET ME DOWN, PETER.
I THINK YOU'VE LET YOURSELF DOWN.
AND WHAT WOULD YOU HAVE ME *DO?*
I DON'T KNOW.
YOU DON'T KNOW.
NOT THIS, CERTAINLY. NOT THIS NONSENSE.
YOU COULD HELP PEOPLE SOMEHOW. NOT JUST ENTERTAIN THEM.
I HELP THEM *BY* ENTERTAINING THEM. I...

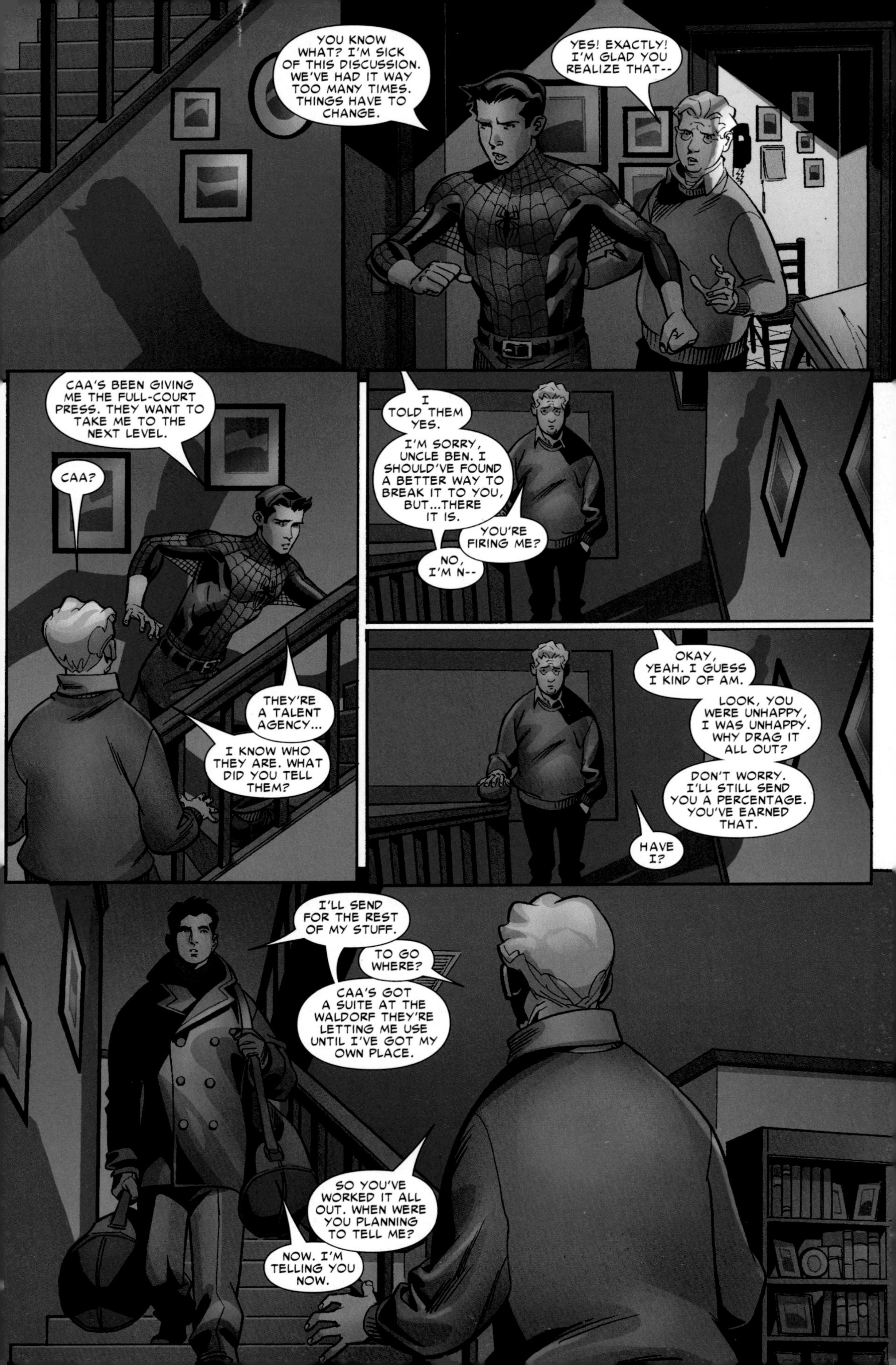
YOU KNOW WHAT? I'M SICK OF THIS DISCUSSION. WE'VE HAD IT WAY TOO MANY TIMES. THINGS HAVE TO CHANGE.
YES! EXACTLY! I'M GLAD YOU REALIZE THAT--
CAA'S BEEN GIVING ME THE FULL-COURT PRESS. THEY WANT TO TAKE ME TO THE NEXT LEVEL.
CAA?
THEY'RE A TALENT AGENCY...
I KNOW WHO THEY ARE. WHAT DID YOU TELL THEM?
I TOLD THEM YES.
I'M SORRY, UNCLE BEN. I SHOULD'VE FOUND A BETTER WAY TO BREAK IT TO YOU, BUT...THERE IT IS.
YOU'RE FIRING ME?
NO, I'M N--
OKAY, YEAH. I GUESS I KIND OF AM.
LOOK, YOU WERE UNHAPPY, I WAS UNHAPPY. WHY DRAG IT ALL OUT?
DON'T WORRY. I'LL STILL SEND YOU A PERCENTAGE. YOU'VE EARNED THAT.
HAVE I?
I'LL SEND FOR THE REST OF MY STUFF.
TO GO WHERE?
CAA'S GOT A SUITE AT THE WALDORF THEY'RE LETTING ME USE UNTIL I'VE GOT MY OWN PLACE.
SO YOU'VE WORKED IT ALL OUT. WHEN WERE YOU PLANNING TO TELL ME?
NOW. I'M TELLING YOU NOW.

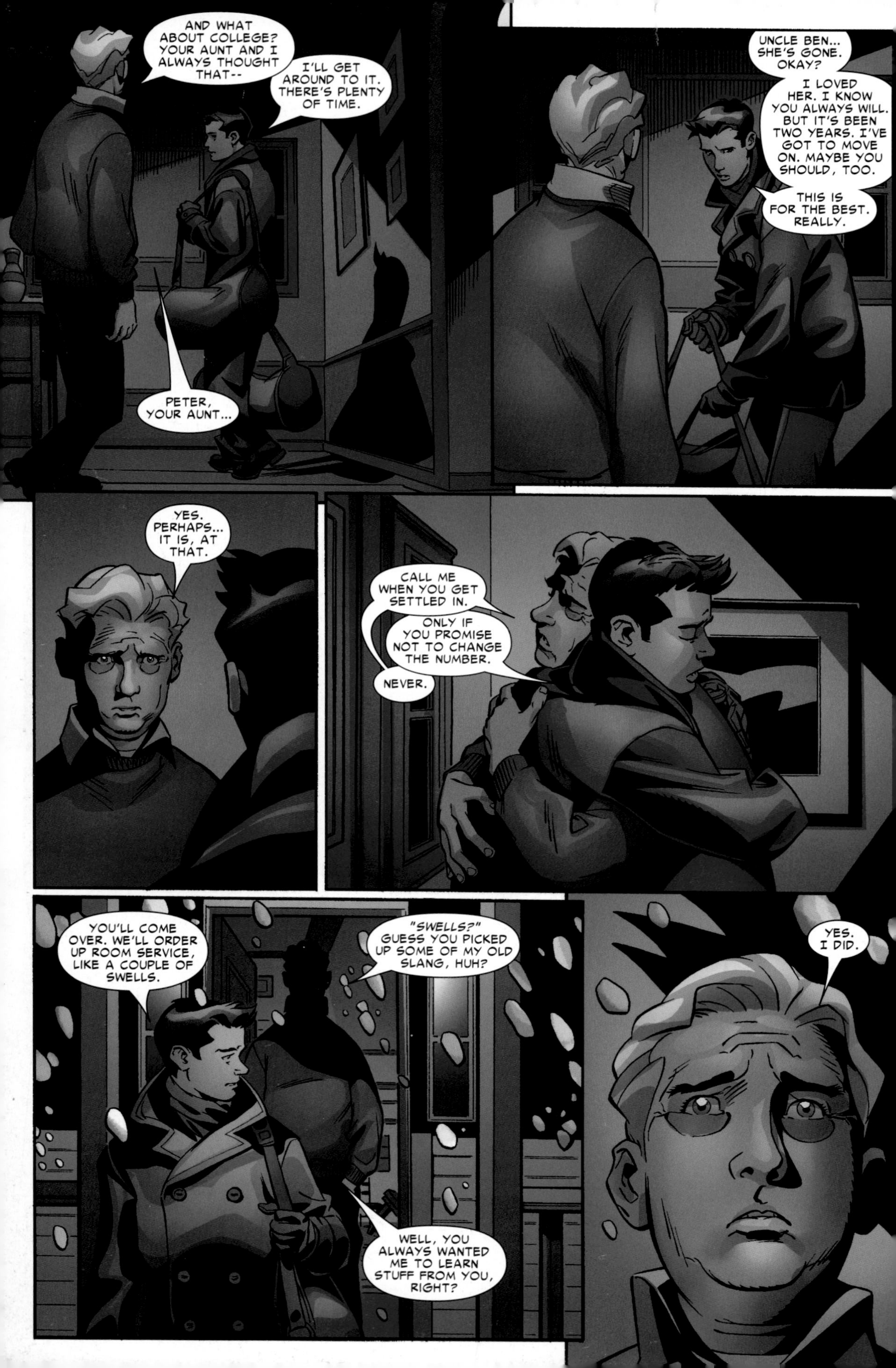
AND WHAT ABOUT COLLEGE? YOUR AUNT AND I ALWAYS THOUGHT THAT--
I'LL GET AROUND TO IT. THERE'S PLENTY OF TIME.
PETER, YOUR AUNT...
UNCLE BEN... SHE'S GONE. OKAY?
I LOVED HER. I KNOW YOU ALWAYS WILL. BUT IT'S BEEN TWO YEARS. I'VE GOT TO MOVE ON. MAYBE YOU SHOULD, TOO.
THIS IS FOR THE BEST. REALLY.
YES. PERHAPS... IT IS, AT THAT.
CALL ME WHEN YOU GET SETTLED IN.
ONLY IF YOU PROMISE NOT TO CHANGE THE NUMBER.
NEVER.
YOU'LL COME OVER. WE'LL ORDER UP ROOM SERVICE, LIKE A COUPLE OF SWELLS.
"SWELLS?" GUESS YOU PICKED UP SOME OF MY OLD SLANG, HUH?
WELL, YOU ALWAYS WANTED ME TO LEARN STUFF FROM YOU, RIGHT?
YES. I DID.

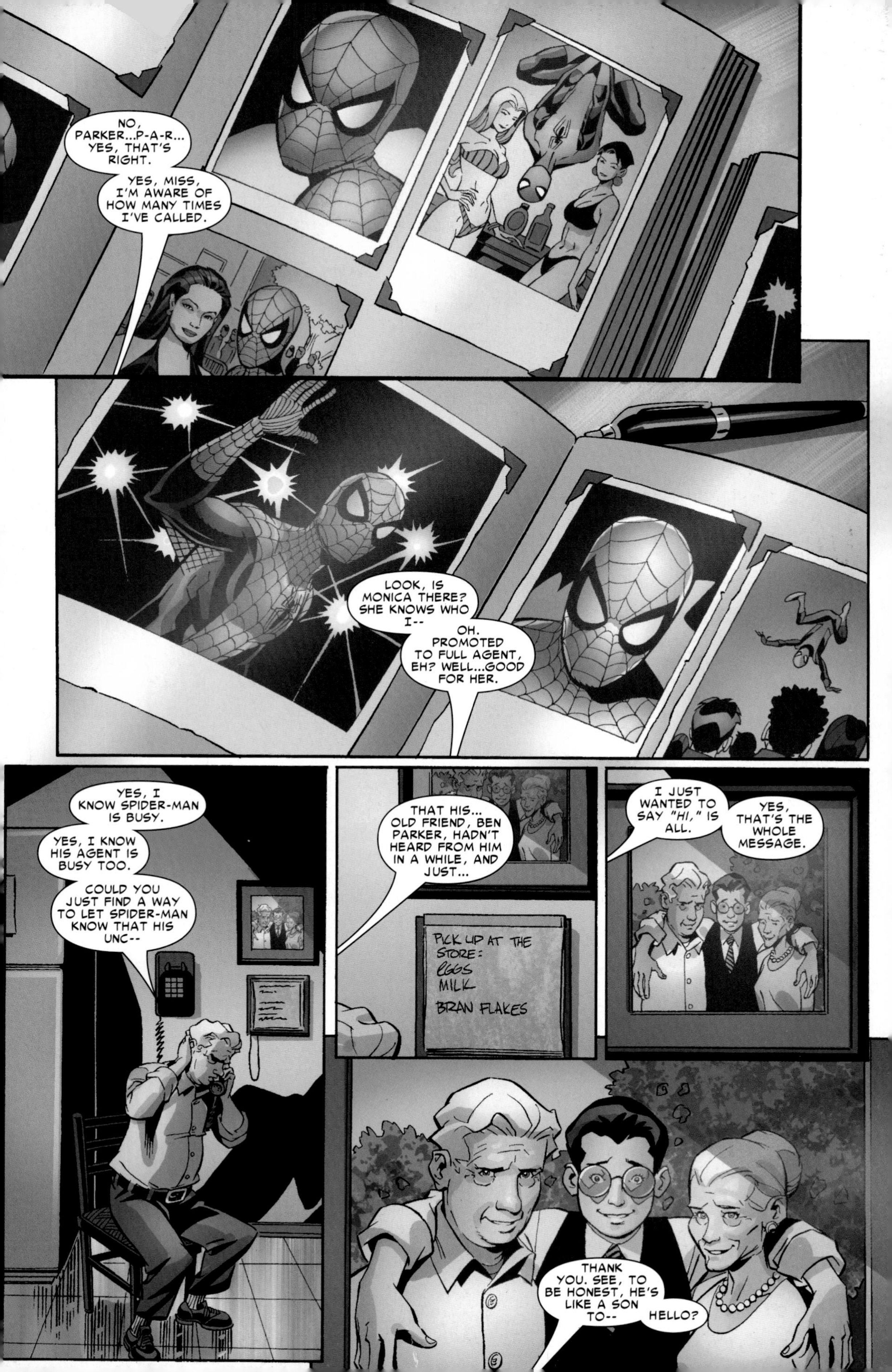
NO, PARKER...P-A-R... YES, THAT'S RIGHT.
YES, MISS, I'M AWARE OF HOW MANY TIMES I'VE CALLED.
LOOK, IS MONICA THERE? SHE KNOWS WHO I--
OH. PROMOTED TO FULL AGENT, EH? WELL...GOOD FOR HER.
YES, I KNOW SPIDER-MAN IS BUSY.
YES, I KNOW HIS AGENT IS BUSY TOO.
COULD YOU JUST FIND A WAY TO LET SPIDER-MAN KNOW THAT HIS UNC--
THAT HIS... OLD FRIEND, BEN PARKER, HADN'T HEARD FROM HIM IN A WHILE, AND JUST...
PICK UP AT THE STORE:
EGGS
MILK
BRAN FLAKES
I JUST WANTED TO SAY "HI," IS ALL.
YES, THAT'S THE WHOLE MESSAGE.
THANK YOU. SEE, TO BE HONEST, HE'S LIKE A SON TO--
HELLO?

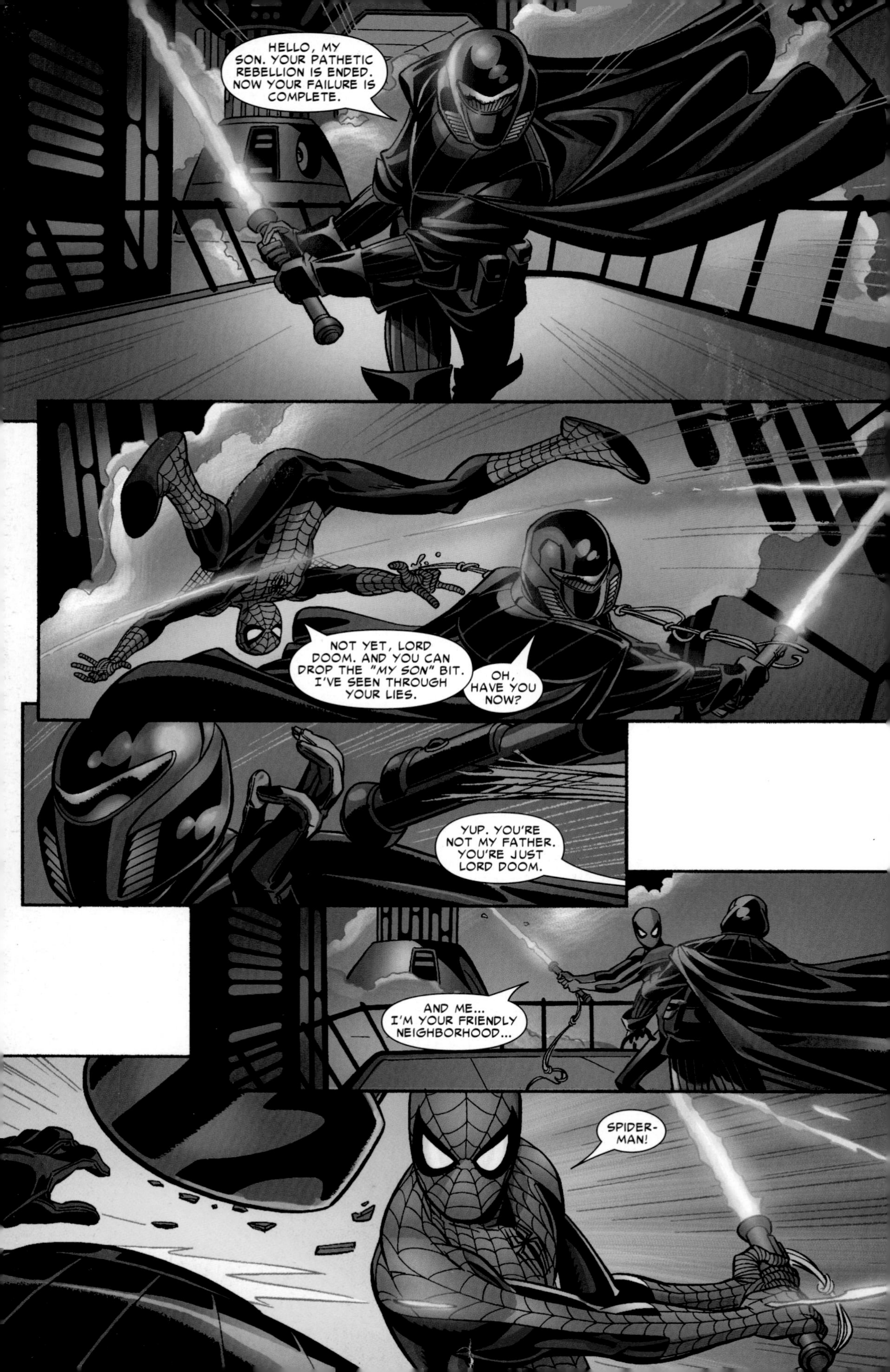
HELLO, MY SON. YOUR PATHETIC REBELLION IS ENDED. NOW YOUR FAILURE IS COMPLETE.
NOT YET, LORD DOOM. AND YOU CAN DROP THE "MY SON" BIT. I'VE SEEN THROUGH YOUR LIES.
OH, HAVE YOU NOW?
YUP. YOU'RE NOT MY FATHER. YOU'RE JUST LORD DOOM.
AND ME... I'M YOUR FRIENDLY NEIGHBORHOOD...
SPIDER-MAN!

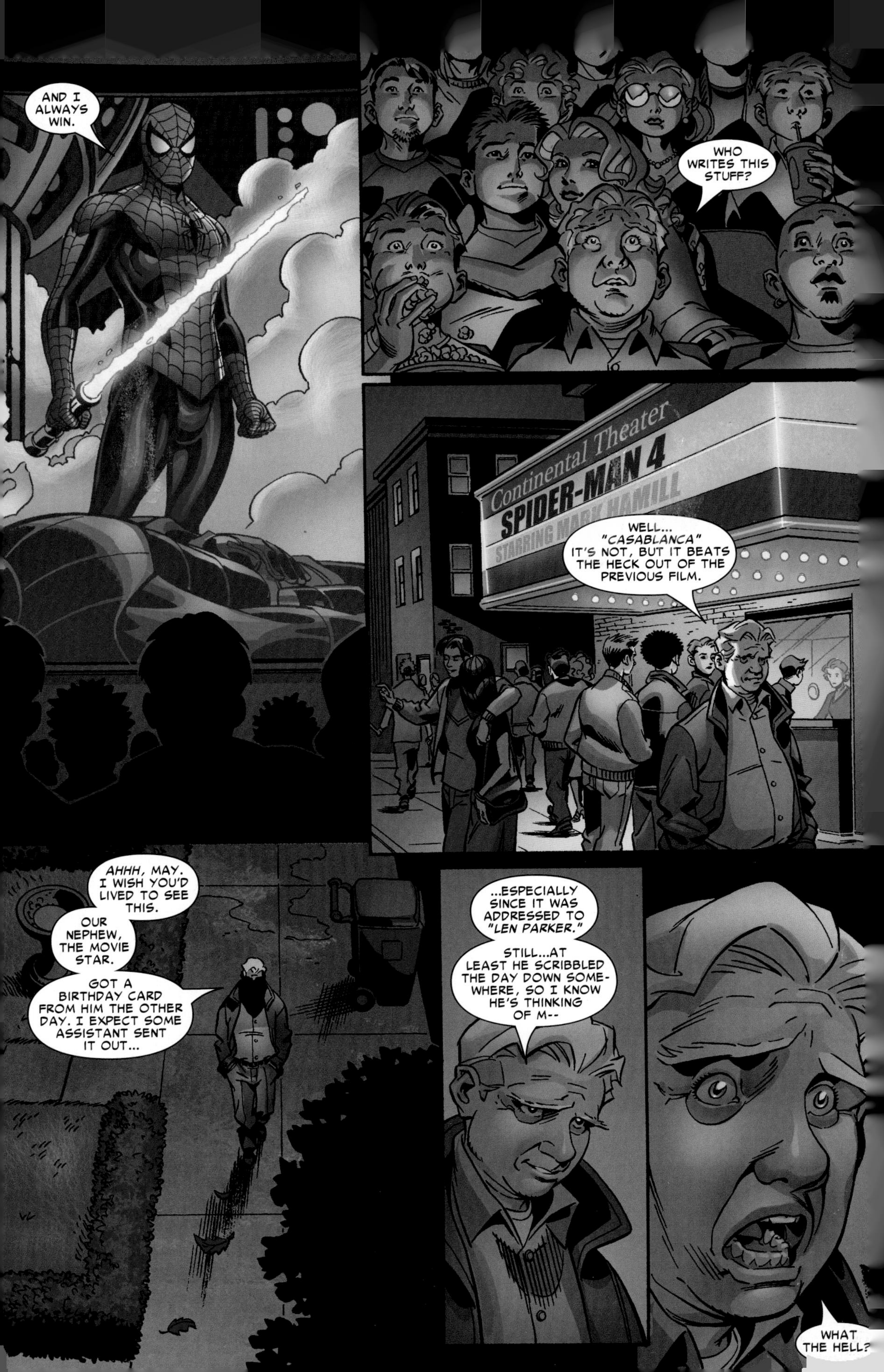
AND I ALWAYS WIN.
WHO WRITES THIS STUFF?
Continental Theater
SPIDER-MAN 4
STARRING MARK HAMILL
WELL... "CASABLANCA" IT'S NOT, BUT IT BEATS THE HECK OUT OF THE PREVIOUS FILM.
AHHH, MAY. I WISH YOU'D LIVED TO SEE THIS.
OUR NEPHEW, THE MOVIE STAR.
GOT A BIRTHDAY CARD FROM HIM THE OTHER DAY. I EXPECT SOME ASSISTANT SENT IT OUT...
...ESPECIALLY SINCE IT WAS ADDRESSED TO "LEN PARKER."
STILL...AT LEAST HE SCRIBBLED THE DAY DOWN SOME-WHERE, SO I KNOW HE'S THINKING OF M--
WHAT THE HELL?

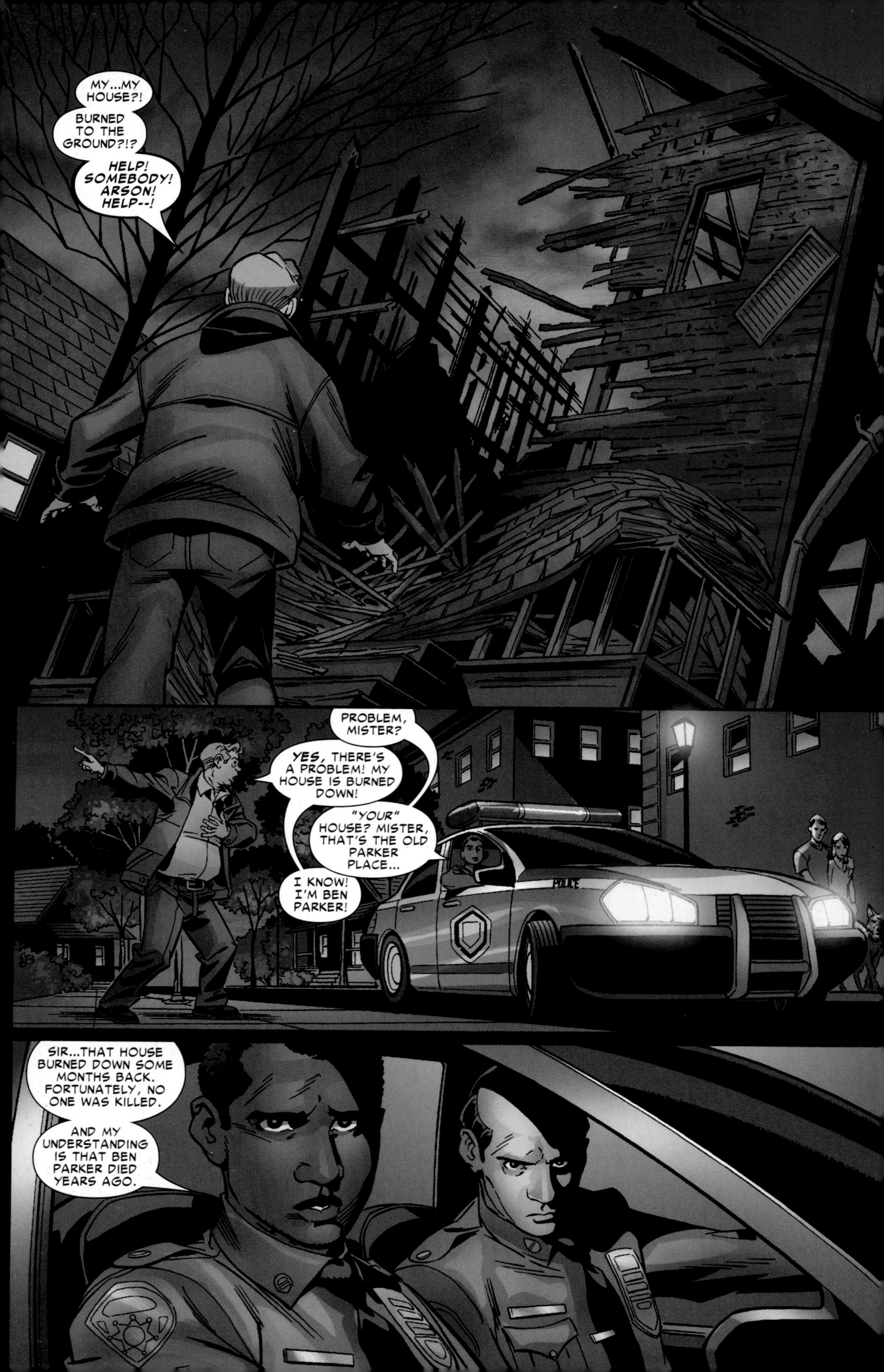
MY...MY HOUSE?!
BURNED TO THE GROUND?!?
HELP! SOMEBODY! ARSON! HELP--!
PROBLEM, MISTER?
YES, THERE'S A PROBLEM! MY HOUSE IS BURNED DOWN!
"YOUR" HOUSE? MISTER, THAT'S THE OLD PARKER PLACE...
I KNOW! I'M BEN PARKER!
POLICE
SIR...THAT HOUSE BURNED DOWN SOME MONTHS BACK. FORTUNATELY, NO ONE WAS KILLED.
AND MY UNDERSTANDING IS THAT BEN PARKER DIED YEARS AGO.

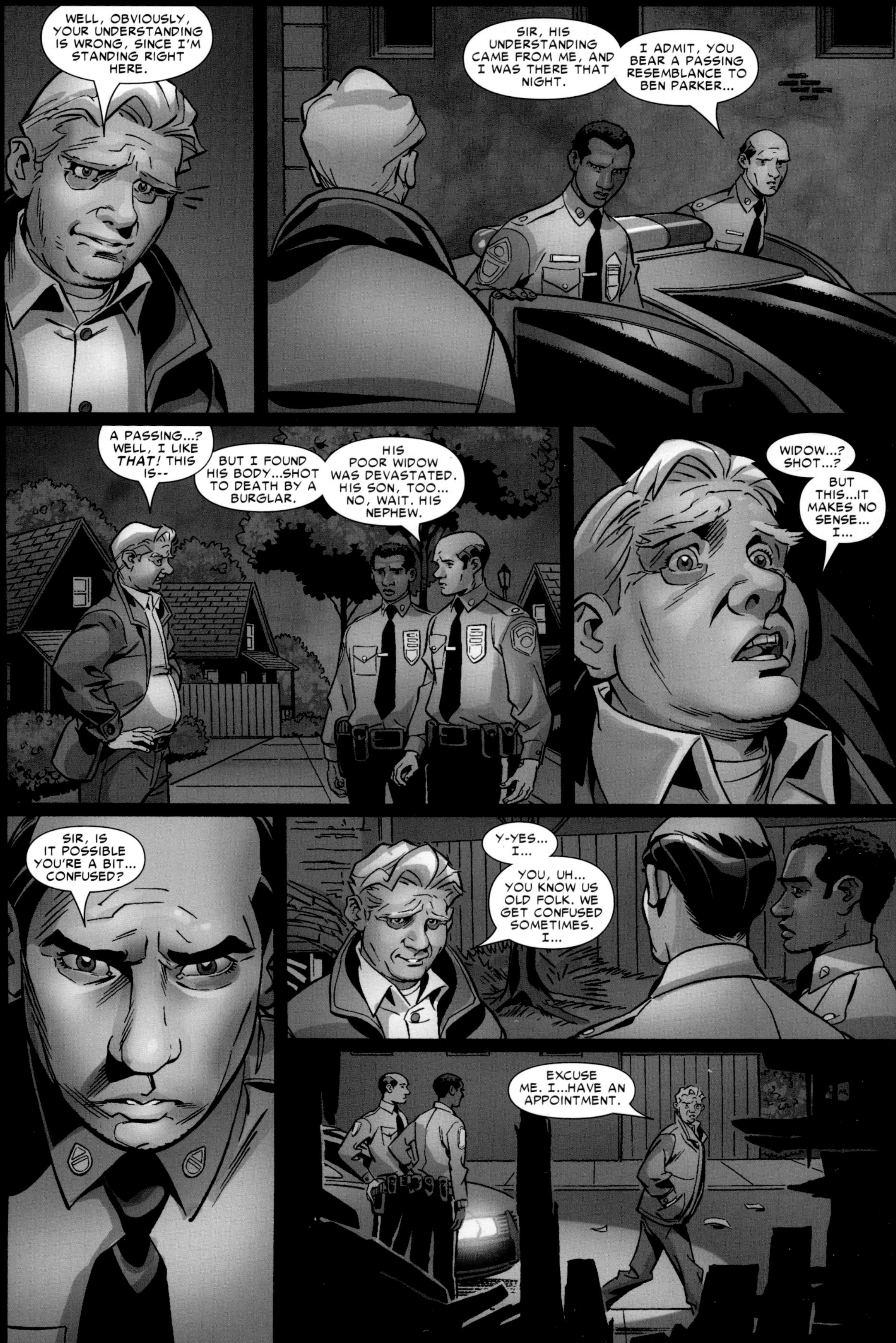
WELL, OBVIOUSLY, YOUR UNDERSTANDING IS WRONG, SINCE I'M STANDING RIGHT HERE.
SIR, HIS UNDERSTANDING CAME FROM ME, AND I WAS THERE THAT NIGHT.
I ADMIT, YOU BEAR A PASSING RESEMBLANCE TO BEN PARKER...
A PASSING...? WELL, I LIKE *THAT!* THIS IS--
BUT I FOUND HIS BODY...SHOT TO DEATH BY A BURGLAR.
HIS POOR WIDOW WAS DEVASTATED. HIS SON, TOO... NO, WAIT. HIS NEPHEW.
WIDOW...? SHOT...?
BUT THIS...IT MAKES NO SENSE... I...
SIR, IS IT POSSIBLE YOU'RE A BIT... CONFUSED?
Y-YES... I...
YOU, UH... YOU KNOW US OLD FOLK. WE GET CONFUSED SOMETIMES. I...
EXCUSE ME. I...HAVE AN APPOINTMENT.

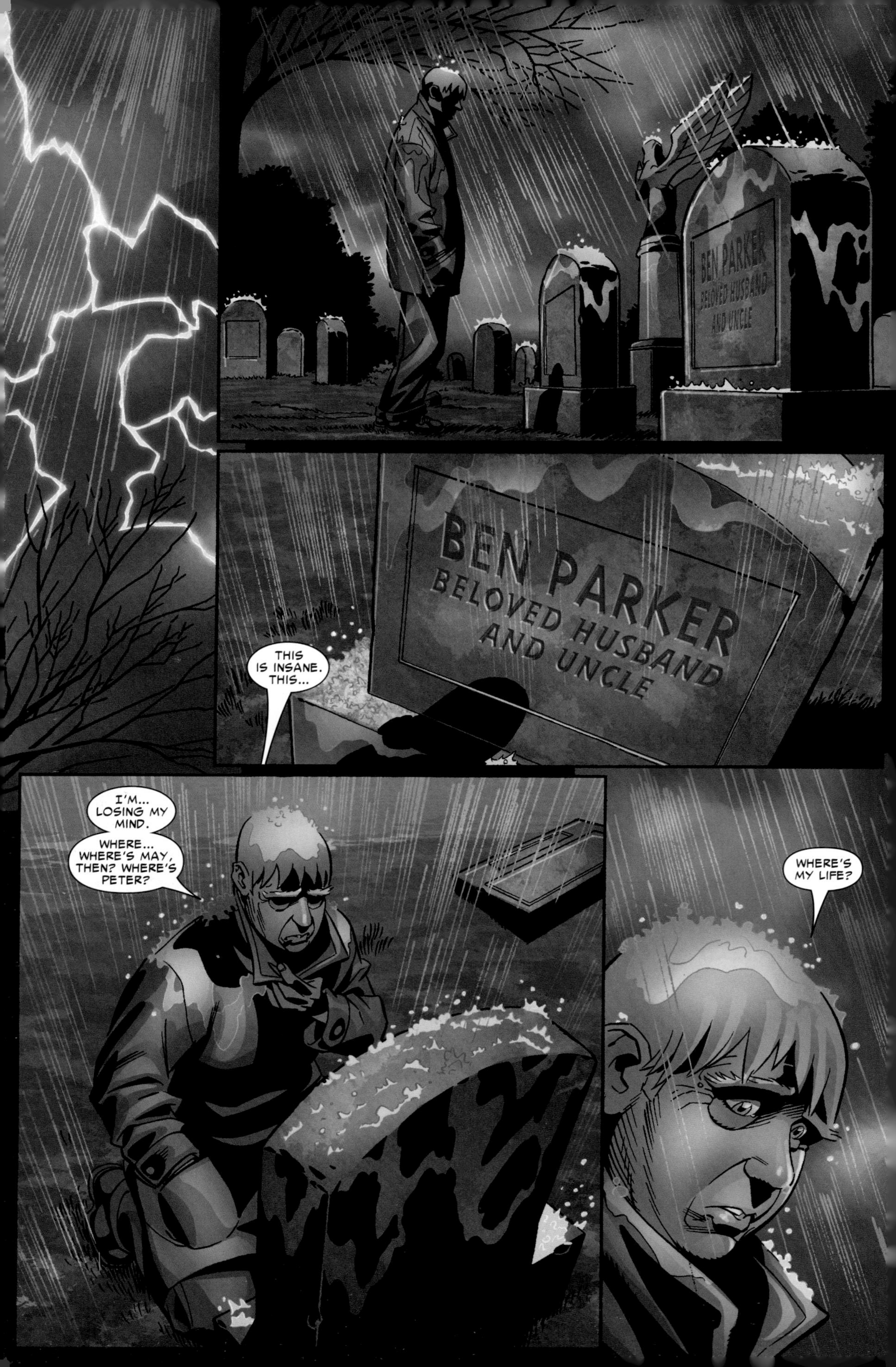
BEN PARKER
BELOVED HUSBAND
AND UNCLE
BEN PARKER
BELOVED HUSBAND
AND UNCLE
THIS IS INSANE. THIS...
I'M... LOSING MY MIND.
WHERE... WHERE'S MAY, THEN? WHERE'S PETER?
WHERE'S MY LIFE?

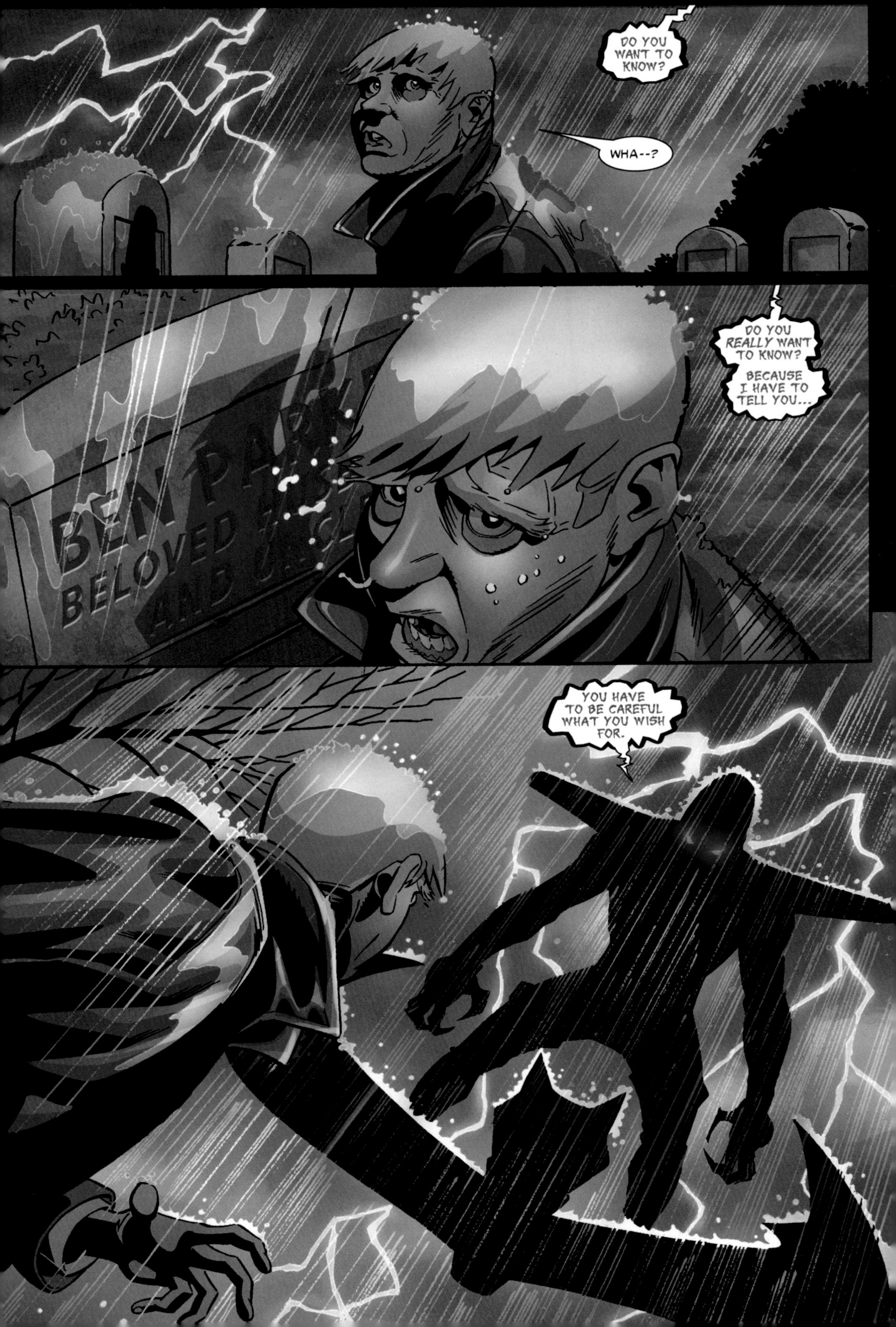
DO YOU WANT TO KNOW?
WHA--?
DO YOU *REALLY* WANT TO KNOW?
BECAUSE I HAVE TO TELL YOU...
BEN PA
BELOVED
AND
YOU HAVE TO BE CAREFUL WHAT YOU WISH FOR.

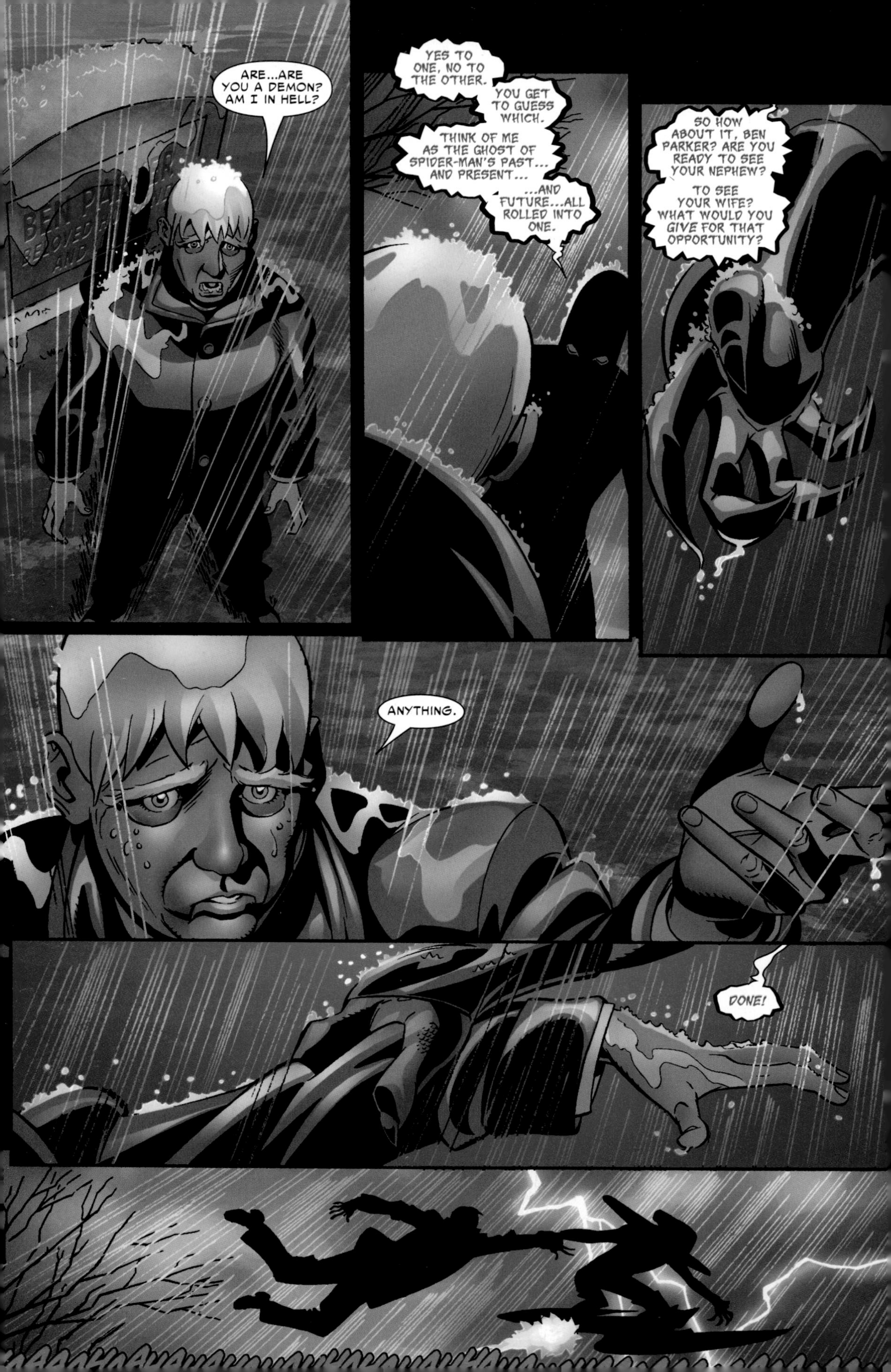
ARE...ARE YOU A DEMON? AM I IN HELL?
YES TO ONE, NO TO THE OTHER.
YOU GET TO GUESS WHICH.
THINK OF ME AS THE GHOST OF SPIDER-MAN'S PAST... AND PRESENT...
...AND FUTURE...ALL ROLLED INTO ONE.
SO HOW ABOUT IT, BEN PARKER? ARE YOU READY TO SEE YOUR NEPHEW?
TO SEE YOUR WIFE? WHAT WOULD YOU GIVE FOR THAT OPPORTUNITY?
ANYTHING.
DONE!

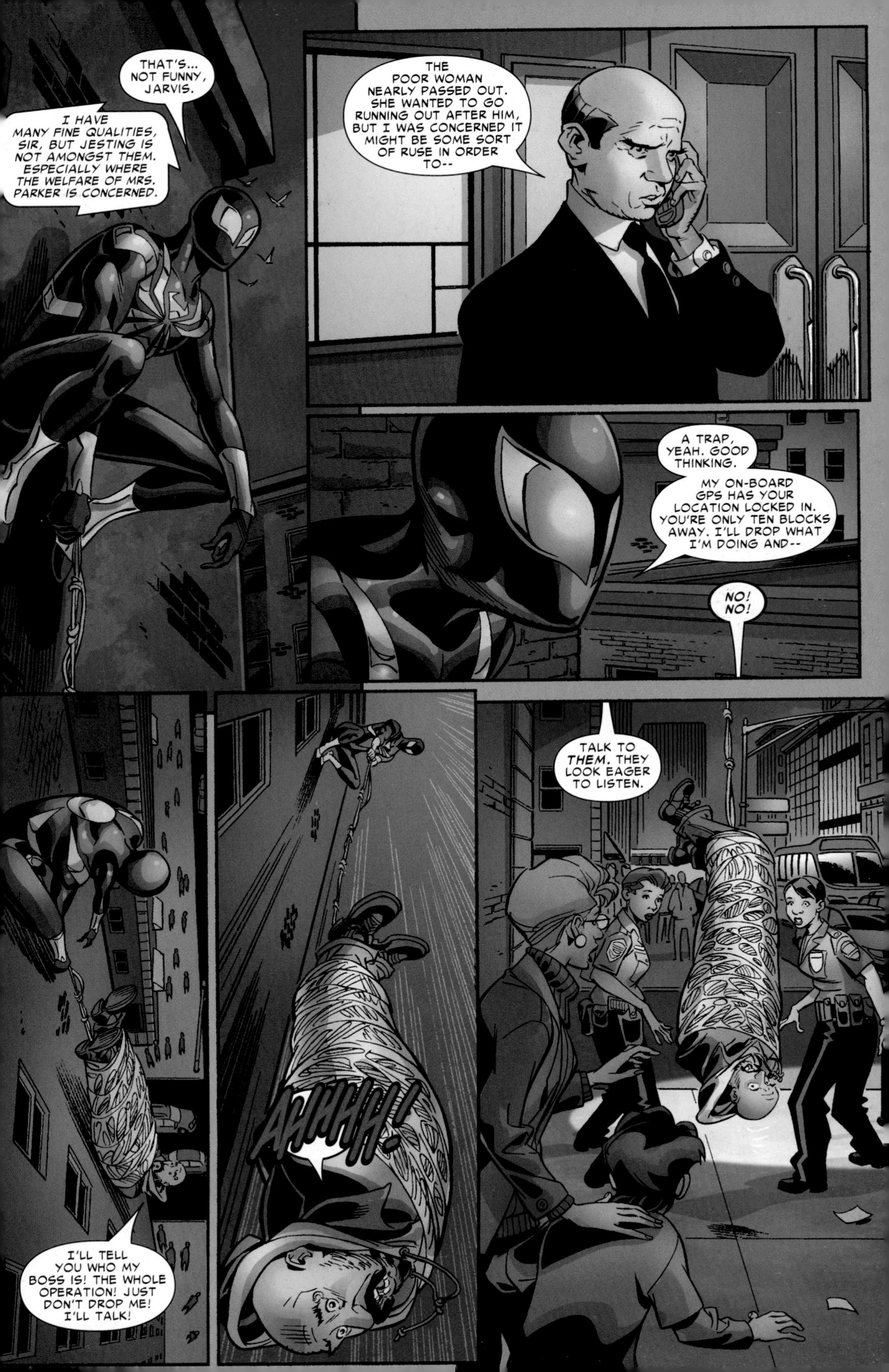
THAT'S... NOT FUNNY, JARVIS.
I HAVE MANY FINE QUALITIES, SIR, BUT JESTING IS NOT AMONGST THEM. ESPECIALLY WHERE THE WELFARE OF MRS. PARKER IS CONCERNED.
THE POOR WOMAN NEARLY PASSED OUT. SHE WANTED TO GO RUNNING OUT AFTER HIM, BUT I WAS CONCERNED IT MIGHT BE SOME SORT OF RUSE IN ORDER TO--
A TRAP, YEAH. GOOD THINKING.
MY ON-BOARD GPS HAS YOUR LOCATION LOCKED IN. YOU'RE ONLY TEN BLOCKS AWAY. I'LL DROP WHAT I'M DOING AND--
NO! NO!
I'LL TELL YOU WHO MY BOSS IS! THE WHOLE OPERATION! JUST DON'T DROP ME! I'LL TALK!
AHHHH!
TALK TO THEM. THEY LOOK EAGER TO LISTEN.

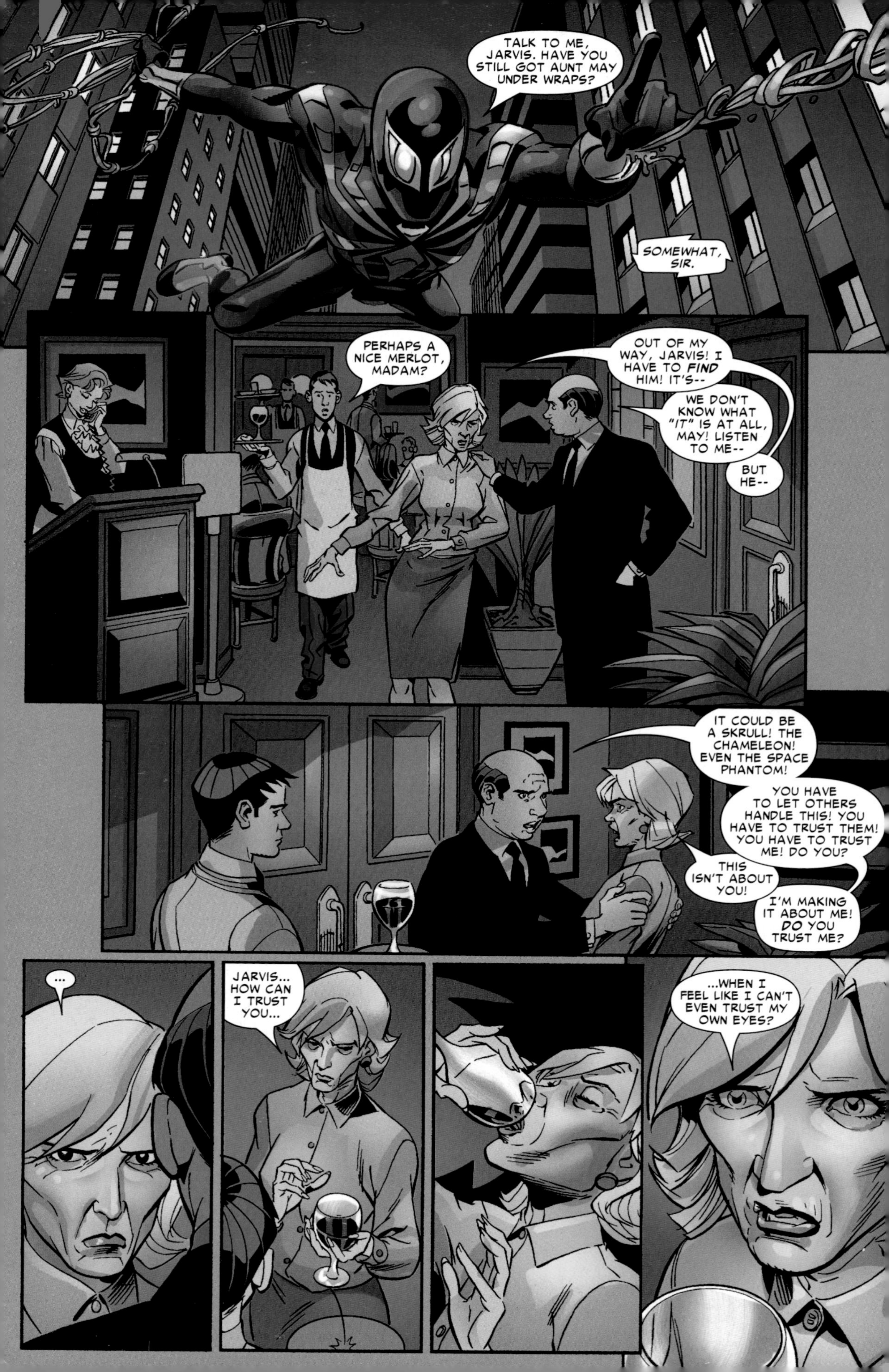
TALK TO ME, JARVIS. HAVE YOU STILL GOT AUNT MAY UNDER WRAPS?
SOMEWHAT, SIR.
PERHAPS A NICE MERLOT, MADAM?
OUT OF MY WAY, JARVIS! I HAVE TO FIND HIM! IT'S--
WE DON'T KNOW WHAT "IT" IS AT ALL, MAY! LISTEN TO ME--
BUT HE--
IT COULD BE A SKRULL! THE CHAMELEON! EVEN THE SPACE PHANTOM!
YOU HAVE TO LET OTHERS HANDLE THIS! YOU HAVE TO TRUST THEM! YOU HAVE TO TRUST ME! DO YOU?
THIS ISN'T ABOUT YOU!
I'M MAKING IT ABOUT ME! DO YOU TRUST ME?
...
JARVIS... HOW CAN I TRUST YOU...
...WHEN I FEEL LIKE I CAN'T EVEN TRUST MY OWN EYES?

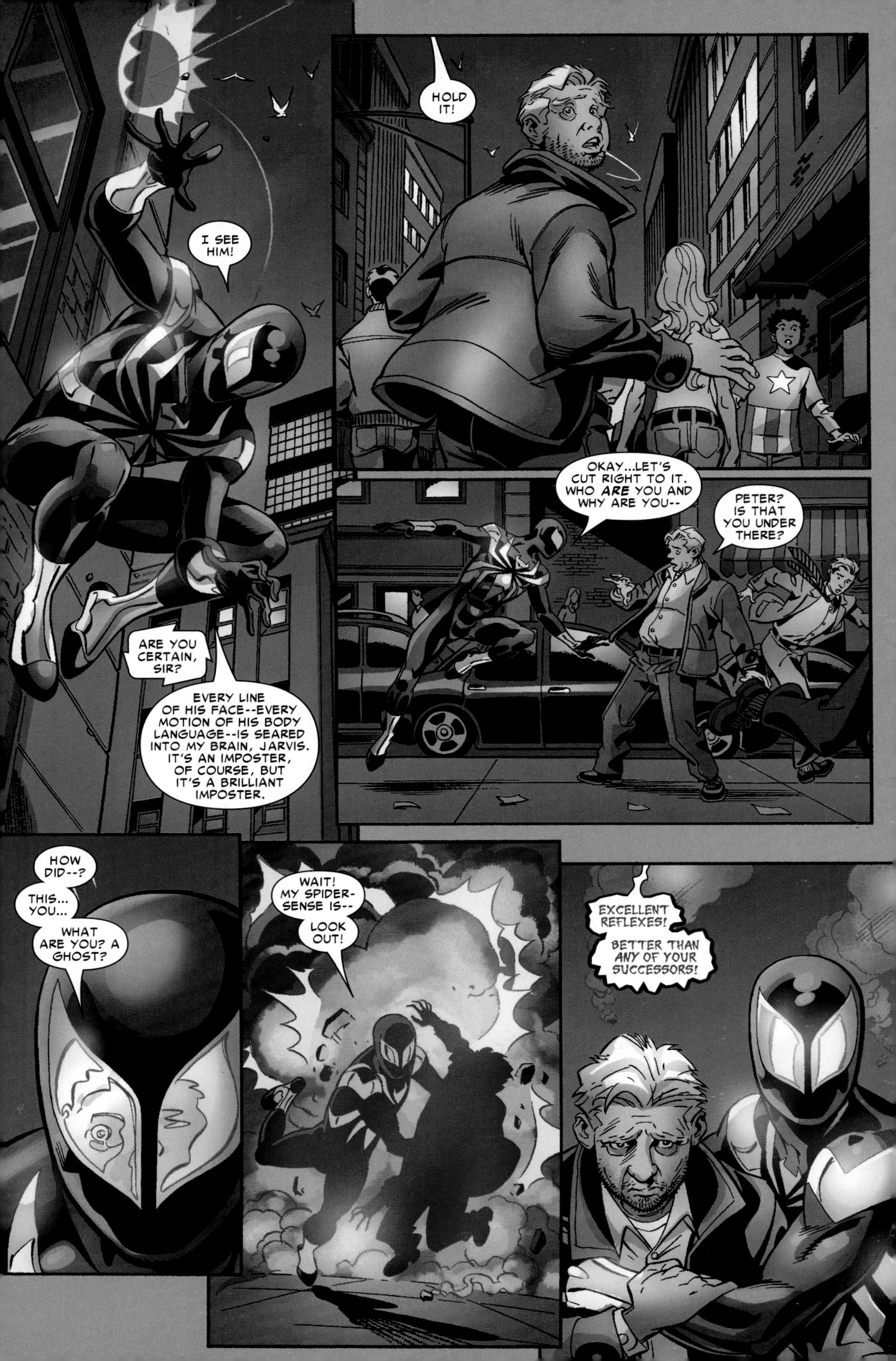
I SEE HIM!
HOLD IT!
ARE YOU CERTAIN, SIR?
EVERY LINE OF HIS FACE--EVERY MOTION OF HIS BODY LANGUAGE--IS SEARED INTO MY BRAIN, JARVIS. IT'S AN IMPOSTER, OF COURSE, BUT IT'S A BRILLIANT IMPOSTER.
OKAY...LET'S CUT RIGHT TO IT. WHO ARE YOU AND WHY ARE YOU--
PETER? IS THAT YOU UNDER THERE?
HOW DID--?
THIS... YOU...
WHAT ARE YOU? A GHOST?
WAIT! MY SPIDER-SENSE IS--
LOOK OUT!
EXCELLENT REFLEXES!
BETTER THAN ANY OF YOUR SUCCESSORS!

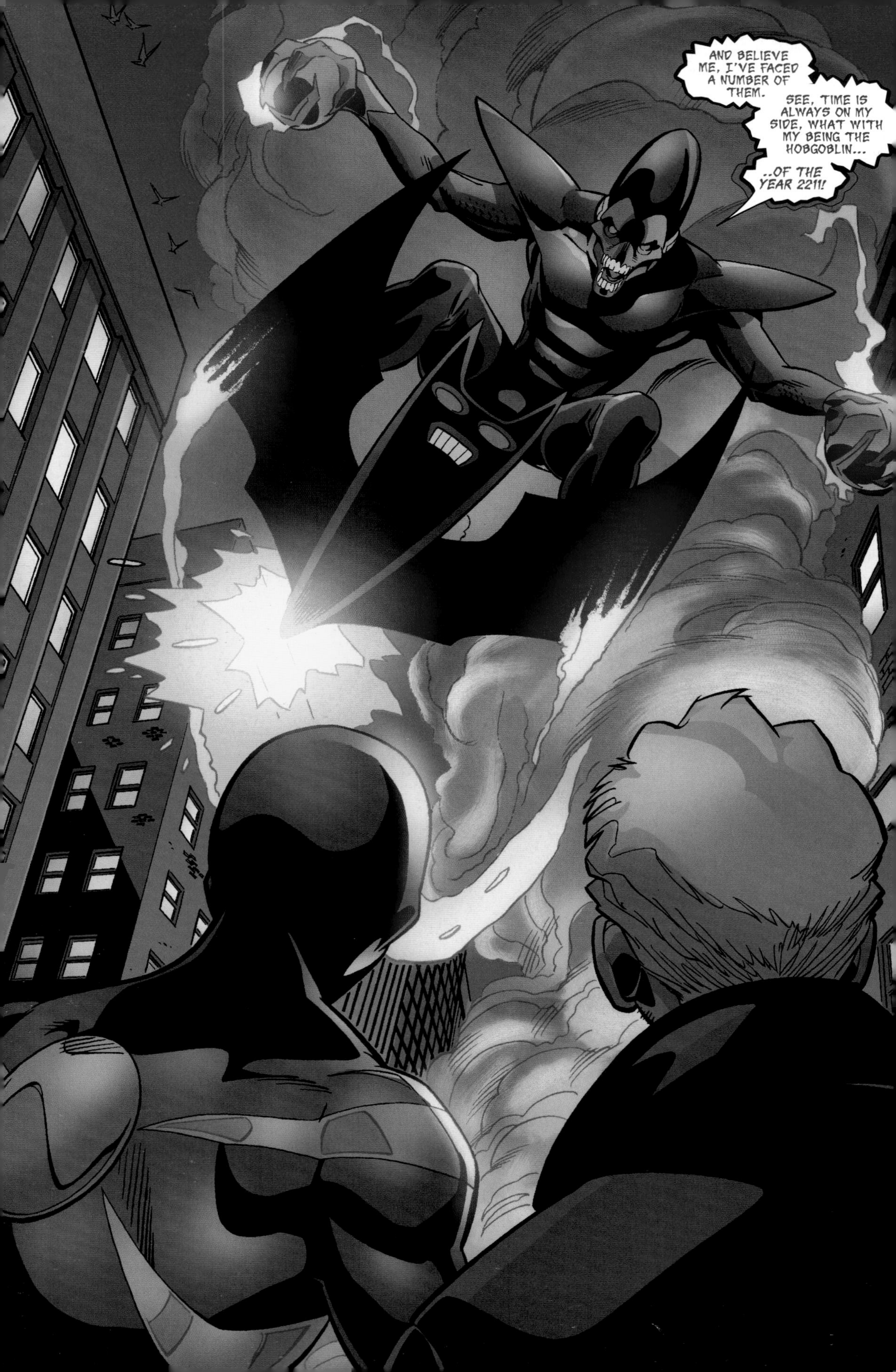
AND BELIEVE ME, I'VE FACED A NUMBER OF THEM.
SEE, TIME IS ALWAYS ON MY SIDE, WHAT WITH MY BEING THE HOBGOBLIN...
..OF THE YEAR 2211!

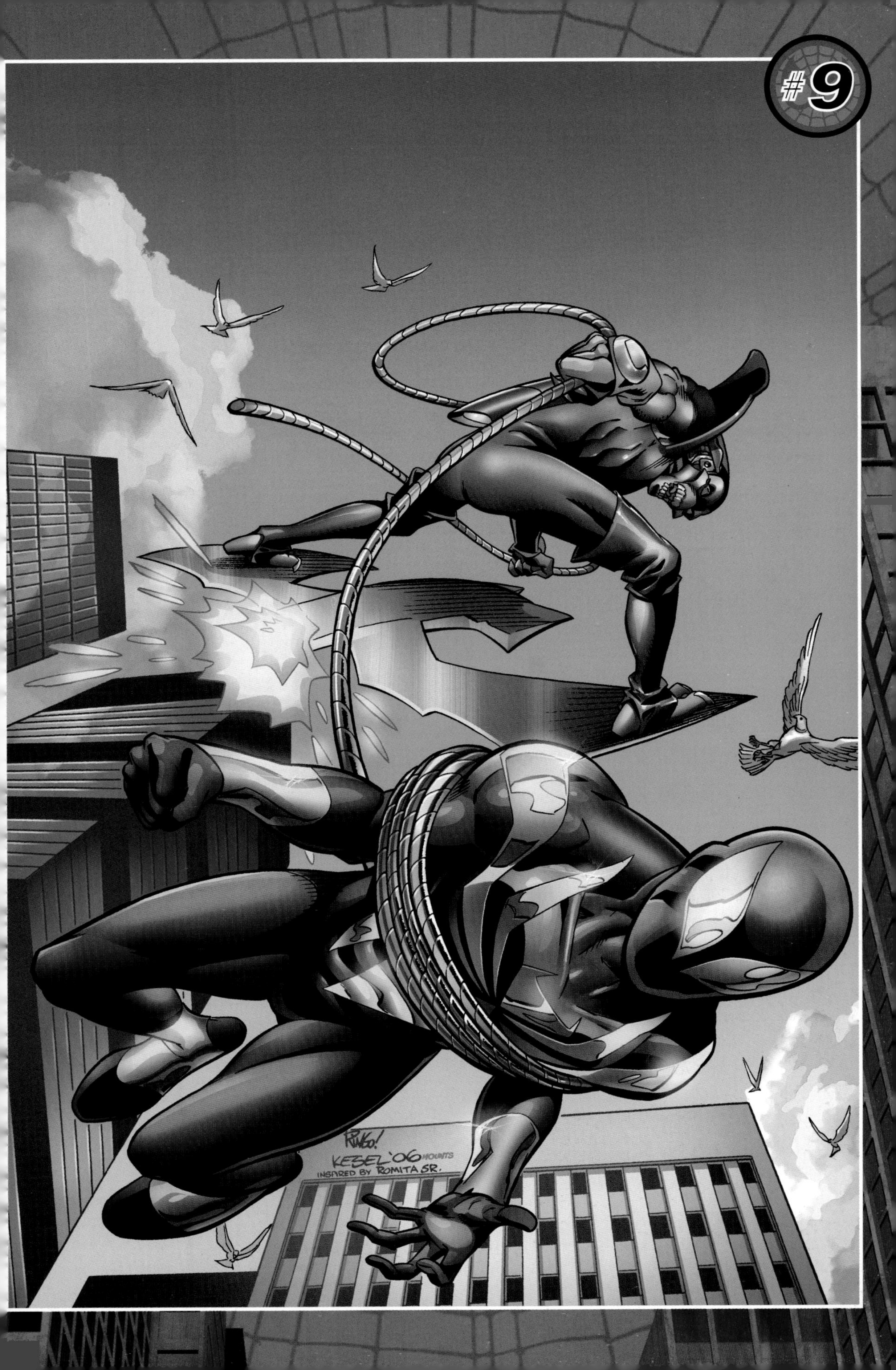
#9
RINGO!
KESEL '06 MOUNTS
INSPIRED BY ROMITA SR.

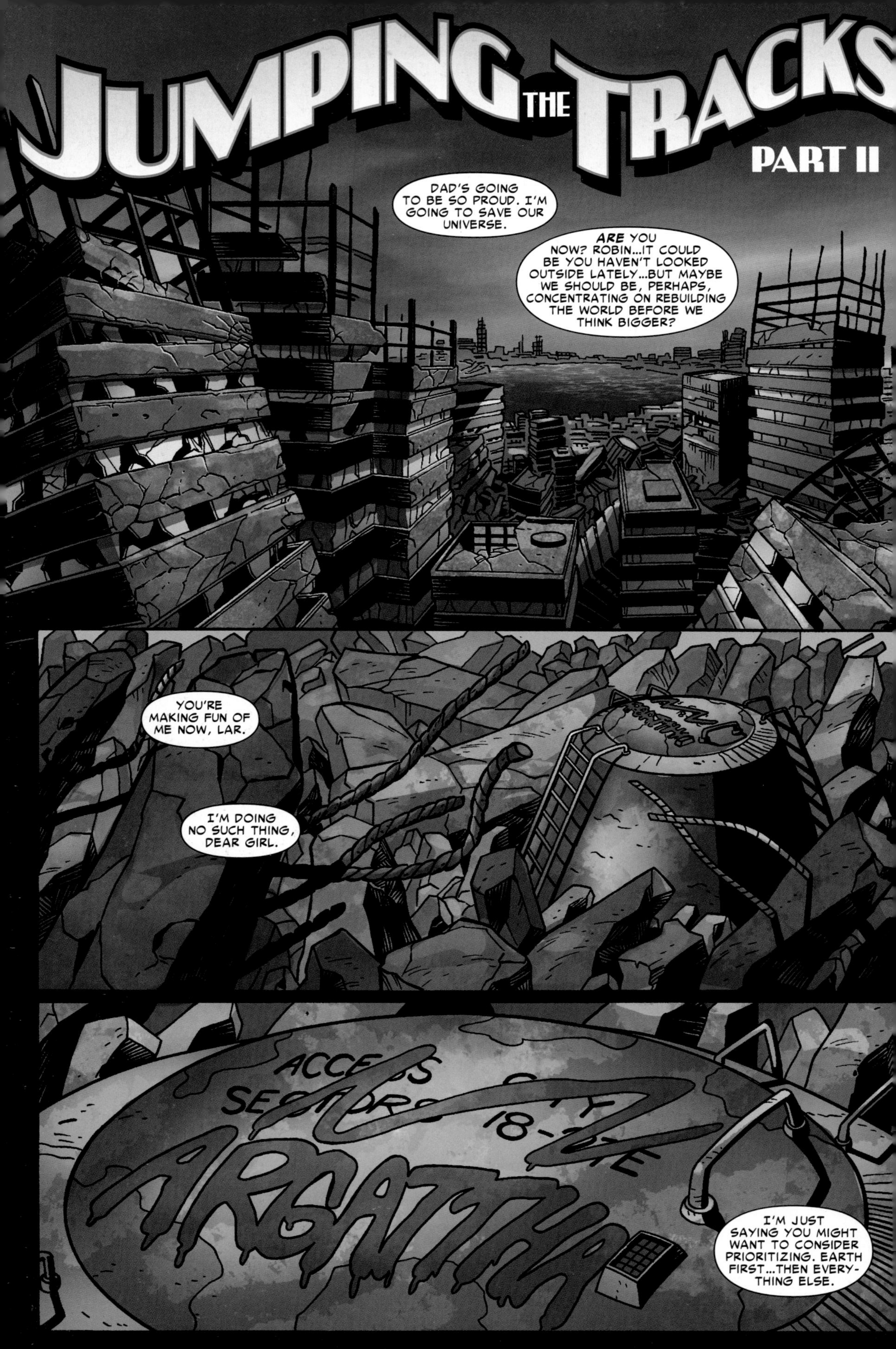
JUMPING THE TRACKS
PART II
DAD'S GOING TO BE SO PROUD. I'M GOING TO SAVE OUR UNIVERSE.
ARE YOU NOW? ROBIN...IT COULD BE YOU HAVEN'T LOOKED OUTSIDE LATELY...BUT MAYBE WE SHOULD BE, PERHAPS, CONCENTRATING ON REBUILDING THE WORLD BEFORE WE THINK BIGGER?
YOU'RE MAKING FUN OF ME NOW, LAR.
I'M DOING NO SUCH THING, DEAR GIRL.
I'M JUST SAYING YOU MIGHT WANT TO CONSIDER PRIORITIZING. EARTH FIRST...THEN EVERYTHING ELSE.

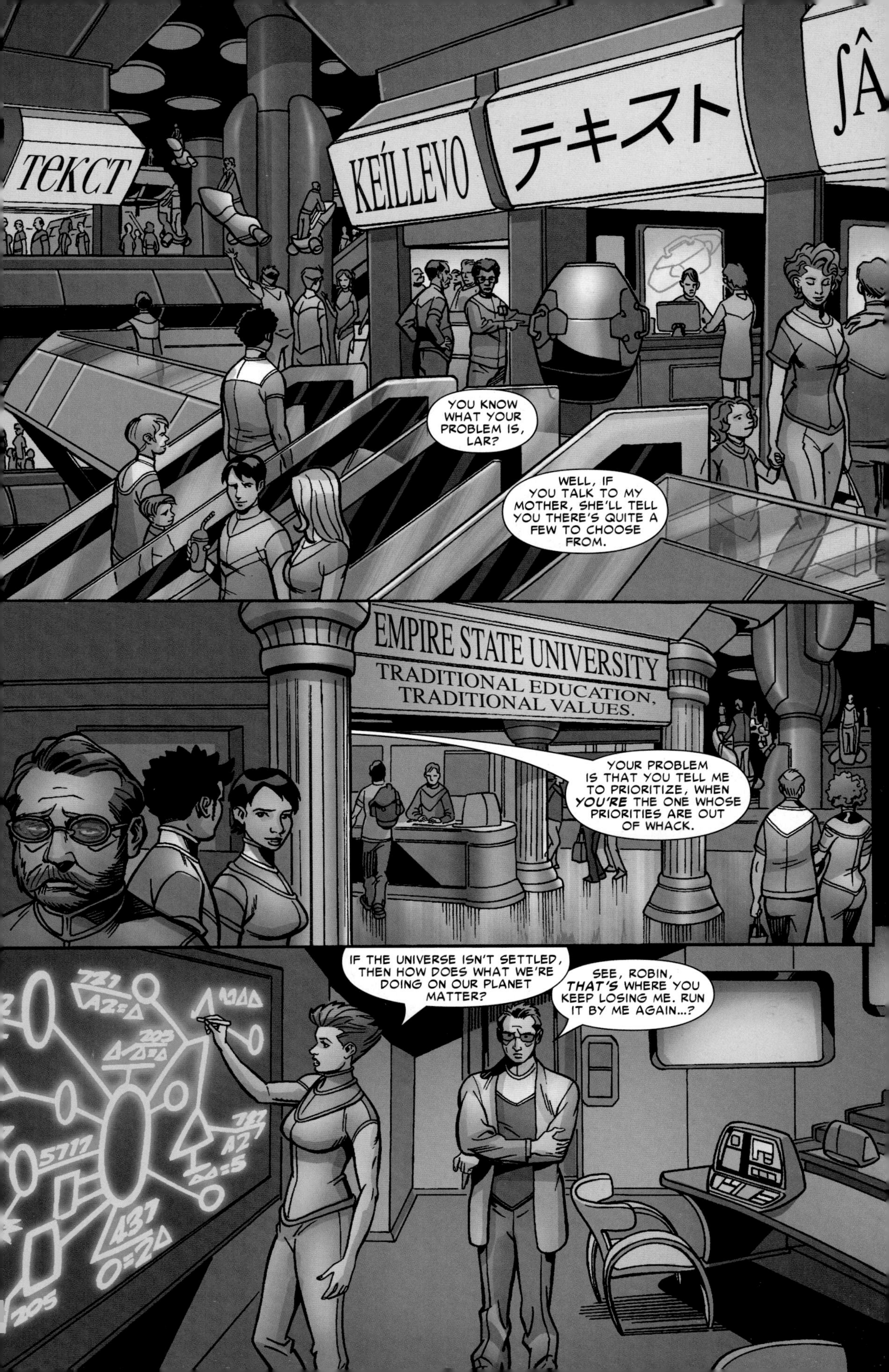
TEKCT
KEÍLLEVO
テキスト
YOU KNOW WHAT YOUR PROBLEM IS, LAR?
WELL, IF YOU TALK TO MY MOTHER, SHE'LL TELL YOU THERE'S QUITE A FEW TO CHOOSE FROM.
EMPIRE STATE UNIVERSITY
TRADITIONAL EDUCATION, TRADITIONAL VALUES.
YOUR PROBLEM IS THAT YOU TELL ME TO PRIORITIZE, WHEN *YOU'RE* THE ONE WHOSE PRIORITIES ARE OUT OF WHACK.
IF THE UNIVERSE ISN'T SETTLED, THEN HOW DOES WHAT WE'RE DOING ON OUR PLANET MATTER?
SEE, ROBIN, *THAT'S* WHERE YOU KEEP LOSING ME. RUN IT BY ME AGAIN...?

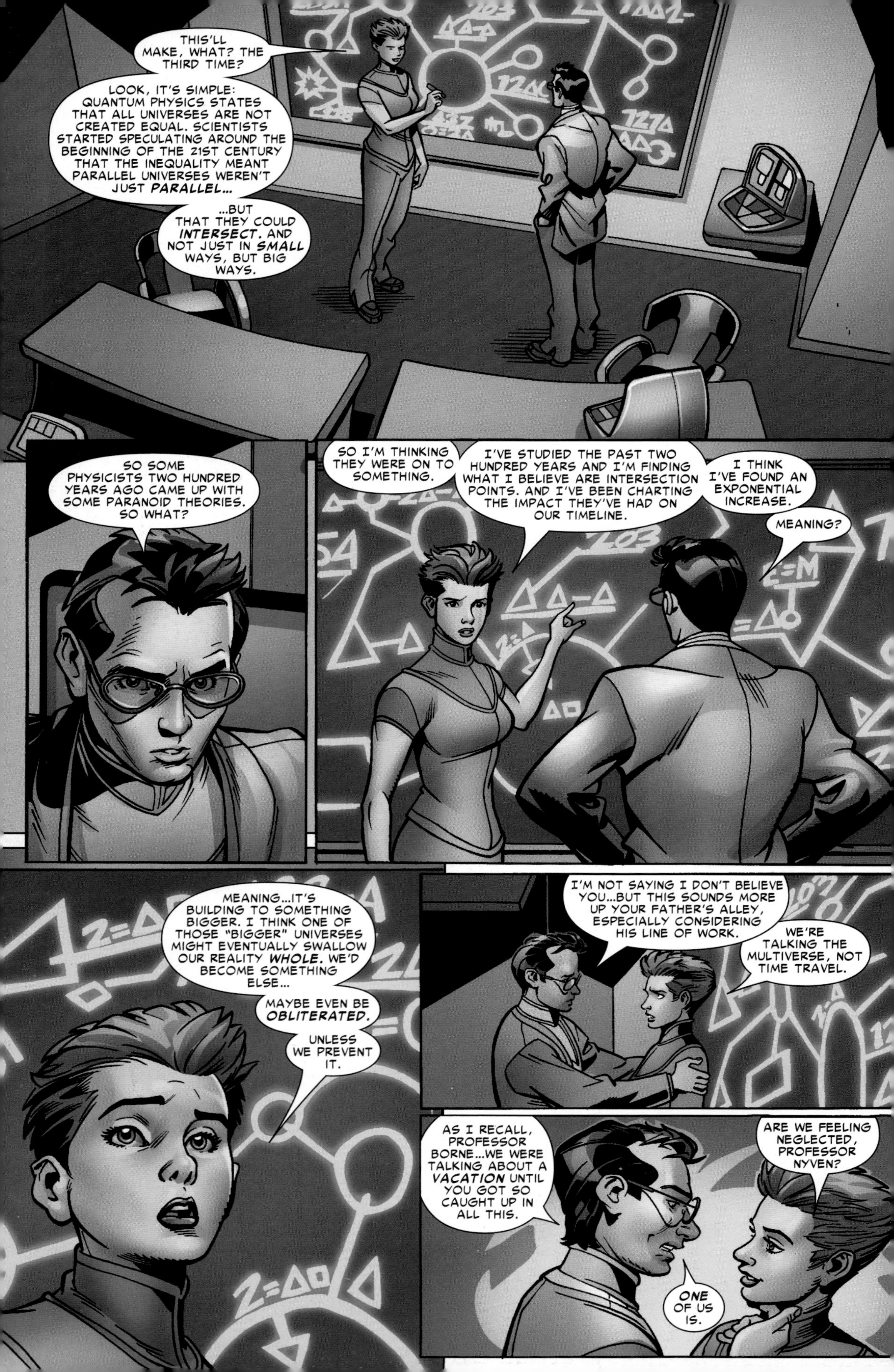
THIS'LL MAKE, WHAT? THE THIRD TIME?
LOOK, IT'S SIMPLE: QUANTUM PHYSICS STATES THAT ALL UNIVERSES ARE NOT CREATED EQUAL. SCIENTISTS STARTED SPECULATING AROUND THE BEGINNING OF THE 21ST CENTURY THAT THE INEQUALITY MEANT PARALLEL UNIVERSES WEREN'T JUST *PARALLEL*...
...BUT THAT THEY COULD *INTERSECT.* AND NOT JUST IN *SMALL* WAYS, BUT BIG WAYS.
SO SOME PHYSICISTS TWO HUNDRED YEARS AGO CAME UP WITH SOME PARANOID THEORIES. SO WHAT?
SO I'M THINKING THEY WERE ON TO SOMETHING.
I'VE STUDIED THE PAST TWO HUNDRED YEARS AND I'M FINDING WHAT I BELIEVE ARE INTERSECTION POINTS. AND I'VE BEEN CHARTING THE IMPACT THEY'VE HAD ON OUR TIMELINE.
I THINK I'VE FOUND AN EXPONENTIAL INCREASE.
MEANING?
MEANING...IT'S BUILDING TO SOMETHING BIGGER. I THINK ONE OF THOSE "BIGGER" UNIVERSES MIGHT EVENTUALLY SWALLOW OUR REALITY *WHOLE.* WE'D BECOME SOMETHING ELSE...
MAYBE EVEN BE *OBLITERATED.*
UNLESS WE PREVENT IT.
I'M NOT SAYING I DON'T BELIEVE YOU...BUT THIS SOUNDS MORE UP YOUR FATHER'S ALLEY, ESPECIALLY CONSIDERING HIS LINE OF WORK.
WE'RE TALKING THE MULTIVERSE, NOT TIME TRAVEL.
AS I RECALL, PROFESSOR BORNE...WE WERE TALKING ABOUT A *VACATION* UNTIL YOU GOT SO CAUGHT UP IN ALL THIS.
ARE WE FEELING NEGLECTED, PROFESSOR NYVEN?
ONE OF US IS.

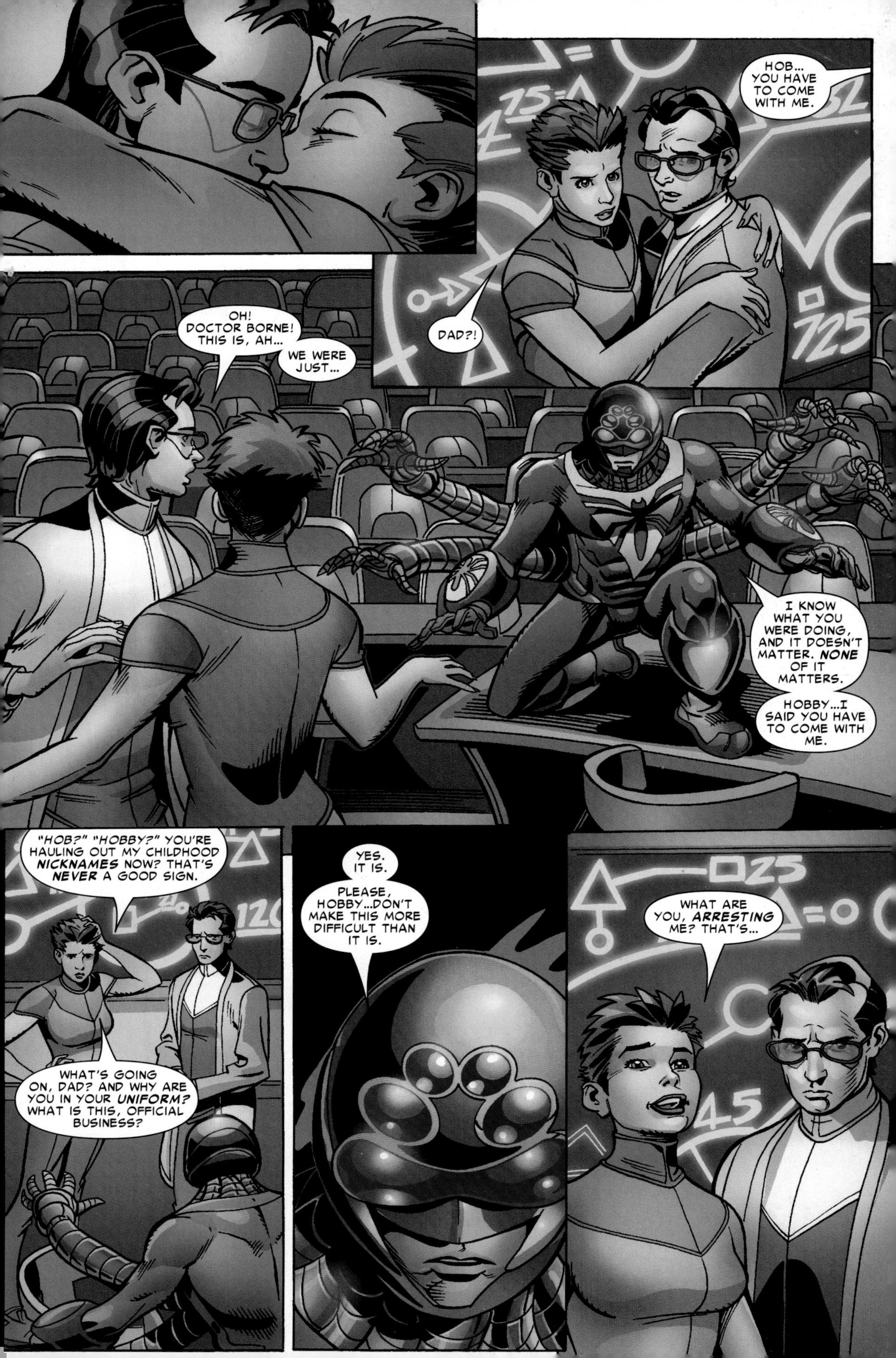
HOB... YOU HAVE TO COME WITH ME.
DAD?!
OH! DOCTOR BORNE! THIS IS, AH...
WE WERE JUST...
I KNOW WHAT YOU WERE DOING, AND IT DOESN'T MATTER. *NONE* OF IT MATTERS.
HOBBY...I SAID YOU HAVE TO COME WITH ME.
"HOB?" "HOBBY?" YOU'RE HAULING OUT MY CHILDHOOD *NICKNAMES* NOW? THAT'S *NEVER* A GOOD SIGN.
WHAT'S GOING ON, DAD? AND WHY ARE YOU IN YOUR *UNIFORM?* WHAT IS THIS, OFFICIAL BUSINESS?
YES. IT IS.
PLEASE, HOBBY...DON'T MAKE THIS MORE DIFFICULT THAN IT IS.
WHAT ARE YOU, *ARRESTING* ME? THAT'S...

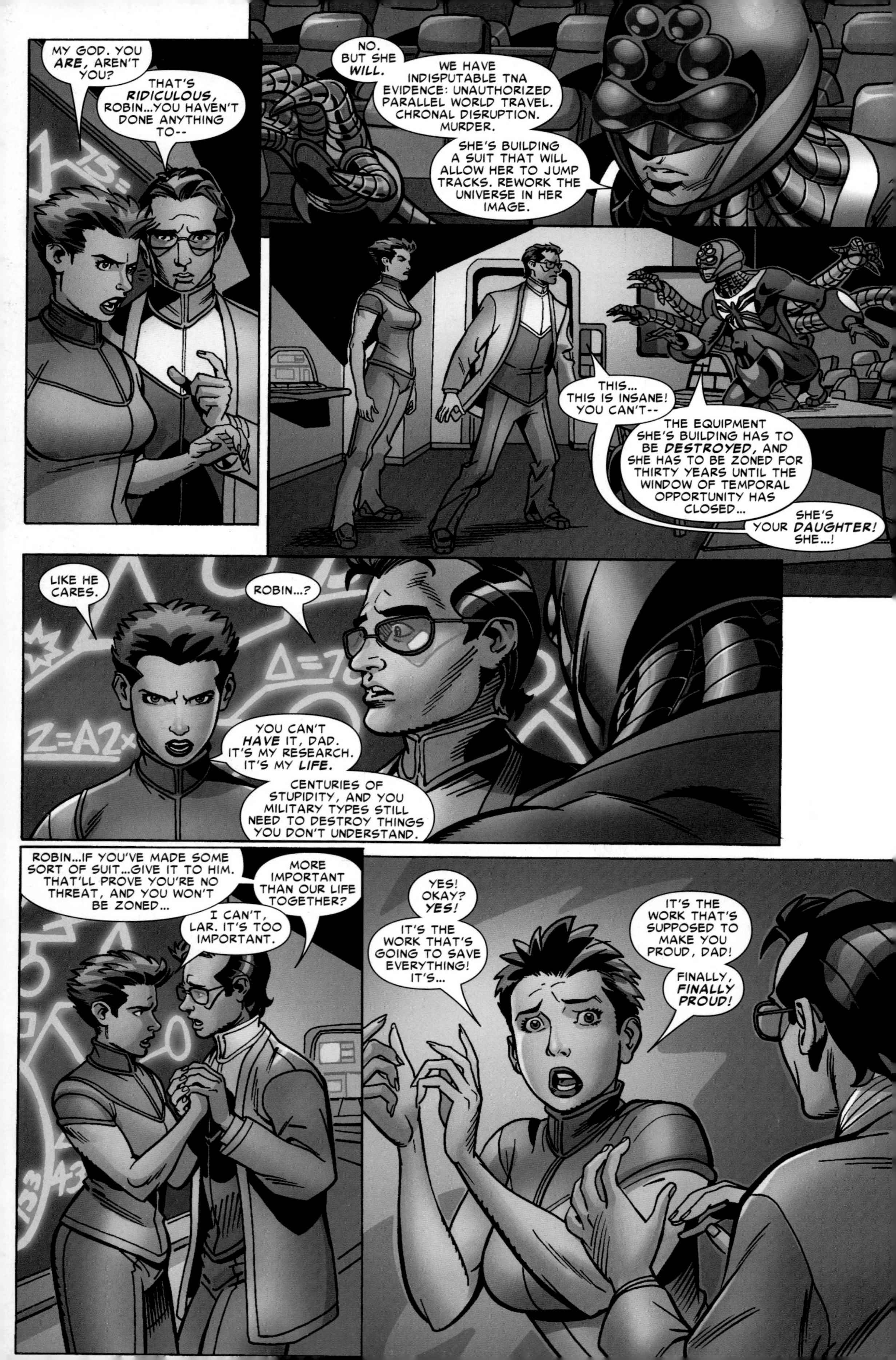

MY GOD. YOU *ARE*, AREN'T YOU?
THAT'S *RIDICULOUS*, ROBIN...YOU HAVEN'T DONE ANYTHING TO--
NO. BUT SHE *WILL*.
WE HAVE INDISPUTABLE TNA EVIDENCE: UNAUTHORIZED PARALLEL WORLD TRAVEL. CHRONAL DISRUPTION. MURDER.
SHE'S BUILDING A SUIT THAT WILL ALLOW HER TO JUMP TRACKS. REWORK THE UNIVERSE IN HER IMAGE.
THIS... THIS IS INSANE! YOU CAN'T--
THE EQUIPMENT SHE'S BUILDING HAS TO BE *DESTROYED*, AND SHE HAS TO BE ZONED FOR THIRTY YEARS UNTIL THE WINDOW OF TEMPORAL OPPORTUNITY HAS CLOSED...
SHE'S YOUR *DAUGHTER!* SHE...!
LIKE HE CARES.
ROBIN...?
YOU CAN'T *HAVE* IT, DAD. IT'S MY RESEARCH. IT'S MY *LIFE*.
CENTURIES OF STUPIDITY, AND YOU MILITARY TYPES STILL NEED TO DESTROY THINGS YOU DON'T UNDERSTAND.
ROBIN...IF YOU'VE MADE SOME SORT OF SUIT...GIVE IT TO HIM. THAT'LL PROVE YOU'RE NO THREAT, AND YOU WON'T BE ZONED...
I CAN'T, LAR. IT'S TOO IMPORTANT.
MORE IMPORTANT THAN OUR LIFE TOGETHER?
YES! OKAY? *YES!*
IT'S THE WORK THAT'S GOING TO SAVE EVERYTHING! IT'S...
IT'S THE WORK THAT'S SUPPOSED TO MAKE YOU PROUD, DAD!
FINALLY, *FINALLY PROUD!*

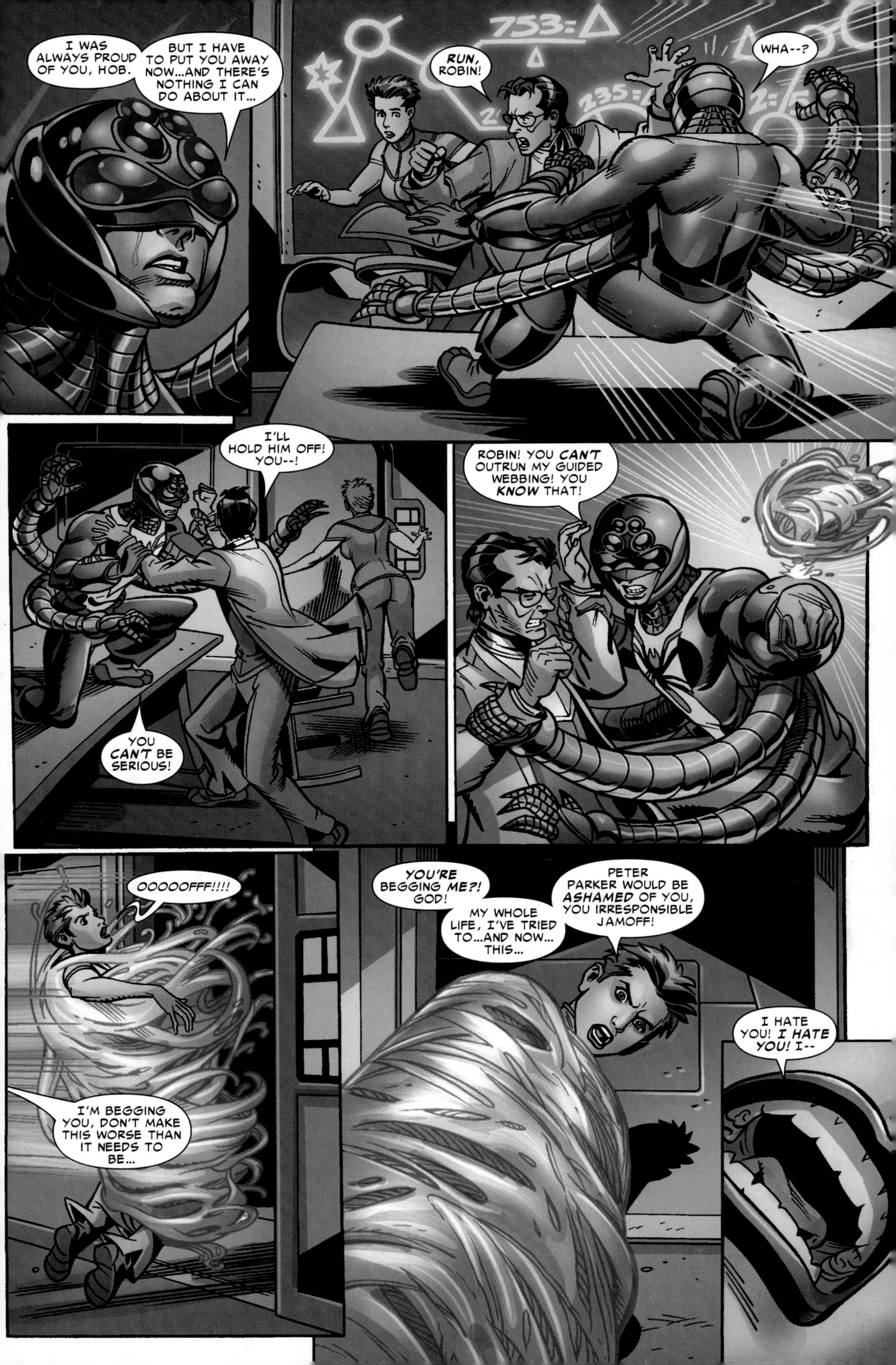

I WAS ALWAYS PROUD OF YOU, HOB.
BUT I HAVE TO PUT YOU AWAY NOW...AND THERE'S NOTHING I CAN DO ABOUT IT...
RUN, ROBIN!
WHA--?
I'LL HOLD HIM OFF! YOU--!
YOU CAN'T BE SERIOUS!
ROBIN! YOU CAN'T OUTRUN MY GUIDED WEBBING! YOU KNOW THAT!
OOOOOFFF!!!!
I'M BEGGING YOU, DON'T MAKE THIS WORSE THAN IT NEEDS TO BE...
YOU'RE BEGGING ME?! GOD!
MY WHOLE LIFE, I'VE TRIED TO...AND NOW... THIS...
PETER PARKER WOULD BE ASHAMED OF YOU, YOU IRRESPONSIBLE JAMOFF!
I HATE YOU! I HATE YOU! I--

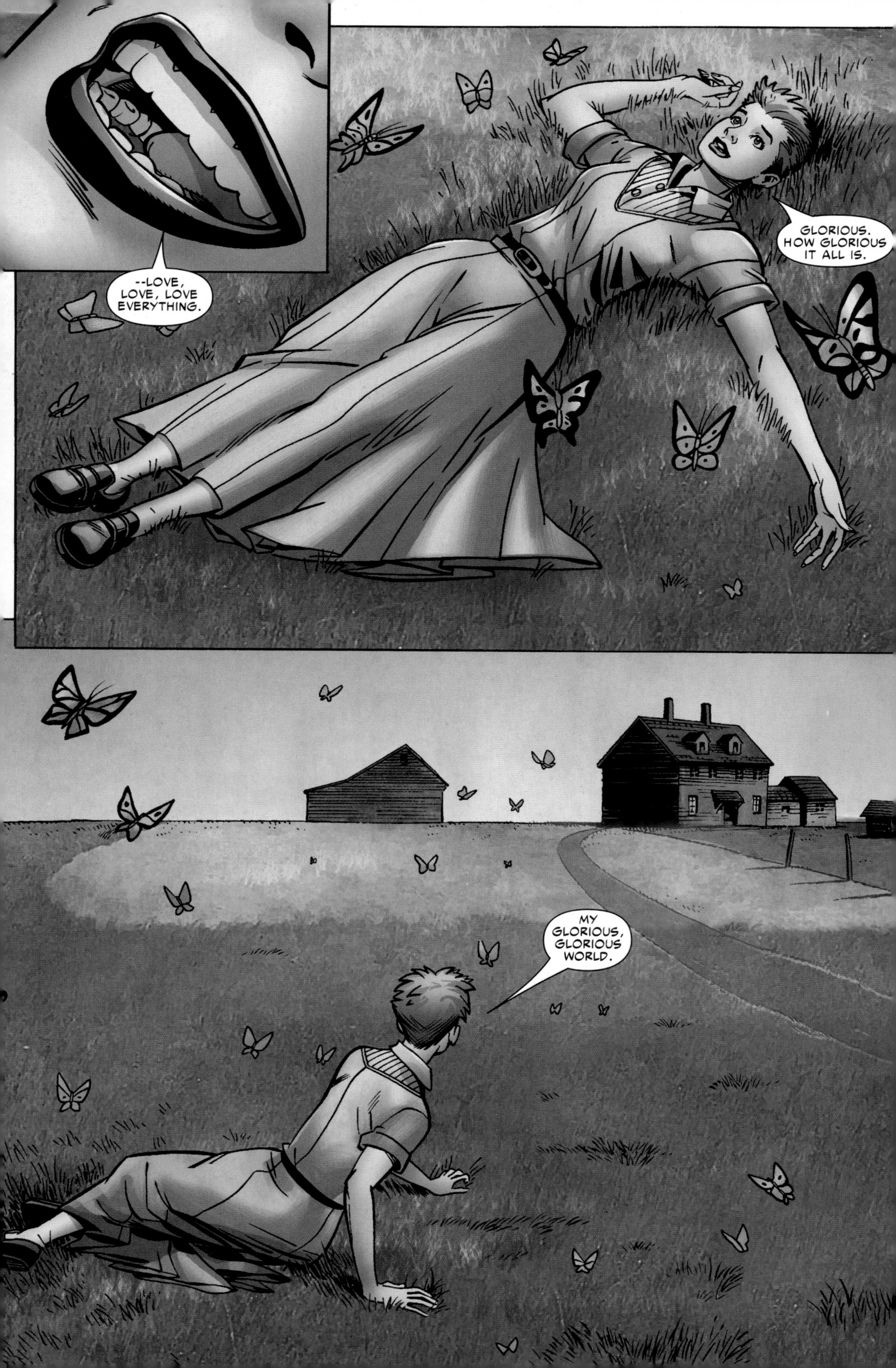
--LOVE, LOVE, LOVE EVERYTHING.
GLORIOUS. HOW GLORIOUS IT ALL IS.
MY GLORIOUS, GLORIOUS WORLD.

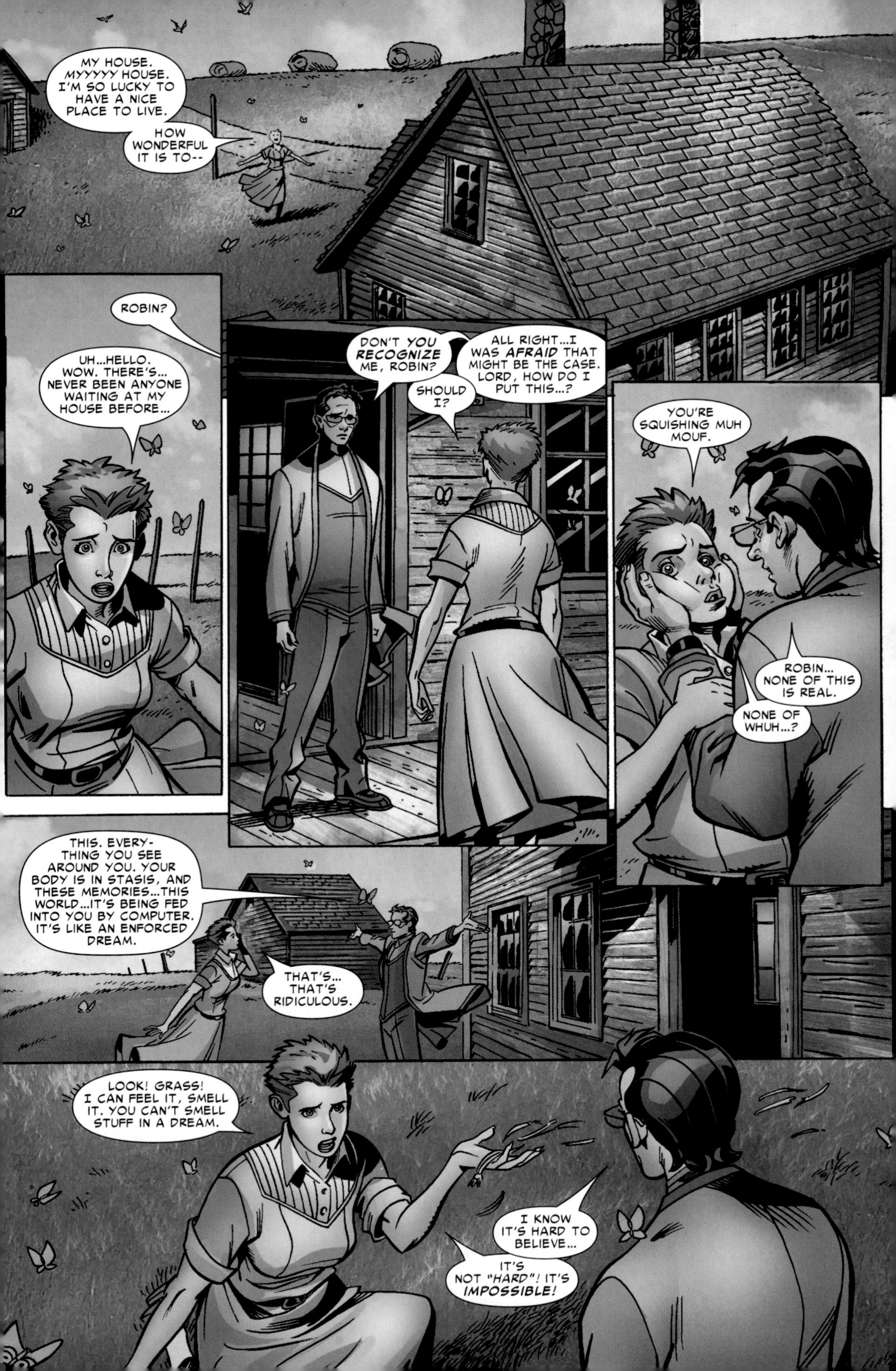
MY HOUSE. MYYYYY HOUSE. I'M SO LUCKY TO HAVE A NICE PLACE TO LIVE.
HOW WONDERFUL IT IS TO--
ROBIN?
UH...HELLO. WOW. THERE'S... NEVER BEEN ANYONE WAITING AT MY HOUSE BEFORE...
DON'T YOU RECOGNIZE ME, ROBIN?
SHOULD I?
ALL RIGHT...I WAS AFRAID THAT MIGHT BE THE CASE. LORD, HOW DO I PUT THIS...?
YOU'RE SQUISHING MUH MOUF.
ROBIN... NONE OF THIS IS REAL.
NONE OF WHUH...?
THIS. EVERYTHING YOU SEE AROUND YOU. YOUR BODY IS IN STASIS, AND THESE MEMORIES...THIS WORLD...IT'S BEING FED INTO YOU BY COMPUTER. IT'S LIKE AN ENFORCED DREAM.
THAT'S... THAT'S RIDICULOUS.
LOOK! GRASS! I CAN FEEL IT, SMELL IT. YOU CAN'T SMELL STUFF IN A DREAM.
I KNOW IT'S HARD TO BELIEVE...
IT'S NOT "HARD"! IT'S IMPOSSIBLE!

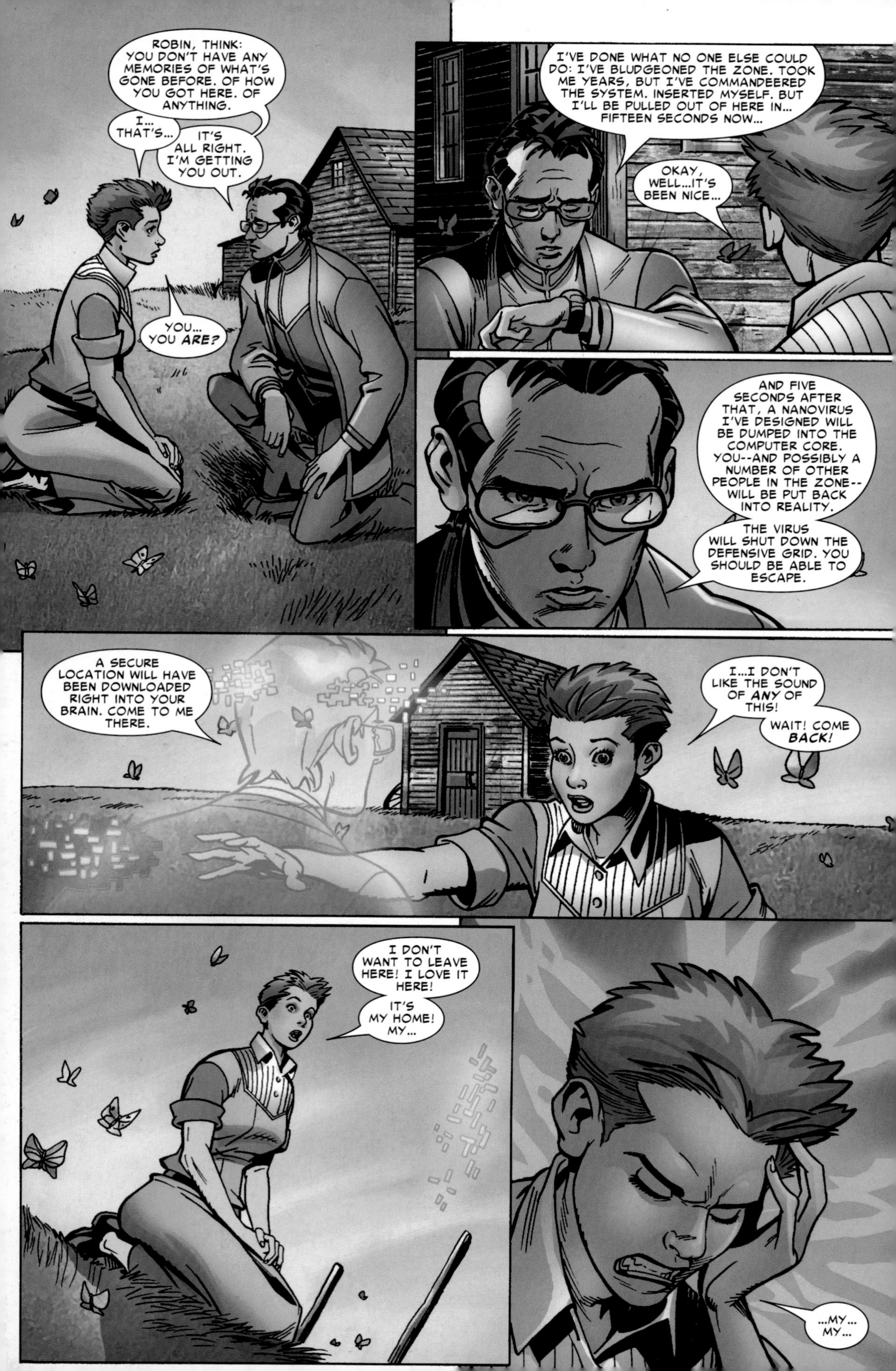
ROBIN, THINK: YOU DON'T HAVE ANY MEMORIES OF WHAT'S GONE BEFORE. OF HOW YOU GOT HERE. OF ANYTHING.
I... THAT'S...
IT'S ALL RIGHT. I'M GETTING YOU OUT.
YOU... YOU ARE?
I'VE DONE WHAT NO ONE ELSE COULD DO: I'VE BLUDGEONED THE ZONE. TOOK ME YEARS, BUT I'VE COMMANDEERED THE SYSTEM. INSERTED MYSELF. BUT I'LL BE PULLED OUT OF HERE IN... FIFTEEN SECONDS NOW...
OKAY, WELL...IT'S BEEN NICE...
AND FIVE SECONDS AFTER THAT, A NANOVIRUS I'VE DESIGNED WILL BE DUMPED INTO THE COMPUTER CORE. YOU--AND POSSIBLY A NUMBER OF OTHER PEOPLE IN THE ZONE--WILL BE PUT BACK INTO REALITY.
THE VIRUS WILL SHUT DOWN THE DEFENSIVE GRID. YOU SHOULD BE ABLE TO ESCAPE.
A SECURE LOCATION WILL HAVE BEEN DOWNLOADED RIGHT INTO YOUR BRAIN. COME TO ME THERE.
I...I DON'T LIKE THE SOUND OF ANY OF THIS!
WAIT! COME BACK!
I DON'T WANT TO LEAVE HERE! I LOVE IT HERE!
IT'S MY HOME! MY...
...MY... MY...

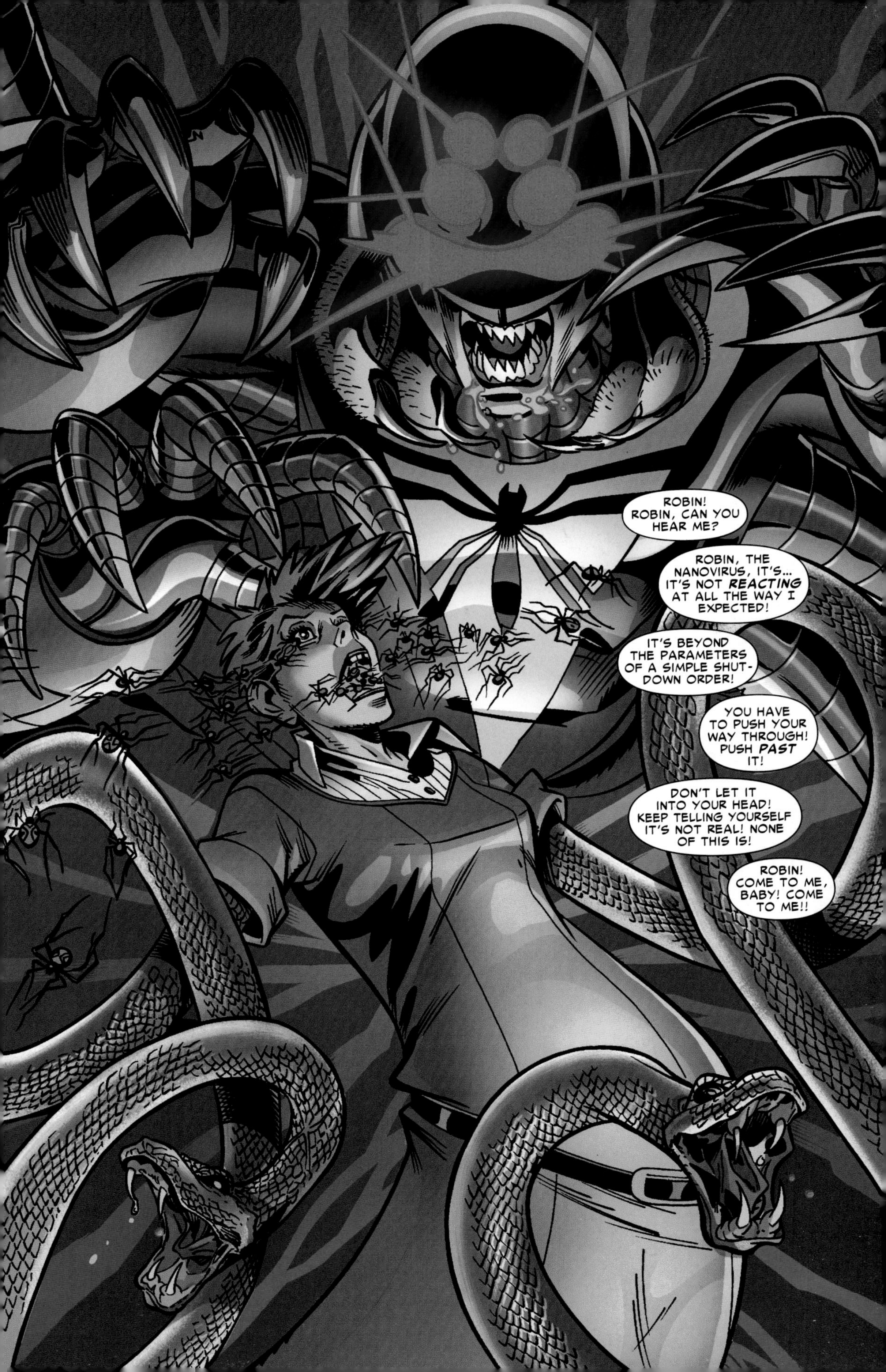
ROBIN! ROBIN, CAN YOU HEAR ME?
ROBIN, THE NANOVIRUS, IT'S... IT'S NOT REACTING AT ALL THE WAY I EXPECTED!
IT'S BEYOND THE PARAMETERS OF A SIMPLE SHUT-DOWN ORDER!
YOU HAVE TO PUSH YOUR WAY THROUGH! PUSH PAST IT!
DON'T LET IT INTO YOUR HEAD! KEEP TELLING YOURSELF IT'S NOT REAL! NONE OF THIS IS!
ROBIN! COME TO ME, BABY! COME TO ME!!

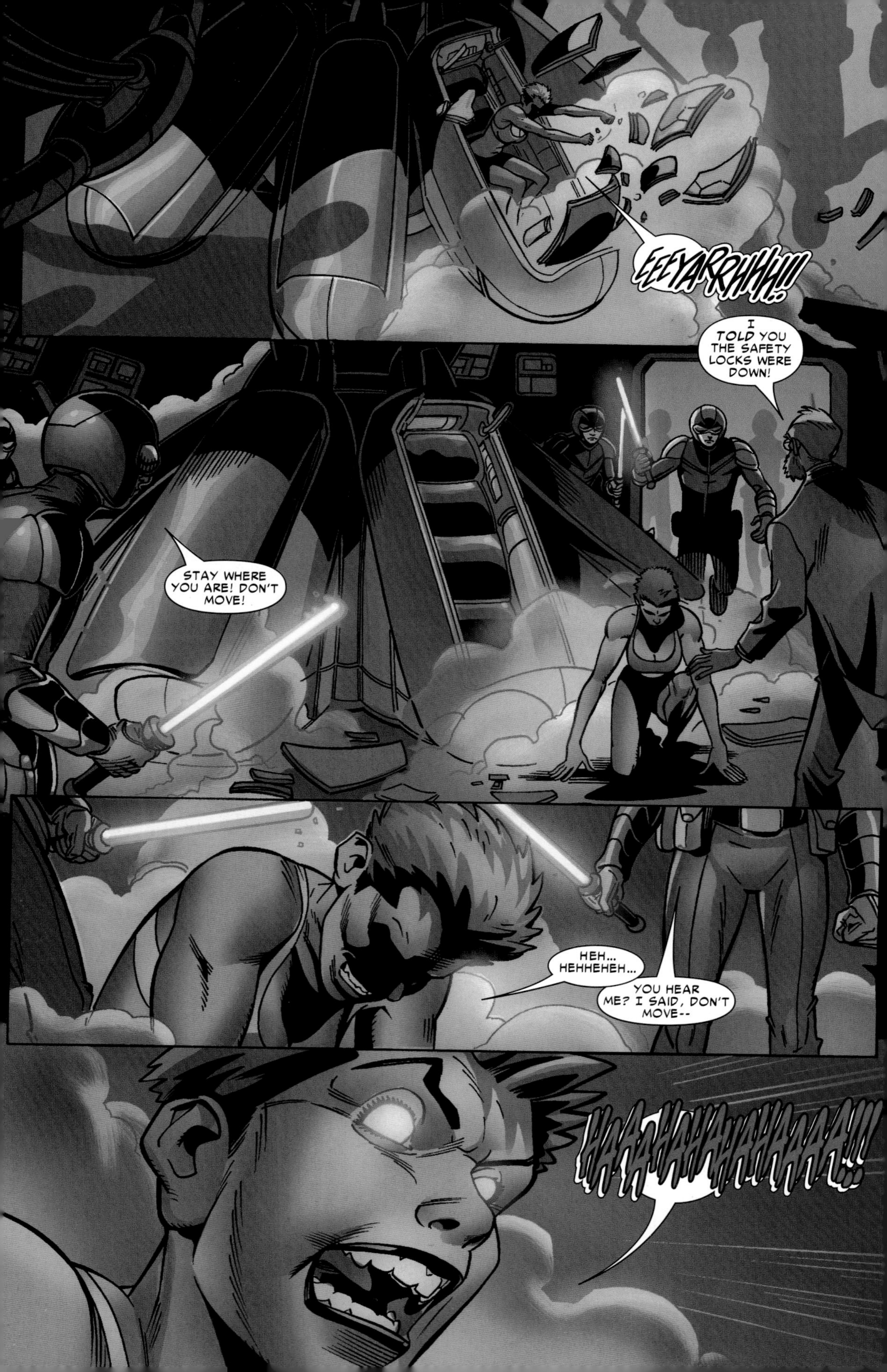
EEEYARRHHH!!
I TOLD YOU THE SAFETY LOCKS WERE DOWN!
STAY WHERE YOU ARE! DON'T MOVE!
HEH... HEHHHEHEH...
YOU HEAR ME? I SAID, DON'T MOVE--
HAAAHAHAHAHAAAA!!

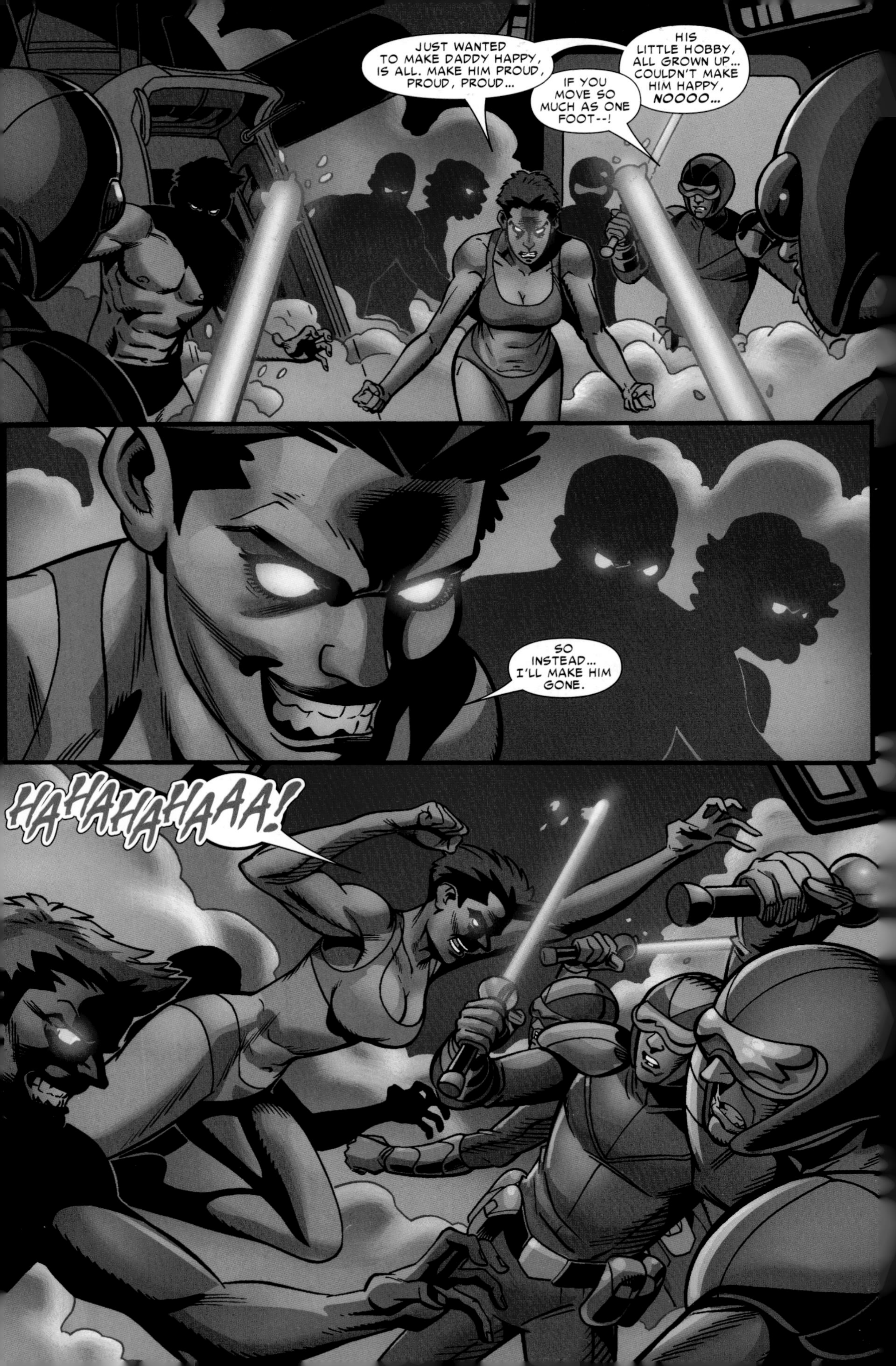
JUST WANTED TO MAKE DADDY HAPPY, IS ALL. MAKE HIM PROUD, PROUD, PROUD...
IF YOU MOVE SO MUCH AS ONE FOOT--!
HIS LITTLE HOBBY, ALL GROWN UP... COULDN'T MAKE HIM HAPPY, NOOOO...
SO INSTEAD... I'LL MAKE HIM GONE.
HAHAHAHAHAAA!

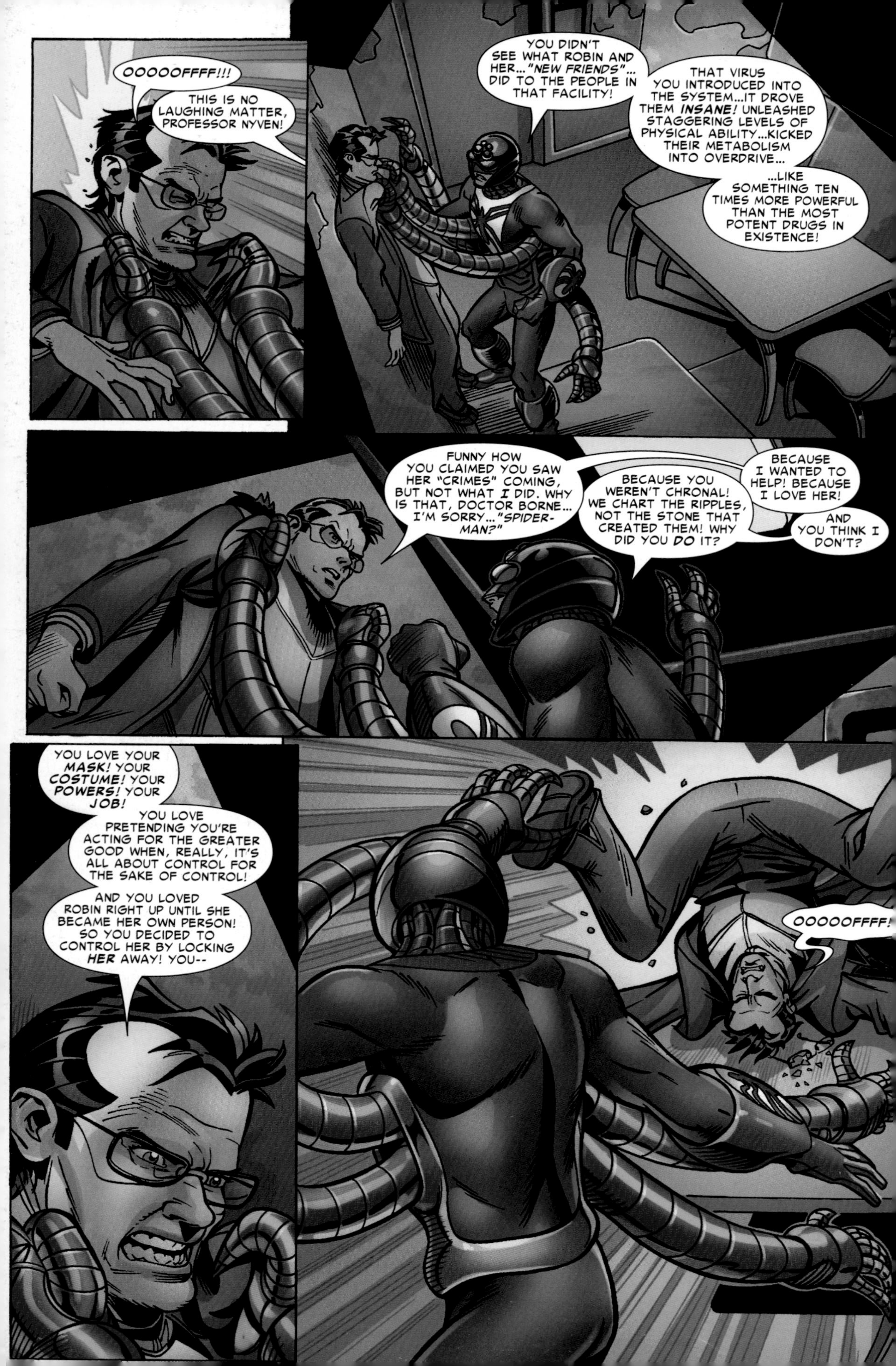
OOOOOFFFF!!!
THIS IS NO LAUGHING MATTER, PROFESSOR NYVEN!
YOU DIDN'T SEE WHAT ROBIN AND HER... "NEW FRIENDS"... DID TO THE PEOPLE IN THAT FACILITY!
THAT VIRUS YOU INTRODUCED INTO THE SYSTEM...IT DROVE THEM INSANE! UNLEASHED STAGGERING LEVELS OF PHYSICAL ABILITY...KICKED THEIR METABOLISM INTO OVERDRIVE...
...LIKE SOMETHING TEN TIMES MORE POWERFUL THAN THE MOST POTENT DRUGS IN EXISTENCE!
FUNNY HOW YOU CLAIMED YOU SAW HER "CRIMES" COMING, BUT NOT WHAT I DID. WHY IS THAT, DOCTOR BORNE... I'M SORRY... "SPIDER-MAN?"
BECAUSE YOU WEREN'T CHRONAL! WE CHART THE RIPPLES, NOT THE STONE THAT CREATED THEM! WHY DID YOU DO IT?
BECAUSE I WANTED TO HELP! BECAUSE I LOVE HER!
AND YOU THINK I DON'T?
YOU LOVE YOUR MASK! YOUR COSTUME! YOUR POWERS! YOUR JOB!
YOU LOVE PRETENDING YOU'RE ACTING FOR THE GREATER GOOD WHEN, REALLY, IT'S ALL ABOUT CONTROL FOR THE SAKE OF CONTROL!
AND YOU LOVED ROBIN RIGHT UP UNTIL SHE BECAME HER OWN PERSON! SO YOU DECIDED TO CONTROL HER BY LOCKING HER AWAY! YOU--
OOOOOFFFF!

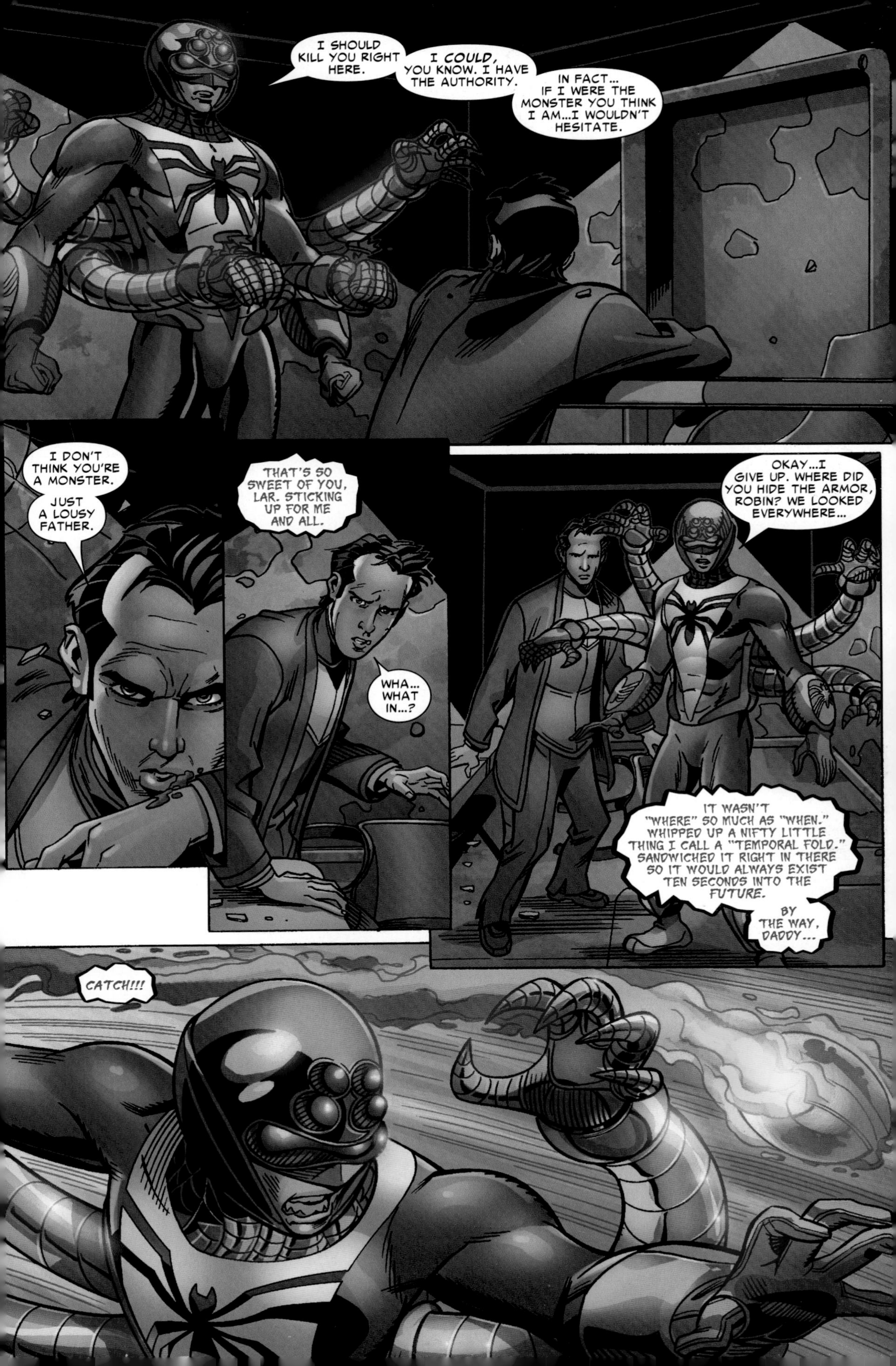
I SHOULD KILL YOU RIGHT HERE.
I *COULD*, YOU KNOW. I HAVE THE AUTHORITY.
IN FACT... IF I WERE THE MONSTER YOU THINK I AM...I WOULDN'T HESITATE.
I DON'T THINK YOU'RE A MONSTER.
JUST A LOUSY FATHER.
THAT'S SO SWEET OF YOU, LAR. STICKING UP FOR ME AND ALL.
WHA... WHAT IN...?
OKAY...I GIVE UP. WHERE DID YOU HIDE THE ARMOR, ROBIN? WE LOOKED EVERYWHERE...
IT WASN'T "WHERE" SO MUCH AS "WHEN." WHIPPED UP A NIFTY LITTLE THING I CALL A "TEMPORAL FOLD." SANDWICHED IT RIGHT IN THERE SO IT WOULD ALWAYS EXIST TEN SECONDS INTO THE FUTURE.
BY THE WAY, DADDY...
CATCH!!!

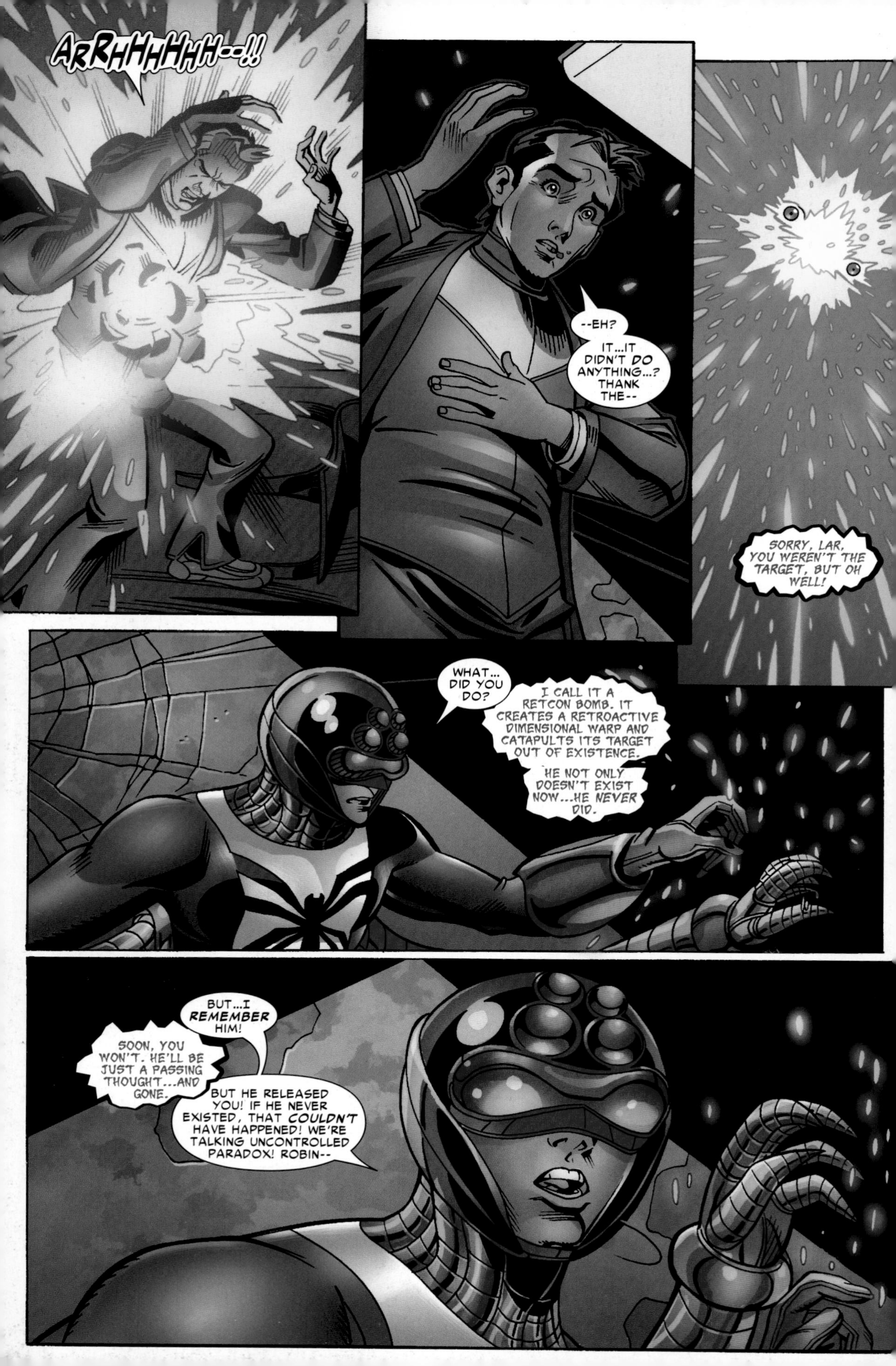
ARRHHHHHH--!!
--EH?
IT...IT DIDN'T DO ANYTHING...? THANK THE--
SORRY, LAR, YOU WEREN'T THE TARGET, BUT OH WELL!
WHAT... DID YOU DO?
I CALL IT A RETCON BOMB. IT CREATES A RETROACTIVE DIMENSIONAL WARP AND CATAPULTS ITS TARGET OUT OF EXISTENCE.
HE NOT ONLY DOESN'T EXIST NOW...HE NEVER DID.
BUT...I REMEMBER HIM!
SOON, YOU WON'T. HE'LL BE JUST A PASSING THOUGHT...AND GONE.
BUT HE RELEASED YOU! IF HE NEVER EXISTED, THAT COULDN'T HAVE HAPPENED! WE'RE TALKING UNCONTROLLED PARADOX! ROBIN--

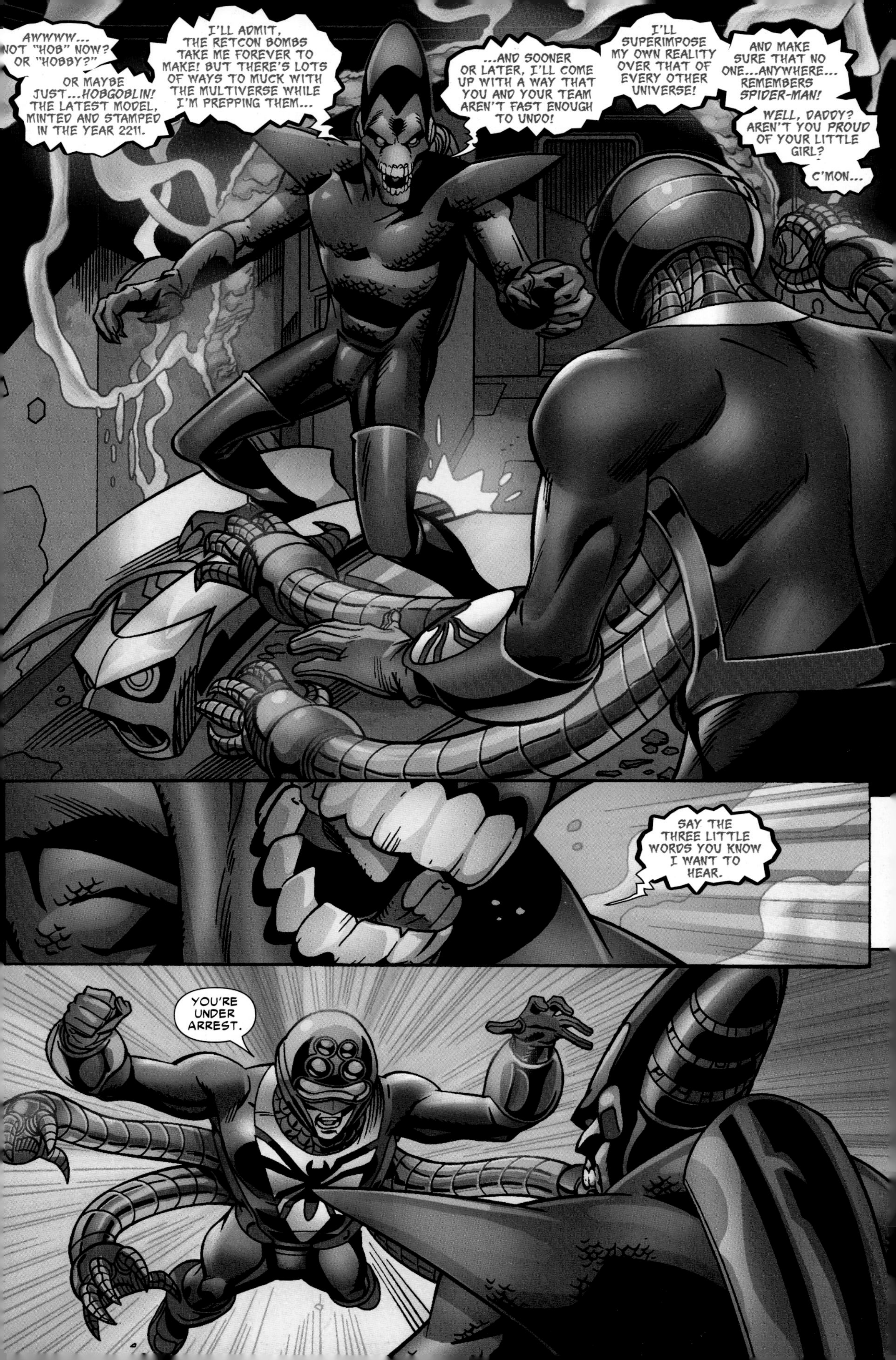
AWWWW... NOT "HOB" NOW? OR "HOBBY?"
OR MAYBE JUST...HOBGOBLIN! THE LATEST MODEL, MINTED AND STAMPED IN THE YEAR 2211.
I'LL ADMIT, THE RETCON BOMBS TAKE ME FOREVER TO MAKE! BUT THERE'S LOTS OF WAYS TO MUCK WITH THE MULTIVERSE WHILE I'M PREPPING THEM...
...AND SOONER OR LATER, I'LL COME UP WITH A WAY THAT YOU AND YOUR TEAM AREN'T FAST ENOUGH TO UNDO!
I'LL SUPERIMPOSE MY OWN REALITY OVER THAT OF EVERY OTHER UNIVERSE!
AND MAKE SURE THAT NO ONE...ANYWHERE... REMEMBERS SPIDER-MAN!
WELL, DADDY? AREN'T YOU PROUD OF YOUR LITTLE GIRL?
C'MON...
SAY THE THREE LITTLE WORDS YOU KNOW I WANT TO HEAR.
YOU'RE UNDER ARREST.

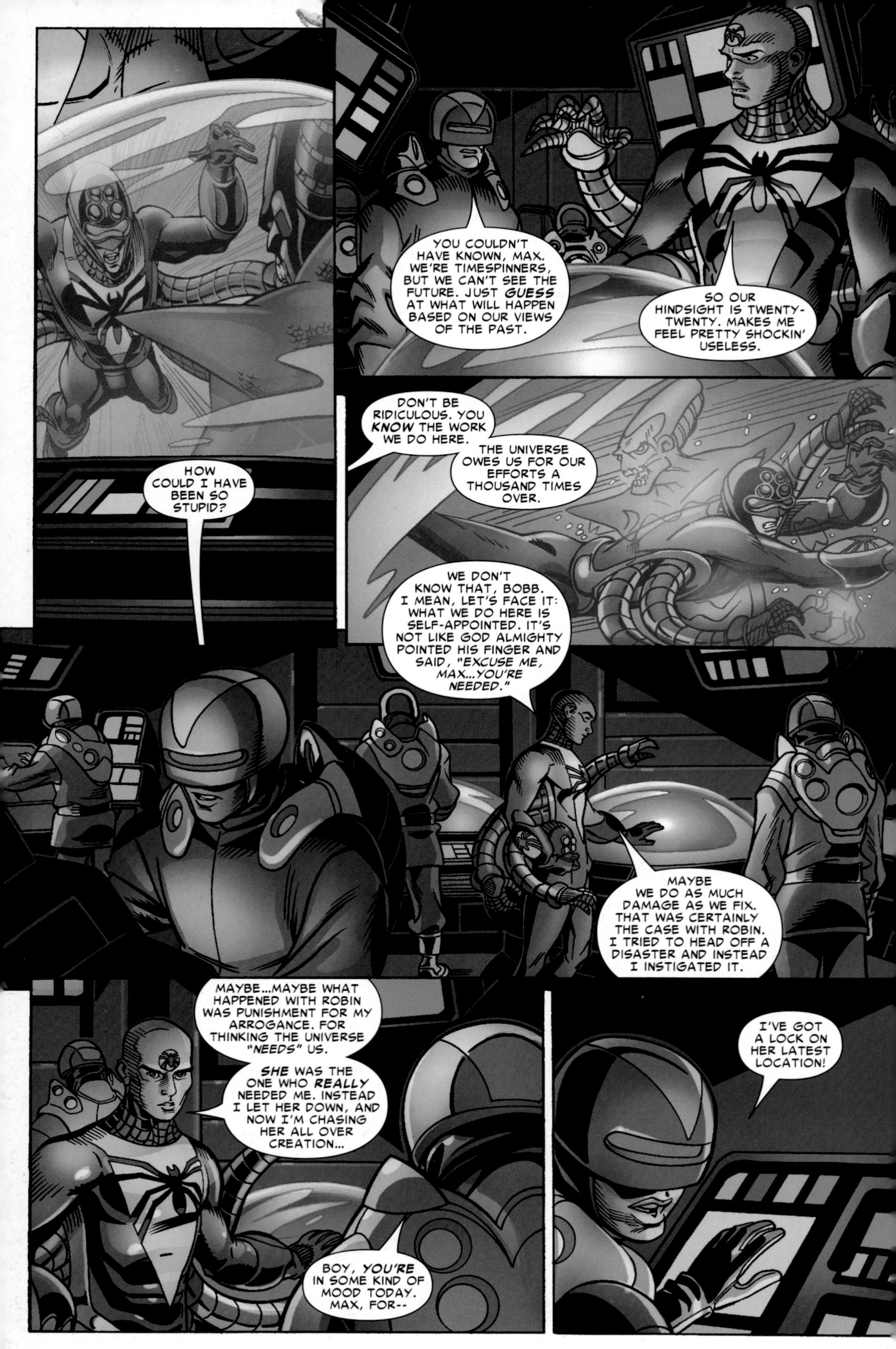
HOW COULD I HAVE BEEN SO STUPID?
YOU COULDN'T HAVE KNOWN, MAX. WE'RE TIMESPINNERS, BUT WE CAN'T SEE THE FUTURE. JUST GUESS AT WHAT WILL HAPPEN BASED ON OUR VIEWS OF THE PAST.
SO OUR HINDSIGHT IS TWENTY-TWENTY. MAKES ME FEEL PRETTY SHOCKIN' USELESS.
DON'T BE RIDICULOUS. YOU KNOW THE WORK WE DO HERE.
THE UNIVERSE OWES US FOR OUR EFFORTS A THOUSAND TIMES OVER.
WE DON'T KNOW THAT, BOBB. I MEAN, LET'S FACE IT: WHAT WE DO HERE IS SELF-APPOINTED. IT'S NOT LIKE GOD ALMIGHTY POINTED HIS FINGER AND SAID, "EXCUSE ME, MAX...YOU'RE NEEDED."
MAYBE WE DO AS MUCH DAMAGE AS WE FIX. THAT WAS CERTAINLY THE CASE WITH ROBIN. I TRIED TO HEAD OFF A DISASTER AND INSTEAD I INSTIGATED IT.
MAYBE...MAYBE WHAT HAPPENED WITH ROBIN WAS PUNISHMENT FOR MY ARROGANCE. FOR THINKING THE UNIVERSE "NEEDS" US.
SHE WAS THE ONE WHO REALLY NEEDED ME. INSTEAD I LET HER DOWN, AND NOW I'M CHASING HER ALL OVER CREATION...
BOY, YOU'RE IN SOME KIND OF MOOD TODAY. MAX, FOR--
I'VE GOT A LOCK ON HER LATEST LOCATION!

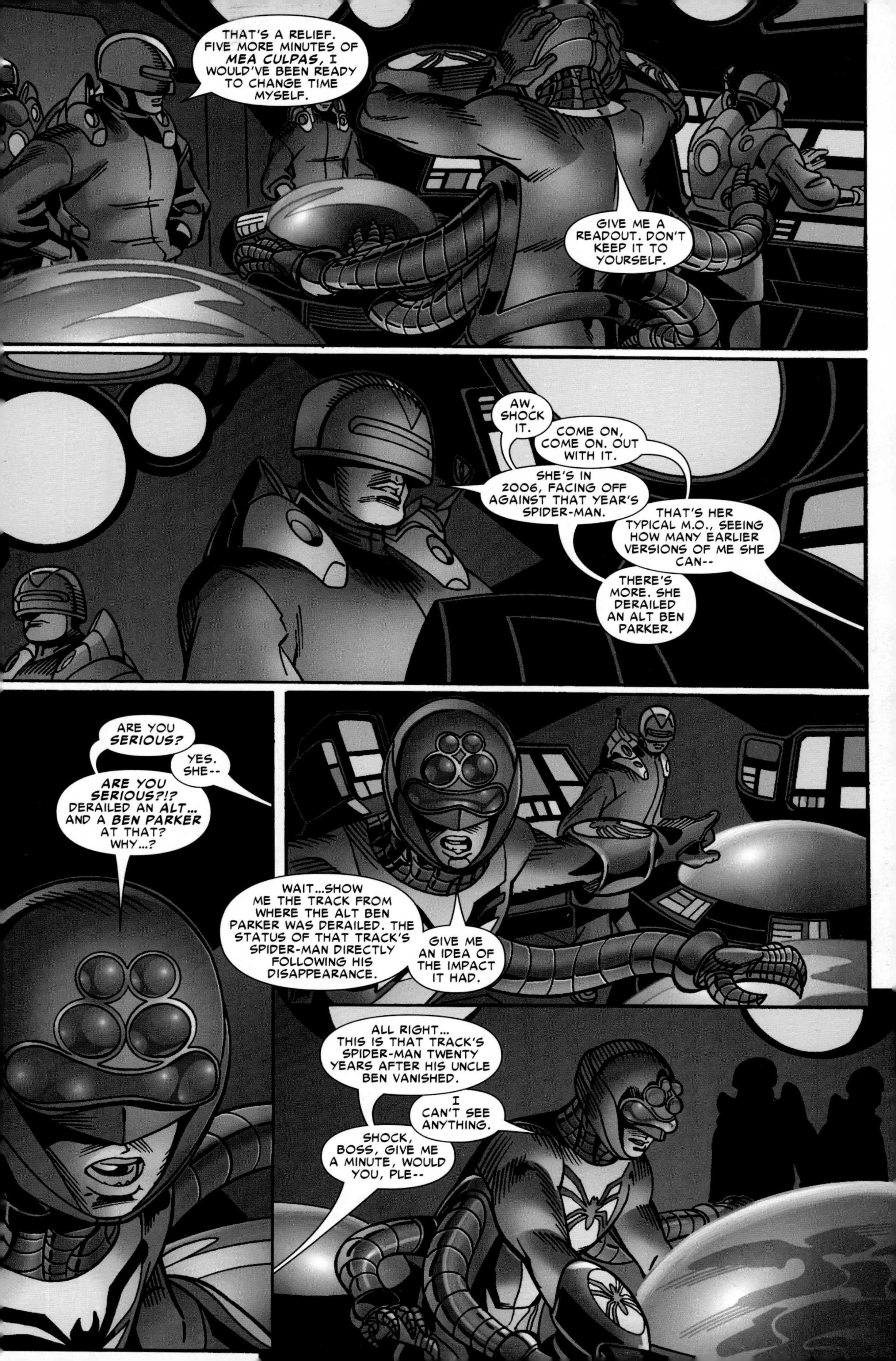

THAT'S A RELIEF. FIVE MORE MINUTES OF MEA CULPAS, I WOULD'VE BEEN READY TO CHANGE TIME MYSELF.
GIVE ME A READOUT. DON'T KEEP IT TO YOURSELF.
AW, SHOCK IT.
COME ON, COME ON. OUT WITH IT.
SHE'S IN 2006, FACING OFF AGAINST THAT YEAR'S SPIDER-MAN.
THAT'S HER TYPICAL M.O., SEEING HOW MANY EARLIER VERSIONS OF ME SHE CAN--
THERE'S MORE. SHE DERAILED AN ALT BEN PARKER.
ARE YOU SERIOUS?
YES. SHE--
ARE YOU SERIOUS?!? DERAILED AN ALT... AND A BEN PARKER AT THAT? WHY...?
WAIT...SHOW ME THE TRACK FROM WHERE THE ALT BEN PARKER WAS DERAILED. THE STATUS OF THAT TRACK'S SPIDER-MAN DIRECTLY FOLLOWING HIS DISAPPEARANCE.
GIVE ME AN IDEA OF THE IMPACT IT HAD.
ALL RIGHT... THIS IS THAT TRACK'S SPIDER-MAN TWENTY YEARS AFTER HIS UNCLE BEN VANISHED.
I CAN'T SEE ANYTHING.
SHOCK, BOSS, GIVE ME A MINUTE, WOULD YOU, PLE--

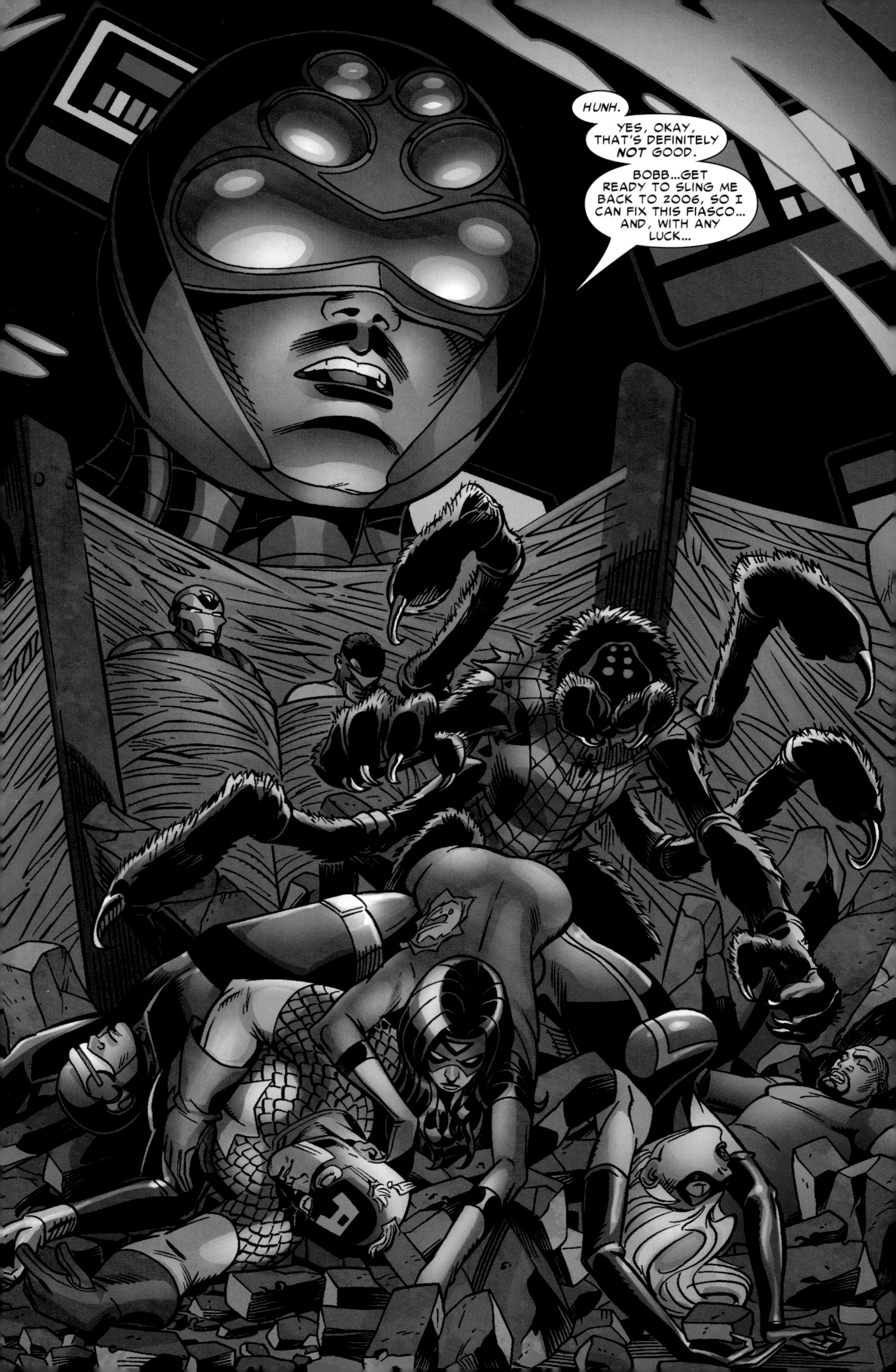
HUNH.
YES, OKAY, THAT'S DEFINITELY *NOT* GOOD.
BOBB...GET READY TO SLING ME BACK TO 2006, SO I CAN FIX THIS FIASCO... AND, WITH ANY LUCK...

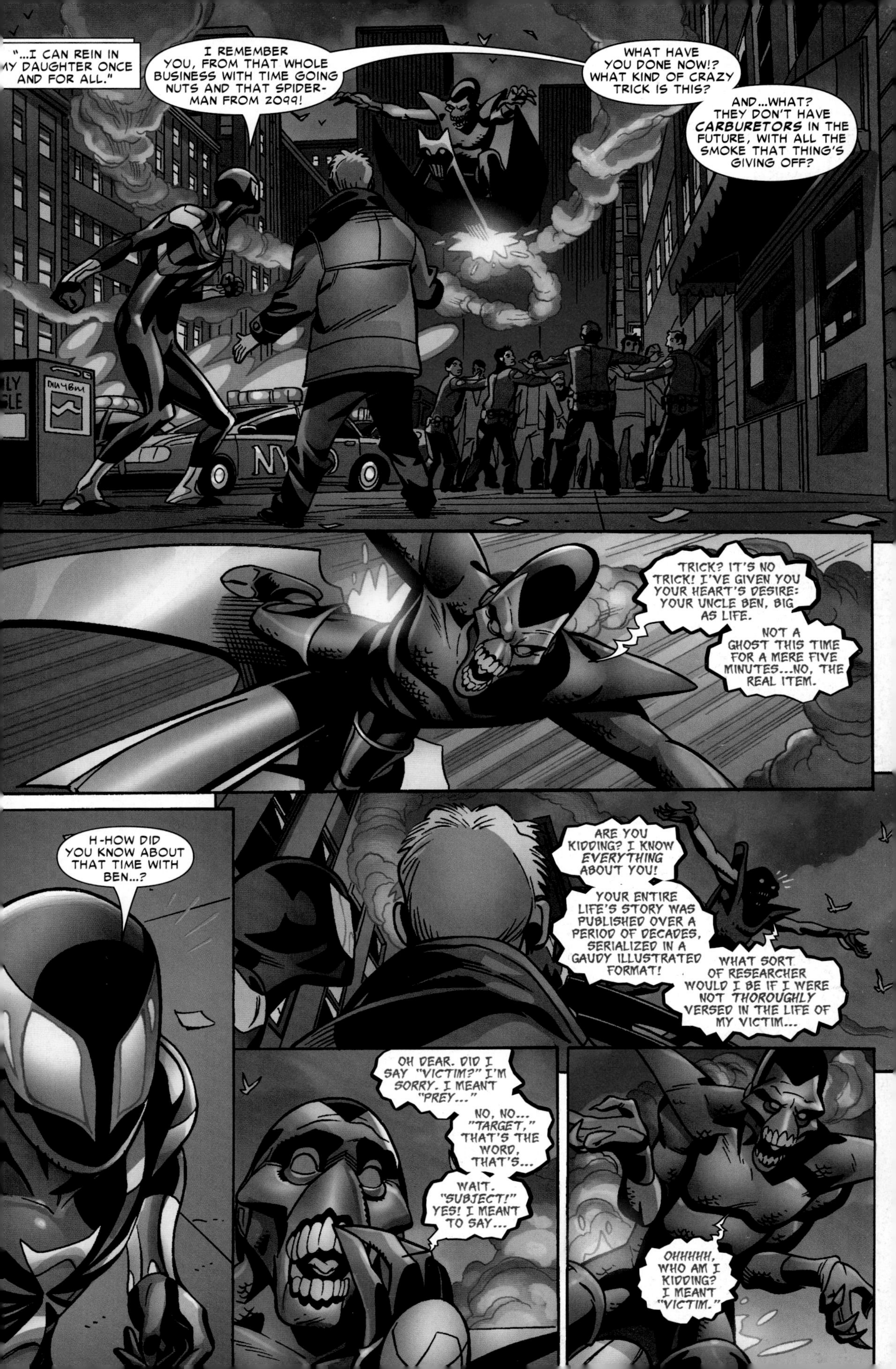
"...I CAN REIN IN MY DAUGHTER ONCE AND FOR ALL."
I REMEMBER YOU, FROM THAT WHOLE BUSINESS WITH TIME GOING NUTS AND THAT SPIDER-MAN FROM 2099!
WHAT HAVE YOU DONE NOW!? WHAT KIND OF CRAZY TRICK IS THIS?
AND...WHAT? THEY DON'T HAVE CARBURETORS IN THE FUTURE, WITH ALL THE SMOKE THAT THING'S GIVING OFF?
TRICK? IT'S NO TRICK! I'VE GIVEN YOU YOUR HEART'S DESIRE: YOUR UNCLE BEN, BIG AS LIFE.
NOT A GHOST THIS TIME FOR A MERE FIVE MINUTES...NO, THE REAL ITEM.
H-HOW DID YOU KNOW ABOUT THAT TIME WITH BEN...?
ARE YOU KIDDING? I KNOW EVERYTHING ABOUT YOU!
YOUR ENTIRE LIFE'S STORY WAS PUBLISHED OVER A PERIOD OF DECADES, SERIALIZED IN A GAUDY ILLUSTRATED FORMAT!
WHAT SORT OF RESEARCHER WOULD I BE IF I WERE NOT THOROUGHLY VERSED IN THE LIFE OF MY VICTIM...
OH DEAR. DID I SAY "VICTIM?" I'M SORRY. I MEANT "PREY..."
NO, NO... "TARGET," THAT'S THE WORD, THAT'S...
WAIT. "SUBJECT!" YES! I MEANT TO SAY...
OHHHHH, WHO AM I KIDDING? I MEANT "VICTIM."

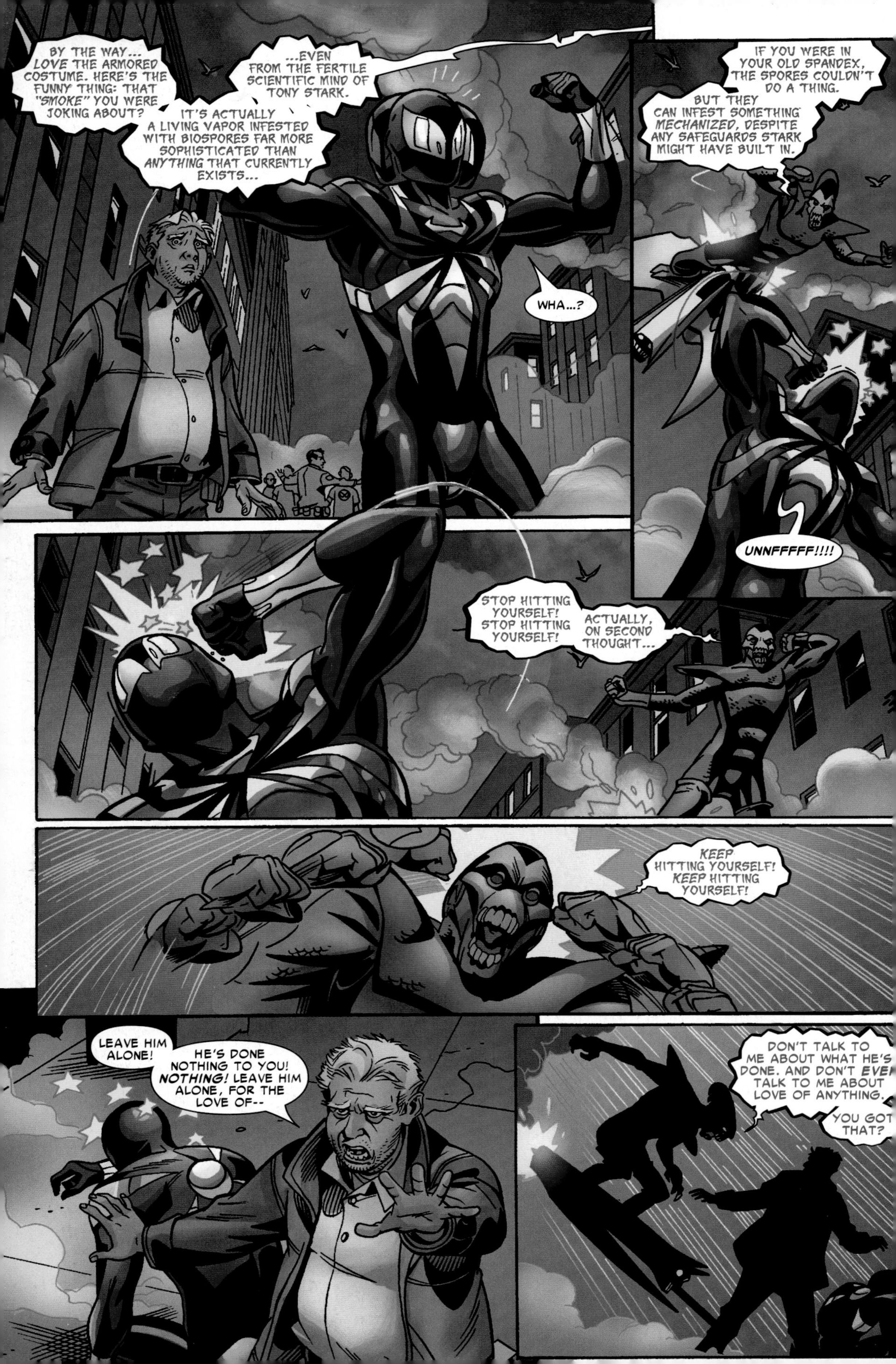
BY THE WAY... LOVE THE ARMORED COSTUME. HERE'S THE FUNNY THING: THAT "SMOKE" YOU WERE JOKING ABOUT?
IT'S ACTUALLY A LIVING VAPOR INFESTED WITH BIOSPORES FAR MORE SOPHISTICATED THAN ANYTHING THAT CURRENTLY EXISTS...
...EVEN FROM THE FERTILE SCIENTIFIC MIND OF TONY STARK.
WHA...?
IF YOU WERE IN YOUR OLD SPANDEX, THE SPORES COULDN'T DO A THING.
BUT THEY CAN INFEST SOMETHING MECHANIZED, DESPITE ANY SAFEGUARDS STARK MIGHT HAVE BUILT IN.
UNNFFFFF!!!!
STOP HITTING YOURSELF! STOP HITTING YOURSELF!
ACTUALLY, ON SECOND THOUGHT...
KEEP HITTING YOURSELF! KEEP HITTING YOURSELF!
LEAVE HIM ALONE!
HE'S DONE NOTHING TO YOU! NOTHING! LEAVE HIM ALONE, FOR THE LOVE OF--
DON'T TALK TO ME ABOUT WHAT HE'S DONE. AND DON'T EVEN TALK TO ME ABOUT LOVE OF ANYTHING.
YOU GOT THAT?

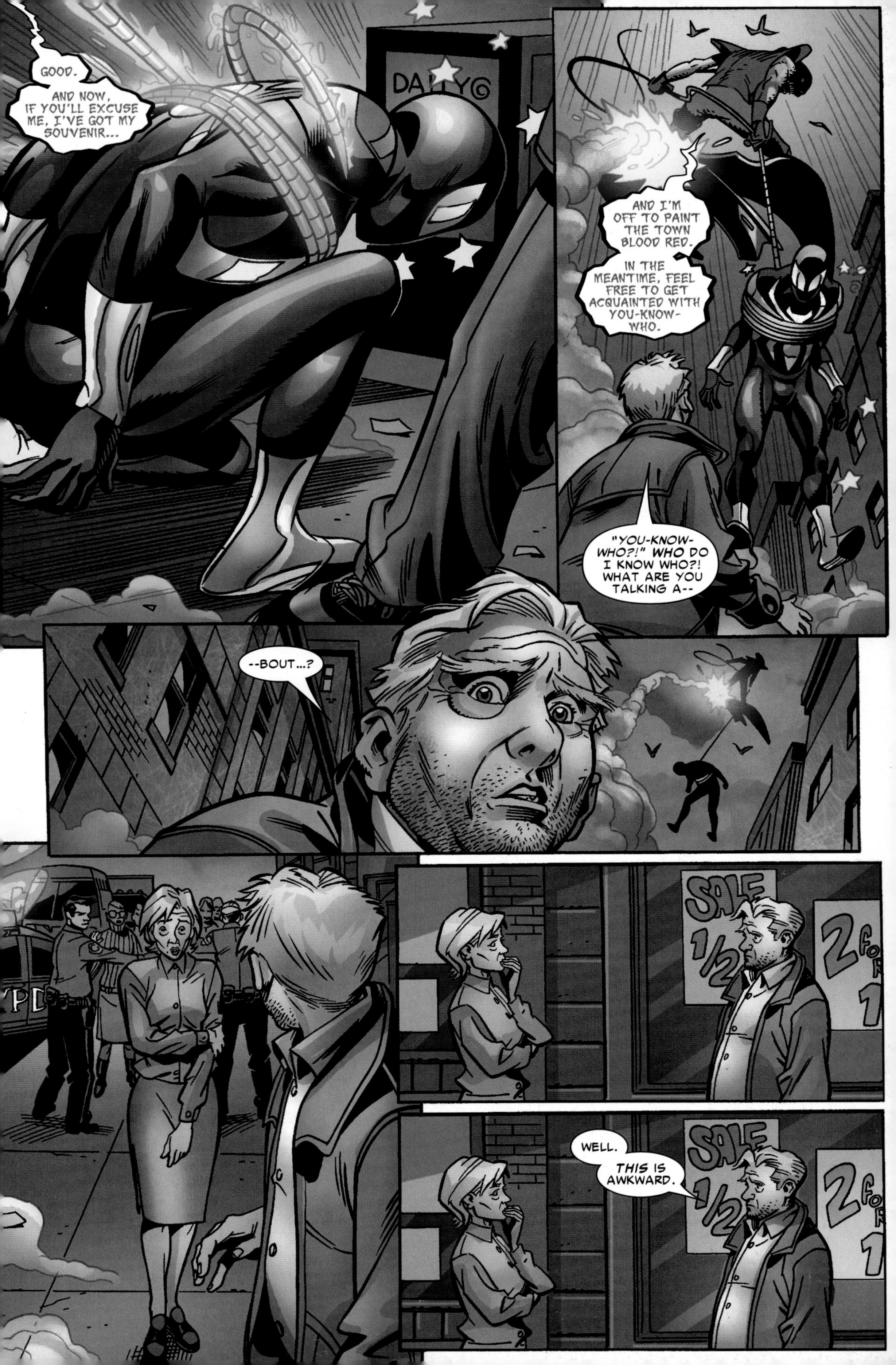

GOOD.
AND NOW, IF YOU'LL EXCUSE ME, I'VE GOT MY SOUVENIR...
AND I'M OFF TO PAINT THE TOWN BLOOD RED.
IN THE MEANTIME, FEEL FREE TO GET ACQUAINTED WITH YOU-KNOW-WHO.
"YOU-KNOW-WHO?!" WHO DO I KNOW WHO?! WHAT ARE YOU TALKING A--
--BOUT...?
DAILY G
SALE
1/2
2 FOR 1
WELL.
THIS IS AWKWARD.

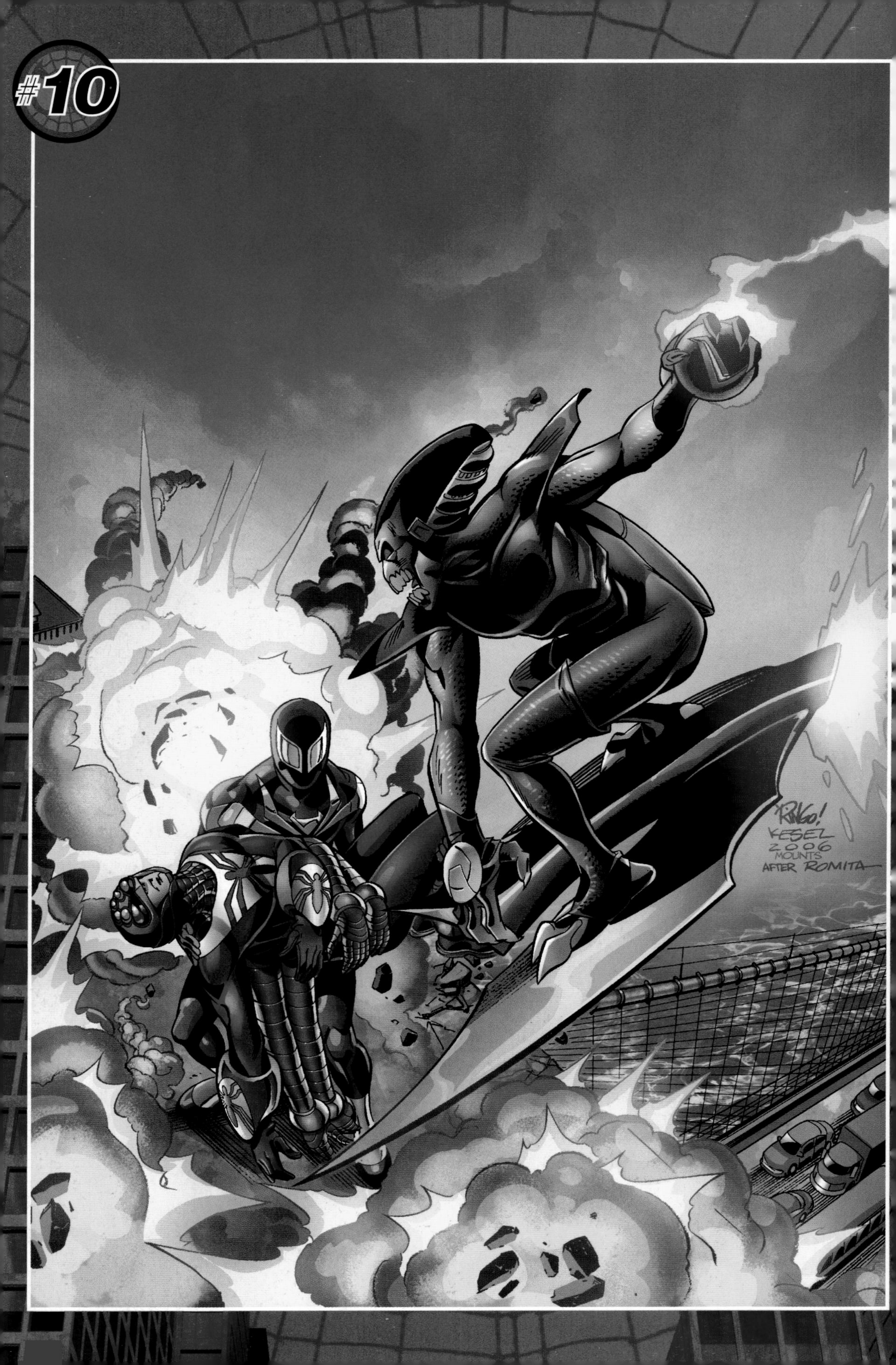
#10
RINGO!
KESEL
2006
MOUNTS
AFTER ROMITA

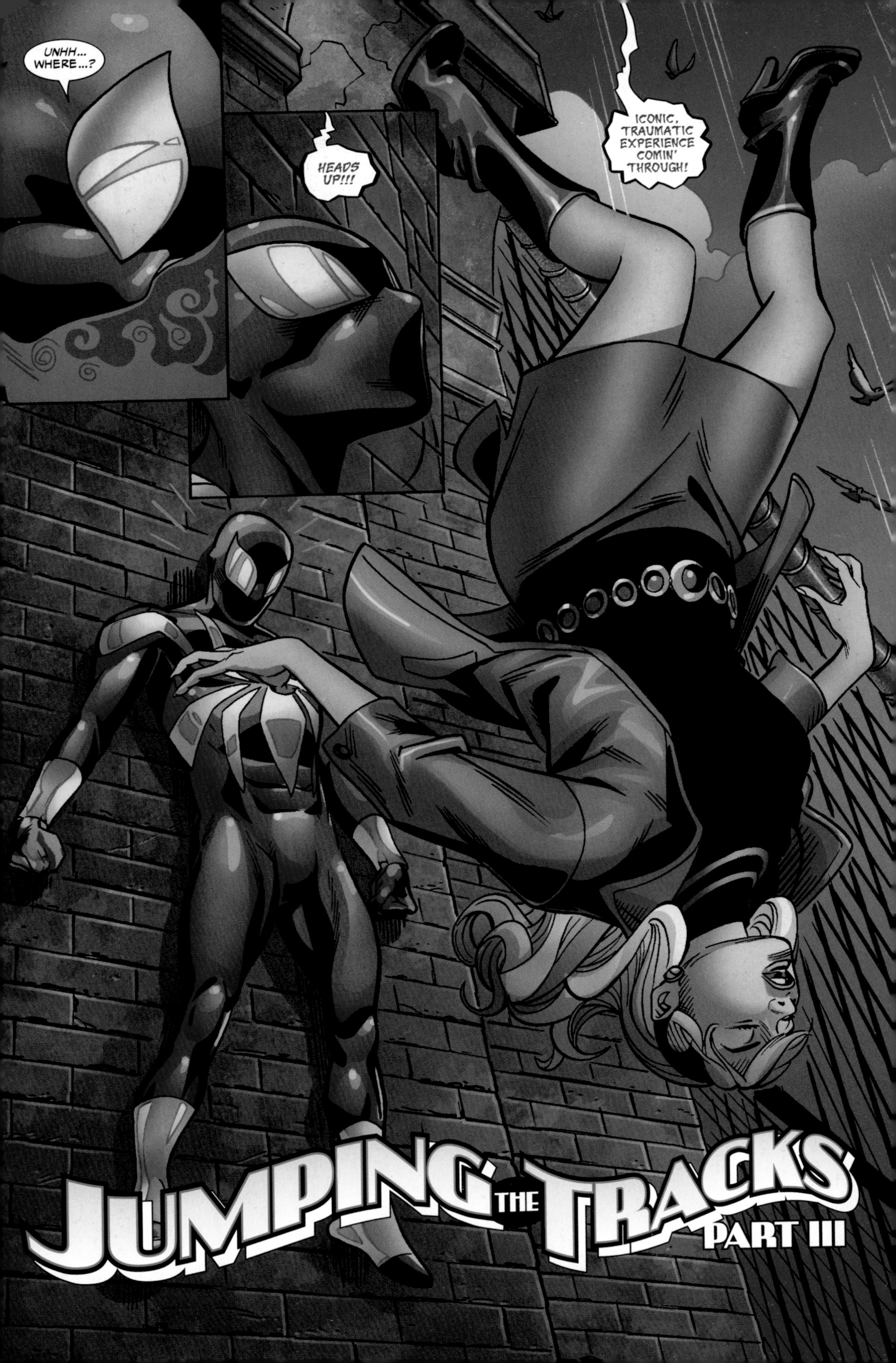
UNHH... WHERE...?
HEADS UP!!!
ICONIC, TRAUMATIC EXPERIENCE COMIN' THROUGH!
JUMPING THE TRACKS
PART III

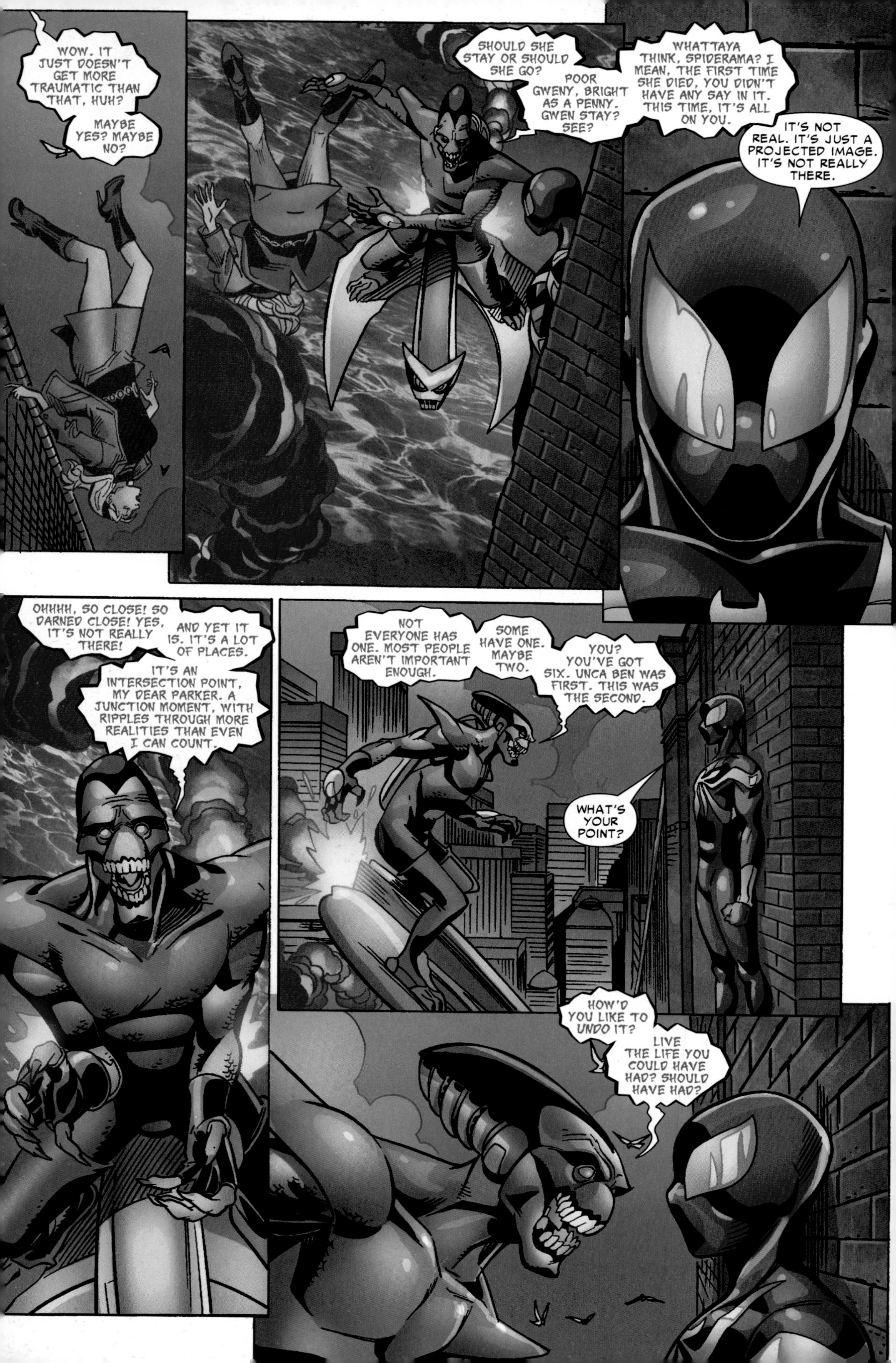
WOW. IT JUST DOESN'T GET MORE TRAUMATIC THAN THAT, HUH?
MAYBE YES? MAYBE NO?
SHOULD SHE STAY OR SHOULD SHE GO?
POOR GWENY, BRIGHT AS A PENNY. GWEN STAY? SEE?
WHATTAYA THINK, SPIDERAMA? I MEAN, THE FIRST TIME SHE DIED, YOU DIDN'T HAVE ANY SAY IN IT. THIS TIME, IT'S ALL ON YOU.
IT'S NOT REAL. IT'S JUST A PROJECTED IMAGE. IT'S NOT REALLY THERE.
OHHHH, SO CLOSE! SO DARNED CLOSE! YES, IT'S NOT REALLY THERE!
AND YET IT IS. IT'S A LOT OF PLACES.
IT'S AN INTERSECTION POINT, MY DEAR PARKER. A JUNCTION MOMENT, WITH RIPPLES THROUGH MORE REALITIES THAN EVEN I CAN COUNT.
NOT EVERYONE HAS ONE. MOST PEOPLE AREN'T IMPORTANT ENOUGH.
SOME HAVE ONE. MAYBE TWO.
YOU? YOU'VE GOT SIX. UNCA BEN WAS FIRST. THIS WAS THE SECOND.
WHAT'S YOUR POINT?
HOW'D YOU LIKE TO UNDO IT?
LIVE THE LIFE YOU COULD HAVE HAD? SHOULD HAVE HAD?

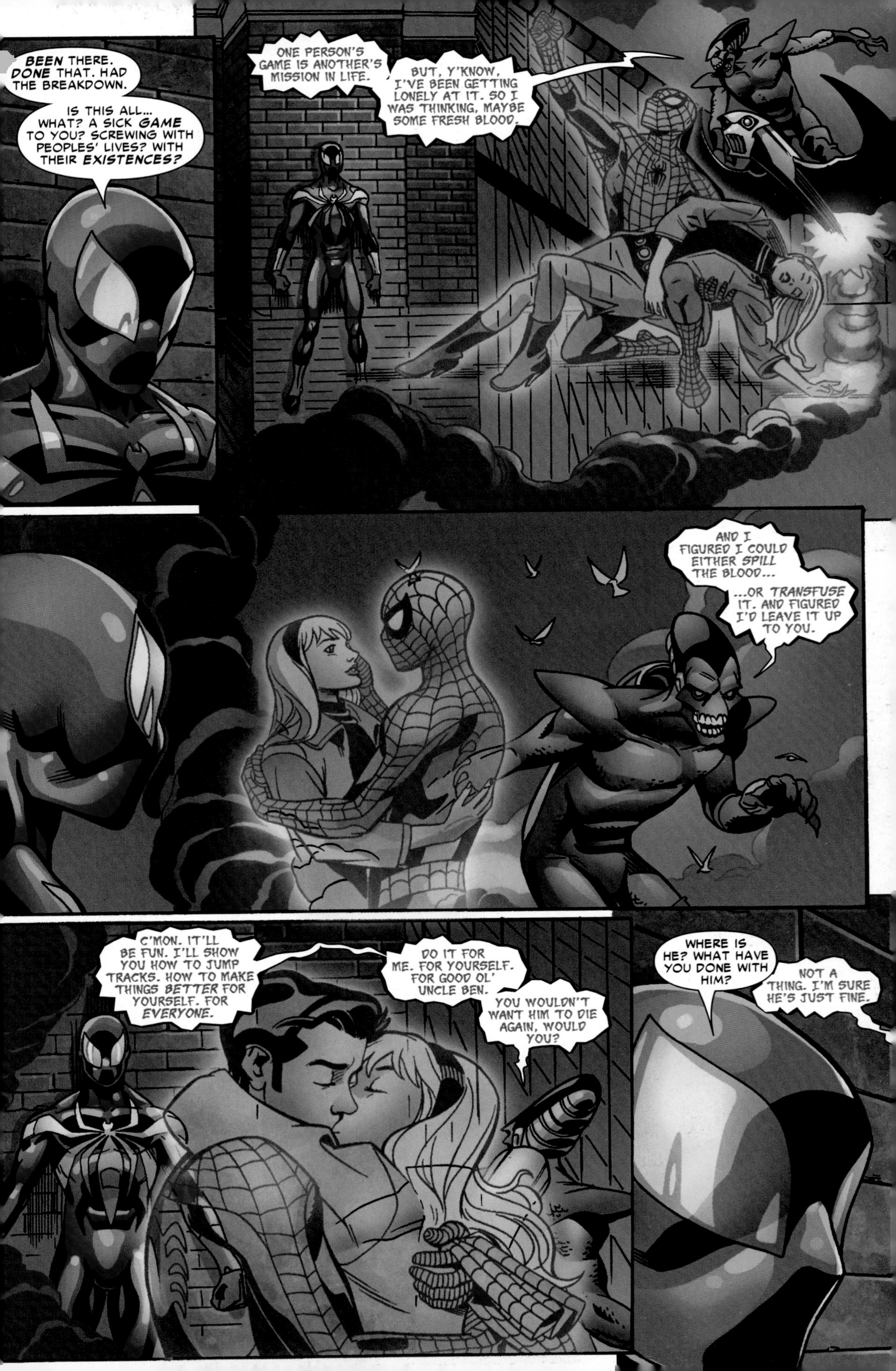
BEEN THERE. DONE THAT. HAD THE BREAKDOWN.
IS THIS ALL... WHAT? A SICK GAME TO YOU? SCREWING WITH PEOPLES' LIVES? WITH THEIR EXISTENCES?
ONE PERSON'S GAME IS ANOTHER'S MISSION IN LIFE.
BUT, Y'KNOW, I'VE BEEN GETTING LONELY AT IT. SO I WAS THINKING, MAYBE SOME FRESH BLOOD.
AND I FIGURED I COULD EITHER SPILL THE BLOOD...
...OR TRANSFUSE IT. AND FIGURED I'D LEAVE IT UP TO YOU.
C'MON. IT'LL BE FUN. I'LL SHOW YOU HOW TO JUMP TRACKS. HOW TO MAKE THINGS BETTER FOR YOURSELF. FOR EVERYONE.
DO IT FOR ME. FOR YOURSELF. FOR GOOD OL' UNCLE BEN.
YOU WOULDN'T WANT HIM TO DIE AGAIN, WOULD YOU?
WHERE IS HE? WHAT HAVE YOU DONE WITH HIM?
NOT A THING. I'M SURE HE'S JUST FINE.

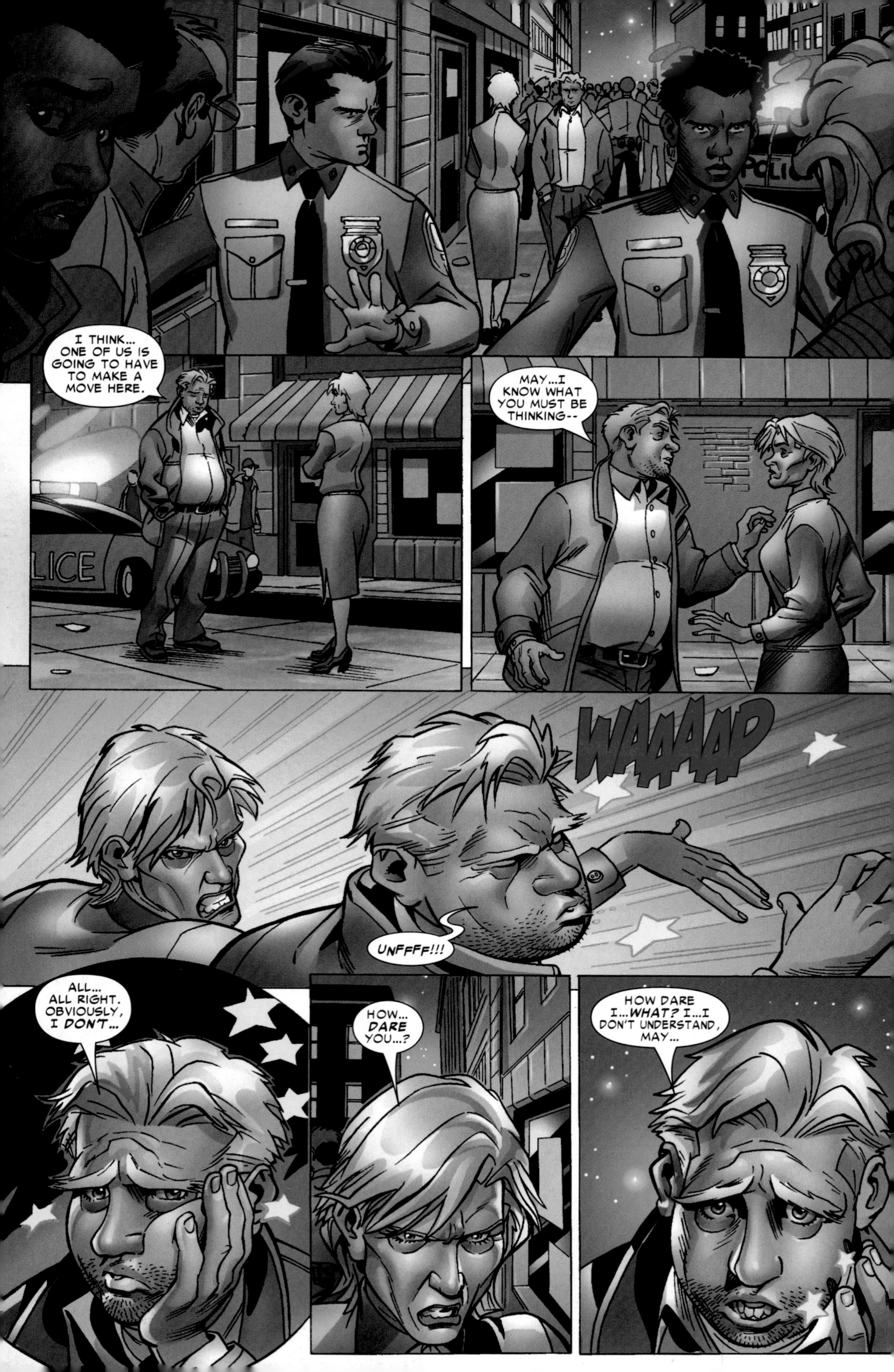

I THINK... ONE OF US IS GOING TO HAVE TO MAKE A MOVE HERE.
LICE
MAY...I KNOW WHAT YOU MUST BE THINKING--
WAAAAP
UNFFFF!!!
ALL... ALL RIGHT. OBVIOUSLY, I DON'T...
HOW... DARE YOU...?
HOW DARE I...WHAT? I...I DON'T UNDERSTAND, MAY...

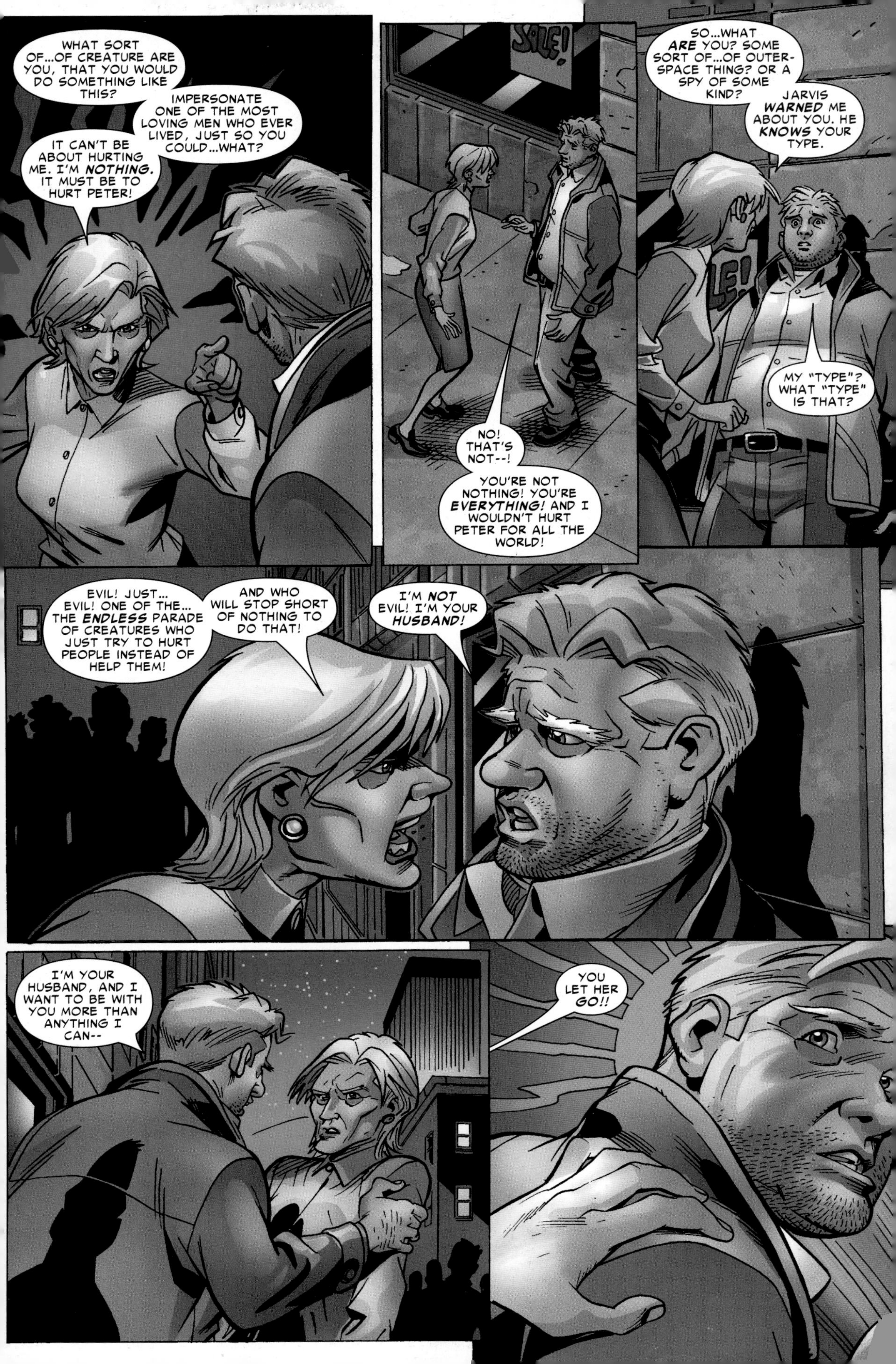
WHAT SORT OF...OF CREATURE ARE YOU, THAT YOU WOULD DO SOMETHING LIKE THIS?
IMPERSONATE ONE OF THE MOST LOVING MEN WHO EVER LIVED, JUST SO YOU COULD...WHAT?
IT CAN'T BE ABOUT HURTING ME. I'M NOTHING. IT MUST BE TO HURT PETER!
SALE!
NO! THAT'S NOT--!
YOU'RE NOT NOTHING! YOU'RE EVERYTHING! AND I WOULDN'T HURT PETER FOR ALL THE WORLD!
SO...WHAT ARE YOU? SOME SORT OF...OF OUTER-SPACE THING? OR A SPY OF SOME KIND?
JARVIS WARNED ME ABOUT YOU. HE KNOWS YOUR TYPE.
MY "TYPE"? WHAT "TYPE" IS THAT?
EVIL! JUST... EVIL! ONE OF THE... THE ENDLESS PARADE OF CREATURES WHO JUST TRY TO HURT PEOPLE INSTEAD OF HELP THEM!
AND WHO WILL STOP SHORT OF NOTHING TO DO THAT!
I'M NOT EVIL! I'M YOUR HUSBAND!
I'M YOUR HUSBAND, AND I WANT TO BE WITH YOU MORE THAN ANYTHING I CAN--
YOU LET HER GO!!

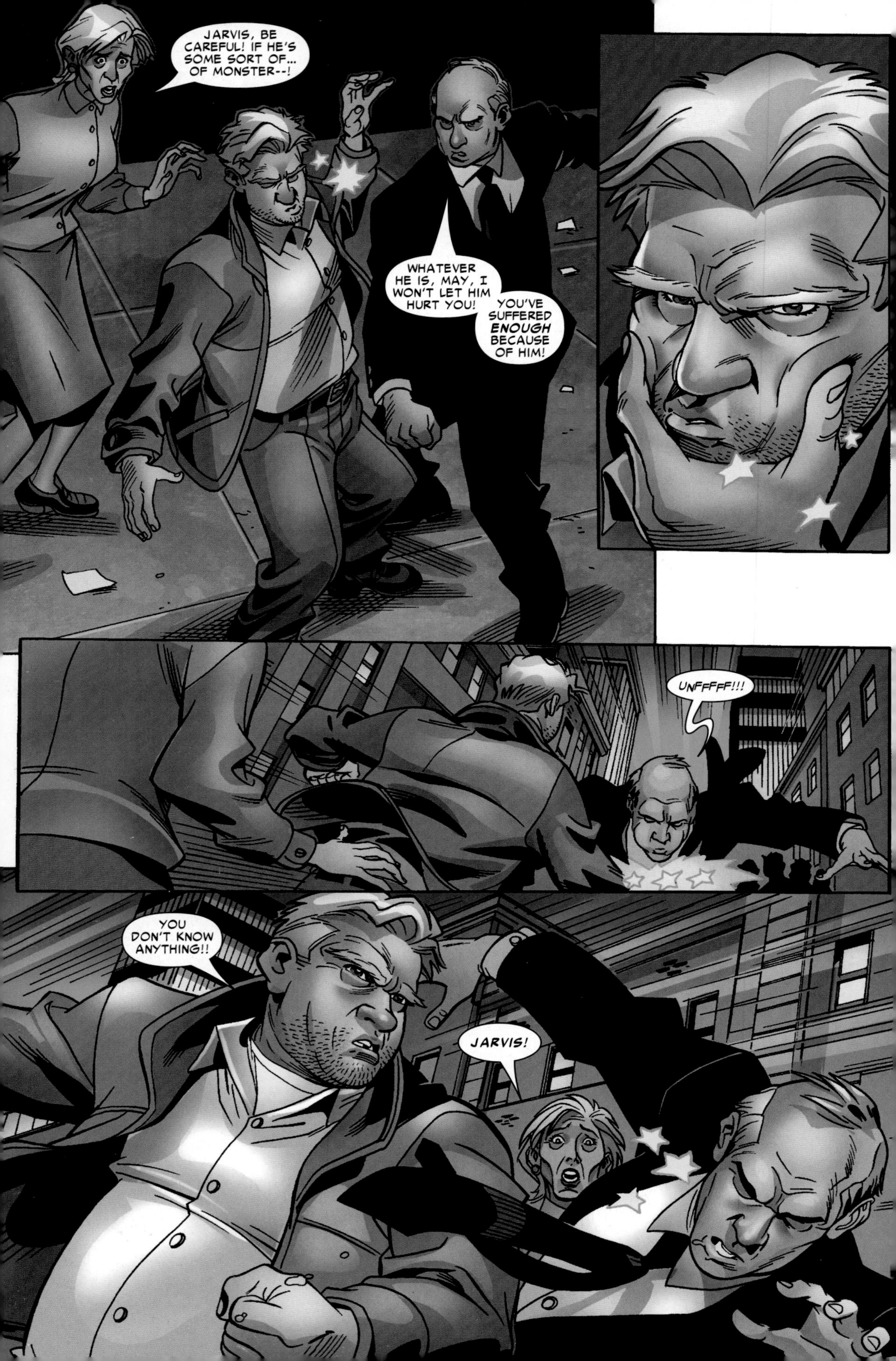
JARVIS, BE CAREFUL! IF HE'S SOME SORT OF... OF MONSTER--!
WHATEVER HE IS, MAY, I WON'T LET HIM HURT YOU!
YOU'VE SUFFERED ENOUGH BECAUSE OF HIM!
UNFFFFF!!!
YOU DON'T KNOW ANYTHING!!
JARVIS!

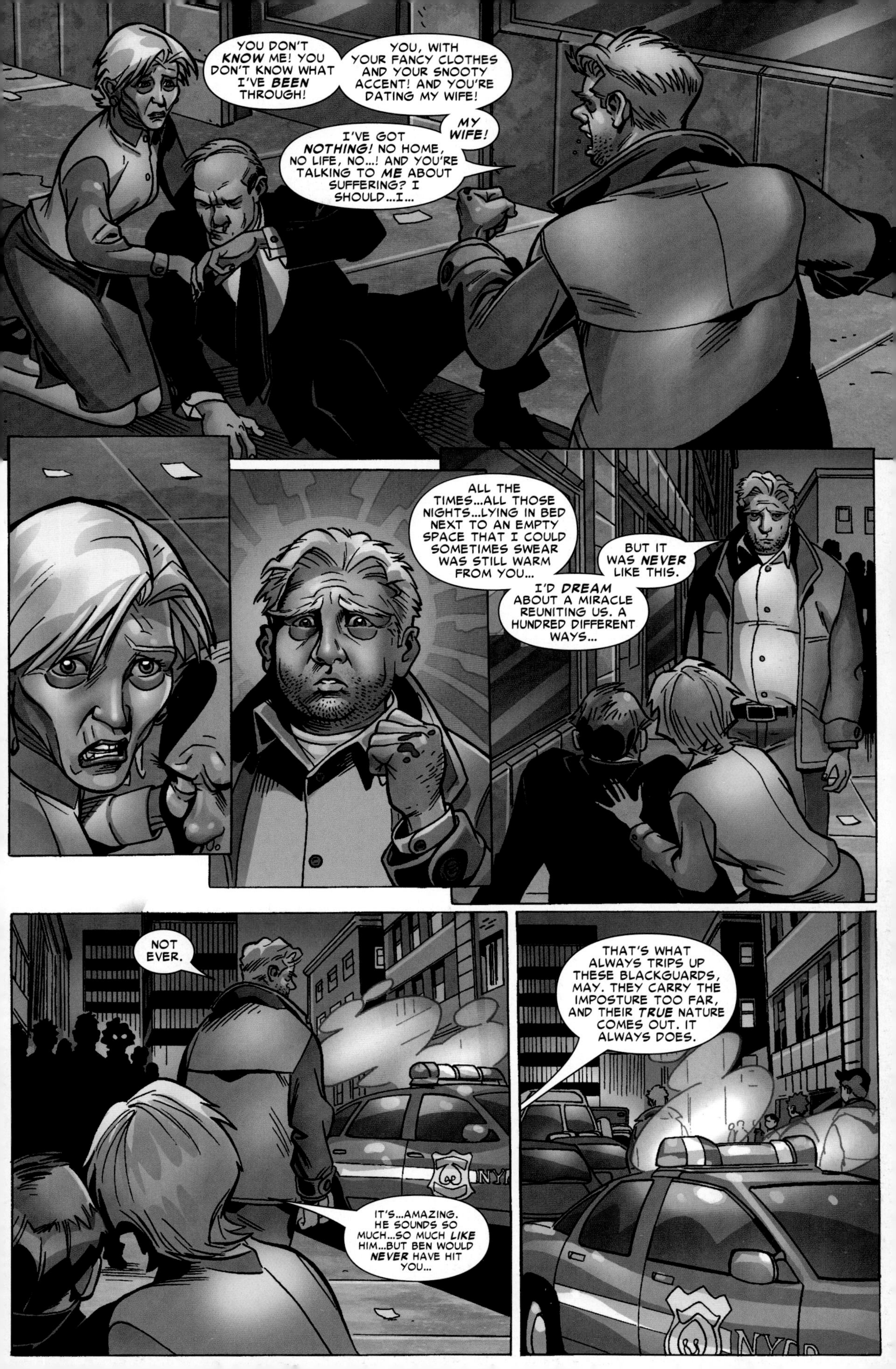

YOU DON'T ***KNOW*** ME! YOU DON'T KNOW WHAT I'VE ***BEEN*** THROUGH!
YOU, WITH YOUR FANCY CLOTHES AND YOUR SNOOTY ACCENT! AND YOU'RE DATING MY WIFE!
MY WIFE!
I'VE GOT ***NOTHING!*** NO HOME, NO LIFE, NO...! AND YOU'RE TALKING TO ***ME*** ABOUT SUFFERING? I SHOULD...I...
ALL THE TIMES...ALL THOSE NIGHTS...LYING IN BED NEXT TO AN EMPTY SPACE THAT I COULD SOMETIMES SWEAR WAS STILL WARM FROM YOU...
I'D ***DREAM*** ABOUT A MIRACLE REUNITING US. A HUNDRED DIFFERENT WAYS...
BUT IT WAS ***NEVER*** LIKE THIS.
NOT EVER.
IT'S...AMAZING. HE SOUNDS SO MUCH...SO MUCH ***LIKE*** HIM...BUT BEN WOULD ***NEVER*** HAVE HIT YOU...
THAT'S WHAT ALWAYS TRIPS UP THESE BLACKGUARDS, MAY. THEY CARRY THE IMPOSTURE TOO FAR, AND THEIR ***TRUE*** NATURE COMES OUT. IT ALWAYS DOES.

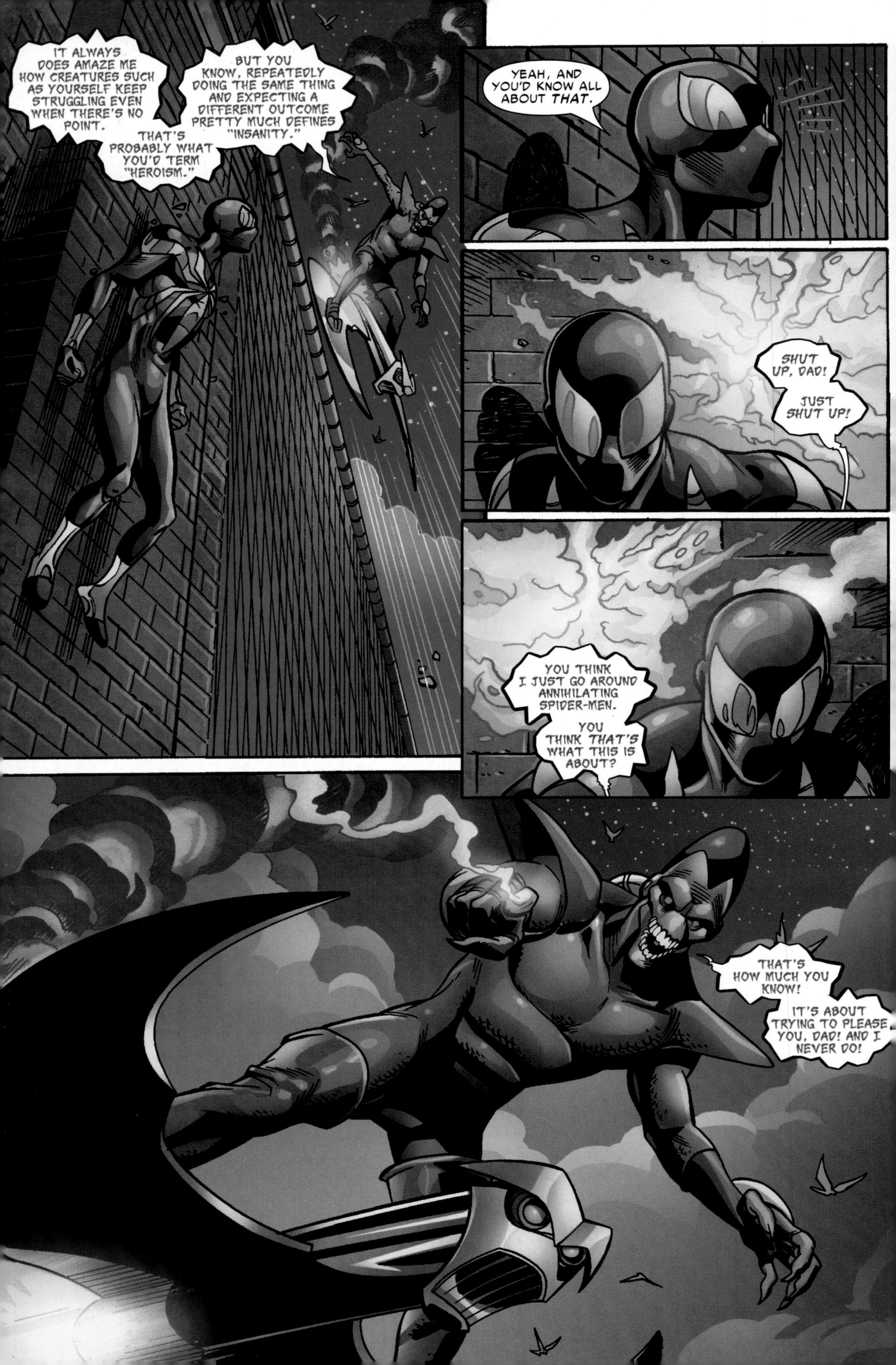
IT ALWAYS DOES AMAZE ME HOW CREATURES SUCH AS YOURSELF KEEP STRUGGLING EVEN WHEN THERE'S NO POINT.
THAT'S PROBABLY WHAT YOU'D TERM "HEROISM."
BUT YOU KNOW, REPEATEDLY DOING THE SAME THING AND EXPECTING A DIFFERENT OUTCOME PRETTY MUCH DEFINES "INSANITY."
YEAH, AND YOU'D KNOW ALL ABOUT THAT.
SHUT UP, DAD!
JUST SHUT UP!
YOU THINK I JUST GO AROUND ANNIHILATING SPIDER-MEN.
YOU THINK THAT'S WHAT THIS IS ABOUT?
THAT'S HOW MUCH YOU KNOW!
IT'S ABOUT TRYING TO PLEASE YOU, DAD! AND I NEVER DO!

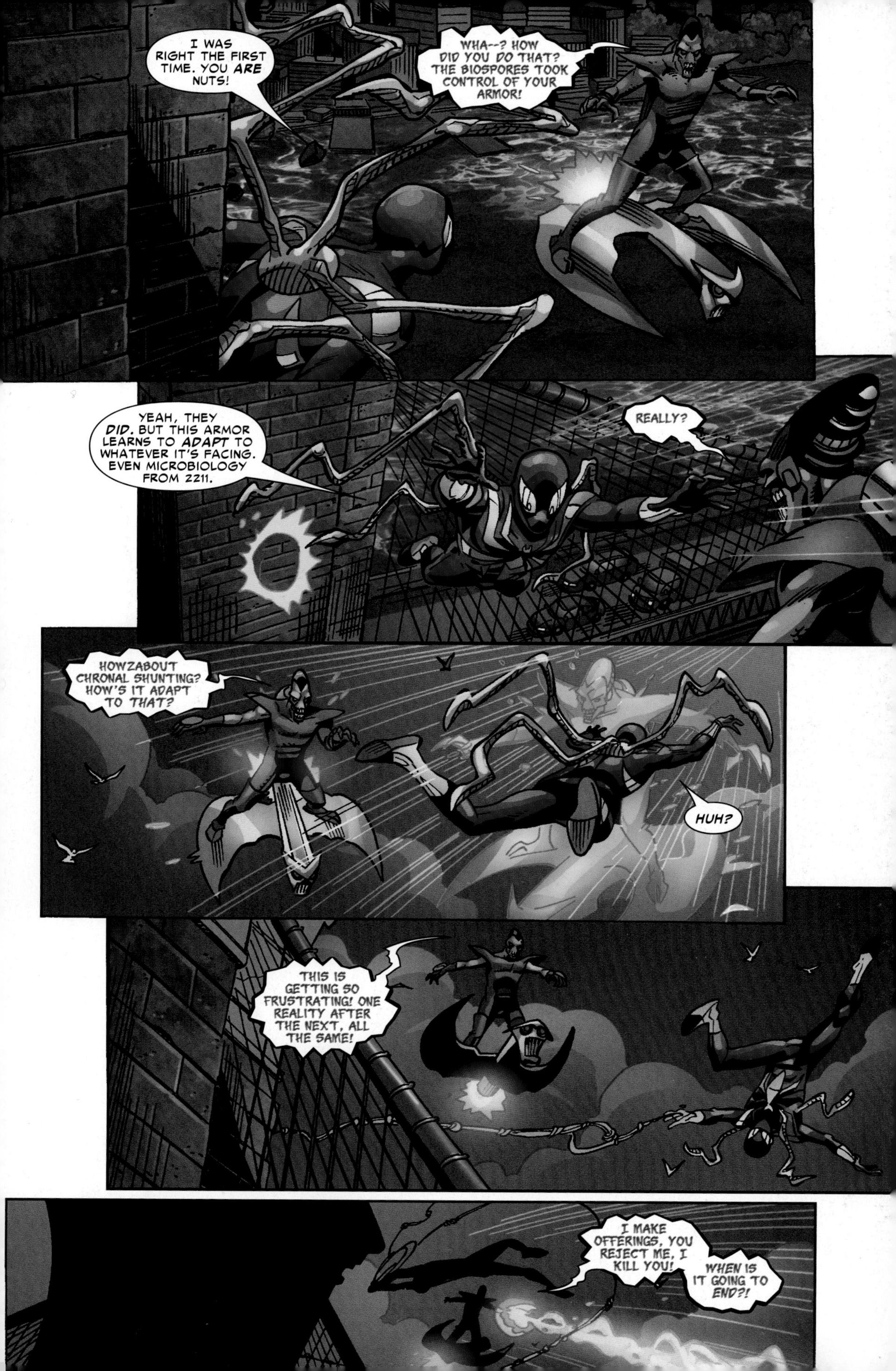
I WAS RIGHT THE FIRST TIME. YOU ARE NUTS!
WHA--? HOW DID YOU DO THAT? THE BIOSPORES TOOK CONTROL OF YOUR ARMOR!
YEAH, THEY DID. BUT THIS ARMOR LEARNS TO ADAPT TO WHATEVER IT'S FACING. EVEN MICROBIOLOGY FROM 2211.
REALLY?
HOWZABOUT CHRONAL SHUNTING? HOW'S IT ADAPT TO THAT?
HUH?
THIS IS GETTING SO FRUSTRATING! ONE REALITY AFTER THE NEXT, ALL THE SAME!
I MAKE OFFERINGS, YOU REJECT ME, I KILL YOU!
WHEN IS IT GOING TO END?!

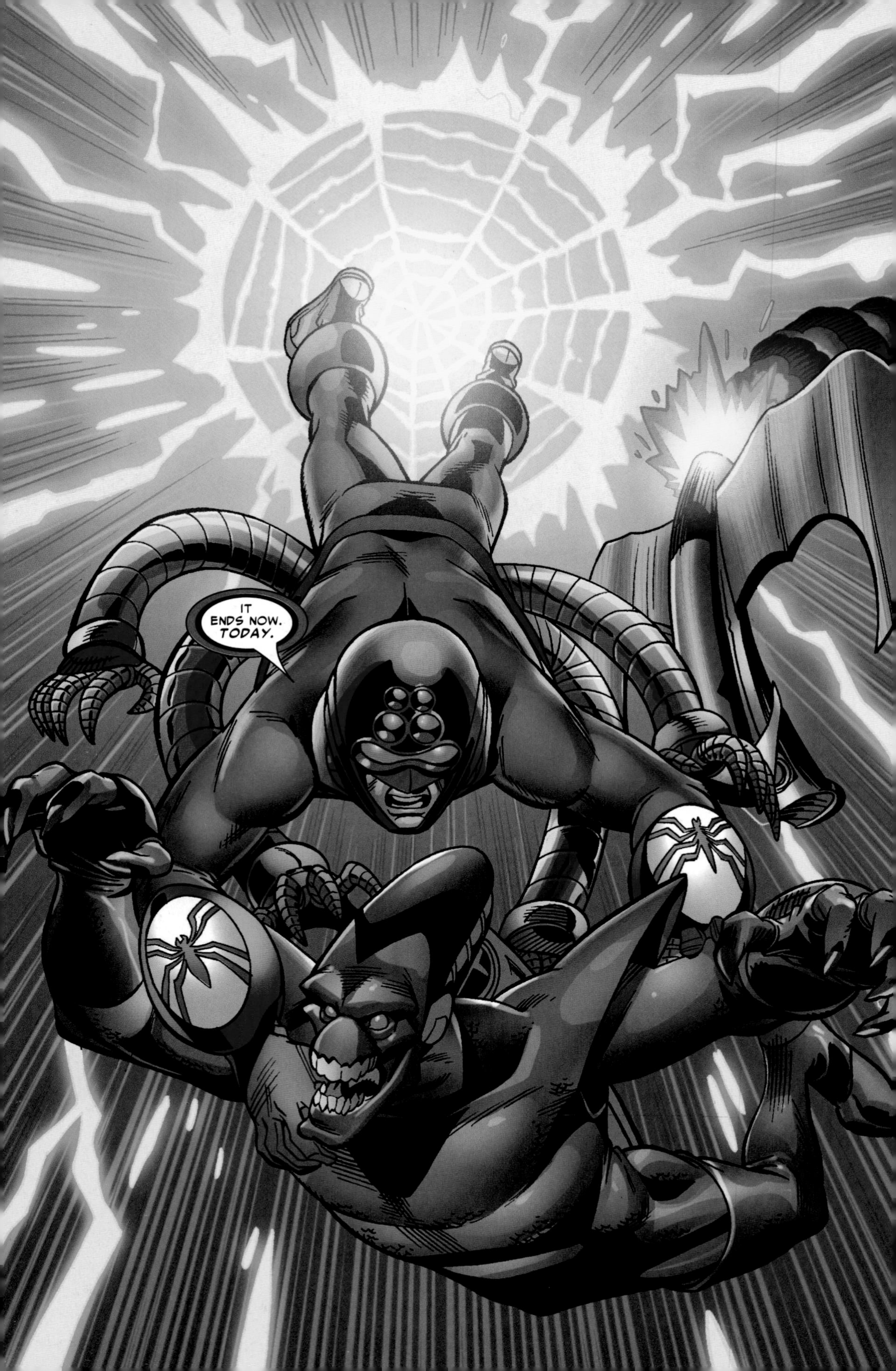
IT ENDS NOW. TODAY.

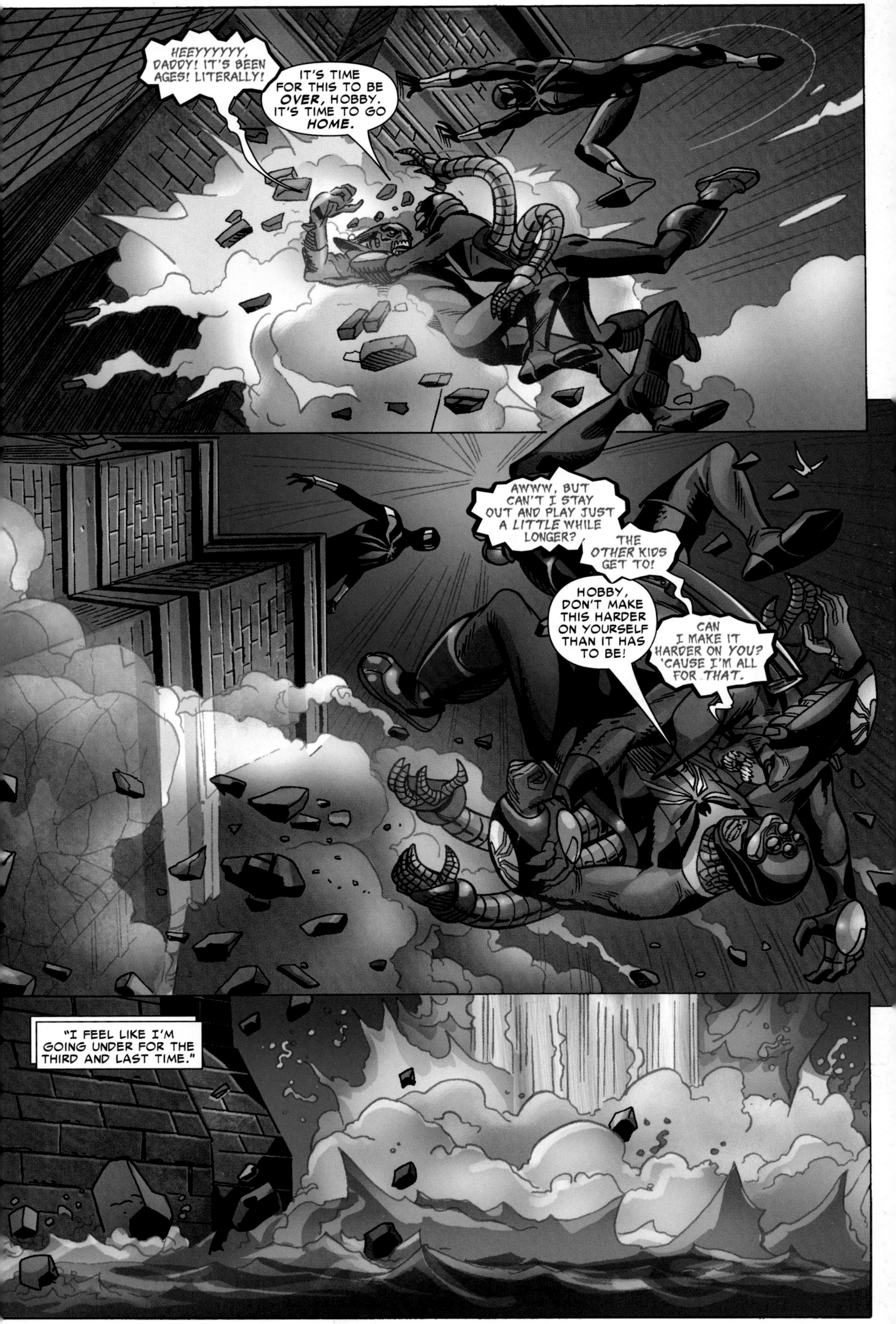
HEEYYYYYYY, DADDY! IT'S BEEN AGES! LITERALLY!
IT'S TIME FOR THIS TO BE OVER, HOBBY. IT'S TIME TO GO HOME.
AWWW, BUT CAN'T I STAY OUT AND PLAY JUST A LITTLE WHILE LONGER?
THE OTHER KIDS GET TO!
HOBBY, DON'T MAKE THIS HARDER ON YOURSELF THAN IT HAS TO BE!
CAN I MAKE IT HARDER ON YOU? 'CAUSE I'M ALL FOR THAT.
"I FEEL LIKE I'M GOING UNDER FOR THE THIRD AND LAST TIME."

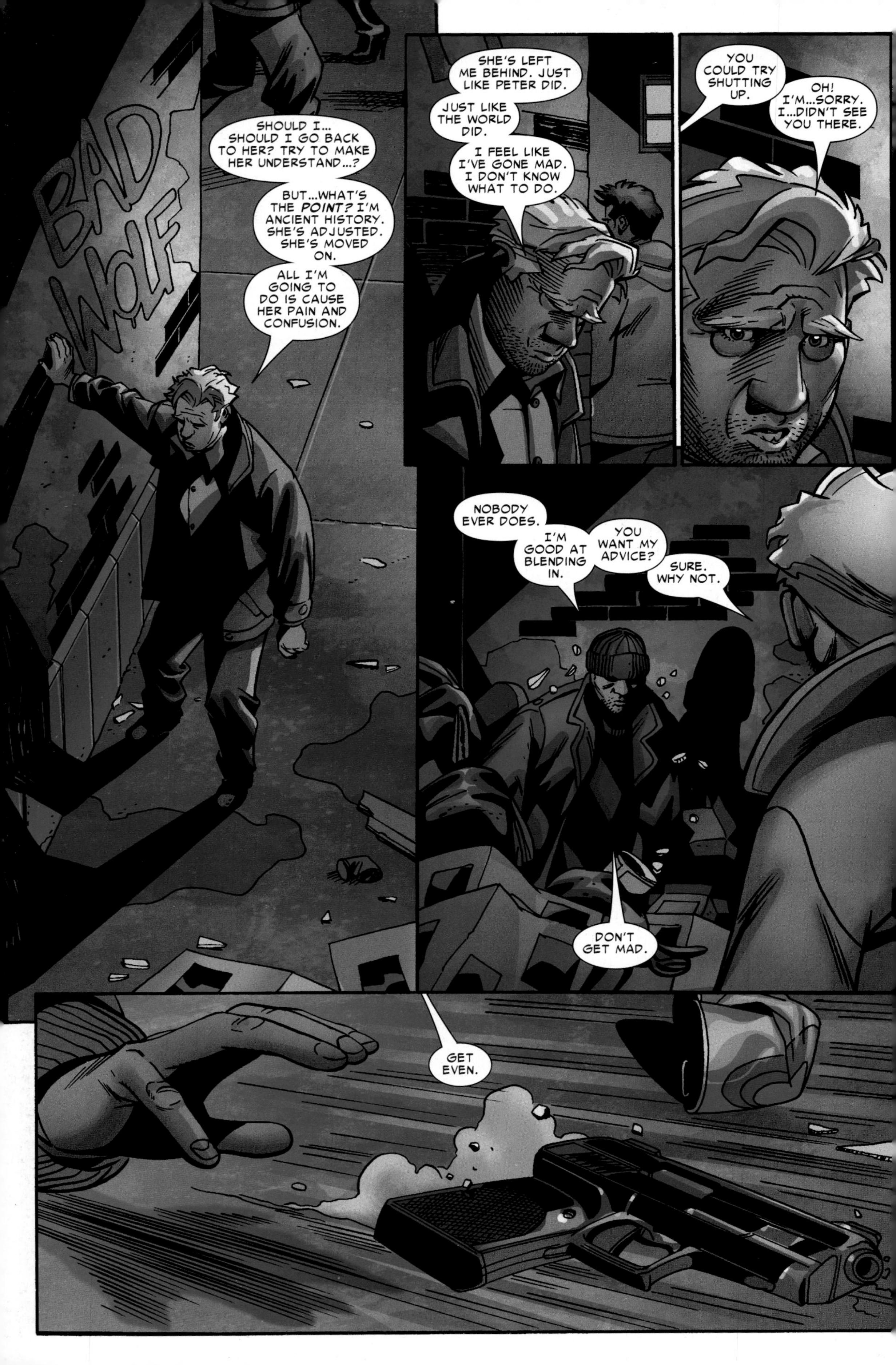
BAD WOLF
SHOULD I... SHOULD I GO BACK TO HER? TRY TO MAKE HER UNDERSTAND...?
BUT...WHAT'S THE POINT? I'M ANCIENT HISTORY. SHE'S ADJUSTED. SHE'S MOVED ON.
ALL I'M GOING TO DO IS CAUSE HER PAIN AND CONFUSION.
SHE'S LEFT ME BEHIND. JUST LIKE PETER DID.
JUST LIKE THE WORLD DID.
I FEEL LIKE I'VE GONE MAD. I DON'T KNOW WHAT TO DO.
YOU COULD TRY SHUTTING UP.
OH! I'M...SORRY. I...DIDN'T SEE YOU THERE.
NOBODY EVER DOES.
I'M GOOD AT BLENDING IN.
YOU WANT MY ADVICE?
SURE. WHY NOT.
DON'T GET MAD.
GET EVEN.

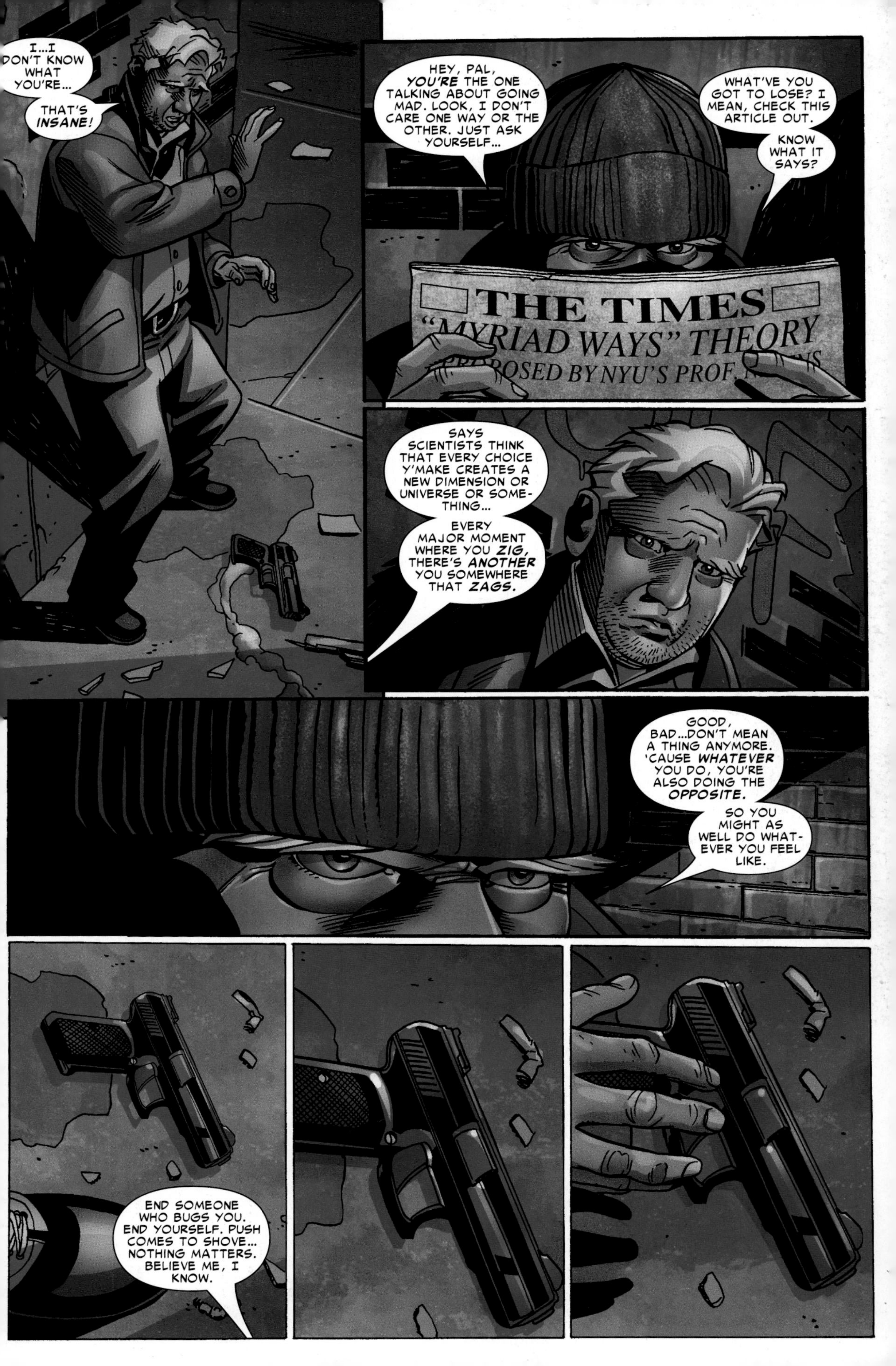

I...I DON'T KNOW WHAT YOU'RE...
THAT'S *INSANE!*
HEY, PAL, *YOU'RE* THE ONE TALKING ABOUT GOING MAD. LOOK, I DON'T CARE ONE WAY OR THE OTHER. JUST ASK YOURSELF...
WHAT'VE YOU GOT TO LOSE? I MEAN, CHECK THIS ARTICLE OUT.
KNOW WHAT IT SAYS?
THE TIMES
"MYRIAD WAYS" THEORY
SAYS SCIENTISTS THINK THAT EVERY CHOICE Y'MAKE CREATES A NEW DIMENSION OR UNIVERSE OR SOMETHING...
EVERY MAJOR MOMENT WHERE YOU *ZIG,* THERE'S *ANOTHER* YOU SOMEWHERE THAT *ZAGS.*
GOOD, BAD...DON'T MEAN A THING ANYMORE. 'CAUSE *WHATEVER* YOU DO, YOU'RE ALSO DOING THE *OPPOSITE.*
SO YOU MIGHT AS WELL DO WHATEVER YOU FEEL LIKE.
END SOMEONE WHO BUGS YOU. END YOURSELF. PUSH COMES TO SHOVE... NOTHING MATTERS. BELIEVE ME, I KNOW.

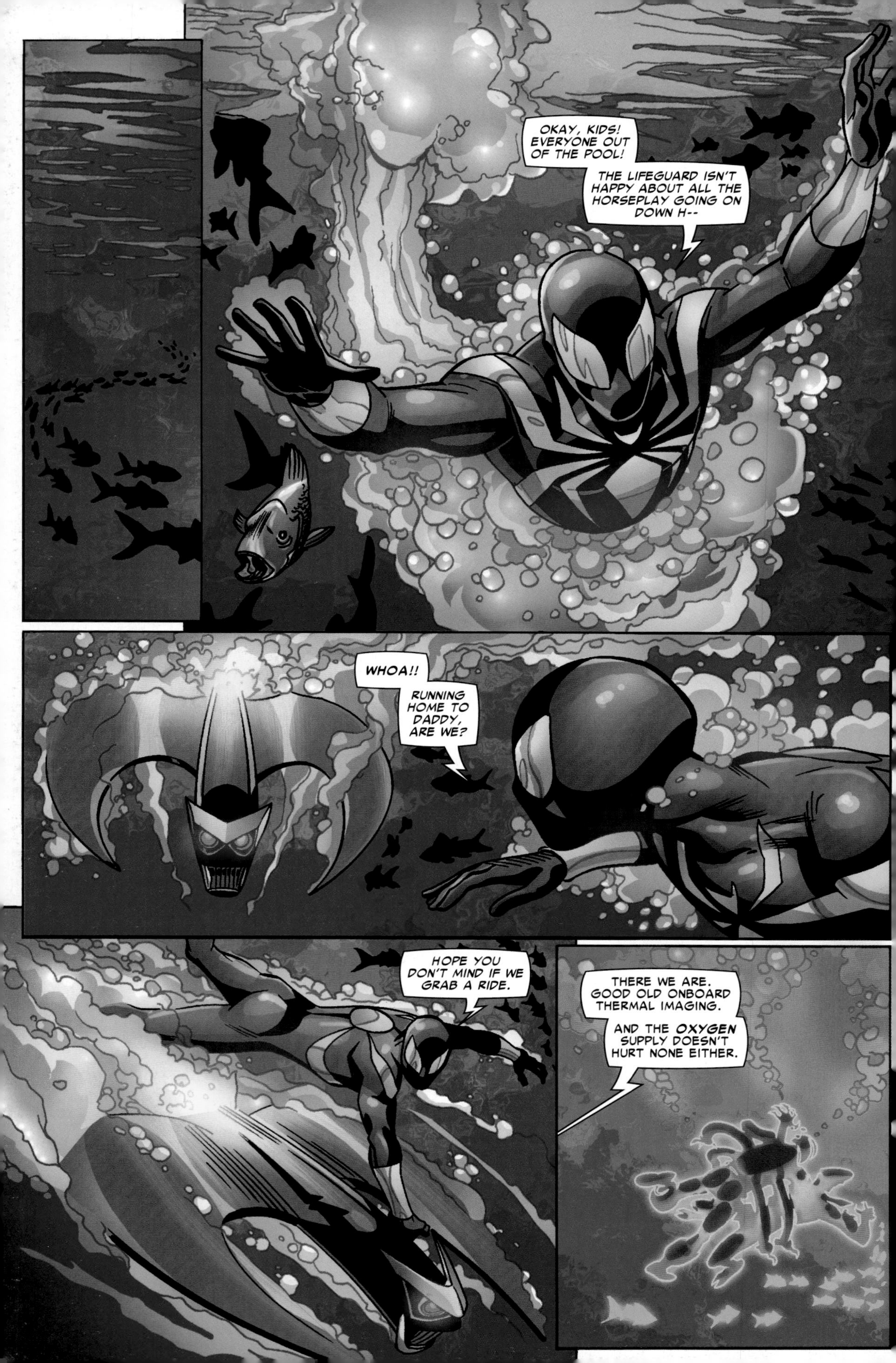
OKAY, KIDS! EVERYONE OUT OF THE POOL!
THE LIFEGUARD ISN'T HAPPY ABOUT ALL THE HORSEPLAY GOING ON DOWN H--
WHOA!!
RUNNING HOME TO DADDY, ARE WE?
HOPE YOU DON'T MIND IF WE GRAB A RIDE.
THERE WE ARE. GOOD OLD ONBOARD THERMAL IMAGING.
AND THE OXYGEN SUPPLY DOESN'T HURT NONE EITHER.

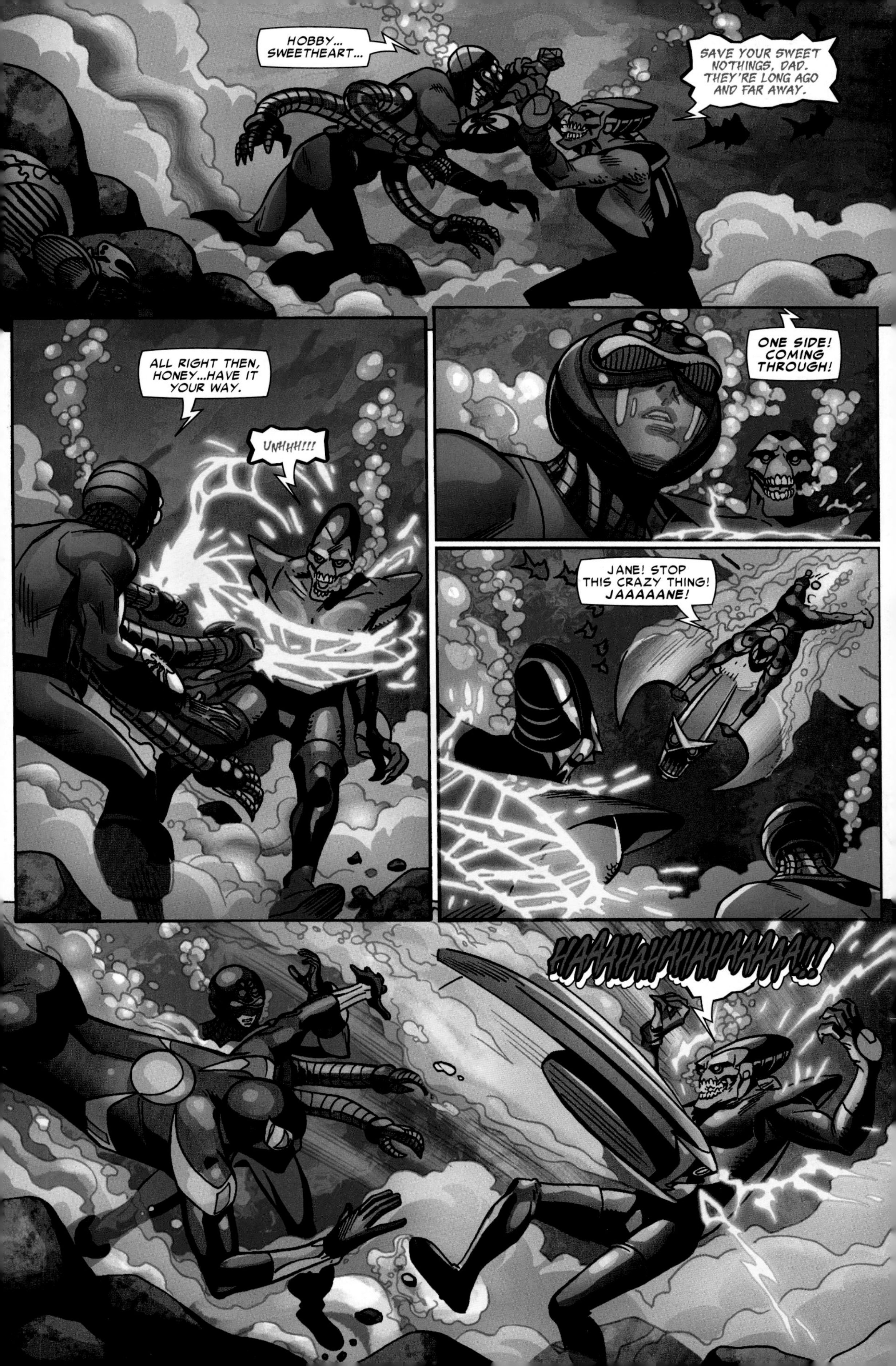
HOBBY... SWEETHEART...
SAVE YOUR SWEET NOTHINGS, DAD. THEY'RE LONG AGO AND FAR AWAY.
ALL RIGHT THEN, HONEY...HAVE IT YOUR WAY.
UNHHH!!!
ONE SIDE! COMING THROUGH!
JANE! STOP THIS CRAZY THING! JAAAAANE!
HAAAHAHAHAHAAAAA!!!

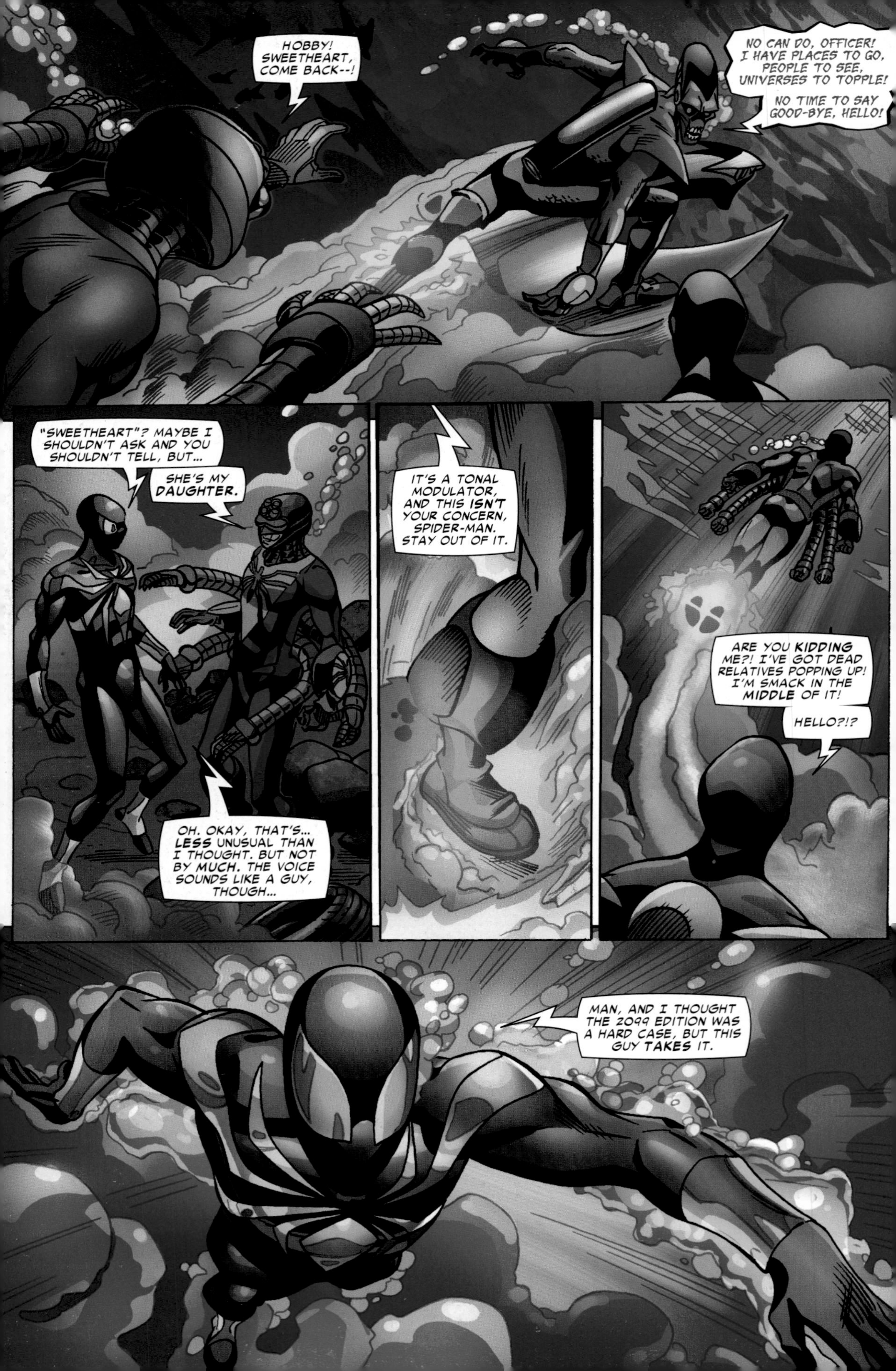
HOBBY! SWEETHEART, COME BACK--!
NO CAN DO, OFFICER! I HAVE PLACES TO GO, PEOPLE TO SEE, UNIVERSES TO TOPPLE!
NO TIME TO SAY GOOD-BYE, HELLO!
"SWEETHEART"? MAYBE I SHOULDN'T ASK AND YOU SHOULDN'T TELL, BUT...
SHE'S MY DAUGHTER.
OH. OKAY, THAT'S... LESS UNUSUAL THAN I THOUGHT. BUT NOT BY MUCH. THE VOICE SOUNDS LIKE A GUY, THOUGH...
IT'S A TONAL MODULATOR, AND THIS ISN'T YOUR CONCERN, SPIDER-MAN. STAY OUT OF IT.
ARE YOU KIDDING ME?! I'VE GOT DEAD RELATIVES POPPING UP! I'M SMACK IN THE MIDDLE OF IT!
HELLO?!?
MAN, AND I THOUGHT THE 2099 EDITION WAS A HARD CASE, BUT THIS GUY TAKES IT.

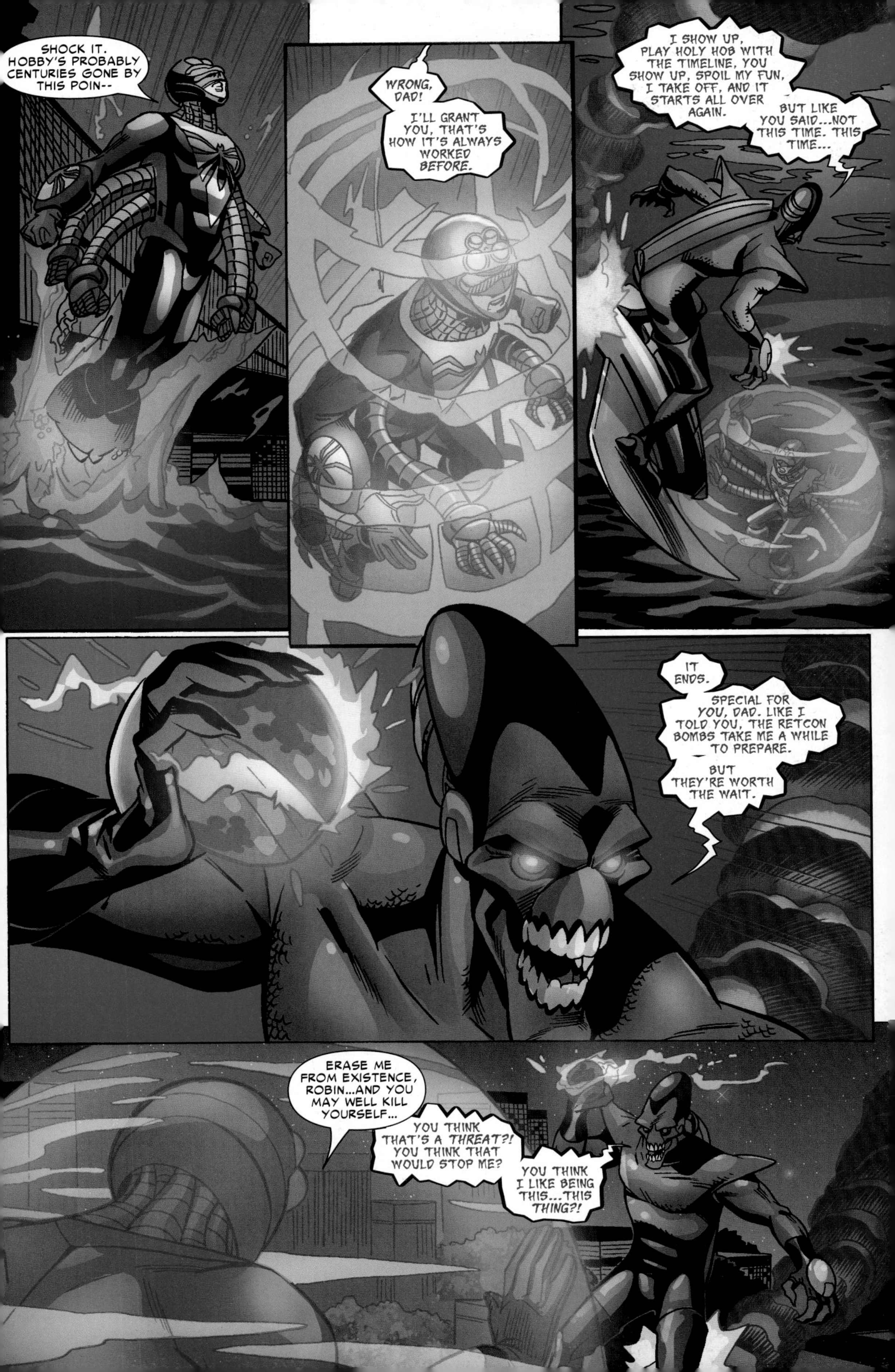
SHOCK IT. HOBBY'S PROBABLY CENTURIES GONE BY THIS POIN--
WRONG, DAD!
I'LL GRANT YOU, THAT'S HOW IT'S ALWAYS WORKED BEFORE.
I SHOW UP, PLAY HOLY HOB WITH THE TIMELINE, YOU SHOW UP, SPOIL MY FUN, I TAKE OFF, AND IT STARTS ALL OVER AGAIN.
BUT LIKE YOU SAID...NOT THIS TIME. THIS TIME...
IT ENDS.
SPECIAL FOR YOU, DAD. LIKE I TOLD YOU, THE RETCON BOMBS TAKE ME A WHILE TO PREPARE.
BUT THEY'RE WORTH THE WAIT.
ERASE ME FROM EXISTENCE, ROBIN...AND YOU MAY WELL KILL YOURSELF...
YOU THINK THAT'S A *THREAT*?! YOU THINK THAT WOULD STOP ME?
YOU THINK I LIKE BEING THIS...THIS *THING*?!

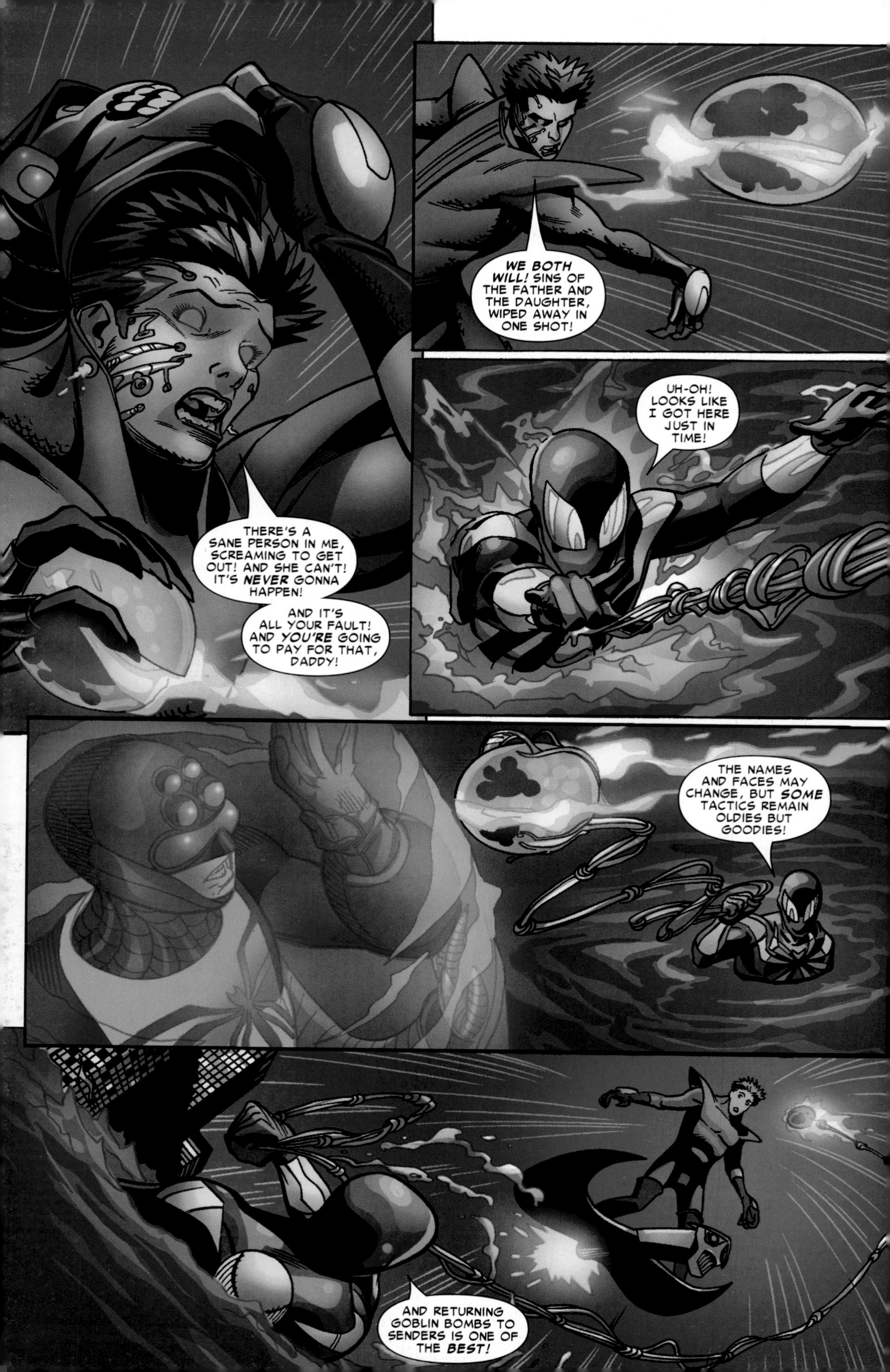
THERE'S A SANE PERSON IN ME, SCREAMING TO GET OUT! AND SHE CAN'T! IT'S NEVER GONNA HAPPEN!
AND IT'S ALL YOUR FAULT! AND YOU'RE GOING TO PAY FOR THAT, DADDY!
WE BOTH WILL! SINS OF THE FATHER AND THE DAUGHTER, WIPED AWAY IN ONE SHOT!
UH-OH! LOOKS LIKE I GOT HERE JUST IN TIME!
THE NAMES AND FACES MAY CHANGE, BUT SOME TACTICS REMAIN OLDIES BUT GOODIES!
AND RETURNING GOBLIN BOMBS TO SENDERS IS ONE OF THE BEST!

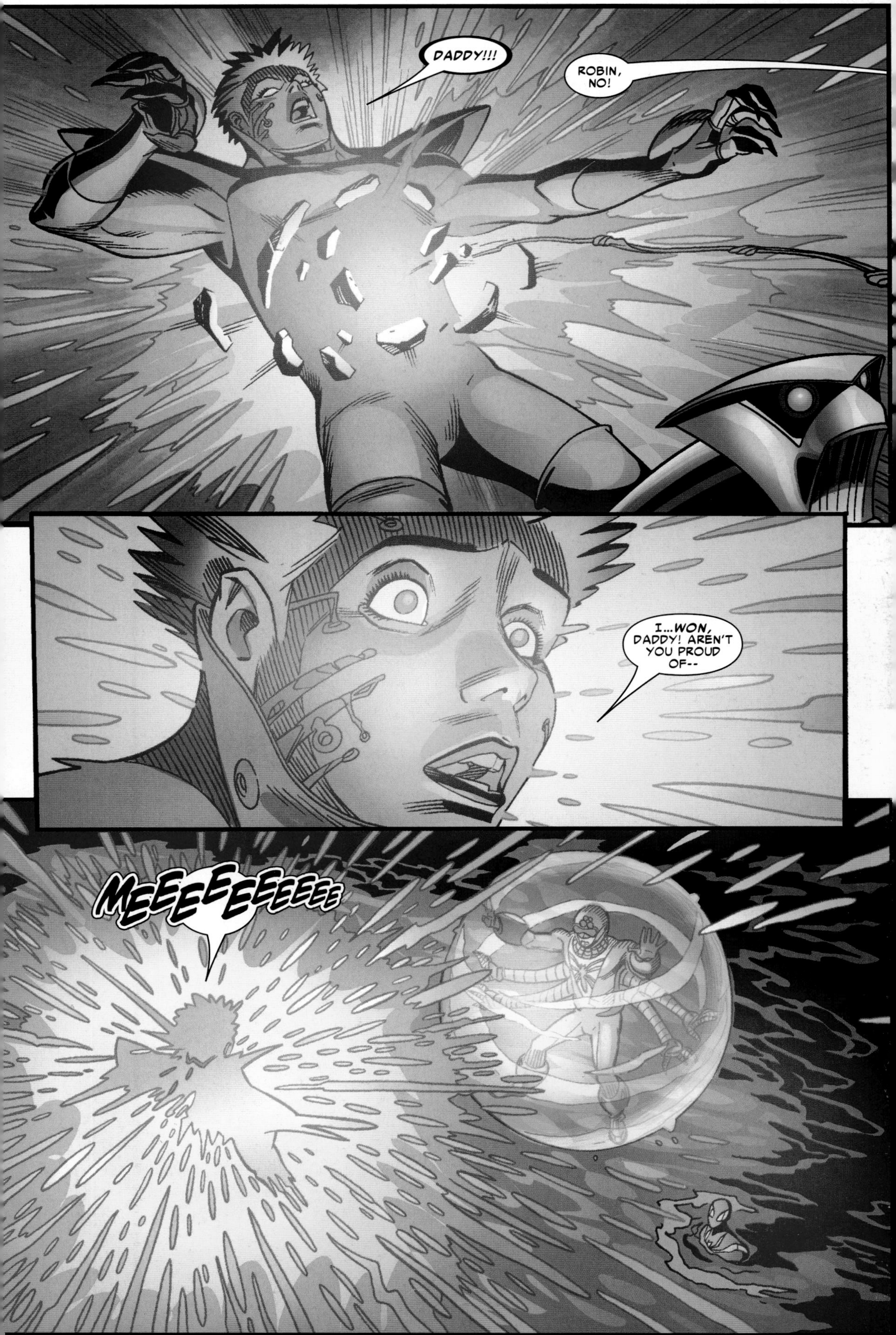
DADDY!!!
ROBIN, NO!
I...WON, DADDY! AREN'T YOU PROUD OF--
MEEEEEEEEEEE

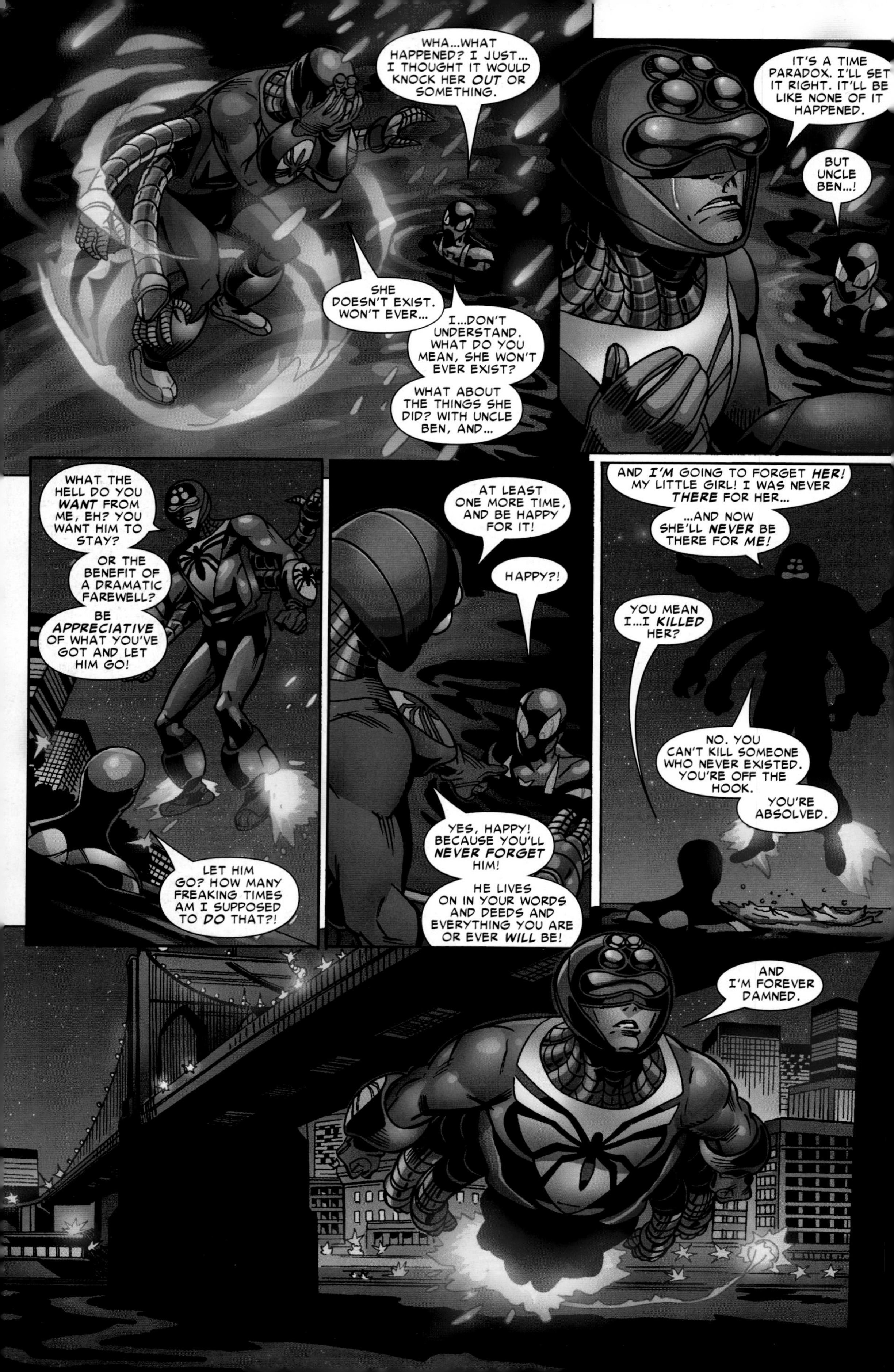
WHA...WHAT HAPPENED? I JUST... I THOUGHT IT WOULD KNOCK HER OUT OR SOMETHING.
SHE DOESN'T EXIST. WON'T EVER...
I...DON'T UNDERSTAND. WHAT DO YOU MEAN, SHE WON'T EVER EXIST?
WHAT ABOUT THE THINGS SHE DID? WITH UNCLE BEN, AND...
IT'S A TIME PARADOX. I'LL SET IT RIGHT. IT'LL BE LIKE NONE OF IT HAPPENED.
BUT UNCLE BEN...!
WHAT THE HELL DO YOU WANT FROM ME, EH? YOU WANT HIM TO STAY?
OR THE BENEFIT OF A DRAMATIC FAREWELL?
BE APPRECIATIVE OF WHAT YOU'VE GOT AND LET HIM GO!
LET HIM GO? HOW MANY FREAKING TIMES AM I SUPPOSED TO DO THAT?!
AT LEAST ONE MORE TIME, AND BE HAPPY FOR IT!
HAPPY?!
YES, HAPPY! BECAUSE YOU'LL NEVER FORGET HIM!
HE LIVES ON IN YOUR WORDS AND DEEDS AND EVERYTHING YOU ARE OR EVER WILL BE!
AND I'M GOING TO FORGET HER! MY LITTLE GIRL! I WAS NEVER THERE FOR HER...
...AND NOW SHE'LL NEVER BE THERE FOR ME!
YOU MEAN I...I KILLED HER?
NO. YOU CAN'T KILL SOMEONE WHO NEVER EXISTED. YOU'RE OFF THE HOOK.
YOU'RE ABSOLVED.
AND I'M FOREVER DAMNED.

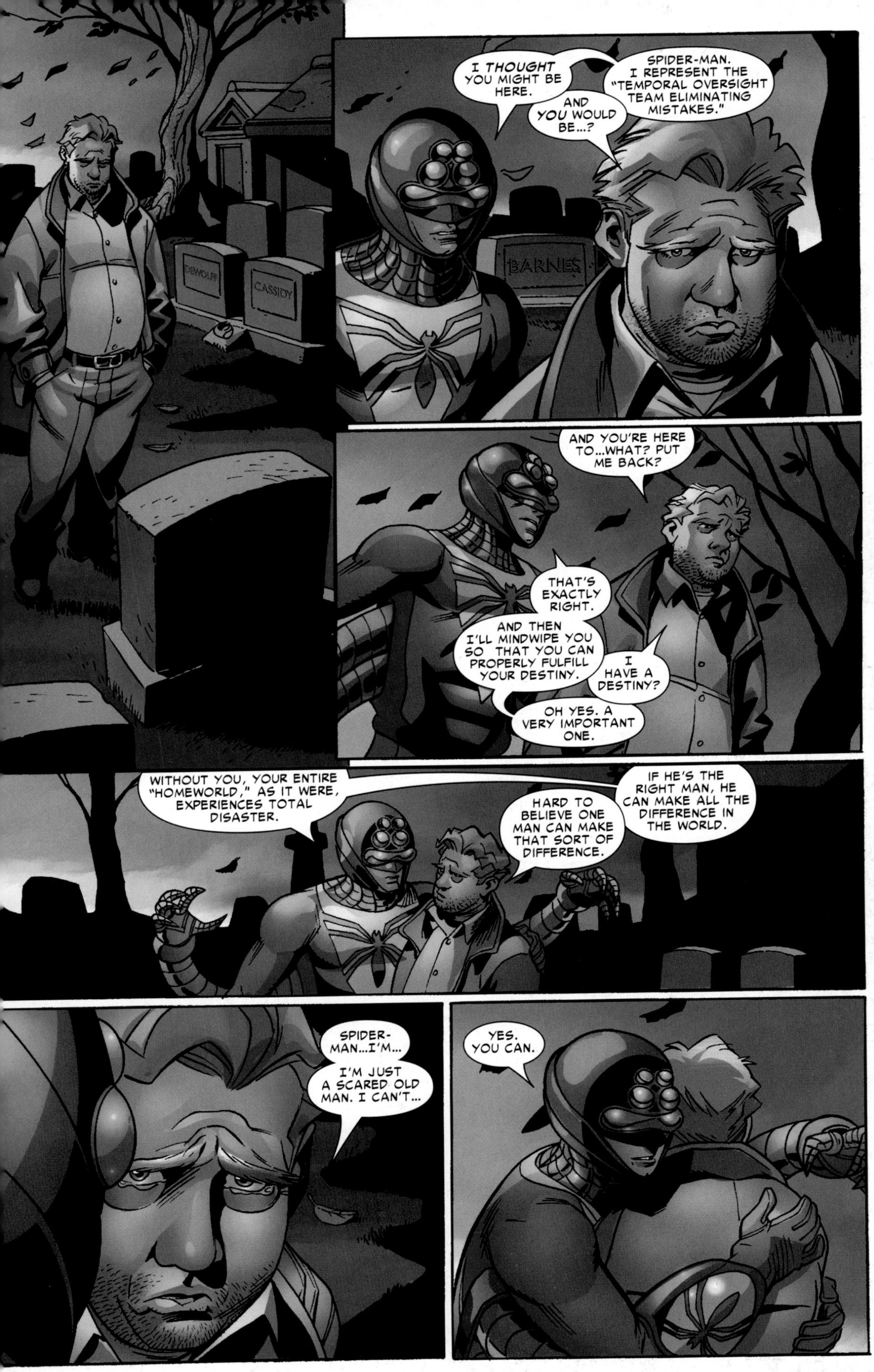

I THOUGHT YOU MIGHT BE HERE.
AND YOU WOULD BE...?
SPIDER-MAN. I REPRESENT THE "TEMPORAL OVERSIGHT TEAM ELIMINATING MISTAKES."
BARNES
DEWOLFF
CASSIDY
AND YOU'RE HERE TO...WHAT? PUT ME BACK?
THAT'S EXACTLY RIGHT.
AND THEN I'LL MINDWIPE YOU SO THAT YOU CAN PROPERLY FULFILL YOUR DESTINY.
I HAVE A DESTINY?
OH YES. A VERY IMPORTANT ONE.
WITHOUT YOU, YOUR ENTIRE "HOMEWORLD," AS IT WERE, EXPERIENCES TOTAL DISASTER.
HARD TO BELIEVE ONE MAN CAN MAKE THAT SORT OF DIFFERENCE.
IF HE'S THE RIGHT MAN, HE CAN MAKE ALL THE DIFFERENCE IN THE WORLD.
SPIDER-MAN...I'M...
I'M JUST A SCARED OLD MAN. I CAN'T...
YES. YOU CAN.

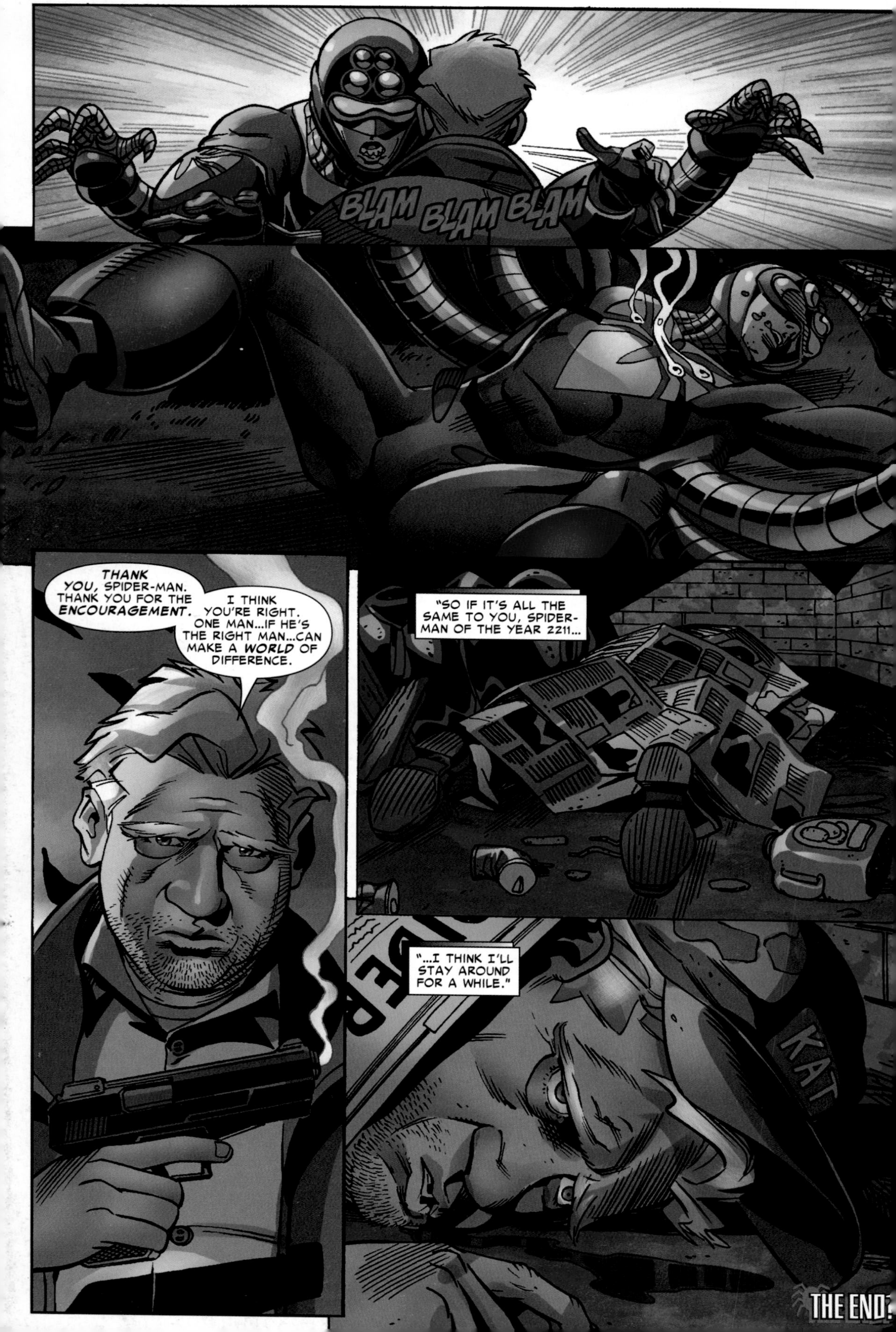
BLAM BLAM BLAM
THANK YOU, SPIDER-MAN. THANK YOU FOR THE ENCOURAGEMENT.
I THINK YOU'RE RIGHT. ONE MAN...IF HE'S THE RIGHT MAN...CAN MAKE A WORLD OF DIFFERENCE.
"SO IF IT'S ALL THE SAME TO YOU, SPIDER-MAN OF THE YEAR 2211...
"...I THINK I'LL STAY AROUND FOR A WHILE."
THE END.

ISSUE #8 COVER PENCILS
BY MIKE WIERINGO

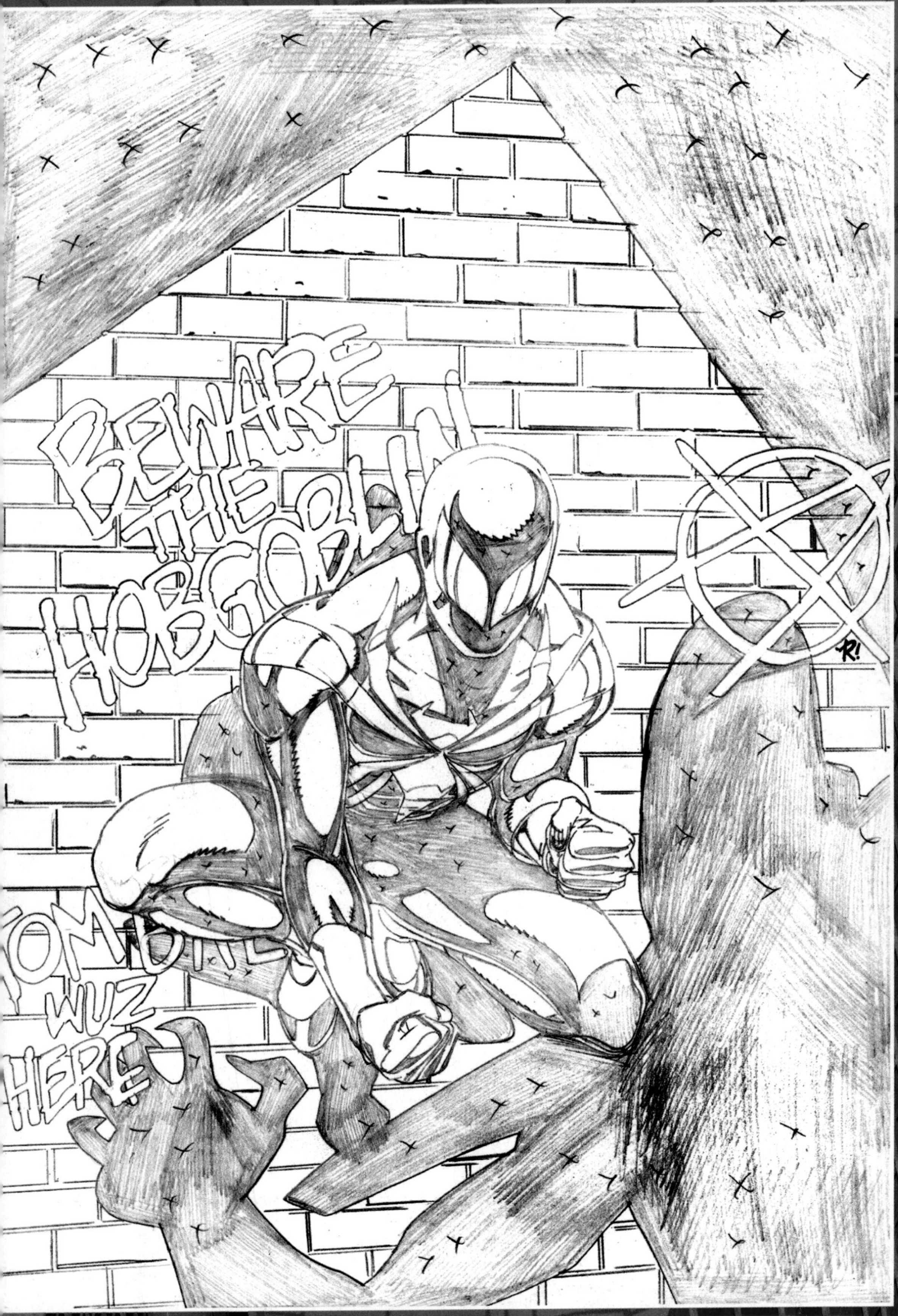
BEWARE THE HOBGOBLIN
WUZ HERE

ISSUE #9 COVER SKETCH
BY MIKE WIERINGO

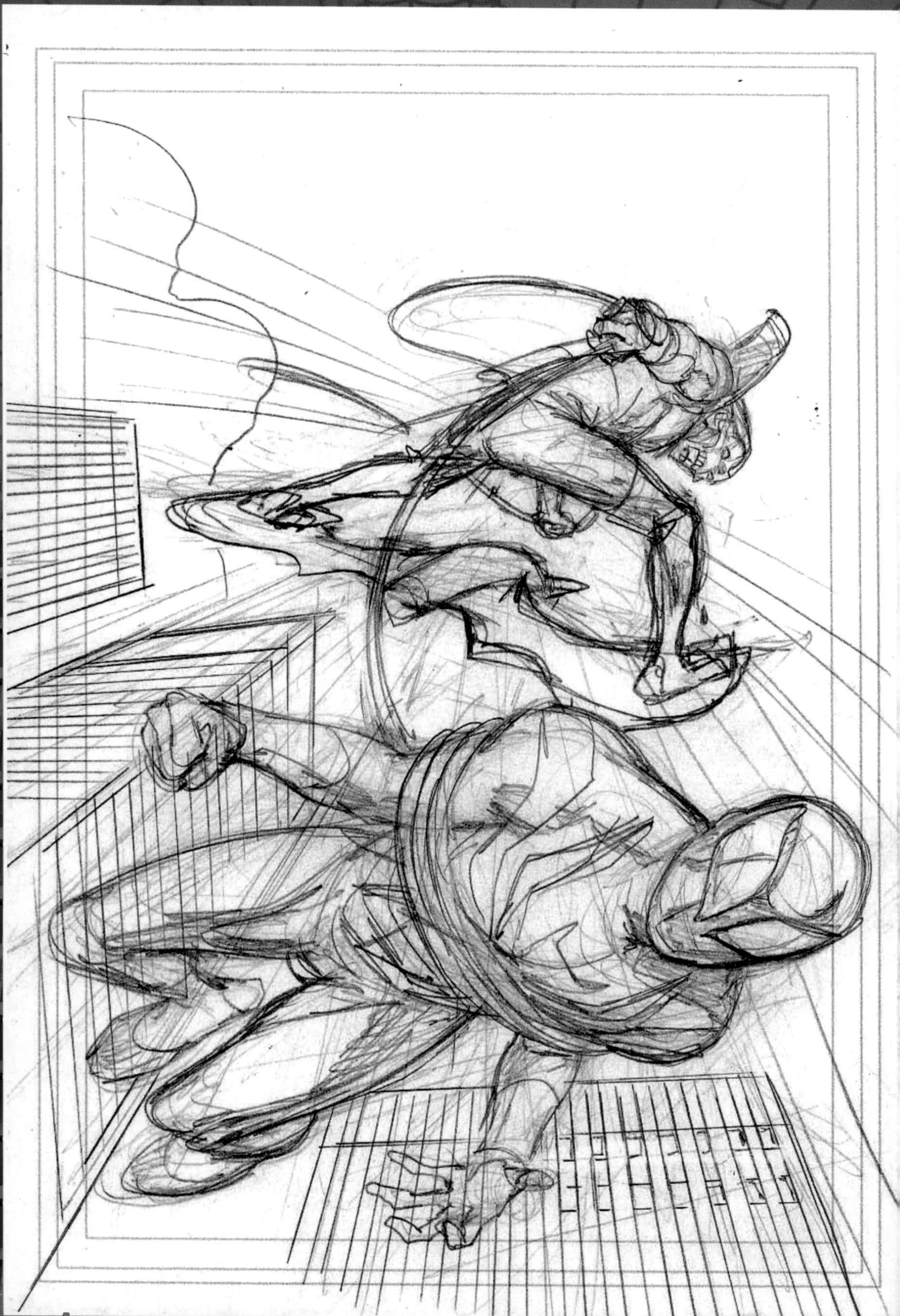